FIFTH EDITION

Eileen N. Whelan Ariza
Florida Atlantic University
Boca Raton, Florida

Maria R. Coady
University of Florida
Gainesville, Florida

WHY TESOL?

Past Contributing Authors

Carmen A. Morales-Jones

Noorchaya Yahya

Hanizah Zainuddin

Theories and Issues
in Teaching English to
Speakers of Other Languages
in K-12 Classrooms

Kendall Hunt
publishing company

Book Team

Chairman and Chief Executive Officer   *Mark C. Falb*
President and Chief Operating Officer   *Chad M. Chandlee*
Vice President, Higher Education   *David L. Tart*
Director of Publishing Partnerships   *Paul B. Carty*
Vice President, Operations   *Timothy J. Beitzel*
Senior Production Coordinator   *Michelle Bahr*
Senior Permissions Coordinator   *Jade Sprecher*
Senior Cover Designer   *Faith Walker*

Cover image © Shutterstock.com

www.kendallhunt.com
Send all inquiries to:
4050 Westmark Drive
Dubuque, IA 52004-1840

Printed in the United States of America

DEDICATION

We wish to dedicate this book to all the English learners who become students in our schools. It is our strong belief that they deserve the most qualified teachers possible. This book is our contribution to the education of teachers who will make a positive difference in the lives of these students, who in turn will significantly influence the future of this great nation.

The Authors

Contents

Foreword

As cultural and linguistic diversity has increased in classrooms across North America and in other parts of the world, it has become clear that the knowledge base required to effectively teach in these classrooms must include specialized information about second language development and its relationship to academic success. It is a pleasure to write a foreword for a book that articulates this expanding knowledge base in a clear, accessible, and comprehensive manner.

This book is particularly timely in view of the increased concern about accountability in our schools. The requirement in states such as Florida, that all teachers of English language learners (ELs) obtain appropriate qualifications to prepare them to teach these students effectively, reflects this concern for accountability. We still, however, face many challenges in implementing appropriate educational reforms that create effective and equitable learning environments for culturally and linguistically diverse students. Among these challenges are the following:

- Ensuring that statewide assessment mandates are valid and realistic for ELs, in addition to students for whom English is their first language (L1).
- Providing appropriate instructional support for ELs, not only in the early stages of learning conversational English, but also in the longer process of catching up in academic aspects of English.
- Building flexibility into instruction and assessment provisions that recognizes the diversity among ELs and avoids slotting these students into a "one-size-fits-all" school system intended for "generic" monolingual, monocultural, English L1 students.
- Ensuring that special education assessment procedures are valid for ELs so that these students are not overrepresented in categories such as "learning disability" or "communicative disorder" as has happened in the past.
- Providing encouragement and opportunities for students to continue to develop their home language ability, as this is the foundation upon which we construct English academic development.

Because issues related to immigration and increasing diversity have been controversial, it is not surprising that there are many misconceptions regarding the language and academic development of bilingual students. For example, students are often assumed to have overcome the "language barrier" when they have acquired the ability to converse relatively fluently in English. We know, in fact, that it can take much longer (5 or more years) for students to bridge the gap in academic aspects of English.

Similarly, students' first languages are still frequently seen as either irrelevant or detrimental to their academic progress. Nothing could be further from the truth. For more than 30 years, research has shown that bilingual students who continue to develop their L1 as they acquire English experience linguistic advantages such as increased awareness of how language works and how to use language effectively. As one example, students from Spanish-speaking backgrounds have a significant potential advantage in gaining access to the low-frequency Latin and Greek-based lexicon of academic English, since most of these words have cognates in Spanish. The word *encuentro* in Spanish is a cognate of the English word encounter, which is much less frequently used than its Anglo-Saxon derived synonym *meet*. As students progress through the grades and learn ever more complex concepts in science, math, and social studies, the proportion of low-frequency Latin-and Greek-derived vocabulary that they must learn increases dramatically. Spanish-speaking students' L1 can be a significant advantage in this process. If we are aware of these extensive L1/L2 linkages, we can help students to search for cognate connections in texts, thereby increasing their ability to infer the meanings of unknown words.

This volume is clearly not intended as a recipe book for implementing appropriate instruction for ELs. There are no recipes or formulas that can be applied to every student or situation. Rather, the intent is to provide educators with the information necessary to make informed and skillful decisions regarding the school policies and instructional practices that are likely to be effective in addressing the learning needs of a very diverse group of students. This implies that we must see ourselves individually and collectively as researchers who are learning from our own experiences in teaching bilingual students. Our goal should be not only to implement a knowledge base, but also to contribute to it.

In order to apply the existing knowledge base to our own unique context, and to contribute to the expansion and refinement of this knowledge base, we must engage in a collective problem-posing and problem-solving process. What approaches have worked for us in the past? What strategies are in place in our schools for involving parents and the community? Are there ideas that have been implemented elsewhere that might improve our practice in this and other areas? Do we, as a school faculty, have a consistent set of beliefs and assumptions about language and literacy teaching for bilingual students? If not, how can we discuss and resolve inconsistencies so that students are not confused by very different instructional strategies from 1 year or classroom to the next? What accommodations and/ or instructional strategies might be helpful to enable ELs to succeed on state-mandated assessments, despite the fact that they may be required to undergo these assessments long before they have had time to catch up academically in English?

There are no easy answers to many of these questions, but we are much more likely to pursue reasonable directions if we are discussing the issues within our own faculty, drawing on our collective experience, and brainstorming possible solutions. In other words, every school can benefit from articulating a language policy—a set of beliefs and practices about language learning and academic achievement that have been formulated specifically with the students we teach in mind. Such a policy should be sensitive, both to the unique situation of our students (and faculty) and the general knowledge base that exists from research and theory. The present volume provides an excellent starting point to understanding the knowledge base that already exists. As educators, we should see ourselves as adding to this knowledge base as a result of our individual and collective actions to implement the best possible instruction for all our students.

In conclusion, it is common these days to hear policymakers and school administrators talk of the school as a learning institution. In doing so they usually try to imply not only that schools are institutions where pupils are engaged in learning, but also that the school itself must continue to learn from its own collective experiences if it is to adapt to the changing cultural, economic, technological, and global challenges of the 21st century. As educators, we are in the vanguard of this learning process when we welcome new students and families into our society. We have to learn from our own experiences—our successes and failures—if we are to implement effective instruction and contribute significantly to the knowledge base regarding the education of linguistically and culturally diverse students.

Jim Cummins
The University of Toronto

Preface

AUDIENCE AND PURPOSE

We have written *WHY TESOL? Theories and Issues in Teaching English to Speakers of Other Languages in K–12 Classrooms* to provide current and prospective teachers who have English learners (ELs) in their classrooms with a knowledge base in the field of teaching English as a second/new language (TESOL). Today, more than ever, when teachers enter their classrooms they encounter a diversity in the student body that brings richness, and at the same time challenges, that teachers must address. The intent of this book is to provide an in-depth theoretical background for teachers as they learn and continue to address the needs of ELs in their classrooms.

In the 5th edition of *WHY TESOL? Theories and Issues in Teaching English to Speakers of Other Languages in K–12 Classrooms* we provide:

- Two completely new chapters, *Literacy Development and the English Learner*, and *Engaging Families of English Learners*, which address current needs of English learners (ELs) students and their families
- National statistics that help clarify the global nature of our American society in the 21st century
- A historical perspective on the laws that have influenced the teaching of ELs in today's schools, including Every Student Succeeds Act (ESSA) policies that address the learning progress of ELs
- A description of a variety of English as a second/new language (ESL/ENL) programs
- A profile of ELs and the needs they bring to today's classrooms
- An analysis and explanation of the nature of language and first or native language acquisition
- A discussion of second language theories and models

- A look at assessment, testing, and other relevant assessment issues as they relate to ELs
- Description and application the **WIDA** framework for English language proficiency, used in more than 38 states at the time of this printing
- The benefits of translanguaging, which fosters the development of multilingual students' various languages and supports English language development

ORGANIZATION

WHY TESOL? Theories and Issues in Teaching English to Speakers of Other Languages in K–12 Classrooms, fifth edition, has five parts. Part One develops an essential knowledge base for readers. It describes the legal rights of ELs and gives a historical overview of the laws that have had an impact on today's educational environment and how to address the needs of ELs in the United States. Part One also provides a clear classification of ESL/ENL programs available throughout the United States, as well as a discussion of factors that affect the design of these programs. Lastly, Part One offers a profile of ELs in the United States.

Part Two provides a basic grounding in the core areas of linguistics: phonology, morphology, syntax, pragmatics, discourse, and other related areas, such as nonverbal communication, dialectal variation, English language development, and World Englishes. This section is not intended to be an exhaustive examination of the language system; rather, it attempts to get the reader's "feet wet" when it comes to the nature of the English language. Such an understanding of how language works and what it means to know a language will help the reader understand the complexities involved in acquiring a language. This section begins with a general introduction of the universals across languages. Despite the linguistic divergence of the world's languages, human languages are remarkably similar in many ways. All languages share the same common properties and components, such as phonology, morphology, syntax, and semantics which make up the grammar of a language and make human communication possible. Part Two then provides a description of the sound systems of a language, including all the possible sound sequences and constraints, and discusses why certain sounds are difficult for foreign speakers to produce. Next, it introduces concepts related to the process of word creation within a language and how we learn to recognize words or nonwords in a language. It also examines how we recognize and form grammatical sentences and interpret potential ambiguities within a sentence and highlights potential difficulties that second language learners may have with English sentences. A chapter is also devoted to a discussion of how speakers arrive at meanings of words and sentences in their native language and how this process is filtered through the experience, culture, and worldview of the speakers.

The second half of this section looks at a number of related issues. It examines how speakers use language to carry out specific linguistic and social tasks and how the context of a language event influences meaning. It also describes differences in nonverbal communication across cultures and how these differences may result in misunderstandings between native and non-native speakers. Cross-cultural conversational and rhetorical patterns are also discussed with implications for teachers to facilitate second language learners' communicative abilities in their target language. Part Two then discusses how variation in human languages is influenced by factors related to socioeconomic status, region, and ethnicity and takes a brief look at the sociolinguistic and linguistic profiles of the different varieties of English used around the world.

Finally, the section ends with a brief overview of the historical development of the English language, how language families are established based on lexical similarities between languages, and the influence of other languages on English as demonstrated by extensive loan words in English.

Part Three contains first and second language theories and applications. Issues discussed focus on first and second/new language processes with the developmental milestones in first and second language learning compared from a linguistic perspective. The nonlinguistic factors affecting second language acquisition, such as age, personality, cognitive factors, sociocultural factors, motivation, and learning environment, are also discussed. Another section explains the complexity of the second language acquisition process through first language acquisition theories such as the behaviorist, innatist, cognitivist, social interactionist, and brain-based approaches. It also discusses second language acquisition theories and models such as Krashen's Monitor Model, Cummins' Second Language Framework, Selinker's Interlanguage Theory, McLaughlin's Attention-Processing Model, and Bialystok's Analysis/Automatic Processing Model. Examples of common linguistic problems faced by ELs of different language backgrounds are in Chapters 17 and 18 to help teachers recognize that ELs' errors may be attributed to first language interference and/or difficulties with learning complex, less predictable, and highly irregular structures in English. Strategies and styles in language learning such as Gardner's Multiple Intelligence Model, Cognitive Academic Language Learning Approach (CALLA), and second language communication strategies are also explored. Sources of error and error treatment are discussed to help teachers understand the difficulty learners experience when learning a new language. The development of methodologies in foreign language teaching and ESL teaching is traced, starting with the more traditional methods, such as the Grammar Translation Method, to the later approaches, such as the Natural Approach and the Whole Language Approach. The section ends with a chapter that argues the significance of meeting the needs of ELs.

Part Four of this book addresses the importance of assessment, evaluation, and the "missing link" of EL family engagement. These topics are especially important when we consider effective instruction for EL students and must ensure that students are learning both English and academic content. This topic is thoroughly explored, as it is important to understanding the appropriateness of standardized tests versus alternative assessments when determining the success of instruction and learning for ELs.

Part Five is a short section in which a new teacher and an experienced teacher share their classroom experiences. They tell how they adapt themselves and their teaching strategies to better measure the academic successes of the second language learners in their mainstream classrooms.

WHY TESOL? Theories and Issues in Teaching English to Speakers of Other Languages in K–12 Classrooms contains the following pedagogical features designed to make the material accessible and lasting for the reader:

- Readers should have an idea of what the chapters will be addressing, each chapter begins with "Learning Objectives" that can be used to guide the chapter content.
- Each chapter opens with a "real life" scenario intended to capture the essence of the chapter. The reader can later go back to this scenario and consider the content of the chapter and how it was reflected in the opening scenario.
- In our effort to help the reader acquire the most essential knowledge base, each chapter ends with a list of key "Points to Remember."
- Each chapter ends with "Reflection Questions and Discussion" as well as follow up "Activities" that can be completed after reading to extend readers' knowledge.
- Finally, each chapter offers "Web Resources" that readers can access immediately to deepen their connection to external resources.

Instructors using this book as a text for an English to Speakers of Other Languages (ESOL) class may require students to complete these assignments as indication of their understanding and reflection of the topics.

Glossary of Terms

At the back of *WHY TESOL? Theories and Issues in Teaching English to Speakers of Other Languages in K–12 Classrooms*, an in-depth definition of key acronyms employed throughout the book has been included. In addition, key terms have been listed and defined for quick reference.

POINTS FOR CLARIFICATION

Typically, ELs speak a primary language other than English at home. ELs vary in their proficiency in their primary languages, as well as in English. Beginners to intermediates in English in the past were referred to as limited English proficient (LEP), a term that was used in federal legislation and other official documents (Peregoy & Boyle, 2005). In more recent years, the federal government has shifted its terminology to ELL. In this book, the terms English language learners, English learners, second language learners, non-native speakers of English, language minority students, and language enriched pupils can be used synonymously to refer to students who are in the process of acquiring English as a new language and whose primary language is not English. (Refer to Glossary of Professional Terms for further clarification.)

Acknowledgments

We wish to thank Dr. Cummins for taking the time to read this manuscript, and for writing the foreword. It gives us great personal pleasure and professional satisfaction to know an individual of his stature endorses the work we are doing, as we prepare teachers to graduate with TESOL competency ready to teach linguistically, ethnically, and culturally diverse students in the classrooms of today, and of the future.

Eileen N. Whelan Ariza, Ed.D
Maria R. Coady, PhD

Writing a book can be a delightful torture that lasts for years, as life goes on around you. Deadlines loom as your family and friends wait patiently for you to finish that one last word or thought, before it escapes you forever. Papers, articles, books, and references are strewn about the house and office with wild abandon. Neatness, such as it was, becomes an elusive goal. But although I write alone, I cannot do it alone. I write for pleasure, as my incredible children, Stefani and Nico, take a temporary back seat, but they always show their pride in my work. I am deeply grateful to them and they are the loves of my life. I dedicated this book to them. I am so proud of them as they have grown up to become productive international members of society.

My recently deceased mother, Nancy Whelan, I thank as well, because she always told me I could be anything I wanted to be. She was the one who told me: "go travel, see the world …" and "Bring any of your friends home … I don't care where they are from, or what color, or faith they are …" and "Why don't you learn Spanish," which led me to my life and career today. Awesome woman that she is, she made the first cross-cultural leap in the family by having the audacity to be an Anglo Protestant who married an Irish Catholic bar owner in the 1940s—a radical move! She truly was the wind beneath the wings and I will be forever grateful that she was my mother.

Finally, I have to thank my co-author, Dr. Maria Coady, who contributed great knowledge and expertise in the field. She brings a new outlook to this book and shares her years of valuable experience with English learners (ELs), especially from working to promote literacy for migrant workers.

Eileen N. Whelan Ariza
Professor, Teaching and Learning
Florida Atlantic University
Boca Raton, Florida, Spring 2018

Writing a book that prepares a wide range of educators—teachers, leaders, and staff—for linguistically-diverse students and families is no small feat. In today's sociopolitical climate, teachers and diverse learners are under constant scrutiny. I wish to acknowledge the hard work, dedication, and accomplishments of the many teachers, students, and families who brave this environment and who hold hope for a brighter future. I especially thank Eileen N. Whelan Ariza, my close professional colleague and friend, whose insight in academia has kept me afloat over many years. I wish to acknowledge my colleagues and doctoral students in the field for their ongoing professional encouragement. I also acknowledge and thank my loving and loyal family: husband, Tom, and children, Thomas and Rachel, Austin and Emily.

Maria R. Coady
Associate Professor
ESOL/Bilingual Education
University of Florida
Gainesville, Florida, Spring 2018

Special thanks go to Marci Maher, who offered insights based on being a new teacher, and Betty Lacayo, a veteran teacher of English to Speakers of Other Languages (ESOL) students, who is an expert on literacy-based curriculum in St. Lucie County, for sharing her insights with us, and thanks also go to Bianca Swanson for sharing her rubric in the appendices (which was a class assignment).

Finally, to all the educators trying to become ESOL endorsed or certified thank you for making the effort to learn how to successfully teach the delightfully diverse ELs.

The Authors

About the Authors

Eileen N. Whelan Ariza, EdD

Dr. Eileen N. Whelan Ariza is a professor in the Department of Teaching and Learning, and English for Speakers of Other Languages (ESOL) Infusion Coordinator in the College of Education at Florida Atlantic University (FAU), Boca Raton, Florida. She received her doctorate in multicultural/multilingual education at the University of Massachusetts, Amherst; a Master's in Teaching English to ESOL; MA in Teaching Spanish as a Foreign Language; and a Bilingual/Multicultural Endorsement from the School for International Training, Brattleboro, Vermont. Her undergraduate degree, from Worcester State College, MA (summa cum laude) is in elementary education.

© Eileen N. Whelan Ariza

She completed her student teaching at the American School in Madrid, where she first learned about bilingual education through English as a foreign language. She holds two levels of certifications by the Cervantes Institute, Ministry of Education, Spain, as a teacher of Spanish as a Foreign Language.

Ariza has over 30 years of experience teaching English as a second/foreign language (ESL/EFL) to students with varying backgrounds and experience from around the world, including Eurasia, Latin America, Europe, the Middle East, and Asia. At FAU for the last 23 years, she has taught graduate and undergraduate courses with a focus on ESOL training and foreign language methodology to preservice and in service teachers. She specializes in cross-cultural and intercultural training for educators who are unfamiliar with "non-mainstream" students and spent several years teaching ESOL/EFL, both overseas, and at Harvard University's English Language Institute. She has taught, lived in, presented and/or given workshops in many cultures, including the Philippines, Colombia, Mexico, Ecuador, Thailand, Costa Rica, Brazil, Hong Kong, France, Ireland, Malta, and the Commonwealth of Puerto Rico, which has shown her the significance and power of cultural sensitivity. Additionally, she taught English as an additional language to multicultural guests on two transatlantic voyages on the Queen Mary 2, from London to New York.

Ariza is a three-time Fulbright Scholar, first at the Universidad de las Americas in Puebla (Fulbright-García Robles), in Spring 2009. Her second Fulbright was in Costa Rica (Spring, 2016), working with the American Embassy, the Ministry of Education, and the University of Costa Rica in San Jose. Her third Fulbright is at the University of Malta, Spring 2018, where she is involved in the study of mainstream teachers of refugee and migrant students, parents of migrants, refugees, and displaced families in Syria, and contributing to the national policy for pathways to Maltese residency for migrants.

Ariza is dedicated to the Fulbright mission and is awestruck by the impact it makes on participants. Her other Fulbright experiences have included: Fulbright-Hayes Seminar, Alternate Reviewer, January 2016; Fulbright Presentation and Public Speaking Certificate, Poynter News University, September 2015; Fulbright Alumni Ambassador, Fall 2013–Fall 2015 (invited); Fulbright U.S. ETA Reviewer, March 2014, 2015; 2017, Fulbright Peer Reviewer (TEFL) 2014–2015; Fulbright Candidate Specialist Roster, 2010–2014; Fulbright Specialist Peer Reviewer, 2006–2009; and is a member of the Fulbright Oversight Committee (Scholar-in-Residence, SIR) at Florida Atlantic University. She also is involved as an external reviewer for English teachers at Nazarbayev University in Kazakhstan, through the Kazakhstan Embassy in Washington, DC.

Over the span of her career, Dr. Ariza has won multiple teaching awards and recognition by her students, teachers, and colleagues (FAU undergraduate excellence; FAU College of Education Distinguished Teacher of the Year; FAU university-wide, Distinguished Teacher of the Year; outstanding alumni award at Worcester State College; and excellence in teaching at Harvard University). She has authored or coauthored 12 well-received books and materials that focus on training teachers of English learners (several that are recommended by the Florida Department of Education), authored or coauthored over 62 peer reviewed publications/chapters on TESOL, and has presented several times a year nationally or internationally, on TESOL and language learning issues, since 1998. Her personal life is dedicated to her children, Stefani and Nico, and her professional life is devoted to the constant mission of helping mainstream teachers understand students who are learning through English as a new language.

Maria R. Coady, PhD

© Thomas Bedard

Dr. Maria Coady is an associate professor and program coordinator of English for Speakers of Other Languages (ESOL) and Bilingual Education at the University of Florida, Gainesville. She received her doctor of philosophy (PhD) degree from the University of Colorado, Boulder in 2001, where she was a U.S. Department of Education Title VII Fellow from 1997 to 2001. She also received her Master's degree in education (MEd) from Boston University in 1993 and Bachelor's degree in business administration and international perspectives from the University of New Hampshire, Durham.

Coady was among the first group of U.S. students to live, work, and study in Buenos Aires, Argentina under the auspices of the Organization of American States in 1987 after the democratic presidential election. She subsequently lived in Paris, France, where she studied at the University of the Sorbonne and began her teaching career in English. Upon return to the United States, Coady taught Spanish and English to students ranging from elementary to higher education; her teaching career has spanned 30 years. Coady continued to work and study abroad. Her dissertation work at the University of Colorado, Boulder, investigated bilingual education programs called *Gaelscoileanna* in the Republic of Ireland. Findings have been published in the prestigious journal *Language Policy*.

Upon completion of her doctorate degree, Coady worked at Brown University's Education Alliance from 2001 to 2003 providing technical assistance to school districts and teachers. She subsequently joined the faculty at the University of Florida, Gainesville, as a scholar of bilingualism and bilingual education. Coady was awarded a competitive position on the U.S. Department of State Fulbright Specialist Scholar roster in 2012. Her first Fulbright Specialist assignment was in teacher education at Kryvyi Rih University in Ukraine, where she was awarded an honorary diploma in teaching in 2013. Coady completed a second Fulbright Specialist assignment at the University of Witwatersrand in Johannesburg, South Africa. Coady has also consulted internationally in teacher education in Ireland, China, Costa Rica, the Dominican Republic, and the United Arab Emirates.

In Florida, Coady works closely with immigrant students and families, at the intersection of teacher education, bilingualism and biliteracy development, and social justice issues. In 2007, she became coprincipal Investigator of a prestigious 5-year $1.2 million U.S. Department of Education National Professional Development (NPD) grant, Project DELTA, that investigated the relationship between preservice teacher education and the academic learning of English learner (EL) students. In 2016, she was awarded a second 5-year NPD grant as Principal Investigator ($2.4 million), which examines the rural context of education, prepares teacher-leaders for ELs, and builds rural family engagement (Project STELLAR, Supporting Teachers of English Language Learners Across Rural Settings). In addition, she is working on the first cross national study of meta-literacy development among multilinguals in South Africa and the United States (with Dr. Leketi Makalela). Coady is completing a book on rural multilingual family engagement. Her publications can be found in the first *TESOL Encyclopedia of English Language Teaching* and the journals *TESOL Quarterly*; the *Bilingual Research Journal, TESOL Journal*; *Language Policy*; and the *Journal of Language, Culture, and Communication*. In 2018, she was appointed the Iriving and Rose Fien Endowed Professorship at the University of Florida College of Education. Coady's personal life is dedicated to the memory of her son Thomas (1992–2014), daughter Rachel, husband Tom, stepchildren Austin and Emily, and Nori, her multilingual, multicultural mini-labradoodle.

A Knowledge Base for English Language Teaching

Why TESOL?

LEARNING OBJECTIVES

Readers will be able to

- ❖ Define the key terms TESOL and English learner (EL)
- ❖ Describe changes in immigration to the United States over time and its implications for teachers in classrooms
- ❖ Describe "diversity" and different facets of diversity among the U.S. school-aged population
- ❖ Describe the number ELs and consider its implication for teaching

Ms. Hathaway enters her middle school science classroom in early August and looks around at the blank walls. Within a week, the classroom space will be transformed, as students arrive and begin a new academic year. Before reviewing changes to the curriculum and lesson planning for unit 1, Ms. Hathaway reviews the roster of students on her skyward dashboard. The dashboard on her computer displays students' names, individualized learning plans, English language status, and prior year test scores. Ms. Hathaway notes students named Jennifer, Jing, Abdul, Steven, Juana, and Paolo. In fact, her dashboard data indicate that eight of her 22 students are English learners or "ELs" with various degrees of English language proficiency. Of the six, two are listed as "beginner," three are "intermediate," and one is "advanced." Her EL students represent countries as far as China and the United Arab Emirates and as near as Cuba. Five of her eight ELs are Spanish speakers. Ms. Hathaway enjoys having the ELs in her science classroom. The Spanish speakers often learn scientific terminology fairly quickly because of the similarities of words and word-roots between English and Spanish in scientific vocabulary. She embraces with enthusiasm the new challenges and resources that the students bring. Ms. Hathaway thinks to herself, "This is why I became a teacher—to learn about my students and see them grow academically and socially."

INTRODUCTION

The education of diverse learners is more important today than ever before. Educational programs and policies are increasingly complex, due in part to changes in global migration patterns that affect schools and teachers; the diverse backgrounds of students' languages, race, ethnicities, religions, and cultures; and the reality of educational standards and student achievement outcomes that teachers of diverse learners must address. In short, in today's 21st century global environment, teachers, administrators, students, and parents face pressures and demands in education, as well as simultaneous access to vast quantities information, materials, and resources.

One question you may have right away is the same as the title of this book: *Why TESOL?* Why is it important for teachers and educators to understand and address issues of language for English learners (Els)? What exactly do teachers need to *do*?

TESOL stands for **T**eachers of **E**nglish to **S**peakers of **O**ther **L**anguages, and if you're reading this book, it is likely that you are—or may soon be—a teacher of ELs in an educational setting. As educators ourselves, we frequently hear people state that "good teaching for ELs is 'just good teaching.'" If that were the case, why would teachers need to know about TESOL? We argue that good teaching *is* good for all students, and it is a helpful start to working with ELs. However, good teaching for all students is likely *not* enough to support the language and content learning needs of ELs in today's schools. ELs have specific language and cultural learning needs, and those needs should guide teachers' instructional decisions and strategies.

In this book we aim to address these questions and many more that you may have. To get started, in this chapter we provide an overview of 21st century immigration patterns and trends in the United States, which help to situate diversity and immigration for teachers and educators. Next, we discuss diversity in U.S. schools and give you a sense of diverse learners and their rich and varied backgrounds. Finally, we describe "English learners" as a subgroup of diverse learners and outline the linguistic landscape of U.S. schools and classrooms in the United States today.

21ST CENTURY (IM)MIGRATION

In the great sweep of American history, immigration has proven to be a positive influence for the United States overall. The diversity that immigrants have brought, and continue to bring, is an asset to the American way of life. These contributions are not only evident in the performing arts, literature, religion, and scientific research, but in the areas of international business and economic growth, as well as in education. As immigrants have settled into geographic areas ranging from sleepy towns to vibrant international metropolises, they have had a significant impact on the development of the United States.

Immigration, however, is not without its challenges. A common caricature of the United States of America is its relationship to new immigrants, whether arriving to Ellis Island in New York City on 19th century ships, landing in California on airplanes from the Pacific Rim, or driving over the U.S. border from Canada. The truth is that immigration has been an important part of American history from its early founding to today. In fact, the "forefathers" of America were immigrants themselves and settled on land already inhabited by native people.

Twenty-first century America is no different today, generally speaking, in terms of the contribution of immigration to U.S. culture. Immigrants continue to provide great benefits to American society, including contributing to labor and the overall economy. Immigrants add to America's intellectual resources, diversity in language, thinking, culture, and religion. Figure 1.1 provides data on rates of immigration to the United States from 1850 to present.

Based on this graph, you may see that the overall number of immigrants to the United States has increased (refer to the blue line). However, the percentage of immigrants as part of the overall U.S. population remains fairly steady, between 5% and 15% of the native, U.S.-born population. It is curious, then, that in the United States there is a rising sense of **nativism**, that is, political policies that protect the interests of native-born people against the interests of immigrants. The perception of the general public about immigrants and immigration continues to be contentious and heated.

Notice on this graph that the total number of immigrants in the United States continues to rise and is predicted to increase into the year 2020, yet the percentage of immigrants is about the same. This is due to the relational increase in the overall U.S. population. So as the United States continues to receive more immigrants, the number of U.S.-born citizens is also increasing (Figure 1.2).

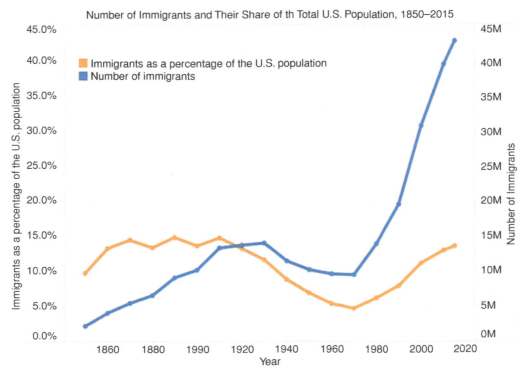

Figure 1.1: Immigrants ("Foreign Born") to the United States 1850–2020

Top Ten Largest U.S. Immigrant Groups, 2016, MPI Data Hub, www.migrationpolicy.org/programs/data-hub/charts/largest-immigrant-groups-over-time.; and, Number of Immigrants and Their Share of the Total U.S. Population, 1850-2016, MPI Date Hub, www.migrationpolicy.org/programs/data-hub/charts/immigrant-population-over-time.

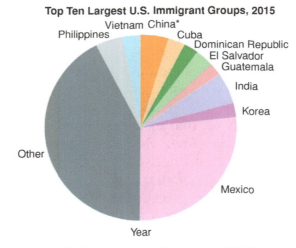

Figure 1.2: Top Ten Largest U.S. Immigrant Groups, 2015

Top Ten Largest U.S. Immigrant Groups, 2016, MPI Data Hub, www.migrationpolicy.org/programs/data-hub/charts/largest-immigrant-groups-over-time.; and, Number of Immigrants and Their Share of the Total U.S. Population, 1850-2016, MPI Date Hub, www.migrationpolicy.org/programs/data-hub/charts/immigrant-population-over-time.

You may be curious about the countries from which the largest number of people emigrate. The U.S.-based Migration Policy Institute (MPI) tracks those data. According to the MPI (2017a), in 2015, the largest sending country was Mexico, which accounted for 29.3% of total immigrants. India accounts for 5.5% of immigrants, and China accounts for 4.8%. However, "Other" sending countries taken as a whole accounts for the majority of immigrants at 42.3%.

The public's perception of immigrants may not be in alignment with actual backgrounds of immigrants to the United States today. The caricature in Figure 1.3 captures some of the public sentiment regarding immigrants over time. Over time the countries that send immigrants to the United States has also changed and will continue to do so in this century with changing migration policies. For example, in 2016, the United Nations has noted that there were more than six million Syrians who were displaced as refugees from their war-torn country (United Nations High Commissioner for Refugees [UNHRC], 2016). International crises have rippling effects in U.S. schools, as the U.S. immigration policies address these events and change to meet the demands and needs of the international community.

Figure 1.3: Caricature of Perceptions in Immigration 1780 to Present

From leftycartoons.com by Barry Deutsch. Copyright © 2017 by Barry Deutsch. Reprinted by permission.

KEY DEFINITION

Immigration—shifts in population due to movement *into* a country
Emigration—shifts in population due to movement *out of* a country

One of the greatest assets of immigrants in the United States is the global perspective so critical in the 21st century. Global independence is a thing of the past; global interdependence is omnipresent. It is a reality, though, that despite its positive effects, immigration also signals an increase in numbers of students from diverse backgrounds, that is, students who speak multiple languages and represent different cultural ways of life.

Diverse students who contribute such richness of culture to our schools, classrooms, and communities also bring considerable difference that can be challenging to teachers who have had limited experience with diverse students. In addition to language diversity, which is the focus of this book, U.S. students are vastly diverse in terms of race, ethnicity, religion, and ability. Figure 1.4 demonstrates the ways in which the school-aged population is shifting racially and ethnically. What is interesting about this graph is the projected decrease by 2026 in students considered "White" and the increase in students identified as "Hispanic" and/or as "Two or more races." Racial categories are considered "constructs," or human-generated ideas, or in this case categories, that are created. Simple classifications such as Black, White, Asian, and Hispanic mask the reality of human diversity in ways that can be harmful. For example, former President Barak Obama was frequently considered "Black" or African American. However, in reality he was biracial.

Some problems with those classifications include associating students with one (inaccurate) race when they may be multiracial; grouping all Hispanics or Asians into one

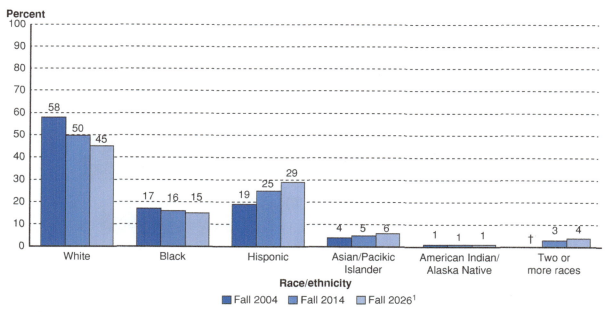

Figure 1.4: Public School Students' Race and Ethnicity, 2014

Source: National Center for Education Statistics (2017b).

classification without acknowledging the rich diversity within those proposed categories; and believe that all "Hispanics" speak Spanish or that all "Asians" speak Chinese. As a teacher, your role is to learn about your students as individuals and to apply your knowledge to the instructional decisions you make that benefit those students.

Like global interdependence, diversity is now the mainstay of classrooms across the United States. In fact, the U.S. Department of Education data show that White students are no longer a majority in U.S. schools; students of color are now considered the "majority–minority." Moreover, by the year 2022, non-White students are projected to account for 55% of the school population (Pew Research Center, 2014).

THE ENGLISH LEARNER

Much more could be noted about diversity in the United States. Our review here is limited but we encourage you to explore other facets of diversity including religious diversity, ableism, and social class. ELs are represented in all of those categories.

Now that you have a general sense of the trends in diversity in U.S. schools, it is helpful to define who ELs are and what that population looks like. One definition of an EL is "students who are unable to communicate fluently or learn effectively in English, who often come from non-English-speaking homes and backgrounds, and who typically require specialized or modified instruction in both the English language and in their academic courses" (Great Schools Partnership, 2017). From this definition you can note the emphasis on communicating fluently or learning effectively through the medium of English. This broad definition should ensure that EL students' learning needs are captured by schools and districts around the United States in order to provide the appropriate high-quality instruction for those students, based on their language learning needs.

Currently, ELs represent about 10% of the overall U.S. school-aged population, or more than five million students. Figure 1.5, shows the percentage of ELs by state during the 2014–2015 school years. California's ELs comprise about one in every four students, the largest in the United States. California is followed by the states of Nevada, Texas, and New Mexico, and Florida's EL population is approaching 300,000 students. All states across the United States, however, have EL students, and with the projected growth in number of ELs, having strong teacher preparation for ELs is increasingly important.

The top five languages spoken by ELs in U.S. schools are Spanish or Castilian, Chinese, Arabic, Vietnamese, and Haitian or Haitian Creole. Those language groups account for about four million ELs in the country (Figure 1.6). That said, there are hundreds of different languages and language varieties spoken and written in the United States, including lesser-used languages of native peoples.

Following our theme on diversity, there is likewise great diversity within the EL student population in the United States. For example, in addition to the need to learn oral and written English for multiple purposes, such as for social interaction and for academic performance, some immigrant EL students may need added academic support. This could be due to students relocating to the United States who have had limited or interrupted formal

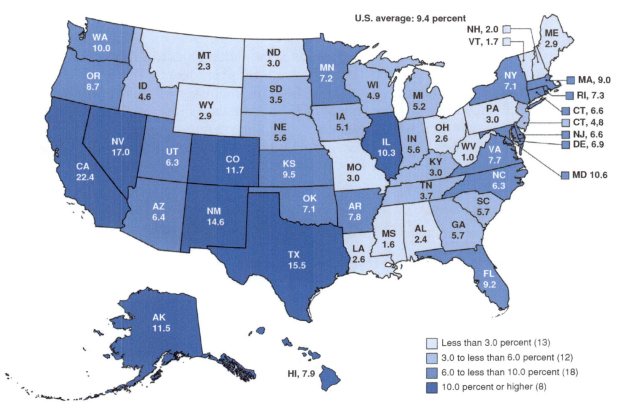

Figure 1.5: English Learners in Public Schools as Percentage of Total Students

Source: National Center for Education Statistics (2017a).

Language	Number
Spanish/Castilian	3,659,501
Chinese	97,117
Arabic	96,572
Vietnamese	75,529
Haitian/Haitian Creole	25,129

Figure 1.6: Five Most Common EL Languages, 2014–2015

Source: National Center for English Language Acquisition (NCELA, 2017).

education (SIFE). We discuss the special learning needs of those students later in this book. Importantly, schools and teachers need to make major adjustments and accommodations to their everyday instructional practices to ensure that those students are able to learn.

But thinking about EL students as *all* coming from immigrant families and backgrounds would be inaccurate. The fact is that many ELs—more than 50% in many states across the United States—were born in the United States but speak a language other than English in the home. Recent data from 2013 indicate that 85% of EL students in grades prekindergarten through grade five were born in the United States, and 62% in grades six through 12 were U.S.-born (MPI, 2013). Those students also represent diverse backgrounds, languages, experiences, and cultures. For teachers of ELs, the key idea is that it is essential to learn about your individual students' home languages and home literacy practices, home culture, and diverse backgrounds. Teachers' instructional decisions should follow from that information.

CONCLUSION

It is important to understand that not all ELs are alike. Many are born in the United States, and many are immigrants. EL students have diverse racial, ethnic, religious, cultural, and linguistic backgrounds, and they contribute to the intellectual and cultural resources of the United States. For students who have had formal education outside of the United States, they can transfer their academic knowledge to the subjects they are taking in the United States. Other immigrants may not be literate in their home language but bring oral traditions and communication patterns and practices with them.

As a teacher, you can nurture, celebrate, and challenge EL students. Some ways to do this are to study their cultures, familiarize yourself with their linguistic and cultural backgrounds as well as their home literacy practices (Coady, 2009), involve ELs in all classroom activities, ensure that ELs' home languages and cultures are a visible resource in the classroom and in the learning materials that you use. Finally, you can engage parents in culturally and linguistically appropriate ways. We give more examples of parent engagement in Chapter 25 of this book.

POINTS TO REMEMBER

✔ Immigrants to the United States bring rich linguistic and cultural resources.
✔ Not all EL students are immigrants.
✔ EL students are a racially, ethnically, linguistically, religious, and culturally diverse group, although Spanish speakers are the largest EL language group.
✔ Teachers of ELs must know their students' language and cultural backgrounds in order to effectively teach ELs.

REFLECTION QUESTIONS AND DISCUSSION

1. Define EL in your own words.

2. In what ways have U.S. immigration patterns changed and how might this affect teachers of immigrant students?

3. Name five different facets of diversity. What is the "majority–minority" trend in the United States and how does it relate to diversity?

ACTIVITIES

1. Review Figure 1.2, Top Ten Immigrant Groups, 2015. What factors do you believe contribute to immigrants' desire to come to the United States? How do you think those factors differ across the top countries? (b) Identify the MPI table online (www .migrationpolicy.org/programs/data-hub/charts/largest-immigrant-groups-over-time) and use their tool to identify immigrant groups from 1960. How have the countries changed between 1960 and the present?

2. Review Figure 1.3 of the caricatures of U.S. immigration in the chapter. Which do you subscribe to? Why? Do you think that perceptions of new immigrants have changed over the past century?

WEB RESOURCES

Changing Face of America. www.ngm.nationalgeographic.com/2013/10/changing-faces/funderburg-text

Migration Policy Institute. www.migrationpolicy.org

Teaching Tolerance. www.tolerance.org

REFERENCES

ALAS! (2008). Cartoon: Immigrants are ruining the economy. Retrieved from http://www.amptoons.com/blog/?p=4113

Coady, M. R. (2009). "*Solamente libros importantes*": Literacy practices and ideologies of migrant farmworking families in north central Florida. In G. Li (Ed.), *Multicultural families, home literacies and mainstream schooling* (pp. 113–128). Charlotte, NC: New Age.

Great Schools Partnership. (2017). Glossary of education reform. Retrieved from http://edglossary.org/english-language-learner

Migration Policy Institute. (2013). The limited English proficient population in the United States. Retrieved from http://www.migrationpolicy.org/article/limited-english-proficient-population-united-states#LEP%20Children

Migration Policy Institute. (2017a). Largest U.S. immigrant groups over time, 1960–present. Retrieved from http://www.migrationpolicy.org/programs/data-hub/charts/largest-immigrant-groups-over-time

Migration Policy Institute. (2017b). U.S. immigrant population and share over time, 1850–present. Retrieved from http://www.migrationpolicy.org/programs/data-hub/charts/immigrant-population-over-time

National Center for Education Statistics. (2017a). Digest of education statistics. Retrieved from https://www.nces.ed.gov/programs/digest/d16/tables/dt16_216.55.asp

National Center for Education Statistics. (2017b). English language learners in public schools. Retrieved from https://www.nces.ed.gov/programs/coe/indicator_cgf.asp

National Center for English Language Acquisition (NCELA). (2017). Fast facts on English learners. Retrieved from http://www.ncela.us/fast-facts

Pew Research Center. (2014). *Fact tank*. Retrieved from http://www.pewresearch.org/fact-tank/2014/08/18/u-s-public-schools-expected-to-be-majority-minority-starting-this-fall

United Nations High Commissioner for Refugees (UNHRC). (2016). *Data on Syrian refugee crisis*. Retrieved from http://www.data.unhcr.org/syrianrefugees/regional.php

Legal Rights of English Learners (ELs) in the United States: An Historical Overview

Readers will be able to

- ❖ Recognize laws that protect the constitutional rights of English learners (ELs)
- ❖ Reflect upon court cases that have had a major impact in the education of ELs
- ❖ Define terminology that describes language proficiency
- ❖ Discuss attitudes and policies of the federal administration and how they determine the ways schools and districts should govern themselves
- ❖ The Florida Consent Decree

THE UNITED STATES CONSTITUTION

AMENDMENT I, THE CONSTITUTION OF THE UNITED STATES, ADOPTED IN 1791

Congress shall make no law . . . abridging freedom of speech . . .

AMENDMENT 14, THE CONSTITUTION OF THE UNITED STATES, ADOPTED IN 1868

No state shall make or enforce any law, which shall abridge the privileges or immunities of citizens of the United States; nor shall any state deprive any person of life, liberty, or property, without due process of law; nor deny to any person within its jurisdiction the equal protection of the laws.

MEYER V. NEBRASKA, UNITED STATES SUPREME COURT, 1923

The protection of the Constitution extends to all those who speak other languages as well as to those born as native English speakers. Perhaps it would be highly advantageous if all had ready understanding of our ordinary speech, but this cannot be coerced with methods which conflict with the Constitution—a desirable end cannot be promoted by prohibited means.

TITLE VI, CIVIL RIGHTS ACT, 1964

No person in the United States shall, on the grounds of race, color, or national origin, be excluded from participation in, be denied the benefits, or be subjected to discrimination under any program or activity receiving Federal financial assistance.

In 1970, the Office of Civil Rights informed school districts with more than 5% national-origin minority children that they had to take affirmative steps to rectify these students' language "deficiencies." This memo mandated that districts offer some type of special language instruction for EL students (Diaz-Rico & Weed, 1995; Gándara & Orfield, 2012). The federal courts began to enforce Title VI of the Civil Rights Act which outlaws discrimination in federally supported programs. In *Serna v. Portales Municipal Schools*, a 1972 case, a federal judge ordered native language instruction as part of a desegregation plan.

LANDMARK CASE

LAU V. NICHOLS, U.S. SUPREME COURT, 1974

There is no equality of treatment merely by providing students with the same facilities, textbooks, teachers, and curriculum, for students who do not understand English are effectively excluded from any meaningful education. Basic English skills are at the very core of what these public schools teach. Imposition of a requirement that demands that a student must already have acquired basic skills before he or she can effectively participate in the educational program is to make a mockery of public education.

The failure of the San Francisco school system to provide English language instruction or other adequate instructional procedures to approximately 1,800 students of Chinese ancestry who did not speak English, denied them a meaningful opportunity to participate in the public educational system. Thus, this neglect violated Section 601 of the 1964 Civil Rights Act, which banned discrimination based "on the ground of race, color, or national origin," in "any program or activity receiving federal financial assistance," and the implementation of the regulations from the Department of Health, Education, and Welfare. This resulted in the national landmark case *Lau v. Nichols*.

The 1974 case made it extraordinarily clear that a student may not be denied equal access to basic subject instruction or to any program offered by an educational entity because of that student's limited English proficiency (LEP). There is not a prescribed threshold of English competency that a student must reach before receiving curricular and extracurricular offerings for which such a student is qualified, irrespective of English proficiency.

OTHER RELEVANT CASES

Castañeda v. Pickard, 1981

Castañeda v. Pickard was a class-action complaint brought against the Raymondville Independent School District in Texas. This complaint alleged that the district's educational policies discriminated against Mexican American students by failing to implement adequate instruction to overcome the linguistic barriers that prevented their equal participation in the district's educational program. In defining "adequate instruction," the court provided the criteria by which a school system's program for EL students could be deemed appropriate to the needs of those students.

These criteria are:

1. Whether the program is based on sound educational theory; that is, one accepted as sound by experts in the field.
2. Whether the program provides adequate resources and personnel to effectively implement the educational theory adopted by the school system.
3. Whether the school system adequately monitors the effectiveness of the program and takes appropriate actions to modify the program as necessary (Garcia, 1995; Smiley & Salsberry, 2007).

Plyler v. Doe, United States Supreme Court, 1982

Plyler v. Doe, a 1982 District Court class-action suit, was filed on behalf of school-aged Mexican children in Smith County, Texas who could not establish that they had been legally admitted into the United States. The action complained of the exclusion of these children from the public schools of the Tyler Independent School District 2.

The appellants argued that because of their immigration status as undocumented aliens, they are not "persons within the jurisdiction" of the State of Texas, and therefore, they had no right to equal protection under Texas law. This argument was rejected by the Court of Appeals. It was reiterated that whatever the status under the immigration laws, an "alien" is surely a "person" in any ordinary sense of that term. Aliens, even aliens whose presence in this country is unlawful, have long been recognized as "persons" and are guaranteed due process of law by the Fifth and Fourteenth Amendments.

After making extensive findings of fact, the District Court held that undocumented people were entitled to the protection of the equal protection clause of the Fourteenth Amendment, and that the Texas statute violated the clause. Thus, the Texas statute withholding funds from local school districts for the education of children not legally admitted into the United States, and authorizing districts to deny enrollment to such children, violated this clause. On appeal, the United States Supreme Court affirmed such violation. However, one can only assume this longstanding law will become a target of abolishment by the anti immigrant presidential administration currently in power. As such, we see the struggle for DACA (Deferred Action for Childhood Arrivals, founded by the Obama administration in June 2012), which calls for the rights of undocumented immigrants to higher education, work permits, deferred action concerning deportation, and whether they should be allowed to pay in-state college tuition (Yates, 2004).

FLORIDA EDUCATIONAL EQUITY ACT, 1984

Discrimination on the basis of race, national origin, sex, handicap, or marital status against a student or an employee in the State system of public education is prohibited. No person in this state shall . . . be excluded from participation in, be denied benefits of, or be subjected to discrimination under any education program or activity, or in any employment conditions or practices, conducted by a public educational institution which receives or benefits from federal or state financial assistance.

All public education classes shall be available to all students without regard to race, national origin, sex, handicap, or marital status; however, this is not intended to eliminate the provision of programs designed to meet the needs of students with limited proficiency in English or exceptional education students.

Although the Constitutional rights of ELs have long been established, further clarification is needed to ensure that all states respect these rights and provide the access to instruction that ELs are guaranteed under the United States Constitution.

Even identifying ELs is a difficult task. There is no federally mandated definition of English proficiency (formerly called LEP). While the federal Bilingual Education Act included an operational definition of LEP, determination of EL status depends largely on state and local agencies. The lack of a mandated uniform definition of LEP has led to a wide range of identification procedures to determine eligibility for services across states, districts, and schools. It also leads to inconsistent reporting of information on ELs within and across states. As a result, states are found noncompliant in court cases for not providing the mandated and necessary services to all ELs.

In 1999–2000, of 55 state education agencies (SEAs) who responded to the question on EL definition and criteria, 90% reported having used Home Language Survey, teacher observation, teacher interviews, and parent information. Eighty percent of the remainder reported the use of student records, grades, informal assessments, and referrals. Although there seems to be more consistency in the identification procedures, there are still inconsistencies reported.

The federal definition of "LEP" is found in Section 7501 of the Bilingual Education Act, Title VII of the Elementary and Secondary Education Act as amended in the Improving America's Schools Act of 1994. See the box that follows.

Improving America's Schools Act of 1994 Title VII

"PART E—GENERAL PROVISIONS" SEC. 7501. DEFINITIONS; REGULATIONS.

"Except as otherwise provided for purposes of this title—

"(8) Limited English proficiency and limited English proficient.—The terms 'limited English proficiency' and 'limited English proficient', when used with reference to an individual, mean an individual—

"(A) who—

"(i) was not born in the United States or whose native language is a language other than English and comes from an environment where a language other than English is dominant; or "(ii) is a Native American or Alaska Native or who is a native resident of the outlying areas and comes from an environment where a language other than English has had a significant impact on such individual's level of English language proficiency; or "(iii) is migratory and whose native language is other than English and comes from an environment where a language other than English is dominant; and "(B) who has sufficient difficulty speaking, reading, writing, or understanding the English language and whose difficulties may deny such individuals the opportunity to learn successfully in classrooms where the language of instruction is English, or to participate fully in our society.

Each state has its own mandates about how to address ELs, however, each state has a different process about determining their proficiency, and appropriate instructional procedures (Samson & Collins, 2012). The Florida Consent Decree provides distinct guidelines for stakeholders in the state of Florida. (See the chapter: *Responding to a Court Imposed Consent Decree: A Look at Initial Placement and Assessment* for further discussion of the Florida Consent Decree.)

Source: National Clearinghouse for Bilingual Education (1992/2002).

League of United Latin American Citizens (LULAC) et al. v. State Board of Education, United States Court of the Southern District, Florida 1990

Like similar laws in other states, the Florida Consent Decree addresses the civil rights of ELs. Foremost among those civil rights is equal access to all education programs. It does not grant ELs any new rights. It simply provides a structure for compliance with the following federal and state laws regarding the education of ELs:

- Title VI and VII of the Civil Rights Act of 1964
- Office of Civil Rights Memorandum (Standards for Title VI Compliance) of May, 1970
- Section 504 of the Rehabilitation Act, 1973
- Requirements based on the Supreme Court decision in *Lau v. Nichols*, 1974
- Equal Education Opportunities Act, 1974
- Requirement of Vocational Education Guidelines, 1979
- Requirements based on the Fifth Circuit Court decision in *Castañeda v. Pickard*, 1981
- Requirements based on the Supreme Court decision in *Plyler v. Doe*, 1982
- Americans with Disabilities Act (PL 94–142)
- Florida Education Equity Act, 1984

In providing the framework for compliance with the above jurisprudence regarding the rights of ELs to equal access to educational programs, the Florida Consent Decree ensures the delivery of the comprehensible instruction to which these students are entitled.

The Florida Consent Decree addresses six broad areas. These are listed below with a synopsis of each area.

- **Section I: Identification and Assessment**
  Synopsis: All students with varied English proficiency must be properly identified and assessed to ensure the provision of appropriate services. The Consent Decree details the procedures for placement of students in the ESOL program, their exit from the program, and the monitoring of students who have exited the program.
- **Section II: Equal Access to Appropriate Programming**
  Synopsis: All ELs enrolled in Florida public schools are entitled to programming appropriate to their level of English proficiency, their level of academic achievement, and to any special needs they may have. ELs shall have equal access to appropriate English language instruction, as well as instruction in basic subject areas that is understandable to the students, given their respective level of English proficiency, and equal and comparable in amount, scope, sequence, and quality to that provided to English proficient (or non-EL) students.
- **Section III: Equal Access to Appropriate Categorical and Other Programs for EL Students**
  Synopsis: EL students are entitled to equal access to all programs appropriate to their academic needs, such as compensatory, exceptional, adult, vocational, or early

childhood education programs, as well as dropout prevention programs and other support services, regardless of their level of English proficiency.

- **Section IV: Personnel**
  Synopsis: This section details the certificate coverage and in-service training teachers must have to be qualified to instruct ESOL students. Teachers may obtain the necessary training through university course work or through school district-provided in-service training. The Consent Decree details specific requirements for ESOL certification and in-service training and sets standards for personnel delivering ESOL instruction.

  As a result of the Florida Consent Decree, all Florida teachers are required to have training in the field of ESOL commensurate with what they teach. At a minimum, this training must involve three university credit hours (or sixty in-service points). The breakdown is as follows:

Elementary, English, Exceptional Education Teachers	15 credits (or 300 in-service points)
Secondary Teachers (Except English Teachers) and Administrators	3 credits (or 60 in-service points)
Secondary Content Area Teachers	3 credits (or 60 in-service points)
Art, Music, Physical Education (PE), Vocational Education, Media Specialists School Counselors and Administrators	3 credits (or varied in-service points)

A state-approved ESOL Endorsement program consists of fifteen credit hours which may be broken down as follows:

Methods of Teaching ESOL
Curriculum Development in ESOL
Testing and Evaluation in ESOL
Applied Linguistics and TESOL
Multicultural Education

- **Section V: Monitoring Issues**
  Synopsis: The Florida Department of Education is charged with the monitoring of local school districts to ensure compliance with the provisions of the Consent Decree pursuant to federal and state law and regulations, including Section 229.565, Florida Statutes (Educational Evaluation Procedures), and Section 228.2001, Florida Statutes (Florida Educational Equity Act). This monitoring is to be carried out by the Office of Multicultural Student Language Education (OMSLE), Division of Public Schools, Florida Department of Education.

- **Section VI: Outcome Measures**
  Synopsis: The Florida Department of Education is required to develop an evaluation process to address equal access and program effectiveness. This evaluation system shall collect and analyze data regarding the progress of EL students and include comparisons between the EL population and the non-EL population regarding

retention rates, graduation rates, dropout rates, grade point averages, and state assessment scores.

(Florida Department of Education, 1990; Samson & Collins, 2012)

Undergraduate/Graduate Teacher Preparation ESOL Infused Programs

Graduates from state approved programs that lead to initial teacher certification are able to qualify for the ESOL endorsement without having to complete the required five courses as listed in Section V, if they complete a state approved ESOL infused program. In these infused programs, some of the required TESOL competencies are infused in the methods courses, and students complete two or three ESOL specific courses.

History of the No Child Left Behind Act of 2001

On January 8, 2002, President Bush signed into law the No Child Left Behind Act (NCLB). No Child Left Behind was a comprehensive plan to reform schools, change school culture, empower parents, and improve education. NCLB applied to all children who attended public schools, including children with disabilities as well as children who traditionally have been excluded, such as minorities, immigrants, and ELs.

NCLB required annual testing of reading and math skills. Beginning with the 2005–2006 school years, students in grades 3–8 were tested in each grade and at least once for those students in grades 10–12. In 2007–2008, NCLB also included testing of science skills and knowledge. This requires students to be tested in science at least once in grades 3–5, 6–9, and 10–12 (U.S. Department of Education, 2008).

At the time, the NCLB act attempted to make efforts to increase academic success for all students and over the years, it became less and less successful while stakeholders agreed there was too much testing and not enough learning. It was intended to reduce the gap between race and class, but that did not happen.

PRESIDENT BUSH OFFERED THIS ADVICE TO PARENTS

"We know that every child can learn. Now is the time to ensure that every child does learn. As parents, you are your children's first teachers and their strongest advocates. You have a critical role to play in how you raise your children and in how you work for meaningful and accurate accountability in their schools. Too many children are segregated in schools without standards, shuffled from grade to grade . . . This is discrimination, pure and simple.

Some say it is unfair to hold disadvantaged children to rigorous standards. I say it is discrimination to require anything less. It is a soft bigotry of low expectations."

Former President George W. Bush

Under the NCLB Act's accountability provisions, states had to describe how they would close the achievement gap and make sure all students, including those who were disadvantaged, achieved academic proficiency. They had to produce annual state and school district report cards that inform parents and communities about state and school progress. Schools that did not make progress needed to provide supplemental services, such as free tutoring or after school assistance, and take corrective actions. If, after 5 years, they were still not making adequate yearly progress (AYP), they had to make dramatic changes to the way the schools were run.

Local Freedom

Under NCLB, states and school districts had unprecedented flexibility in how they used federal education funds, in exchange for greater accountability results.

It was possible for most school districts to transfer up to 50% of the funds they received under the Improving Teacher Quality State Grants, Educational Technology, Innovative Programs, and Safe and Drug-Free Schools programs to any of these programs or to their Title I programs, without separate approval. This allowed school districts to use funds for their particular needs, such as hiring new teachers, increasing teacher pay, and improving teacher training and professional development. Similarly, the law's consolidation of bilingual education programs gave states and districts more control in planning programs to benefit all ELs.

Proven Methods

No Child Left Behind put special emphasis on determining what educational programs and practices had been proven effective through rigorous scientific research. Federal funding was targeted to support these programs and teaching methods that worked to improve student learning and achievement.

Choices for Parents

"...School choice was part of the strategy to give every child an excellent education..."

Former U.S. Secretary of Education Margaret Spellings

The NLBA provided new education options for many families. This federal law allowed parents to choose other public schools or take advantage of free tutoring if their child attended a school that needed improvement. Also, parents could choose another public school if the school their child attends was unsafe. The law also supported the growth of more independent charter schools, funds for some services for children in private schools, and certain protections for home schooling parents. Finally it required that states and local school districts provide information to help parents make informed educational choices for their children.

NCLB and EL Classification

The rapid growth of ELs in the United States demands consistent and accurate measurement of their academic progress and determination of the areas where they need the most assistance. Accordingly, NCLB had mandated inclusion of these students in national and state assessments using reliable and valid measures (Abedi, 2004). Unfortunately, criteria for identifying ELs are still not uniform across the nation. This is problematic since there is not a national definition of LEP.

NCLB provided an operational definition of LEP (NCLB, 2002). (The term "LEP" is no longer used because it denotes a "deficiency" instead of language proficiency.) According to this definition:

The term "LEP," when used with respect to an individual, means an individual
A. who is aged 3 through 21;
B. who is enrolled or preparing to enroll in an elementary school or secondary school;
C.   i. who was not born in the United States or whose native language is a language other than English;
   ii. I. who is a Native American or Alaska Native, or native resident of the outlying areas; and
     II. who comes from an environment where a language other than English has had a significant impact on the individual's level of English language proficiency; or
  iii. who is migratory, whose native language is a language other than English, and who comes from an environment where a language other than English is dominant; and
D. whose difficulties in speaking, reading, writing, or understanding the English language may be sufficient to deny the individual
  i. the ability to meet the State's proficient level of achievement on State assessments;
  ii. the ability to successfully achieve in classrooms where the language of instruction is English; or
  iii. the opportunity to participate fully in society

(Abedi, 2004)

NCLB and ELs

While the NCLB definition of EL seems to be operationally defined, different states, school districts, and schools may interpret these criteria differently (Abedi, 2004).

Based on the inclusion instructions described in NCLB, the National Assessment of Educational Progress (NAEP) excluded ELs who had received reading or mathematics instruction primarily in English for fewer than three school years and could not demonstrate their knowledge of reading or mathematics in English even with the accommodations permitted by NCLB/NAEP. However, the high rate of transience in schools with large numbers of ELs may have caused inaccuracy in reporting the number of years in English-only classes for these students (Nevárez-La Torre, 2012; Pandya, 2011).

Two other problems were the type of assessment instruments being employed to judge ELs' ability to demonstrate their knowledge, and the fact that the reporting of the students' ability may be inaccurate since it may be subjective.

A provision of NCLB allowed states to test ELs in their native language for up to three years (or five on a case-by-case basis) appeared to add a measure of flexibility to the system. There are different kinds of assessment in the native language: translations of tests, adaptations of tests, and parallel development tests.

Translated tests pose problems since these only differ from the English version in the language in which they are written, not in the content or the constructs intended to be measured. Only minor changes are done from the English version; these changes may not even be accurate across all "dialects" of the same language. For example, a translated version of a mathematics test may simply reverse the use of commas and periods, that is, from the number 12,215.64 (in English) to 12.215,64 (in Spanish). This example is totally incorrect for a Hispanic student coming from Puerto Rico, where all numbers are written in the same fashion as in the United States.

Adapted tests involve more substantial changes, such as replacement of a number of items with others that are more appropriate for either culture or language of the new test. Changes in the content thus raise concerns regarding test validity, especially if substantial changes have been made. Since the adaptation process is long and costly, adaptations are rarely used in state assessments in the United States.

Parallel development tests are the least commonly used of the three kinds of native language assessments. This kind of test usually involves a native language version developed concurrently with the English version. The test content and specifications are similar since they are based on the same content standards; however, all items are developed separately in each language. While the items are unique and original, the tests should exhibit similar validities, since they measure similar content (Bowles & Stansfield, 2008).

A review of state assessment practices in in the past revealed that only 11 states offered written native language versions of their statewide assessments. These were: Delaware, Kansas, Massachusetts, Minnesota, Nebraska, New Mexico, New York, Ohio, Rhode Island, Texas, and Wisconsin. Additionally, Texas and New Mexico offered parallel Spanish language versions of some statewide assessments. All states offered native language versions in Spanish, but few states offered versions in Chinese, Haitian Creole, Hmong, Korean, Russian, Somali, and Vietnamese, depending upon the needs of the minority population. By 2012, American Council on Teaching Foreign Languages (ACTFL) was offering written proficiency test in Albanian, Arabic, English, French, German, Italian, Japanese, Russian, and Spanish. However, written translations are limited to students who have had formal education in their native languages and are literate in the L1, but not proficient enough in English for testing.

The reality is that native language assessments are not plentiful and are rarely aligned with state standards. Some are merely translations from English language tests, a procedure that, as already indicated, is considered invalid. In addition, native language tests are inappropriate for ELs who often have limited literacy development in their native language.

It is fair to say that existing instruments for assessing the academic achievement of ELs, whose validity and reliability are questionable at best, cannot be counted on to generate meaningful information for accountability purposes. Yet, state plans that were approved under NCLB relied heavily on such inaccurate and invalid achievement tests (NCLB, 2004).

No Accountability without Reasonable Expectations

In NCLB's accountability system, the EL subgroup itself was a problematic construct. This was, and still is, a highly diverse population in terms of socioeconomic status, linguistic, and cultural background, level of English proficiency, amount of prior education, and instructional programs experience. It is also a highly fluid population, as newcomers often enter programs speaking little English and others leave after being reclassified as fully proficient in English when in actuality they are not. A common exit criterion was the 36th percentile in English reading/language arts. In other words, ELs were *defined* by their low achievement level. When they have acquired minimal English proficiency, they exited the subgroup and their scores were no longer counted in the computation of AYP. So it was not merely unrealistic—it was a mathematical impossibility—for the EL subgroup to "hold schools accountable" for failing to achieve the impossible. Indeed, lumping virtually all schools with significant EL enrollments in the same "needs improvement" category would defeat the purpose of accountability.

Another difficulty in setting reasonable AYP targets was the variability in the time it takes children to acquire a second language, especially the kind of academic language needed for success in school. Research has shown that students in bilingual and English as a second language (ESL) programs require 5 to 7 years to achieve grade-level academic achievement (Crawford, 2004; Cummins & Swain, 2014; García & Kleifgen, 2010).

From NCLB to Every Student Succeeds Act

As you can see by reading about all the problematic issues regarding NCLB, stakeholders complained about the over prescriptive and inflexible laws that every state educational administrators had to comply with. President Barack Obama, along with political consensus from both parties, signed into effect the Every Student Succeeds Act (ESSA) act on December 10, 2015, and ESSA went into full effect in the 2017–2018 school years.

It is hoped that the ESSA will help the overlooked and underserved students who would finally be able to achieve academically by making standards, assessments, and teacher evaluations less restrictive, and ideas more positive. Federal governance will now allow each state to be more innovative and individualist according to their own needs. ESSA still requires annual testing in reading and mathematics in grades 3–8, and only once in high school. But the big plus is that states may overhaul their accountability systems and use their own interventions to increase the success of their lower performing schools. They must keep track of their neediest and most underserved learners, such as ELs, minoritized students, and exceptional education students help improve their academic performance. Schools must show innovative improvements that will help students learn and may even eliminate teachers' salaries that are determined by test scores. Federal government may not dictate how states and districts must follow standards.

All schools must include systems that show they are accountable using multiple measures, academic outcomes, and allow stakeholders to share in the process. Schools can choose their own measures that are research driven, but the problem will be that each school may determine their outcomes individually, so there will be no way to tell if each school has gained the same measures and some may be more rigorous than others (Hess & Eden, 2017; Klein, 2016).

✔ The United States Constitution protects the rights of all who live in the United States.

✔ All legal and undocumented people are protected under federal laws. (This may be changing due to the new presidential administration.)

✔ Numerous court cases have resulted in clarification of peoples' rights in the United States.

✔ *Lau v. Nichols* is considered the landmark case that served as the catalyst that forced districts to provide adequate educational opportunities for EL students in the United States.

✔ *Lau v. Nichols* clarified what is meant by "equal access" under the law.

✔ There is no federally mandated definition of LEP. This causes serious problems, especially when trying to identify ELs and make decisions about programs to serve them.

✔ The Florida Consent Decree is one example of an agreement between the Florida State Board of Education and a coalition of eight groups represented by Multicultural Education, Training, and Advocacy, Inc. (META).

✔ The Florida Consent Decree provides a structure for compliance with all the jurisprudence ensuring the rights of ELs in Florida and equality in educational opportunities as afforded to all native-English-speaking students.

✔ As a result of the Florida Consent Decree, all teachers must receive some type of training in teaching English as a second language.

✔ ESSA has replaced NCLB and each school and district will have more autonomy in making academic gains.

✔ NCLB placed ELs at a testing disadvantage.

REFLECTION QUESTIONS AND DISCUSSION

1. What was the significance of *Plyer v. Doe*, U.S. Supreme Court, 1982?

2. If the Constitution of the United States guarantees the rights of all citizens of the United States, why do you think there has been a need for further clarifying statements resulting from so many court cases?

3. Describe the NCLB of 2002. What did it address? Why? What was the intent? What were the major components?

a. How did NCLB impact education and ELs?

b. What conclusions can you draw from that legislation?

4. Describe ESSA and its main aims.
   a. How is it different from NCLB, particularly for EL students and families?

   b. What issues will school systems have to deal with?

   c. What problems can you anticipate with ESSA?

ACTIVITIES

1. Search the net and study other important cases not discussed in this chapter which have affected the teaching of ELs in the United States the cases and give a brief explanation of their respective impact.

2. Develop a timeline of the major jurisprudence which has affected the teaching of ELs in the United States. Include the cases discussed in this chapter and add a minimum of three others that you researched on your own.
   Be prepared to share your timeline and expand upon the entries you added.

3. Reread the Landmark Case *Lau v. Nichols* of 1974. Explain in writing your interpretation in the space provided.

LAU V. NICHOLS, SUPREME COURT, 1974

There is no equality of treatment merely by providing students with the same facilities, textbooks, teachers, and curriculum; for students who do not understand English, are effectively foreclosed from any meaningful education. Basic English skills are at the very core of what these public schools teach. Imposition of a requirement that, before a child can effectively participate in the educational program, he must already have acquired those basic skills is to make a mockery of public education.

4. Select one of the areas of the Florida Consent Decree and research the area to expand its scope. Interview a teacher and/or an administrator to investigate how the area you selected is being implemented in his or her school. Describe your results in the space provided.

WEB RESOURCES

A Chronology of Federal Law and Policy Impacting Language Minority Students. http://www.colorincolorado.org/article/chronology-federal-law-and-policy-impacting-language-minority-students
ELL Policy and Research. http://www.colorincolorado.org/ell-basics/ell-policy-research
How Educators can Advocate for English Learners. https://www.nea.org/assets/docs/18285_ELL_AdvocacyGuide2015_low-res_updated_6-23.pdf

REFERENCES

Abedi, J. (2004). Inclusion of students with limited English proficiency. In *NAEP: Classification and measurement issues: CSE Report 629, Graduate School of Education and Information Studies*. Los Angeles, CA: University of California.

Bowles, M., & Stansfield, C. W. (2008). *A practical guide to standards-based assessment in the native*. Language. NLA—LEP Partnership. Bethesda, MD: Second Language Testing.

Crawford, J. (2004). *No Child Left Behind: Misguided approach for school accountability for English language learners*. Washington, DC: NABE. http://www.languagepolicy.net/articles.html.

Cummins, J., & Swain, M. (2014). *Bilingualism in education: Aspects of theory, research and practice*. New York, NY: Routledge.

Diaz-Rico, L. T., & Weed, K. Z. (1995). *The crosscultural language and academic development handbook: A complete K–12 reference guide*. Massachusetts, MA: Allyn and Bacon.

Florida Department of Education. (1990). Office of Multicultural Student Language Education. *Consent Decree*. Retrieved from http://www.firn.edu/doe/bin00011/restatem.htm

Gándara, P., & Orfield, G. (2012). Why Arizona matters: The historical, legal, and political contexts of Arizona's instructional policies and US linguistic hegemony. *Language Policy, 11*(1), 7–19.

Garcia, B. (1995). Florida Department of Education. *Issues regarding the education of LEP students . . . A restatement*. Retrieved from http://www.firn.edu/doe/bin/restatem.htm

García, O., & Kleifgen, J. A. (2010). *Educating emergent bilinguals: Policies, programs, and practices for English language learners*. New York, NY: Teachers College Press.

Hess, F. M., & Eden, M. (2017). *The every student succeeds act: What it means for schools, systems, and states*. Cambridge, MA: Harvard Education Press.

Klein, A. (2016). Under ESSA, states, districts to share more power. *Education Week, 35*(15), 10–12.

National Clearinghouse for Bilingual Education. (1992/2002). Retrieved from https://ncela.ed.gov/publications/archived2002

Nevárez-La Torre, A. A. (2012). Transiency in urban schools: Challenges and opportunities in educating ELLs with a migrant background. *Education and Urban Society, 44*(1), 3–34.

No Child Left Behind. (2002). Retrieved from http://www.wrightslaw.com/news/2002nclb.sign.htm

Pandya, J. Z. (2011). *Overtested: How high-stakes accountability fails English language learners*. New York, NY: Teachers College Press.

Samson, J. F., & Collins, B. A. (2012). *Preparing all teachers to meet the needs of English language learners: Applying research to policy and practice for teacher effectiveness*. Center for American Progress. Retrieved from https://files.eric.ed.gov/fulltext/ED535608.pdf

Smiley, P., & Salsberry, T. (2007). *Effective schooling for English language learners: What elementary principals should know and do*. Larchmont, NY: Eye On Education.

U.S. Department of Education, A Nation Accountable: Twenty-five Years After A Nation at Risk, Washington, D.C., 2008. https://www2.ed.gov/rschstat/research/pubs/accountable/accountable.pdfm

Yates, L. S. (2004). Plyler v. Doe and the rights of undocumented immigrants to higher education: Should undocumented students be eligible for in-state college tuition rates. *Washington ULQ, 82*, 585.

Language Education Programs for English Learners

Readers will be able to

- ❖ Historically situate bilingual education programs from the 19th to 21st centuries
- ❖ Understand bilingual education as a political movement
- ❖ Identify and describe key features of various language education programs for English learners (ELs) in the United States
- ❖ Describe the association between bilingual (two language) education programs and student learning outcomes
- ❖ Relate translanguaging to different language education programs

Señora Martinez is a third grade teacher in a dual language program in California. She has 11 students who are native English speakers, eight who are native Spanish speakers from Central America and California, and three who are Portuguese speakers who speak Brazilian Portuguese in the home. Her program provides students instruction in both English and Spanish for about 50% of the time in each language, and the languages are separated across different subjects each day. She notices that her native Spanish and Portuguese speaking students are gaining a good grasp of English reading and writing but their overall literacy is slightly below than that of her native English speakers in English but above the English speakers in Spanish. By the time these students reach fifth grade, their literacy levels will be strong in both English and Spanish.

INTRODUCTION

English learner (EL) students today can be found in every state in the United States, from rural settings in Vermont where there are limited numbers of students who are learning English in mainstream, traditional classrooms to Texas and California in dual language (two way) educational programs where English and a second language such as Spanish are both used as mediums of instruction in school. These different program models have vastly different approaches to the social, emotional, and linguistic development of EL students. In this chapter, we review several of the most common language education program types for EL students in the United States and we discuss ways that teachers and educators who instruct in "English only" classrooms can most effectively support the language and literacy development of ELs.

From the outset, educational programs for students in the process of learning English is a social and political (and arguably an ethical) issue. An individual's or group's ideologies regarding the role of "minority" language use in public schools greatly affect the ways that politicians, educators, parents, and communities support (or not) the development of multiple languages. An example of an ideology or belief that affects language education programs is the misconception that EL students must be "immersed" in English only classrooms in order to learn English more quickly or efficiently. This belief is far from true. Although it seems counterintuitive, ongoing first language and literacy development enhances and supports the development of English as a second or additional language; Thomas & Collier, 1997, 2002).

Imagine your parents were offered a great opportunity for you to live for 3 years in Tajikistan. After weighing their options, they decide to accept the offer because it will bring financial security and safety to your family. You are both scared and excited by the prospect of living in a new environment and culture (Figure 3.1).

You arrive in Dushanbe, the capital, knowing no Tajik. Before arriving, you learned that the Tajik language uses a Cyrillic alphabet, and that many Tajiks also speak Russian. Back in the United States you were in the middle of your eighth grade school year. There are no

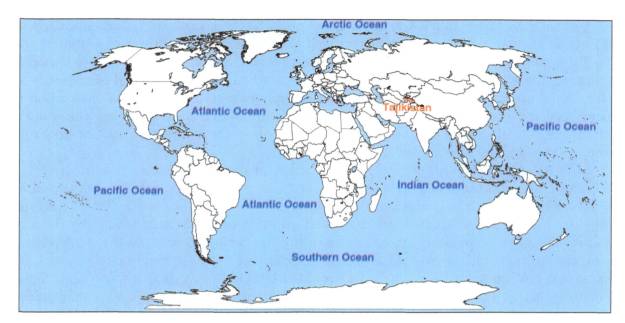

Figure 3.1: Tajikistan on World Map
© ekler/Shutterstock.com

private English language programs for you in Dushanbe, so your parents enroll you in an age appropriate grade at a local school. The first day of school you are brought to your classroom, and the teacher walks you to a desk in the middle of the room. Students seem to be learning history—you think—because the images on the chalkboard look like the outline of a map. The teacher is talking in rapid pace. Your head swarms. You understand none of the language or instruction, but a classmate brings you a textbook after being prompted by the teacher. You stare at the cover of the book. Students around you are writing in their notebooks, but the script is nothing like what you know in English or have ever seen before. It looks like this:

> ҷанг
> сулҳ
> ҳизби сиёсӣ
> ҳукумат
> шартнома

The sounds of Tajik echo around the room, and you are unable to decode or understand what is going on. You feel defeated and alone, like you will never learn the subject or the language.

Now imagine that a classmate pulls up a chair next to you and starts to write some key words on your notebook in English alongside the Tajik words. She writes:

> war—ҷанг
> peace—сулҳ
> political party—ҳизби сиёсӣ
> government—ҳукумат
> treaty—шартнома

You begin to realize that if you learn the school subjects in Tajik alongside some support in English, the language you already know well, you can learn BOTH the subject matter and the Tajik language. Skills learned in one language (such as reading) transfer into a second language (Cummins & Sayers, 1997). This is bilingual education. **Bilingual education is an educational program where two (or more) languages are used as mediums of instruction to learn academic content**. Without being an expert in bilingual education, you can quickly see the benefits of using a language you know to support the acquisition and learning of a second language, or Tajik in this hypothetical case.

Misconceptions regarding bilingual education programs and their benefit, however, abound. One main misconception in the United States is that Spanish-speaking children in Spanish–English bilingual education programs will fail to learn English (Crawford, 2004) if they receive instruction in Spanish. This misconception is generated by the idea that is only possible to development of one language well at a time, or that English will compete with Spanish in overall language development. Another misconception is the social fear that immigrants might "take over" the United States, or that the United States will no longer be a majority English-speaking country. In similar vein, there is a misguided idea that the United States will lose its cultural identity. A brief review of the history of bilingual education in the United States demonstrates that these myths are not true, and that multilingual societies are natural, normal, and characteristic of a global society.

BRIEF HISTORY OF BILINGUAL EDUCATION IN THE UNITED STATES

In contrast to the prevalent "official English" policies adopted by 31 states today (Liu & Sokhey, 2014), the United States has a long history of bilingual education. In fact, from the time of the earliest settlers, educational programs have been organized and promoted through multiple languages. For example, in the late 19th century, German-medium, Dutch-medium, and French-medium schools were not rare, and they existed without conflict with different language education programs (Crawford, 2004). In addition to those languages of settlers, indigenous or native people's languages were and continue to be used in educational programs in the United States. In fact, as early as 1839 the first bilingual education law was established in the state of Ohio, where parents could request German–English instructional programs.

Anti-immigrant sentiment, however, negatively affected bilingual education programs, notably at the onset of World War I in 1914. It became increasingly difficulty to continue German-medium programs, and by World War II, those programs were effectively diminished. Although the growth of immigrants continued, there was little continued support for bilingual education programs during and after World War II, following public anti-immigrant and pro-U.S. nationalist movements. This trend halted to some degree with the 1968 Bilingual Education Act, which established financial support for bilingual programs and the preparation of teachers to work in those programs. However, the shifting tides of bilingual education changed again, and the late 20th century experienced another decline in bilingual programs, as evidenced by anti-bilingual legislation passed in the states of California, Arizona, and Massachusetts.

Current views about bilingual education programs are varied. On the one hand, there has been a steady growth in educational programs where two languages are used as mediums of instruction with non-native English speakers and native English speakers in the same classroom (Center for Applied Linguistics [CAL], 2017). Those programs are generally referred to as dual-language programs, and are located largely in immigrant communities and bilingual settings in California, Texas, and New York. Overall, more than 35 states offered dual-language education programs in 2015–2016 (National Center for English Language Acquisition [NCELA], 2016). Proponents of bilingual education cite the social, emotional, cognitive, and linguistic benefits of children learning to read and write in two languages. On the other hand, opponents of bilingual education argue that the programs undermine a one-nation, one-language ideology and that they are costly to administer. They also argue that bilingual programs delay the reading, writing, and speaking of English because students spend too much time using their native language and fail to learn English rapidly. The data on English language acquisition in dual language, bilingual education programs demonstrate that students take slightly longer to learn to read and write in English and their first language (e.g., Spanish) but by 5th grade those students either perform as well as or outperform native English speakers.

Language Education Programs for ELs

There are nearly five million ELs in the United States, representing approximately 10% of the total K–12 school-age population. Despite this large number, there are no federal laws that mandate a specific type of program to serve the needs of ELs. However, legislation provides funding and support for services for them. In addition, federal court decisions have focused primarily on civil rights for non-English speakers supporting their right to services that offer equal educational opportunity to all ELs (see the legal case Lau v. Nichols, 1974). The vast majority of ELs are served by a type of language education program designed to meet their social and academic needs in school. Regardless of its design, the minimal goal of each program must be to provide each student with the English language skills necessary to function successfully in an academic setting.

There are numerous program models for ELs in the United States. They range from programs that provide no support for students in their native language (or first language, L1) to programs that support the development of bilingualism and biliteracy in the native language and English. In the next section, we describe the most common types of language education programs for ELs in the United States (Table 3.1).

SUBMERSION

When no instructional support is provided to EL students by trained specialists or teachers, we refer to this as "submersion." Unfortunately, under U.S. law, submersion is not an educational program and it is illegal in the United States not to provide specific supports to students in the process of learning English as a second or additional language. Supports under the federal law were outlined by the case *Lau v. Nichols* in 1974 by the U.S. Supreme Court. Subsequent legal cases have further defined the types of supports required under U.S. law.

ENGLISH-DOMINANT PROGRAMS

English as a Second or Additional Language (ESL/EAL) or English to Speakers of Other Languages (ESOL) instruction, with no instruction through the minority language.

ESL/EAL/ESOL Support Programs

These programs are generally used in elementary schools. Under this model, an EL student receives specialized instruction in ESOL. Instruction is conducted by a trained ESOL teacher who employs second language acquisition techniques. EL students may receive instruction primarily in English (language arts), science, and social studies, but not necessarily exclusively in these subjects. Subject areas may vary from district to district. ELs from different minority language backgrounds may be grouped together, and teachers may or may not be bilingual in the language of the students. The amount of time varies from school to school. Instruction may take place in the mainstream classroom or in a designated ESL classroom.

ESL/EAL/ESOL Taught as a Subject

This approach is generally used in middle or high schools. The EL students receive ESOL instruction during a regular class period, often with an English language arts teacher or teacher specialized in ESOL. Students generally receive credit for this course, taken in a departmentalized setting. ELs may be grouped according to their level of English proficiency.

Sheltered English or Content-Based Programs

These programs are used primarily in secondary schools. In these content area classes, such as science or social studies, ELs from different backgrounds, who usually have intermediate English proficiency, come together to receive content instruction especially designed to provide "comprehensible input," or language that is modified to be understandable to students. A trained teacher who is not necessarily bilingual provides the instruction. Sheltered English or content-based programs may parallel virtually all mainstream academic curricular offerings or may consist of only one or two subjects.

Structured Immersion Programs

These programs may be offered either in elementary or secondary schools. Immersion programs include, in varying degrees, development of language skills and content area instruction in English. No structured ESL component is included, since content area instruction is based on the notion of "comprehensible input" in which the teacher uses second language acquisition strategies, including sheltered English. In these programs, teachers may be bilingual; students may address them in their native language, although the teacher will generally respond in English. Again, there is great variation in these programs based on the number of ELs, resources, preparation of the teaching staff, and parental and community support.

NATIVE/FIRST LANGUAGE AND ENGLISH LANGUAGE DEVELOPMENT PROGRAMS

Early-Exit or Transitional Bilingual Programs

In this program model, academic instruction is provided in the first language (such as Spanish) of young children, with gradual transition to all English language instruction in approximately 2–3 years. The goal is not bilingualism or biliteracy development but to support the first language until the student has acquired "enough" English to function in a mainstream, "English only" classroom. It is known that it takes more than 3 years to acquire a second language (Cummins, 1981). Thus, this type program is ineffective in providing for the long-term language development needs of the EL student.

Late-Exit or Maintenance Bilingual Programs

In this model, academic instruction is provided in the first language for elementary EL students in grades K–6, with a gradual decrease in first language instruction and a corresponding increase in English language instruction. Students are transitioned into all English instruction by the end of elementary or into the middle or high school years. The goal is to provide extended support for the first language and literacy development; however, the long-term goal is not to support high levels of literacy in two languages.

Immersion Bilingual Programs

Immersion bilingual programs provide academic instruction through both L1 and L2 for grades K–12 and originally were developed for language majority students in Canada and used as a model for two-way bilingual education in the United States. Two-way bilingual programs are those programs where language majority students, as well as language minority students, are both being taught in two languages, that is, bilingually. The goal is for both student populations to become bilingual.

Dual Language or Two-Way Immersion Programs

In this program model, native English speakers and language minority students (e.g., Spanish speakers) are schooled together in the same bilingual class. This model is implemented with many variations including coteaching models; models where the two languages of instruction are strategically varied terms of input (listening or reading) and output (speaking or writing); and daily or weekly instructional shifts in language to ensure that both languages are used equally as mediums of instruction. Some advocates of this model prefer a 50–50 balance between native- and non-native speakers of English; however, a challenge to implementing this model is identifying areas where those proportions of students live.

Table 3.1 summarizes the information discussed in the previous section. Although bilingualism appears as the linguistic goal for the late-exit or developmental bilingual education, this goal is unattainable if this type of program is only provided at the elementary school level. Thus, although the goal is bilingualism, and the benefits of bilingualism and

Table 3.1: Language Education Programs

Type of Program	Typical Child	Language of the Classroom	Aim in Language Outcome
English-Dominant Programs			
Submersion (Mainstreaming with no differentiation)	Language minority	English	Monolingualism
Mainstream classrooms — with ESL pull-out—with ESL push-in	Language minority	English	Monolingualism
Structured English immersion	Language minority	English	Monolingualism
Native/First Language Development Programs			
Transitional bilingual education (TBE)	Language minority	From minority to majority language (English)	Relative monolingualism, limited bilingualism
Developmental bilingual education (DBE)	Language Minority	From minority to majority (English)	Limited bilingualism and biliteracy
Two-way immersion (TWI)/dual language	Language minority and majority (may be 50/50)	Both minority and majority languages	Bilingualism and biliteracy

biliteracy are great, in reality, that goal may not be achieved unless students continue to be taught in both languages throughout high school.

FACTORS THAT AFFECT THE DESIGN OF ESOL PROGRAMS

District Demographics

Some districts have large, relatively stable populations of ELs from a single language or cultural background. Others have large groups of ELs representing several language backgrounds. Still other districts may experience a sudden increase in the number of ELs from a given group: the number of Vietnamese, Hmong, Cubans, Haitians, and Guatemalans in many districts has increased significantly in direct response to social and political changes in these students' countries of origin. Some districts have very small numbers of ELs from many different language groups, whereas others report more than one hundred language groups with very few students from each scattered across grade levels and schools. The characteristics of these populations, including the numbers and kinds of students per language group, the size of language groups and the mobility of their members, as well as geographic and grade distribution of students influence the type of EL instructional program design that a district may develop.

Teacher Preparation

Another important factor is the preparation of teachers to teach in bilingual education programs. Across the United States, different states hold various requirements for teachers to work with children in the process of learning English as a second language. In the State of Florida, for example, the preparation of teachers is governed by a legal requirement called the Florida Consent Decree, signed in 1990. That decree requires all elementary teachers to have 300 hours of preparation, whereas secondary content teachers require 60 hours of professional preparation. States such as California, Texas, and New York also have legal requirements that govern teacher preparation. It is important to note that individual states determine the preparation requirements of teachers to work with EL students. Increasingly, states across the country are including goals of bilingualism and biliteracy development for students.

Individual Student Characteristics

Some ELs enter U.S. schools with strong academic preparation in their native language. They have attended schools in their own country, have learned to read and write well in their native language, and are at comparable (or better) levels as native English speakers of the same grade level and age. Others may not have such extensive academic preparation. Due to social, economic, or cultural factors, their schooling may have been interrupted or nonexistent. This means some students at every age level come with little or no exposure to reading and writing, and may be unable to do even basic mathematical computations. Thus, designing an instructional program to serve students of such diverse needs becomes an increasingly complex task.

District Resources

The capability of individual districts to provide human and material resources greatly influences the type of program that may be designed to serve ELs. The availability of resources varies from district to district. Some school districts have trained ESL personnel to staff schools as need arises, whereas others have to scramble to find someone who can work with a few students on a volunteer basis. Some districts can draw upon a large stable community group for bilingual personnel to staff immersion bilingual programs, others must look beyond the local area.

Some districts are experiencing declining enrollments, freeing up classroom space to allow magnet schools or resource centers to flourish where ELs from several schools come together at one centrally located school. Other districts are bursting at the seams, making it almost impossible just to find classroom space to house dual language or structured English immersion (SEI) programs. In addition, the preparation of teachers who can teach bilingual is a great concern for districts seeking to add or expand dual language or other bilingual education programs where students are learning to read and write academic content in two languages.

The design of any ESOL/English as a new language (ENL) program must take these factors and others, such as transportation for children, state curricular mandates, and local support for immigrants, into account. Hence, it becomes a complex task to determine which type of program would be best in any given set of circumstances. It can be said that the best program is one which:

- Is tailored to meet the linguistic, academic, and social–emotional needs of EL students;
- Provides ELs with high quality instruction necessary to allow them to progress through school at a rate commensurate to their native English-speaking peers;
- Makes the best use of district and community resources.

However, because researchers have made considerable advances in the fields of psycholinguistics, second language acquisition, bilingual pedagogy, and multicultural education, today we know a great deal more about the challenges faced by ELs and about promising strategies for overcoming them.

A CASE FOR BILINGUAL EDUCATION

Bilingual education is one of the most controversial topics in the field of education. This controversy centers around the role of first language instruction: Should ELs receive instruction in their native language until they are able to comprehend English? Another question relates to the selection of students for the bilingual programs: Which students should enroll and in which programs? Bilingual programs have been criticized for segregating ELs from fluent English-speaking peers for an extended amount of time, restricting opportunities for second-language (L2) acquisition and acculturation.

Meta-analysis, an objective method that weighs numerous variables in each study under review, has yielded positive findings about bilingual education (Goldberg, 2008). A comprehensive review of research regarding the use of first and second languages in education was carried out for the World Bank. The following are among the conclusions drawn from this study:

- Individuals most easily develop literacy skills in a familiar language.
- Individuals most easily develop cognitive skills and master content material when they are taught in a familiar language.
- The best predictor of cognitive/academic language development in a second language is the level of development of cognitive/academic language proficiency in the first language.
- If the ultimate goal is to help the student develop the highest possible degree of content mastery and second language proficiency, time spent instructing the student in a familiar language is a wise investment.
- Development of the mother tongue promotes cognitive development and serves as a basis for learning the second language.

Two major reviews of the research on educating ELs completed in 2006 (one by the national literacy panel [NLP]; the other by the center for research on education, diversity, and excellence, [CREDE]), report the following:

- Primary language instruction (L1) promotes reading achievement in English (L2) and in the primary language.
- More L1 instruction over more years leads to higher levels of EL achievement in English.
- The longer ELs receive instruction in a mix of their L1 and English, the better their achievement in English.
- Learning to read in the home language promotes reading achievement in L2.

The general public may express disbelief at these findings. It seems counterintuitive that if the goal of education is English proficiency, delivering instruction in any other language could be helpful. This is why scientific research is so crucial; common sense does not always turn out to be the truth. If people only relied on common sense, the common belief would still be that the earth is flat.

Although there is much to be learned about the contexts and strategies that facilitate transfer across languages, the fact that transfer of academic concepts already mastered occurs from one language to another is not a topic of debate. The work of Hakuta (1986) and his colleagues provides clear evidence that a student who acquires basic literacy or mathematical concepts in one language can transfer this knowledge easily to a second language. The literature is abundant with examples confirming the importance of nurturing the student's native language. Durgunoğlu (2002), in particular, writes about the need to develop the basic functions of literacy, mathematical concepts, and scientific discourse in the first language to the fullest extent possible, while facilitating the transfer to the second language. Learning time spent in well-designed bilingual programs is time well spent. Knowledge and skills acquired in the native language—literacy in particular—are transferable to the second language. They do not need to be relearned in English (Cummins, 1992; Krashen, 1996). The NLP and CREDE reports (2006) also substantiate the fact that literacy and other skills and knowledge transfer across languages.

Research over the past few decades has determined that, despite appearances, it takes anywhere from 5 to 7 years to develop academic language proficiency or academic language. Often the EL is quick to develop basic interpersonal communication skills (BICS) or social language used on the playground or to communicate simple needs, yet they are nowhere near ready to employ the cognitively demanding decontextualized language used for academic pursuits; this takes much longer to acquire (Cummins, 1981; Goldberg, 2008; Thomas & Collier, 2001).

Bilingual education programs that emphasize a gradual transition to English and offer native language instruction in declining amounts over time provide continuity in the ELs' cognitive growth and lay a foundation for academic success in the second language. However, bilingual education supporters point to two-way immersion (TWI) programs as examples of integration in a bilingual context (de Jong, 2006).

As outlined in Table 3.1, there are a number of programs in which the main focus is on developing literacy in two languages: bilingualism. The framework for two-way bilingual education programs is the interdependent relationship between L1 and L2. Nguyen, Shin, and Krashen (2001) assert that the use of L1 is not detrimental to the development of spoken English. In fact, it may accelerate L2 acquisition and the development of academic skill in L2. Advocates of the two-way bilingual model adhere to the paradigm influence in Cummins' (1996) interdependence hypothesis, which purports that (a) there is a transfer of knowledge, skill, and processes across languages; (b) the development of L1 literacy skill facilitates the acquisition of academic skills in the L2, and, hence (c) proficiency in L2 is a function of the level of L1 proficiency at the time when instruction in L2 begins (López & Tashakkori, 2006).

If bilingual education appears to be the most effective model in teaching ELs, then why is it not the most widely employed? Bilingual education continues to be a political and social issue in many societies and communities. Some incorrectly equate "bilingual" education programs with children learning only Spanish.

One of the most commonly alluded to fallacies about bilingual programs is that they are far more costly than English language instruction. All programs serving ELs require additional staff, training, instructional materials, and administration; thus, they cost a little more than regular programs for native English speakers. Yet, in most cases the difference is minimal. In fact, there is typically the same number of teachers and staff per student in a well-implemented dual language program as there is in an English only classroom with ESL support. An additional challenge to the growth in bilingual or dual language programs is the shortage of bilingual teachers, or the lack of expertise in bilingual methodologies. Nevertheless, the following propositions have strong empirical support:

- Native-language instruction does not hinder the acquisition of English language or literacy; in fact, ongoing first language literacy instruction supports English language literacy development.

- Well-developed skills in the native language are associated with high levels of academic achievement.
- Bilingualism is a valuable skill for the individuals and for the country and is an essential characteristic of a global society.

All teachers working with EL students can benefit from practices and pedagogies in translanguaging. Translanguaging is the strategic use of two or more languages, as an integrated language system, by multilingual students. García describes bilingual classrooms where EL students can use translanguaging practices, such as reading in one language about a topic and writing about that topic in a second/different language. She also describes mainstream, English language classrooms where teachers create strategic spaces for their multilingual students to use languages for learning, sharing, and assessment purposes (García & Kleyn, 2016). The work on translanguaging is emerging; however, teachers of bi- and multilingual students can use student's linguistic repertoires as a resource for education and learning.

SUMMARY

This chapter has described multiple and varied educational programs that support EL students and that hold potential for bilingualism and biliteracy development. Importantly, teachers cannot simply "do nothing" with their EL students; that form of linguistic submersion is illegal in the U.S. context. There are multiple program models, from dual language to transitional bilingual, that support language and literacy development of ELs. Teachers and educators also benefit from these programs, because they value the culture and linguistic identities of their students. The decision to design and implement bilingual education programs is based on multiple factors, including resources, funding, and social support for the programs. Despite having a long history in the United States, bilingual education remains a challenging political issue.

ACTIVITIES

1. Conduct an analysis or investigation of the language(s) used in your community. Identify spaces where bilingual EL students or families gather, including restaurants, stores, transportation stations, airports, and malls. Note the languages you hear spoken around you. How might those languages be used as resources in school settings?

2. Review the Seal of Biliteracy, currently endorsed by over 30 states: http://www.sealofbiliteracy.org/ Investigate your state by clicking on the map. In what stage of adoption of the Seal is your state? Consider ways that your school or district might

support bilingualism and biliteracy of your EL students? How can you implement the Seal at your school or district? What other ways can you value biliteracy development of ELs in your classroom, school, district, or state?

REFLECTION QUESTIONS AND DISCUSSION

1. Read García and Lin (2017) and García and Kleyn's (2016) work on translanguaging. Which program model do you work in with ELs? How does translanguaging relate to your program model? How could you implement translanguaging practices in your instruction?

2. Watch the film on dual language programs and learners, *Speaking in Tongues*, by PatchWork Films http://www.speakingintonguesfilm.info/ What surprised you about the students in dual language programs? What are two key learning points of the film and the academic achievement of the students?

Reread the scenario at the beginning of this chapter. Answer the following questions:

3. What type of program do you think is represented by this scenario?

_____

_____

_____

_____

_____

4. What makes you think that? Explain.

_____

_____

_____

_____

_____

_____

5. Based on what you read, would you recommend this type of program? Why?/Why not?

_____

_____

_____

_____

TEST YOUR LEARNING

1. What models of bilingual programs are described in this chapter? What is the language development goal for each?

      Model Program   Language Development Goal

a. _____

b. _____

c. _____

d. _____

e. _____

2. Describe the differences between the five program models listed above.

3. What models of ESL programs are described in this chapter? What is the language development goal for each?

      Model Program   Language Development Goal

a. _____

b. _____

c. _____

d. _____

4. Describe the differences between the four program models listed above.

5. If you were the superintendent of a school district and had all the necessary resources, which model program would you implement and why?

Answer the following questions:

6. Interview a teacher and/or principal to investigate what model program is offered to ELs in their school. Describe the program.

_____

_____

_____

_____

_____

7. Does the program fall under any of the models described in this chapter? Which one? If not, where would you classify this particular program model?

_____

_____

_____

_____

_____

8. What is your opinion of this program, based on what you have learned in this chapter?

_____

_____

_____

_____

_____

WEB RESOURCES

CAL Dual Language Directory in the United States. www.cal.org/twi/directory/
Center for Applied Linguistics. www.cal.org
Dual Language Education of New Mexico. http://www.dlenm.org/index.php/homepage/what-is-dle

EAL Journal: What Is Translanguaging? https://www.ealjournal.org/2016/07/26/what-is-translanguaging/

Seal of Biliteracy. http://www.sealofbiliteracy.org/

Translanguaging. https://www.youtube.com/watch?v=MmIiq6Bsgqc

REFERENCES

Center for Applied Linguistics. (2017). *Dual language programs*. Retrieved from http://www.webapp.cal.org/duallanguage/

Crawford, J. (2004). *Educating English learners: Language diversity in the classroom*. Houston: Bilingual Education Serv.

Cummins, J. (1981). The role of primary language development in promoting educational success for language minority students. In California State Department of Education (Ed.), *Schooling and language minority students: A theoretical framework*. Los Angeles, CA: Evaluation, Dissemination and Assessment Center, California State University.

Cummins, J. (1992). Language proficiency, bilingualism, and academic achievement. In P. A. Richard-Amato & M. A. Snow (Eds.), *The multicultural classroom: Readings for content-area teachers* (pp. 16–26). New York, NY: Longman.

Cummins, J. (1996). *Negotiating identities: Education for empowerment in a diverse society*. Los Angeles, CA: California Association for Bilingual Education.

Cummins, J., & Sayers, D. (1997). *Brave new schools: Challenging cultural illiteracy through global learning networks*. Palgrave Macmillan.

de Jong, E. (2006). Integrated bilingual education: An alternative approach. *Bilingual Research Journal, 30*(1), 23–44.

Durgunoğlu, A. Y. (2002). Cross-linguistic transfer in literacy development and implications for language learners. *Annals of Dyslexia, 52*(1), 189–204.

EAL Journal. (2016). What is translanguaging? Retrieved from https://www.ealjournal.org/2016/07/26/what-is-translanguaging/

García, O., & Kleyn, T. (Eds.). (2016). *Translanguaging with multilingual students: Learning from classroom moments*. New York, NY: Routledge.

García, O., & Lin, A. M. (2017). Translanguaging in bilingual education. In O. García, A. M. Lin, & S. May (Eds.), *Bilingual and multilingual education* (pp. 117–130). New York, NY: Springer.

Hakuta, K. (1986). *Mirror of language. The debate on bilingualism*. New York, NY: Basic Books.

Krashen, S. D. (1996). *Under attack: The case against bilingual education*. Culver City, CA: Language Education Associates.

Lau v. Nichols (1974). 414 US 563.

Liu, A. H., & Sokhey, A. E. (2014, June 18). When and why do U.S. states make English their official language? *Washington Post*. Retrieved from https://www.washingtonpost.com/news/monkey-cage/wp/2014/06/18/when-and-why-do-u-s-states-make-english-their-official-language/?utm_term=.4f7b38621dab

López, M. G., & Tashakkori, A. (2006). Differential outcomes of two bilingual education programs on English language learners. *Bilingual Research Journal, 30*(1), 123–145.

National Center for English Language Acquisition (NCELA). (2016). Dual language education programs: Current state policies and practices. Retrieved from https://www.ncela.ed.gov/files/rcd/TO20_DualLanguageRpt_508.pdf

Nguyen, A., Shin, F., & Krashen, S. (2001). Development of the first language is not a barrier to second-language acquisition: Evidence from Vietnamese immigrants to the United States. *International Journal of Bilingual Education and Bilingualism, 4*(3), 159–164.

Thomas, W. P., & Collier, V. P. (1997, December). *School effectiveness for language minority students*. Washington, DC: National Clearinghouse for English Language Acquisition (NCELA) Resource Collection Series, No. 9.

Thomas, W. P., & Collier, V. P. (2002). *A national study of school effectiveness for language minority students' long-term academic achievement*. Santa Cruz, CA: Center for Research on Education, Diversity and Excellence, University of California-Santa Cruz.

The English Learner (EL)

LEARNING OBJECTIVES

Readers will be able to

- ❖ Define and describe common characteristics of an English learner (EL)
- ❖ Define various language backgrounds of ELs, including SIFE, SLIFE, refugee, and immigrant
- ❖ Contrast recent arrivals, generation 1.5, and generation 2.0 students
- ❖ Consider and describe implications of English learner (EL) status on for teachers

It is difficult to fathom a concept that is totally unfamiliar to us. A few years ago, I decided to try a shock language activity with my elementary education majors at Florida Atlantic University, hoping to jar them out of their "comfort zone." I began the introduction to my TESOL class in Spanish rather than English. I made no effort to make the input comprehensible but asked the class for a volunteer to come up to the board, take a marker, and draw a large circle. Three of the students understood Spanish and were able to follow along, nodding their heads. I asked them to wait while I made a second request for someone to come up to the board to draw a large circle. I only used words, with no gestures. The rest of the students sat in disbelief, puzzled by what was happening, not knowing what I was asking. I then asked the class again to come up to the board, pick up a marker, and draw a large circle on the board. While I physically showed them what I wanted them to do. When I concluded this short event, I asked them to do the following:

> Please take out a piece of paper and capture in writing your impressions of what just happened; describe your feelings, your thoughts. We will discuss your comments in a few minutes.

After a few minutes of fast writing, they shared and discuss their feelings. The consensus was that they felt "stupid," shy, confused, and frustrated, because they could not follow along. At first, some thought they might have entered the wrong classroom and began to leave, but when the professor wrote the course number TSL 4080 on the whiteboard they realized they were in the right room and began to feel anxious. Although they thought that I would certainly not be teaching the entire semester in Spanish, they were feeling inadequate, and actually upset, while the activity was taking place. They were impatiently waiting for me to finish whatever experiment I was doing with them, but they were not feeling good about it.

This strategy worked, since for the first time, most of these students were able to experience how ELs feel in mainstream classrooms. It also helped the students realize that they, as future teachers, will be the ones who will make a profound impact in their ELs' lives.

TYPES OF ELs

Students may have different proficiency levels in different languages or no proficiency in an additional language at all. They may also have different levels of literacy across different languages. Classrooms today have a diverse mixture of students but we cannot assume they are all from the same backgrounds, nor can we assume that they are literate in the languages that they know.

Students may be immigrants who arrive from other countries under a variety of conditions or migrant workers who were born in the United States but migrate seasonally to harvest crops. They may be native born students whose families speak a language other than English (e.g., Hawaiian, Alaskan, Native American, or Spanish). Students may be unaccompanied minors from other countries (often from Mexico and Central America, but not always) and sometimes represent large groups who seek refugee status, as with the 2014 event described by President Barack Obama as a "humanitarian crisis" (Park, 2014).

Another important consideration for students in our classrooms is those who have experienced interrupted formal education either in other countries or in the United States. Students with limited or interrupted formal education (SLIFE) or students with interrupted formal education (SIFE) face language and educational challenges due to disruptions in schooling. Obvious reasons for migrating might be due to refugee status, but SIFE or SLIFE status is not limited to these populations alone. Students from the United States may be victims of domestic violence or homeless and live in shelters. Migrant students who move from state to state with families who travel where agricultural work can be found are also frequently SIFE/SLIFE students.

Categories of ELs are broad and variable. They can be immigrants by choice, international students, children or temporary foreign workers, displaced persons (refugees) who are being assisted by the government or international agencies, asylum seekers, and many other categories. Students may arrive in our classrooms with previous training from refugee settlements that try to prepare them for the new host country. Some may have little previous knowledge of English, whereas others have quite advanced proficiency, or are even multilingual.

It is not known exactly how many languages are actually spoken in the United States, but the numbers are shockingly high and reflect the reality that multilingualism is a norm worldwide. An even more surprising fact might be that our mainstream teachers are expected to teach students who speak all of these different languages through English, whether they know the students' language or not.

In 2004–2005, the EL population was **9.1%**, (or an estimated **4.3 million** students). In 2013–2014, the number was **9.3%** or an estimated **4.5 million** students who were ELs in the public schools. More recently, in 2014–2015, **9.4%**, (or an estimated **4.6 million** students) were ELs in the public schools. We can see the numbers are growing considerably and mainstream teachers will have the responsibility to ensure these students achieve academically (McFarland et al., 2017).

Previously, 80% of our students were Spanish language speakers. The Asian population (Vietnamese, Hmong, Chinese, Korean, Khmer, Laotian, Hindi, and Tagalog) comprises the second largest group (approximately 8%). There are notable changes in the demographic profiles of school-age children. In more and more states around the country, Latino students are reflecting the fastest growing subgroup, often accounting for a substantial proportion of enrollment increases. This growing national trend has important implications for many aspects of public school education. States that are slow to recognize these and who do not prepare educators for this demographic change do so at their students' peril.

With refugees coming to the United States, we can expect other languages we may not be familiar with. Typical languages spoken are English, Spanish, Vietnamese, Arabic, Lao, Cambodian, Chinese (all varieties), Bengali, Urdu, and Swahili. However, with

Table 4.1: Languages spoken in the United States

Rank	Native Language	Arrivals								Cumulative Total
		FY 2008	FY 2009	FY 2010	FY 2011	FY 2012	FY 2013	FY 2014	FY 2015	
1	Arabic	9,767	13,675	15,199	7,372	9,938	17,230	17,859	4,430	**95,470**
2	Nepali	5,302	13,450	12,355	14,993	15,114	9,164	8,484	1,304	**80,166**
3	Sgaw Karen	7,460	3,331	5,833	6,521	4,148	5,011	4,115	1,046	**37,465**
4	Somali	2,402	3,879	4,787	3,057	4,763	7,295	8,449	2,664	**37,296**
5	Spanish	4,247	4,831	4,951	2,976	2,075	4,429	4,305	778	**28,592**
6	Chaldean	2,897	3,783	2,550	1,392	1,790	1,954	1,328	204	**15,898**
7	Burmese	3,769	2,040	1,414	1,290	1,146	1,523	1,066	233	**12,481**
8	Armenian	3,625	3,444	1,798	747	387	875	1,190	263	**12,329**
9	Kayah	0	5,267	1,922	1,179	595	784	637	136	**10,520**
10	Other Minor Languages	1,788	1,913	1,667	673	1,006	1,277	1,124	242	**9,690**
	Total	**41,257**	**55,613**	**52,476**	**40,200**	**40,962**	**49,542**	**48,557**	**11,300**	**339,907**

more refugees, teachers see students from central Africa, Iraq, Lebanon, Joran, Burma (Myanmar), and varieties of language from Syria.

World Atlas is quick to point out that the original languages of the Native American tribes are being emphasized currently and tribal elders are making a great effort to maintain the native language to be sure the children don't forget their original tongue. They explain that for centuries, Native Americans were persecuted and assimilation was imposed upon them. In fact, they were not allowed to speak their native languages, so unfortunately, no Native American language represents the top 25 languages spoken in the United States (see Table 4.1). The Navajo language was the most widely used language but only about 170,000 speakers of the language remain. It is ironic that Hebrew, which made it to the 25th spot on the list, has close to 213,000 speakers. In a multicultural nation such as the United States, it is critical that indigenous speakers do not lose their languages (e.g., Native Americans, Alaskans, or Inuit, Hawaiians) (Table 4.2).

EL PROFILES

At first, newcomer ELs may seem excited about being in a new country, a new neighborhood, and a new school. The newness of it all creates a sense of adventure, but soon, reality sets in. They may feel lonely, missing family members and friends. They may feel "stupid" because of the language barrier, or angry, since they did not ask to be brought to this country. Many

Table 4.2: Most U.S. Native Speakers by Language (Top Languages Spoken by EL Nationally and by State. EL Information Center Fact Sheet Series. No. 3. Migration Policy Institute.)

Rank	Primary Language Spoken at Home in the United States	Number of Speakers
1	English	231,122,908
2	Spanish	37,458,470
3	Chinese (including Hebrew Cantonese, Mandarin, and other Chinese languages)	2,896,766
4	French and French Creole	2,047,467
5	Tagalog	1,613,346
6	Vietnamese	1,399,936
7	Korean	1,117,343
8	German	1,063,773
9	Arabic	924,374
10	Russian	879,434
11	Italian	708,966
12	Portuguese	693,469
13	Hindi	643,337
14	Polish	580,153
15	Japanese	449,475
16	Urdu	397,502
17	Persian	391,113
18	Gujarati	373,253
19	Greek	304,932
20	Bengali	257,740
21	Punjabi	253,740
22	Telugu	247,760
23	Armenian	237,840
24	Hmong	214,943
25	Hebrew	212,747

Source: Migration Policy Institute (2015) and Snyder and Dillow (2012).

do not understand why they are in this new environment. All they know is that they do not understand what surrounds them. Teachers do know that before coming to this country, ELs could communicate their basic needs and wants, they could laugh and joke, and they had friends; now they are surrounded by sounds and words that are incomprehensible.

Unfortunately, too often EL students sit in school trying to make sense of the world in which they are immersed, without much success. Their emerging English ability does not allow them to participate in what takes place in the classroom, and they may feel intimidated when they observe their native-English-language peers effortlessly involved in the lessons they find so confusing.

In addition, ELs are apprehensive when required to interact with school personnel such as teachers, aides, the school principal, cafeteria workers, and guidance counsellors, who seem to have such a command of the language they are unable to speak. Frequently, the roles of counsellors are unknown to them and their families, making it difficult to understand why anyone would ask them about their transition to school, their home and families, and their prior educational experiences.

SLIFE/SIFE and immigrant students enter U.S. schools with a tremendous language and conceptual development gap when compared with their native-English-language peers. It is critical to understand that the lack of conceptual development stems from the fact that many concepts are neither present in these students' cultures nor part of the everyday culture of their families. Consequently, some experiences from home may never be able to be named at school and certain experiences at school cannot be taken home or explained in Horbury & Cottrell, 1997). The learning within each realm is experienced in separate, noninterchangeable domains (Ariza, 2010). What a student learns at home (e.g.. culturally or personally) may not be relatable in the classroom, and vice versa.

At times, ELs may feel embarrassed about their own heritage. Some do not want to be seen with their parents, sensing that their ways are different from those of the majority culture. Often their parents do not speak English, which from the newcomer's perspective only compounds their problems (Coady & Yilmaz, 2017).

Some educators believe ELs have short attention spans. It is very difficult to remain on task and be attentive when the input received is incomprehensible. Students' short attention spans are not innate, but rather a normal reaction to the classroom situation they are encountering.

Teachers sometimes describe these students as shy; this is normally the result of being in an environment where they are unable to interact and communicate actively in their first language. When these students are observed in mainstream classrooms, they may appear quiet and withdrawn; however, when they are observed among peers of their same language background or by other ELs, the difference is remarkable. In this environment, among peers who speak their language or who are at their same level of English language proficiency, they are eagerly and actively involved in the teaching and learning situation. Additionally, teachers must keep in mind that learning a new language and trying to perform cognitive tasks within that new language is exhausting. For that reason the EL may show physical symptoms of fatigue and actually sleep in the classroom.

Diverse origins, values, capabilities, and needs characterize the EL teacher's clientele. Some EL students have never been to school, despite their advanced age. Some have parents (or caregivers) who value education for all their children; others have parents who believe schooling is worthwhile for males only, and who perceive the school as only a protective holding tank for daughters until they are marriageable. Some parents send their children to school on a regular basis; others keep them home often to look after younger siblings or to serve as interpreters for them. It is important to note that across different cultures, parents believe that teachers are responsible for their child's education, and parents believe that their role is not to interfere. This can lead U.S. teachers to believe that parents don't care about their child's education, when in fact they do (Coady & Yilmaz, 2017).

It is a reality that many ELs eventually learn to accept their new challenges and develop a sense of comfort in their new environment. If they are in schools where their English language development is taken seriously and EL programs are available to them, these students will develop the English language proficiency needed to succeed and remain in school (Ariza, 2010) Others, unfortunately, become frustrated and if not provided the necessary aid, will stop trying, eventually leading them to dropout of school as soon as they become of age.

Research indicates that EL students who enter school with positive self-esteem lose confidence in themselves as a result of the lower expectations they encounter in school (Bankston & Zhou, 2002; It is not known if low self-esteem causes low academic achievement or if low academic achievement causes low self-esteem. A study of migrant farm workers' children compared high and low academic achievers and their responses regarding their memory of having a "bad" teacher ("one who would not go out of the way to help them"). It was found that 40% of low achievers reported having had a "bad" teacher, whereas only 10% of high achievers reported having had a "bad" teacher. Although this study cannot be used as conclusive data to describe the total U.S. immigrant/migrant student population, it is important. Perhaps low achievers have teachers whose mistreatment affected their self-esteem, and as a result, their school performance (Ariza, 2010; Osterman, 2000).

Several million recent immigrants reside in the United States, and more than three and a half million are school-age children (National Center for Education Statistics [NCES], 2016). Immigrant students may have moved to the United States to seek a better life, or more opportunity, but don't necessarily suffer the same trauma that refugee children do. Refugee children usually arrive with severe trauma due to their previous circumstances, which can hinder their learning process. Education is essential for psychosocial and accultural adjustment, but there is no set formula to help with these stages because each student's situation is different.

Unique Characteristics of Refugee Students

The definition of a refugee includes "well-founded fear of being persecuted for reasons of race, religion, nationality, membership of a particular social group or political opinion, is outside the country of his nationality and is unable or, owing to such fear, is unwilling to avail himself of the protection of that country; or who, not having a nationality and being outside the country of his former habitual residence as a result of such events, is unable or, owing to such fear, is unwilling to return to it." Also, refugees are typically "outside their country of nationality or habitual residence and unable to return there owing to serious and indiscriminate threats to life, physical integrity or freedom resulting from generalized violence or events seriously disturbing public order" (United Nations High Commissioner for Refugees [UNHCR], 2018).

Refugee students may demonstrate symptoms of post-traumatic stress disorder, anxiety, sleeplessness, nightmares, flashbacks, cultural practices such as FGM (female genital mutilation) and take a very long time to get over their experiences. These are serious issues that need attention from sensitive professional caregivers and emotional and medical support that will scaffold the new educational experience.

Cultural differences with refugee students will be pronounced as the students have been displaced for a long time, so may have had to make abnormal adjustments just to survive in each new situation. American schools, cultures, and practices will be an entire culture of their own. Students may not be used to using the supplies such as a pencil that needs sharpening. Moreover, their families may be confused by lists of school items that they need to bring during the first week of school, or the teacher's "wish list" of items such as ink for printers, tissues, and hand sanitizer. Sometimes, new students may inadvertently cause disruption due to the newness of the school routine. Students may be misplaced in an incorrectly aligned classroom, or in lower classes because of their emerging English skills.

Teachers will have to make adjustments and must remember that refugee students may have had severely disrupted education due to transience and the limited access to education. They will need more resources, support, and scaffolding due to language and literacy barriers. Try to utilize their native languages literacy as much as possible so knowledge can be transferred into the new language. Be kind, patient, compassionate, and considerate.

Immigrants

Many immigrants settle in urban areas because of family contacts or job opportunities; however, scattered across the country are thousands of children from a variety of ethnic groups who do not attend school in either suburban or rural areas. As reflected in the cities, the bulk of EL students in nonmetropolitan areas represent immigrant or migrant groups. In 1990, 1 in every twenty public school students in grades K–12 was an EL. The EL population has grown from 2 million to 5 million since 1990; however, the overall population increased only 20% by 2006 (National Clearinghouse for English Language Acquisition [NCELA], 2016). In 2014, the number of public school students participating in EL programs was 4,559,323, or 9.4% (NCELA, 2016).

The following best describes the EL population in the United States:

- By far, the majority of ELs (approximately 80%) in the United States are Spanish speaking.
- Spanish speakers in the United States tend to come from lower economic and educational backgrounds than either the general population or other immigrant and language minority populations.

- Twenty percent of immigrants from Mexico and Central America are below poverty level, compared with 9%–14% from other regions of the world.
- Fewer than 40% of immigrants from Mexico and Central America have the equivalent of a high school diploma, in contrast to 80%–90% of other immigrants (and 87.5% of U.S. born residents).
- Students of Asian origin tend to come from families with higher income and educational levels than do other immigrant families.
- Among immigrants from the major world regions, the poverty level of Asian immigrants is the second lowest (11.1%). Only immigrants from Europe have lower rates.
- Over 80% of Asian immigrants have the equivalent of a high school diploma (highest among immigrants from major world regions). These figures hide the diversity among Asian populations: 50% or fewer Cambodian, Laotian, and Hmong adults in the United States have completed the equivalent of high school; fewer than 10% have a college degree.
- In contrast, Filipinos, Indians, and Japanese in the United States have high school completion rates of 90%.
- Over 60% of Taiwanese and Indians in the United States have completed college degrees (Table 4.3).

Researchers (Freeman & Freeman, 2007; Ruiz-de-Velasco, Fix, & Clewell, 2000) have identified three types of ELs: long-term ELs; recent arrivals with limited or interrupted formal schooling; and recent arrivals with adequate schooling. Long-term ELs are those who have attended United States schools for several years; they speak English and are often no longer classified as EL but still struggle academically. These students have mastered social language but are lacking academic language/vocabulary. Recent arrivals with limited or interrupted formal schooling are those ELs who often arrive in the United States in the middle of the school year and possess limited academic knowledge in their native language due to limited or interrupted schooling. These students may have very little or no social language; thus they need to develop academic and social language as well. Those students who are recent arrivals with adequate schooling do not have the social language; however, they do possess academic language and academic content knowledge in their native language (L1). As their English language develops, they are able to draw on this background knowledge and catch up with their classmates.

Generation 1.5 Students

There is another large group of ELs, a relatively new phenomenon that has been identified as Generation 1.5. These students are in a complex situation in terms of coming to the United States, with whom they identify, and how they label themselves. Much of this stems from their in-between position in terms of their language development and literacy. These students are in the middle of two generations of immigrants (Table 4.4).

Table 4.3: States with 80% or More ELs Speaking One Predominant Language, 2008–2009 (Sorted by Share Accounted for by the Top Spoken Language)

State	Language 1	Language 2	Language 3	Language 4	Language 5	Percentage of ELs Speaking the Top Language	Percentage of ELs Speaking Top 5 Languages
Wyoming	Spanish	Arapaho	Korean	Filipino; Pilipino	Japanese	90.4	97.3
Texas	Spanish	Vietnamese	Chinese	Arabic	Urdu	88.5	91.7
Arkansas	Spanish	Marshallese	Hmong	Vietnamese	Lao	87.7	95.7
Nevada	Spanish	Tagalog	Filipino; Pilipino	Chinese	Vietnamese	86.8	96.6
Colorado	Spanish	Vietnamese	Arabic	Chinese	Russian	86.7	91.5
California	Spanish	Vietnamese	Chinese	Tagalog	Hmong	84.8	92.2
Idaho	Spanish	American Indian	Undetermined	Russian	Arabic	84.3	89.5
Alabama	Spanish	Korean	Vietnamese	Arabic	Chinese	83.7	91.2
North Carolina	Spanish	Hmong	Vietnamese	Arabic	Chinese	82.9	89.5
Utah	Spanish	Navajo	Vietnamese	Tonga	Samoan	82.8	89.1
Oklahoma	Spanish	Cherokee	Vietnamese	Hmong	Chinese	81.8	90.5
Kansas	Spanish	Undetermined	Vietnamese	German	Chinese	81.1	93.4
Arizona	Spanish	Navajo	Vietnamese	Arabic	Somali	80.0	83.8

Source: 2008–2009 Consolidated State Performance Reports (CSPR). www2.ed.gov/admins/lead/account/consolidated/index.html.

TABLE 4.4: Generation 1.5

1st Generation	Generation 1.5	2nd Generation
Adult Immigrant	Childhood Immigrant	Children of Immigrants
Foreign Born	Foreign Born	U.S. Born
Foreign Educated	Partially Foreign Educated	U.S. Educated
L1 Dominant	Partially U.S. Educated: L1 or English Dominant	English Dominant

Source: Adapted from Roberge, Siegal, and Harklau (2009).

These 1.5ers come to the United States in their early teenage years; thus, they are partially foreign-educated and partially U.S.-educated. They may develop an unusual pattern of language use; depending on when they have arrived; they may identify with one language but may be actually more proficient in the other. They earn the label of "1.5 generation" because they bring with them characteristics from their home country but continue their assimilation and socialization in the new country. Their identity is a combination of new and old culture and traditions (Cheung, 2017). These students may seek postsecondary education, yet they may lack the necessary cognitive and linguistic demands of discipline-specific academic classes in English language institutions of higher learning (NCELA, 2016) For these reasons, these ELs are considered in between and in the Generation 1.5.

How can Generation 1.5 students be identified? In reality, these 1.5ers cannot be identified by the number of years they have been in the United States, nor by the number of years of schooling either in their L1 or in English. These students can only be identified by asking questions such as: What does their language look like? What do their life experiences look like? How do they label or identify themselves? The boundaries for identifying 1.5ers are not clearly defined. Much depends on factors such as those in the questions posed.

There are other groups of ELs that can also be identified as Generation 1.5ers:

"Immigrants from U.S. territories," for example, Puerto Rico

"Native-born, non-native English speakers—these are U.S.-born students from linguistics enclave communities (very little exposure to English)."

"Transnationals"—those students who have complex patterns of back and forth migration"

Implications for U.S. Schools and Teachers

The description of the U.S. immigrant population has implications for U.S. schools and teachers. The challenges to educate these students, especially those who will become the majority in the K–12 school population, are of great magnitude. The most recommended programs to address the EL's language and academic needs must become a priority if the goal is for these students to be successful in the academic setting.

As explained above, not all ELs are immigrants. Some are in the United States on international exchanges or as international students; they are sons and daughters of wealthy families who want their children to learn English for the status and the professional opportunities it affords. These students tend to be bright and academically oriented—top-notch students who are highly literate in their native language. Their parents value education. Many of these students attend private schools and thus do not pose a financial burden to the public schools' budgets. These students' needs are usually met by private tutors paid by their parents, or provided by the private schools which they attend and where the costs of these tutors is encompassed in the tuition their parents pay. These international students are usually in the United States on a transitory basis; many are here without their parents in boarding schools. These students are in school from the beginning of the school year, and unless there is an extenuating circumstance, until the last day. They are involved in extracurricular activities and they excel at most of their undertakings.

Many of today's classrooms are microcosms of the global situation experienced in the United States in the present times. Teachers, like diplomats, must be prepared to deal with the constant variation and change that this reality imposes on them. Teachers must learn to provide for the needs of this varied student population of native speakers of English, as well as ELs who come with an array of differences that need to be addressed.

POINTS TO REMEMBER

✔ The school/classroom environment has a tremendous impact on ELs' retention and success.
✔ Nonspeakers of English feel intimidated when surrounded by input that is not comprehensible.
✔ There is great diversity among ELs enrolled in the public/private schools of America today.
✔ Most ELs come from 3 main regions: Southeast Asia, eastern Europe, and Latin America (including Mexico and the Caribbean).
✔ Now ELs may be refugees from other parts of the world such as Syria, Iraq, Afghanistan, Middle Eastern, and sub-Saharan countries.
✔ In the agricultural areas of the United States, immigrant children are still found working in the fields.
✔ Many immigrant children serve as interpreters for their parents. However, this is not an ideal situation because it strains the parent–child relationship, and language can be misconstrued, deliberately or inadvertently.
✔ Teachers are legally accountable for providing a comparable education for non-native English speakers.
✔ Teachers have a tremendous impact on the success or failure of their students, especially their ELs.
✔ There are 3 types of ELs: long-term ELs, recent arrivals with limited or interrupted formal schooling, and recent arrivals with adequate schooling.
✔ Generation 1.5 is a phenomenon of ELs who are attending U.S. schools.

REFLECTION QUESTIONS AND DISCUSSION

1. What are the 3 types of ELs as identified by current researchers?

2. Who are the students identified as Generation 1.5ers?

3. How are Generation 1.5 students described? What are some of the problems they face?

ACTIVITIES

1. List the characteristics ELs may display, and list the contributing factors.

   Characteristic example: Contributing factor
   May show excitement   Newness of life situations

   _____   _____
   _____   _____
   _____   _____
   _____   _____

2. If you are completing any type of field experience in a school setting, observe the ELs. Describe their behavior (interactions) in their mainstream classroom. If these students leave their mainstream classroom to receive any type of English language instruction, follow them and observe them in this pull-out setting. Describe their behavior (interactions) in this setting. Compare both descriptions. How do they compare? Do they interact in the same fashion in both environments? Do they differ? How do your descriptions compare with the descriptions given in Chapter 4?

WEB RESOURCES

English Language Learners: A Policy Research Brief produced by the National Council of Teachers of English. http://www.ncte.org/library/NCTEFiles/Resources/PolicyResearch/ELLResearchBrief.pdf
   ESOL in Higher Ed. www.esolinhighered.org

How to Support Refugee Students in the EL Classroom. www.colorincolorado.org/article/how-support-refugee-students-ell-classroom

Program Models for ELS. www.colorincolorado.org/article/program-models-teaching-english-language-learners

Six Different Types of English Learners and How to Teach Them. https://www.eslkidstuff.com/blog/classroom-management/6-different-types-of-esl-learners-and-how-to-teach-them

Teaching Refugee Students: Instructional Resources. www.teachingrefugees.com/instructional-programming/resources

Understanding DACA. http://immigrationimpact.com/2013/11/18/understanding-dacas-education-requirement

Welcoming Refugees Into Your Classroom. http://www.teachmag.com/archives/8880

REFERENCES

Ariza, E. N. (2010). *Not for ESOL teachers: What every classroom teacher needs to know about the linguistically, culturally, and ethnically diverse student* (2nd ed.). Boston, MA: Allyn & Bacon.

Bankston, C. L., & Zhou, M. (2002). Being well vs. doing well: Self-esteem and school performance among immigrant and nonimmigrant racial and ethnic groups. *International Migration Review, 36*(2), 389–415.

Cheung, K. K. (2017). *Chinese American literature without borders: Gender, genre, and form*. New York, NY: Springer.

Coady, M. R., & Yilmaz, T. (2017). Preparing teachers of ELs: Home-school partnerships. In J. I. Liontas (Ed.), *The TESOL encyclopedia of English language teaching*. Hoboken, NJ: TESOL International Association & Wiley. doi:10.1002/9781118784235.eelt0837

Horbury, A., & Cottrell, K. (1997). Cultural factors affecting the acquisition of reading strategies in bilingual children. *Education 3–13, 25*(1), 24–26.

McFarland, J., Hussar, B., de Brey, C., Snyder, T., Wang, X., Wilkinson-Flicker, S., … Hinz, S. (2017). *The condition of education 2017. NCES 2017-144*. Washington, DC: National Center for Education Statistics.

Migration Policy Institute. (2015). Top Languages Spoken by English Language Learners Nationally and by State. ELL Information Center Fact Sheet Series. No. 3. *Migration Policy Institute*. Retrieved from http://www.worldatlas.com/articles/the-most-spoken-languages-in-america.html

National Center for Education Statistics. (2016). Retrieved from https://nces.ed.gov/programs/digest/d16/tables/dt16_204.20.asp

National Clearinghouse for English Language Acquisition. (2016). NCELA. Retrieved from https://ncela.ed.gov/

Osterman, K. F. (2000). Students' need for belonging in the school community. *Review of Educational Research, 70*(3), 323–367.

Park, H. (2014, October 21). Children at the border. *The New York Times*. Retrieved from https://www.nytimes.com/interactive/2014/07/15/us/questions-about-the-border-kids.html

Roberge, M., Siegal, M., & Harklau, L. (Eds.). (2009). *Generation 1.5 in college composition: Teaching academic writing to US-educated learners of ESL*. New York, NY: Routledge.

Ruiz-de-Velasco, J., Fix, M., & Clewell, B. C. (2000). *Overlooked and underserved: Immigrant students in U.S. secondary schools*. Washington, DC: The Urban Institute. Retrieved from http://www.urban.org/UploadedPDF/overlooked.pd

Snyder, T. D., & Dillow, S. A. (2012). *Digest of education statistics 2011 (NCES 2012-001)*. National Center for Education Statistics Institute.

United Nations High Commissioner for Refugees (UNHRC). (2018). The UN Refugee Agency. UNHCR. Retrieved from http://www.UNHCR.org

Linguistic Systems

Human Language

Readers will be able to

- ❖ Understand the different linguistic subsystems of language
- ❖ Describe and delineate key features of universal grammar (UG)
- ❖ Contrast human and animal language
- ❖ Describe key ideas that teachers of English learners (ELs) need to know about human language

SCENARIO

In the Introduction to Linguistics class, Dr. Cruz asks her students the following questions:

Dr. Cruz: *Who can tell me how many spoken languages are there in the world?*
Kim: *Five thousand?*
James: *Ten thousand?*
Dr. Cruz: *Good guesses. There are 6,913 spoken languages in the world, of which less than a thousand have written forms.*
Dr. Cruz: *What features do all languages share?*
Dr. Cruz lists the features on the board as students contribute their answers.

Linguistically speaking, no language is superior to another. All languages in the world have grammars, although it is not unusual to hear the remark that some languages have no grammar or one language is more difficult to learn than another. Because virtually all human languages are spoken, they must have sounds and sound systems, words and word-order systems, and word meanings. One exception to this is a former script used by Chinese women to communicate via cloth books, paper fans, and embroidered items (Ager, 2017). The script, Nüshu, was only used by women, who were unable to travel outside of the home due to foot-binding practices as far back as 700 years.

Most languages, however, are based on sounds. American English is known to have between 14 and 16 vowel sounds, Australian English about 20 vowels sounds, and Spanish has five vowels with about 14 sounds. Walibri (an aboriginal language of Australia) has a more flexible word order than English, but this difference does not make Spanish or Walibri inferior to the English language.

All languages have constraints within their phonemic sequence, the permissible way in which phonemes can be combined. In English, there are no words that begin with the nasalized /ŋ/ sounds like the end of /siŋ/, but in Malay, this sound is found in the initial position, as in the word /ŋantuk/ (sleepy). In Spanish, the /sp/ cluster only appears medially; therefore it is common to hear Spanish speakers say /estop/ or /especial/ for *stop* and *special*. People who are learning English often can be helped with pronunciation if the instructor can relate it to the student's native language. For example, Spanish speakers who have problems trying to say a word like *stop* without saying "estop," can be shown that they do have words that begin with *s*, like *sábado* (Saturday) in their language. But even after much practice, it is difficult to transfer the correct sound without deliberate and constant monitoring (Krashen, 1981; Moyer, 2014).

These languages and a vast majority of other languages share a similar word order pattern, that is, the subject precedes the object. We sometimes refer to these as S–V–O (subject–verb–object). Other languages follow different word pattern orders. In addition, although Spanish and English may "inflect nouns" for plurals and Haitian Creole and Spanish inflect nouns for gender, a process where letters or a combination of letters (morphemes) are added onto existing words, all three languages use the inflectional system to mark different grammatical categories. For example, in English, adding the "ly" ending changes words from adjectives to adverbs, such as changing "happy" to "happily." Thus, even though Spanish, English, and Haitian Creole languages may seem very different from one another, they all share a number of universal features in their grammar.

Many grammatical categories and rules within languages of the world are universal. Noam Chomsky, a Professor Emeritus at the Massachusetts Institute of Technology and laureate professor at the University of Arizona, termed this concept as universal grammar (UG. The intricacies within UG perplex linguists, and they continue to have an ongoing fascination with linguistic analysis as it reflects the structure and organization of the human mind.

Ethnologue, languages of the world, Simmons and Fennig (2017) report that there are about 6,900 distinct languages still spoken in today's world? What are some of the universal properties of human language? White (2003) offers these ideas about UG about human language:

- Language exists wherever humans exist. The main purpose of language is communication.

- Every normal child, regardless of creed, geographical, or socioeconomic background, is capable of acquiring any language to which he or she is exposed. Language is culturally transmitted, it is not biologically transmitted. For example, an adopted Cambodian child in an American family will grow up to speak American English because he or she is exposed to the American language and culture.

- All human languages use a limited set of sounds and gestures to form meaningful sound combinations in words found in unlimited sets of possible sentences. For example, note how many ways you can say this sentence: *The world celebrated President Barack Obama's win in 2008's U.S. presidential election.* One can say, *In the 2008 presidential election in the U.S., President Barack Obama's win as President was celebrated worldwide,* or *There was a world celebration when Barack Obama won the 2008 U.S. Presidential election,* or *The winning of Barack Obama in the 2008 presidential election was celebrated by people around the world.* These are a few ways to communicate this idea, and there are a dozen other ways. This property is called *productivity.* In contrast, animal language does not have this characteristic. A cicada has four fixed sounds, not three or two, and a vervet monkey has 36 signals, not 35 or 37. Animal language has this aspect of permanency, and the animals cannot change their system of communication (Radick, 2007).

- All languages have properties to refer to past time, the ability to negate, use question forms, issue commands, and so on. This property of human language is called *displacement* (Yule, 2016). In contrast, animal language does not have this characteristic. For example, bees use the sophisticated "waggle" dance to direct each other to the location of the nectar, but bees cannot tell each other how sweet and wonderful the nectar was yesterday and that it will be better tomorrow. Only human language has this enabling property: people can talk about historical events and plan for what to do in the future.

- All languages are dynamic; they undergo changes through time. Just listen to the words and slang teenagers use nowadays. Calling someone "BAE" is short for babe, or baby, or it may stand for the acronym Before Anyone Else. When they say something is "lit" they mean something is great. Background knowledge of the social search dating app (Tinder) will clarify the meaning of a phrase such as "swipe left," which refers to manipulating a smart phone or touch screen and clearing an image when you don't like someone's picture, or "swipe right," when you like someone. "Throw shade," is when you say something nasty or mean, or give someone a dirty look. The original meanings of these words are completely changed and each generation develops its own terminology. Nouns can become verbs, such as saying you will "Google" it when you look up something on Google, or you could say you are going to "microwave" something. "Texting" comes from the act of sending a text message. This phenomenon may be referred to as *verbification* (Kuczok, 2011).

- *Arbitrariness* is yet another property of a language. A symbol can be mapped onto any concept or grammatical rule. In other words, most languages' use of sound combinations do not necessarily have inherent meaning—they are merely an agreed-upon convention to represent a certain thing by users of that language. For instance, the sound combination *nada* carries the meaning of "nothing" in the Spanish language and also the meaning "thread" in the Hindi language. There is nothing about the word *nada* itself that forces Hindi speakers to convey the idea of "thread," or the idea of "nothing" for Spanish speakers. Other sets of sounds (e.g., the English words *nothing* and *thread*) could equally be used to represent the same concepts, but all Spanish and Hindi speakers have acquired or learned to correlate their own meanings for this particular sound pattern. Indeed, for speakers of Slovene and other South Slovak languages the sound combination carries the meaning of "hope," whereas in Indonesian it means "tone". People can ascribe meaning to any given sound.

- Human language has the property of *discreteness*, that is, it has distinct sounds. Even though some languages have sounds that others may not have (e.g., /p/ and /b/ sounds are not distinguishable for Arabic speakers), they are distinct sounds to the English speakers because *parking* and *barking* are two different words. When speaking English, Tagalog speakers in the Philippines will say size *porty fants* instead of size *forty pants*, exchanging the sound of p for f and f for p.

Glottogony is a term used for the origin of language. A considerable amount of attention has been given to this topic throughout human history. One of the most significant factors that distinguishes Homosapiens from other species is the use of language. Unlike writing, spoken language leaves no explicit concrete evidence of its nature or even its existence, although it is believed that spoken language predates written language by at least tens of thousands of years. Therefore, scientists use conjecture and assumption (educated guesses) as indirect methods to determine the origins of language (Fischer, 2001).

Linguists agree that there are no existing primitive languages, and that all modern human populations speak languages of comparable complexity. The evolution of modern human language required both the development of the anatomical apparatus for speech and also neurological changes in the brain to support language itself, but other species have some of these capabilities without full language ability. A major debate surrounding the emergence of language is whether language evolved slowly as these capabilities were acquired, resulting in a period of semilanguage, or whether it emerged suddenly once all these capabilities were available (Acuña-Fariña, 2009).

What important factors should teachers of English learners (ELs) know about language to be effective in the classroom?

- Knowing that the purpose of language is communication and it is learned through use, teachers will set a stage for a conducive learning environment in the classroom where ELs are encouraged to take risks when communicating with one another (Akmajian, Farmer, Bickmore, Demers, & Harnish, 2017).
- Knowing that language is culturally transmitted and that people speak the same way as the people around them speak, teachers should embrace the varieties of English that their students bring into the classroom. But at the same time, teachers usually

impart and promote the use of Standard English, which is the prevalent dialect in the academic circle. For the EL whose family members do not speak English, it is vital that they are immersed in an environment where they can actively participate in learning English. Teachers need to involve these students in their lessons even though the ELs regardless of level of English proficiency.

- Human language has the characteristic of *displacement*—the property that enables humans to use language for a variety of functions: talk about past, present, and future events, issue commands, ask questions, seek permission, express condolences, make a factual statement, disagree with others, and so on. Teachers need to understand language from the psycholinguistic and sociolinguistic sense.

What are the components of the human language system? All human languages have phonology, a sound system; morphology, the system upon which words or concepts are built; syntax, the system of how words are arranged in sentences and paragraphs; semantics, the system of word meanings; and pragmatics, the system of how language is used in society.

Within the field of phonology, teachers of ELs, who are aware that not all languages possess the same distinct sounds will understand and appreciate the non-native pronunciation of English words that their students produce. English is a global language, and different English accents exist. Thus, in the context of World Englishes, all pronunciations are correct.

In morphology, teachers who have the knowledge of morphemes across cultures will tolerate ELs' incorrect usage of comparative or superlative adjectives of English, such as more pretty, or more good, instead of prettier or better. They understand that their ELs transfer their L1 (native or first language) morphological rules when using English morphemes.

For syntax, one of the many pieces of information that teachers will have is that the arrangement of words in a sentence is not universal. For example, as noted above English sentences are arranged in subject-verb-object order, whereas Korean sentences have the subject–object–verb word order pattern. Irish has yet another word order pattern—VSO. With this knowledge, teachers can be more effective in their use of appropriate strategies when teaching literacy skills.

How does knowing semantics help teachers? The field of semantics deals with meanings of words. There are many categories of words; the parts of speech such as nouns, adjectives, verbs, adverbs, and so forth, is one category; here are some others: *Homonyms*—words that sound the same but have different meanings (*bat, bank*), *homophones*—words that have the same sound but are spelled differently and have different meanings (*meat, meet*), *homographs*—words that are spelled the same but sound different (*read, read*); synonyms, antonyms, compound words, idioms. ELs find the learning of idioms more challenging as idioms are complex and have meaning that is not necessarily intuitive. The phrase *break a leg* (an expression used when wishing someone good luck before a performance) has a nonliteral meaning which oftentimes confuses ELs. These examples illustrate the complexity of the semantic system.

The nuances of the English language or any other language are mostly apparent in the pragmatic system. The pragmatic system involves social conventions of the speech community where a communicative act or speech act is determined by the particular or distinct speech situation. For example, in the United States, the phrases speakers use to close a conversation are several: *See you later, have a nice day, bye, take care, we should go to lunch some time*, and so on. Some of these phrases such as *we should have lunch some time*, or *see you later* are hollow in nature, meaning that the speaker may not really intend on doing it. ELs who are new to the language and its social conventions may misunderstand these greetings and expect the speakers to follow through with them. Many miscommunications occur because of the limited understanding of pragmatics, and teachers can ease their students' adjustment to the new language and culture by comparing their knowledge of the pragmatics of the English language system to the pragmatics of their students' native language system.

POINTS TO REMEMBER

✔ Linguistically speaking, no language is superior to another.
✔ All languages have constraints within their phonemic sequence.
✔ Grammatical categories and rules in many languages are universal.
✔ Every normal child is capable of acquiring his or her native language.
✔ Languages undergo changes through time.

REFLECTION QUESTIONS AND DISCUSSION

1. What is UG (Universal Grammar)? Describe three properties that all languages share?
2. What are the differences between human language and animal communication?
3. Why do you think idiomatic expressions pose problems for ELs?

ACTIVITIES

1. Complete the knows, wants to know, and has learned (KWL) chart below regarding what you already know, want to know, and learned in this chapter. Reflect on how your knowledge about language has changed.

What do you **know** about human language?	What do you **want** to know about human language?	What did you **learn** in this chapter?

2. Try sounding out these words:
   Malay
   Nyamuk (mosquitoes)
   Ngantuk (sleepy)

   Spanish
   anaranjado (orange)
   amarillo (yellow)

   Philipino or *Filipino / a*
   ngalan (name)

   German
   Pferd (horse)

   Polish
   Gdynia (name of a city)

   Swahilli
   ndiyo (yes)

   Do you think there is a difference between your pronunciation of these words and a native speakers' pronunciation of these words?

3. Search on the web: How are new words in English identified and subsequently graphized (written down)? Who identifies what word(s) are written into English language dictionaries?

WEB RESOURCES

Discovering Language. www.youtube.com/watch?v=850gPKOGWx0

Great Courses on Human Language. https://www.thegreatcourses.com/courses/story-of-human-language.html

How Computers Translate Language. https://www.youtube.com/watch?v=X4BmV2t83SM

Human Language Properties. www.youtube.com/watch?v=m6Zfb_4uTDM

Human Language vs Animal Communication. https://www.youtube.com/watch?v=N8-nUpcoVu4

The Miracle of Human Language. www.youtube.com/playlist?list=
PLzugOrS2Z8op69jva2xxkiEx6JhdbE5T5; www.youtube.com/watch?v=Onp5caCVV6w

Nine Animals Who Can Understand Human Language. www.youtube.com/watch?v=
2T8NSoSOUw4

What Is Human Language? www.bmcbiol.biomedcentral.com/articles/10.1186/s12915-
017-0405-3

REFERENCES

Acuña-Fariña, J. C. (2009). Aspects of the grammar of close apposition and the structure of the noun phrase. *English Language & Linguistics, 13*(3), 453–481.

Ager, S. (2017). *Nüshu*. Retrieved from https://www.omniglot.com/writing/nushu.htm

Akmajian, A., Farmer, A. K., Bickmore, L., Demers, R. A., & Harnish, R. M. (2017). *Linguistics: An introduction to language and communication*. Cambridge, MA: MIT Press.

Dobrin, L. M. (2009). SIL international and the disciplinary culture of linguistics: Introduction. *Language, 85*(3), 618–619.

Fischer, S. R. (2001). *History of language*. London, UK: Reaktion Books.

Krashen, S. D. (1981). *Second language acquisition and second language learning*. Oxford, UK: Oxford University Press.

Kuczok, M. (2011). The interaction of metaphor and metonymy in noun-to-verb conversion. In B. Bierwiaczonek, B. Cetnarowska, & A. Turula (Eds.), *Syntax in cognitive grammar* (pp. 41–54).

Moyer, A. (2014). Exceptional outcomes in L2 phonology: The critical factors of learner engagement and self-regulation. *Applied Linguistics, 35*(4), 418–440.

Radick, G. (2007). *The simian tongue: The long debate about animal language*. Chicago, IL: University of Chicago Press.

Simmons, G. F., & Fennig, C. (Eds.). (2017). *Ethnologue: Languages of the world* (20th ed.). Dallas, TX: SIL International.

White, L. (2003). *Second language acquisition and universal grammar*. Cambridge, UK: Cambridge University Press.

Yule, G. (2016). *The study of language*. Cambridge, UK: Cambridge University Press.

Phonology

Readers will be able to

- ❖ Discriminate the sound systems of a language
- ❖ Predict the English learners' (ELs) transfer of the first language's phonological rules to a second language
- ❖ Distinguish distinctive sounds that make a difference
- ❖ Recognize permissible arrangements of sounds within a language
- ❖ Anticipate problematic sound distinctions
- ❖ Distinguish pitch, stress, tones, and relaxed pronunciation

SCENARIO

Three ELs were standing on a mountaintop. One said, "It's windy," and the other responded, "No, it's Thursday." The third student chimed in, "Yes, let's go and get a drink!"
What phonological explanations can you offer for the above conversational miscommunication?

Now examine the production of sounds in English phonology in the following sentences.

1. Say the word **fan**. How is the first sound of this word produced? The /f/ sound is produced by putting the top teeth and the bottom lip together, and blowing air between them.
2. Say the word **were**. This whole word is produced with one continuous motion of the vocal tract (lungs, tongue, lips, etc.), yet we perceive the production of this word as three separate speech sounds, /w-e-r/.
3. The words **hoe, sew, so**, and **dough** all have the same vowel, even though the vowel is spelled differently in each.
4. The sounds **/m/** and **/b/** are alike in that they are both produced by pursing the lips; /b/ and /g/ are different in that /g/ is not produced with the lips.
5. The vowel sound in the word **fad** is longer than the same vowel sound in **fat**.

Example 1 shows that humans use the vocal tract to produce speech sounds. Example 2 represents the fact that words are psychologically viewed as a series of discrete units called segments, even though, physically, they are produced with one continuous motion. Example 3 displays the fact that a single segment can be spelled in a variety of ways because sound and letter correspondence in English is inconsistent; therefore, the phonetic alphabet is used in place of the English alphabet so that each symbol represents one sound. Example 4 shows the fact that smaller units called *distinctive features* are contained within each segment. Thus, /m/ and /b/ have the same distinctive feature; that is, they are *labial* sounds because they are produced using both *lips*, whereas /b/ and /g/ do not share the same distinctive feature. Substituting /m/ in the word *bat* will result in a different meaning. Example 5 illustrates that the same vowel /a/ can be lengthened in one context but shortened in another. Thus, the same vowel /a/ is pronounced differently in different contexts—long in *fad* but short in *fat*. Examples 1–5 are phonological in nature. In other words, the production of these sounds is governed by underlying phonological rules within the English sound system.

WHAT IS PHONOLOGY?

Phonology is the study of the sound system of a language. It also deals with the rules that govern pronunciation and studies the function and patterning of the sounds of a language.

There are some sounds and sound combinations in English that are not heard or differentiated by non-native speakers, who may have difficulty in producing them. The sounds of English that are mispronounced by non-native speakers oftentimes become a source for jokes and laughter in stand-up comedy. Examine the following dialogue:

Non-native speaker: *Hey, can you pass me the flying pan?*
Native speaker: *I'm sorry. You want what? A frying pan?*

In Chinese, the /r/ sound is not found in unit sound clusters such as /fr/, as in *fried*, or /wr/, as in *wrong*, or /spr/, as in *spring*. Most Chinese speakers of English have difficulty with the pronunciation of /wr/, /fr/, and /str/ sound clusters. Native Chinese speakers who are beginning learners of English will pronounce the words *spring, fried*, and *strawberry* as /spliŋ/, /fleyd/, and /stlɔbɛli/. Moreover, because in English not all sounds have one-to-one correspondence of sound and orthography, non-native speakers often are unsure of the correct English pronunciation, and thus transfer first language (L1) phonological rules to the second language (L2), thereby mispronouncing words in English. For instance, the word *occupy* with the letter *c* in the middle is pronounced with the /k/ sound. However, in the word *proceed*, the letter *c* in the middle position does not take the sound /k/, but instead the sound /s/. Remember that transfer goes on all the time but you will only know when the transfer is incorrect. If the student is able to transfer correctly from the L1, you will not notice it because there will be no obvious mistake.

When these isolated mispronunciations occur in sentences that contain other words from which the listener can guess the meanings from context, communication is not hindered. However, frequent mispronunciations alongside heavily accented words can be major obstacles in communication.

Why are non-native speakers unable to pronounce native sounds of a language as shown in the examples above? Native speakers of any language are generally exposed only to the sounds of their language from birth, they only hear and use the sounds of their native language. Although linguists purport that when a baby is born, he or she has the capacity to hear all the sounds of any language in the world, they also state that as children grow up they will only have formed the connections in the brain for their native language sounds. Because other sounds are not heard or reinforced, connections for these sounds are not formed and will be difficult to learn and to reproduce. This is why non-native speakers of any language may have difficulty in producing the sounds of a target language they are learning. Younger learners may sound like native speakers, whereas older learners usually speak with an accent. Sounding like a native English speaker may prove to be difficult because a teacher may never know that that young student is a second language learner. In addition, there are different varieties of spoken English around the world. Different pronunciations of words are common among distinct groups, for example, Singaporean English and Indian English, and the distinction between "native" and "non-native" speakers is fluid rather than strict.

DESCRIPTION AND ARTICULATION OF CONSONANTS AND VOWELS

The earlier scenarios of non-native speakers encountering difficulties in producing English sounds can be further understood when we examine the sounds that make up a language, called *phonemes*, and *minimal* pairs. *Phonemes* are distinctive sound units that "make a difference" when sounds form words. Minimal pairs are words that differ by only one phoneme. Examples of minimal pairs in English are /pɪn/ *pin* and /bɪn/ *bin*; /stet/ *state* and /sted/ *staid*; /tɛn/ *ten* and /dɛn/ *den*. In Chinese, /ti/ and /di/ are minimal pairs, the former meaning *tears* and the latter *earth*; in Malay *sayang* and *dayang*, the former meaning *love* and the latter *princess's maids*. While in English, /p/ and /b/ sounds are distinguishable, they are not in Arabic. Arab speakers will say *barking lot* instead of *parking lot*, and *bile* instead of *pile*. English speakers are unable to say the word *nyamuk* (mosquitoes) as the

Malays do, because English does not have nasalized sounds in word initial position. The /b/ and /v/ sounds are indistinguishable for some Spanish speakers when /v/ occurs in a medial position; therefore, some Spanish speakers who attempt to say /baklava/ will substitute the /v/ with a /b/ sound in the third syllable, producing /baklaba/ instead.

PHONOTACTIC CONSTRAINTS

In studying *phonology*, it is important to note that each language has permissible ways in which phonemes can be arranged. This permissible arrangement is called *phonemic sequence*. Each language allows only specific sound combinations at initial, mid, or final positions. In English, there can be a single sound in a word, such as *oh*, or multiple consonants can occur successively in final position in a word, such as *texts* /tɛksts/—CVCCCC; three consonants can occur successively in initial position, such as in words like /spriŋ/ *spring* and /striŋ/ *string*—CCCVC. It becomes more complicated when there are only permissible combinations in consonant clusters; for instance, in English there is a word *draft* but not *sraft*; /dr/ is a consonant cluster in English, whereas /sr/ is not. In Spanish, it is permissible to have the *s* cluster such as /sp/ occur in mid position, as in the word *español*, but never in initial position. This may explain why Spanish native speakers may say *espoiled* for *spoiled* or *espace* for *space* when speaking English.

How can we help non-native speakers of English with difficulty in producing words with initial and final consonant clusters that are permitted in English? The most troublesome initial consonant clusters for the largest number of non-native English speakers seem to be those consisting of an initial /s/ followed by one or more other consonants. This large group includes /sf/, /sk/, /sl/, /sm/, /sn/, /sp/, /st/, and /sw/. To compound the problem for non-native speakers of English is the three-consonant clusters at the initial position of words such as /stri/ *string*, /skræp/ *scrape*, and /skwɛr/ *square*. The above examples of initial consonant clusters violate the phonotactic rules of a number of languages, such as Chinese, Japanese, and Iranian.

Two- and three-consonant clusters in word final position also pose a problem for non-native speakers of English. Let us examine some of these sound combinations in the following words: /lb/ *bulb*, /gd/ *tagged*, /nd/ *cleaned*, /vd/ *lived*, /lf/ *self*, /rvd/ *carved*, /mps/ *camps*, /ks/ *links*.

Reed and Levis (2015) suggest two ways of making clusters easier for non-native English speakers to pronounce. First is the process of phonetic syllabication and second is the omission of consonants. Phonetic syllabication can occur when a word ends in a consonant sound and the following word begins with a vowel, as in the sequences *has it* /haezñt/, *hide 'em* /haydəm/, and *give up* /gñvUp/. In these examples, it is suggested that the final consonant of the first word be pronounced at the beginning of the second word: /hæ´ -zñt/, /háy-dəm/, /gñ-v´əp/. In the same way, the last consonant of a final cluster can be moved forward and pronounced with the vowel of the following word. *Find out* can become /faynḏáwt/, *Sixth Avenue* /sɪks-æ´ vənyuw/, and *changed address* can become /c̆eyn j̆-dUdrɛ́s/. Two-consonant clusters are thus reduced to single consonants, three-consonant clusters to two-consonant clusters, and four-consonant clusters to easier, three-consonant clusters. Proper use of phonetic syllabication can not only facilitate a student's pronunciation, it can also do much to make his or her English sound more authentic. The second way to make consonant clusters more pronounceable is simply to omit one of the consonant sounds. Native speakers of English do this more often than they realize: for example, many commonly pronounce $\overline{arctic}$ as /ártñk/, omitting the first c. Probably everyone omits the difficult p in *raspberry*, which is normally pronounced /ræ´ zbɛ́rɪ/. Such omissions happen most frequently and are least noticeable in final three-consonant clusters when the middle consonant (the sound that is omitted) is a voiceless stop: *acts* /ae<u>kt</u>s/ becomes /ae<u>ks</u>/, *lifts* /lñ<u>ft</u>s/ becomes /li<u>fs</u>/, *asked* /æs<u>kt</u>/ becomes /ae<u>st</u>/. These are some ways to assist non-native speakers of English to overcome their problems with the pronunciation of words with initial and final consonant clusters.

Phonemes can be classified into two main categories: consonants (C) and vowels (V), as noted above in phonemic sequence. The third category of sounds that resemble both consonants and vowels is called semivowels. Consonants are made when the airflow is partially or completely obstructed in the mouth by the placement of the tongue and the positioning of the lips. Voiced and voiceless consonants are differentiated by the vibration felt when the larynx is touched. Having students touch where the sounds should be made (lips, throat) will help them with more accurate pronunciation. For example, /s/ does not produce any vibrations, whereas the production of /z/ produces vibration of the vocal folds (muscles). English consonants can be recognized by three modifications to the airstream: the place of articulation of the consonants, the manner in which the airstream is blocked, and voicing. Refer to Figure 6.1 for places and manner of articulation for consonants. Refer to Table 6.1 for consonant symbols and sample words. In the production of vowels, the airflow in the vocal tract is not blocked. English has 14 vowels and five *diphthongs*.

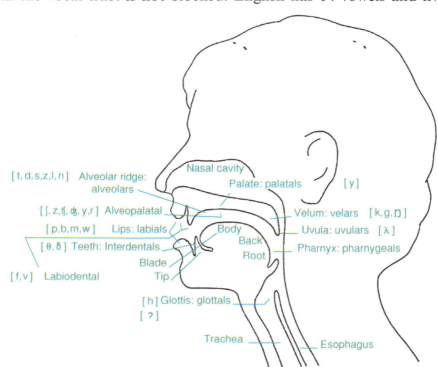

Figure 6.1: Places of Articulation are Listed, Followed by a Term used to Describe Sounds Made at Each Place. Areas of the Tongue are Also Provided

Source: Eileen Ariza

Table 6.1: The International Phonetic Alphabet Symbols for American English Phonemes

Symbol	Sample Words
Stops	
[p]	pot, top, staple
[b]	bet, globe, dabble
[t]	tip, pat, staple
[d]	dense, body, guard
[k]	can't, chemistry, kick
[g]	garden, again, get
[ʔ]	uh-oh
	button, mitten (in some dialects)
Fricatives	
[f]	fan, coffee, enough
[v]	van, dove, gravel
[θ] theta	through, teeth, ether
[ð] epsilon	the, either, leather
[s]	sweet, bask, fuss
[z]	zip, design, kisses
[ʃ]	shred, bashful, mesh
[ʒ]	measure, vision, casualty
[h]	who, cohort, ugh
Affricate	
[tʃ]	choke, batch, catching
[dʒ]	judge, cojole, page
Nasals	
[m]	moose, comb, coming
[n]	nine, banner, snow
[ŋ]	sing, wringer, prong

(Continued)

Table 6.1: The International Phonetic Alphabet Symbols for American English Phonemes (*Continued*)

Symbol	Sample Words
Liquids	
[l]	leaf, hill, piling
[r]	ran, terrain, stare
[D] flap	written, bitter, liter
Glides	
[w] voiced	witch, worm, with
[j]	exhume, yoke, lawyer
[ʍ]	what, whale, white (in some dialects)

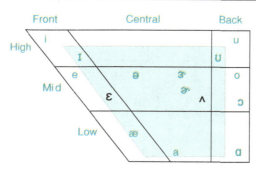

Figure 6.2: The Vowel Quadrilateral. Noncolored: tense vowel, Colored: lax vowels

Source: Eileen Ariza

Diphthongs are two vowels that make up one *phoneme*. Vowels can be described using these characteristics: height, tongue advancement, lip rounding, and tense (long)/lax (short). See Figure 6.2 for symbols and Table 6.2 for sample words for vowels and diphthongs. For example, using the vowel characteristics, let us describe the vowel /e/. Refer to Figure 6.2.

/e/ Description
Height: high-mid
Advancement: front
Lip rounding: retracted
Tense/lax tense

The information on the manner and place of articulation that phonologists provide is important for teachers of non-native speakers of English.

For example, some consonants in English are pronounced with a stronger release of air, such as the /p/ in *pin*. A lighted match placed close to the lips would be put out. However, there is less aspiration in the /sp/ cluster in *spin*. Nevertheless, aspiration is not a distinctive

Table 6.2: The Different Sounds of English Vowels in Sample Words

Symbol	Sample Words
Vowels	
[i]	beat, we, believe, people
[I]	bit, injury, business
[e]	bait, reign, great, they
[ɛ]	bet, reception, says, guest, bury
[æ]	bat, laugh, anger, rally
[u]	boot, who, sewer, through
[ʊ]	put, foot, butcher, could
[o]	boat, beau, grow, though, over
[ɔ]	bought, caught, wrong, stalk
[a]	pot, father, far, car
[ʌ]	but, tough, another
[ə]	among, focus, sofa
[ɜ]	bird, her, stir
Diphthongs	
[au]	how
[ai]	tie
[ɔ]	Boy
[eⁱ]	bake
[oᵘ]	Rose

phoneme in English. Some languages may not produce this sound in the same manner that English does. For example, aspiration is a distinctive feature of the Khmer language—[pʰa]: *father* and [pa]: *silk cloth*. Likewise, when the place of articulation is changed even slightly, the word may not sound correct. For instance, pronounce the word *tin*. Now, move your tongue as far back as you can and pronounce this word again. Continue to place your tongue at different positions and pronounce the same word. What do you notice? In some languages, consonants are pronounced in a more forward position than in English, whereas in others, the places of articulation are further back in the mouth. The difference in the place of articulation contributes to one of the many qualities that make up "foreign accents." Tables 6.3 and 6.4 contain examples of sounds that may pose problems for non-native English speakers, as well as some sounds in different languages that native English speakers have difficulty producing.

Spanish Speakers of English

Spanish and English differ in their phonemic systems, both in terms of vowels and of consonants. English has *14* vowel sounds and five diphthongs approximately, and Spanish has *only five vowel* sounds that are constant. Because of this, Spanish speakers of English will always experience difficulty with vowel production due to interference from their first language. For example, the word *pick* will be pronounced as /pik/, because /ñ/ is nonexistent in Spanish. Other examples are *bake, tack, good,* and *hope.* In *bake,* vowel /ei/—/e/; in *tack,* /ae/ —/a/; in *good,* /ʊ/—/u/, in *hope,* /ou/—/o/. Not all vowel productions are caused by interference; for instance, for the word *feet,* Spanish speakers say *fit,* the substitution of /i/ for /ɛ/ is not caused by interference (Iverson & Evans, 2009). Other similar examples are in words such as *men (/ɛ/—/ae/), room (/u/—/ʊ/),* and *some (/ʌ/—/a/).*

Some examples of common consonant interference are: with, /wit/; those, /douz/; vine, /baɪn/; shoe, /tʃu/, yes, /ɟɛs/. Refer to Table 6.5 for more examples of Spanish-influenced English vowel and consonant productions. Regardless of the language, teachers can identify tricks to help the speaker make the sound easier to produce. In Spanish, it might be easier for Spanish speakers to relate to words that begin with the sound of s, like *sábado* (Saturday) when they are having difficulty saying the word "stop," which they will pronounce as "estop." Have them say the word *sábado* by elongating the front s. Example:

Table 6.3: Problematic Sound Distinctions in English for Spanish and Haitian-Creole Speakers

The first sound is the problem sound; the second is the substituted sound		
Consonant	**Spanish**	**Haitian-Creole**
v/b	x	
θ/s(theta)	x	x
ʃ/ʧ	x	x
j/ʤ	x	
s/z	x	
θ/z(theta)		x
ð/d(epsilon)	x	
m/ŋ	x	
n/ŋ	x	x
w/g	x	
r/w		x

Table 6.4: Problem English Vowel Contrasts for Spanish Speakers

English	Problem Contrast	Spanish
/e/—ate /ʌ/—after	A	/a/—pluma (pen)
/i/—even or /ɛ/—every	E	/ɛ/—enero (January)
/aɪ/—ice or /ɪ/—sick	I	/i/—libro (book)
/o/—open or /ʊ/move	O	/o/—blanco(a) (white)
/ɟu/—use or /ʌ/—under	U	/u/—nuevo(a)

Table 6.5: Common Spanish-Influenced English Vowel and Consonant Productions

English Word	Spanish-Influenced English Transcription	Phonological Pattern
Vowel Articulations		
lid	/lid/	ɪ → i
need	/nɪd/	i → ɪ
mate	/met/(will sound similar to /ɛ/	eɪ → e
late	/lɛt/	eɪ → ɛ
tennis	/teɪnɪs/	ɛ → eɪ
dead	/dæd/	ɛ → æ
bag	/bɑg/ or /bɛg/	æ → ɑ or ɛ
look	/luk/	ʊ → u
pool	/pʊl/	u → ʊ
boat	/bot/ (will sound similar to /ɔ/	oʊ → o
bug	/bɑg/ or /bag/	ʌ → ɑ or a
word	/wɛrd/	ɝ → ɛr

(*Continued*)

Table 6.5: Common Spanish-Influenced English Vowel and Consonant Productions (*Continued*)

English Word	Spanish-Influenced English Transcription	Phonological Pattern
Consonant Articulations		
think	/tiŋk/	θ → t stopping
them	/dɛm/	ð → d stopping
vase	/bes/	v → b stopping
you	/dʒu/	j → dʒ affrication of a glide
sheep	/ʧip/	ʃ → ʧ affrication of africative
choose	/ʃuz/	ʧ → ʃ deaffrication
just	/jʌst/	dʒ → j deaffrication
zoo	/su/	consonant devoicing
was	/wʌs/	consonant devoicing
spot	/əspat/ or /ɛspat/	epenthesis of /ə/
leaks	/lik/	reduction of word-final consonant clusters

SSSSSSS (like *sábado*)—top. It allows them to feel how they can actually make the sounds in "stop" instead of "estop."

Asian Speakers of English

Tables 6.6 and 6.7 summarize common consonant and vowel productions spoken by Asians/Pacific Islanders (Mandarin Chinese, Cantonese, Vietnamese, Korean, Japanese, and Filipino). Several Asian languages are tone languages and intonation is considered phonemic since each tone has a different meaning. In contrast, intonation in English conveys the speaker's mood or intent, statement, or question. There are fewer words that end with consonants in Mandarin Chinese and Cantonese than in English, so Asian speakers of English will delete the final consonants of English words, as they are just transferring their L1 rule to English—applying a no-consonant-endings rule as in their L1. Another important difference between English and most Asian languages is the issue of grammatical rules and phonology.

The phonological system of Chinese is very different from that of English. Some English phonemes do not have Chinese counterparts and are hard to learn. Others resemble Chinese phonemes but are not identical to them in pronunciation, and thus cause confusion. Stress, intonation, and juncture are all areas of difficulty. In general, Chinese speakers find English hard to pronounce, and have trouble learning to understand the spoken language. (Cao, Xu, & Ariza, 2018)

There are more vowel contrasts in English than in Chinese, so English vowels are closer to each other in terms of position of articulation than Chinese vowels. This means that more effort is required to distinguish them. For instance, the contrast between /i:/ and /I/ has no

Table 6.6: Common Consonant Productions for English Phonemes, as Spoken by Chinese, Vietnamese, Korean, Japanese, and Filipino Speakers (Mandarin and Cantonese Dialects of Chinese are Shown Separately)

		Cantonese	Mandarin	Vietnamese	Korean	Japanese	Filipino
Fricatives	θ	s, f	s, f	s		s, z	t
	ð	d	z, d		ʤ	z, j	d
	ʃ	S		s, t	s		s
	ʒ	~				ʤ, ʃ	d, ds
	f	f, w	f, w	p		h	p
	v	S			b, p	b	b
	z			s	s	dz, ʤ, s	s
Affricates	ʧ	z	ʃ	s, t, ʃ	t		ts
	ʤ	I		ʒ			ds
Liquids	r		I	z	I		
	I		r	n	r	r	

Table 6.7: Some Common Vowel Productions in Asian/Pacific Influenced English

Chinese	æ → e or ɛ, ɛ → e, ɪ→ i; ɔ→o; ʊ→ u;ʌ→ɑ /ə/ is added to consonant clusters
Vietnamese	I→ i; æ → ʌ; ʊ→ u
Korean	Problems with the production of /i/,I, u, and /ɔ/
Japanese	Epenthesis of the vowels /ə/ or /u/ to the ends of syllables and words. (Most Japanese words end in an open syllable.) I → i; æ, a or ə → ɑ;ą→ a; ʊ → u; ʌ → æ; eɪ → e; æ → ɛ
Filipino	Tensing of lax vowels, i.e., ɪ→ i; ʊ → u; ɔ→ o (and they switch p for f and vice versa)

equivalent in Chinese. Learners confuse pairs such as *eat* and *it, bean* and *bin*. The same applies to /u/, leading to confusion, for instance, between *fool* and *full, Luke* and *look* (de Jong, 2006).

As for consonants, in the three pairs of stops /p/ and /b/, /t/ and /d/, /k/ and /g/, the unaspirated group/b/, /d/, and /g/ are voiced in English but are on the whole voiceless in Chinese. Chinese students tend to lose the voiced feature in speaking English. /v/ is absent from most Chinese dialects. As a result, it is sometimes treated like /w/ or /f/: *invite* may be pronounced "inwoite"; *live* pronounced /lif/. Many Chinese dialects do not have /n/. Learners speaking these dialects find it difficult to distinguish, for instance, *night* from *light*. /θz/ and /δd/ do not occur in Chinese. /N/ is likely to be replaced by /t/, /f/, or /s/, and /δ/ by /θ/or /z/. So for example, *thin* may be pronounced *tin, fin*, or *sin; this* may be pronounced /dis/ or /zis/

Pitch changes in Chinese (the "tones") are mainly used to distinguish words whose pronunciation is otherwise the same; sentence intonation shows little variation. The English use of intonation patterns to affect the meaning of the whole utterance is therefore difficult for Chinese to grasp. Unfamiliar with these patterns, Chinese learners tend to find them strange and funny. Some add a tonic value (often a high falling tone) to individual syllables. Thus their speech may sound flat, jerky, or "singsong" to English ears (Cao, Ke, & Ariza, 2018; Ploquin, 2013).

In Chinese, each printed character is only one syllable in length; therefore, Chinese speakers of English may pronounce multisyllabic words syllable by syllable in a telegraphic, or faltering rhythm.

Arabic Speakers of English

Unlike English, which has 14 vowel sounds and five diphthongs, Arabic has only three vowels, /i/, /a/, and /u/, in short and long forms. The diphthongs in Arabic are /ei/ and /eu/. Several English consonants do not exist in Arabic, such as the stops /p/ and /g/, the fricatives /v/ and /ʒ/, and the nasal / / (Abdelaal, 2017). Also, in Arabic there are no two or three consonant clusters at the beginning of a word, so Arabic speakers of English will pronounce the word *scream* and *street* as /sikrim/ and /sitrit/—adding a vowel between consonants. Sometimes, Arabic speakers will also pronounce silent letters in English because the Arabic alphabet is phonemic. For example, the words *knot, could*, and *lamb* will be pronounced as /kn:t/, /kuld/, and /laemb/. In English, the /c/ can take on different sounds depending on the surrounding sounds; for example, in the words *city, proceed*, and *proclaim*, /c/ is pronounced as /s/, /s/, and /k/. For Arabic speakers of English, they may pronounce the word *city* as /kiti/ and the word *soccer* as /sɔsə/.

Table 6.8 summarizes common Arabic-influenced English vowel and consonant productions.

Other problems learners of English have are demonstrated by words that have allophones, that is, sound variants of the phonemes.

Say these words and note how the /t/ is pronounced in each word.

bottle (ʔ glottal, t,)
kitten (ɾ, flap)

stop (nonaspirated)

top (aspirated)

hunter (/t/ is not pronounced in some regional dialects)

PITCH, STRESS, AND RELAXED PRONUNCIATION PATTERNS

Other sound qualities like *pitch* and *stress* are also important in the formation of sounds. In English, pitch and stress are important in distinguishing meaning within a sentence. For instance, "José is going to the movies," as a statement, is said with a falling pitch, but when it is used as a question, the pitch rises at the end. Intonation is the rising and falling pitch in a

Table 6.8: Common Arabic-Influenced English Vowel and Consonant Productions

English word	Arabic-Influenced English Transcription	Phonological Pattern
Vowel Articulations		
brought	/brot/	ɔ → o
bit	/bet/	ɪ → e
because	/bikuz/	ʌ → u
cup	/kæp/	ʌ → æ
set	/sæt/	ɛ → æ
bread	/brid/	E → i
note	/nat/	o → a
Consonant Articulations		
party	/bartɪ/	p → b
very	/fɛrɪ/	v → f
thin	/sɪn/	θ → s
lesion	/liʃən/	ʒ → ʃ
witch	/wɪʃ/	ʧ → ʃ
Jim	/ʃɪm/	ʤ → ʃ
bathe	/bez/	ð → z
think	/θɪnk/	θ → t
scream	/sikrim/	epenthesis of i

language that does not change word meaning, but changes the function of a sentence. Patterns of intonation in English are said to resemble waves, with the crest of the wave over those syllables with the greatest stress. Intonation acts very much like punctuation in a sentence; emotions such as anger and impatience are signaled by intonation patterns. However, there are many languages that use pitch in individual syllables to contrast meaning; these languages are called tonal languages. There are more than 1,000 tonal languages in Africa alone. Chinese, Thai, and Burmese are also tonal languages, as are many native American languages (Zeng, 2012). In Mandarin Chinese, the sound /ma/ when used with four different tones produces four different meanings: *horse, mother, hemp*, and *scold*. The word /mai/ can mean buy or sell.

Like pitch, stress also modifies the meaning of words. In English, stress indicates the part of speech of a particular word. Look at the following examples:

Where would you put the stress on the word used in both sentences?

1a. Carol's conduct at the party was the talk of the town.
1b. Carol will conduct a popular orchestra at the opening ceremony.
2a. McCoy is the meanest rebel in the group.
2b. McCoy and Kazaski rebel against the top members of the organization.

Can you figure out the rule for stress placement in the above examples?
Word stress at the sentence level can also change the intended meaning within a sentence. For example,

H/e' did that? (Who did that?)
He d/i'd that? (Did he do that?)
He did th/a't? (What did he do?)

Each statement asks a different question depending on which word is stressed.
Native speakers are seldom taught the explicit phonological rules in their native language, yet they know them. Speakers of any language have different styles of speaking: formal to informal to casual. In English, casual or relaxed speech has three forms in the pronunciation of words: (a) contractions, (b) "dropping" of sounds, and (c) changing of sounds. Examine the following examples of these three categories:

A. Contractions
   1. *Who'd do that?* (Who would do that?)
   2. *We've been there.* (We have been there.)
B. "Dropping" of sounds
   1. *Eat 'em.* (Eat them.)
   2. *She's changin' her clothes.* (changing)
C. Changing of sounds
D. In English, changing of sounds occurs when the final sound of one word and the beginning sound of the following word combine to make a third sound. Examples are:
   1. *Did you do it?* (j → ʤ) or
   2. *Is your brother home?* (j → ʒ)

APPLYING PHONOLOGY IN THE CLASSROOMS

How do teachers apply these phonological concepts when teaching ELs? Understanding that phonemes are individual units of sound in words is having phonological awareness (PA). Skills within PA are concept of spoken word, rhyme, syllables, phonemes, and phoneme manipulation. Children become fluent readers by learning to manipulate these sounds. Phonemic awareness falls under the umbrella of PA, though phonemic awareness and PA are used interchangeably. Research has shown that phonemic awareness is the best single predictor of reading ability in kindergarten, followed by knowledge of letter names and kindergarten teacher predictions (Wade-Woolley, 2016). Phonemic awareness is the first component of effective reading instruction (Ryder, Tunmer, & Greaney, 2008; Ztonc, 2000). Children need solid phonemic awareness training in order for phonics instruction to be effective (Stockall, 2007).

Using the following sample activities, children are taught the following PA skills (Ztonc, 2000):

- **Concept of spoken word**
  (*sentence segmentation*)
  The ability to distinguish words in a sentence. Example: *Juan likes oranges.* (three words) Teachers can use counters (edible ones make cleaning up easier, although check with parents for their approval to allow children to eat whatever counters are being used, e.g, candies, marshmallows, peas,) when teaching this concept. Determine the number of words in the sentences that will be read to students. Give students five counters if you are reading sentences with three to five words. Ask students to lay the counters on their desk and push them up when they hear the words in the sentences. So, for the above example, students will push up three counters. Sentence segmentation is an important skill to teach ELs because, being new to the sounds of English, the words in the sentence may sound as one long word to them.

- **Rhyme**
  The ability to recognize rhyme, complete rhyme, and produce rhyme. Example: *Does hall rhyme with ball?* The teaching of this concept brings in the knowledge of minimal pairs—substituting the phoneme /h/ in /hall/ with /b/ changes the word meaning. An activity for this skill is to distribute two tongue depressors to the students. Have students draw a happy face on one and a sad face on the other. Call the happy face "Happy Harry" and the sad face "Sad Sandy." Read to the children some words with minimal pairs that rhyme and some words that do not rhyme. When they hear the rhyming words, children will hold up "Happy Harry" and when they hear ones that do not, they will hold up "Sad Sandy." Some possible word sets are: *bet-get, go-me, fan-pan, cake-take, gold-back, big-dig, dust-must.* This is a good way to find out if EL students can hear and are able to distinguish sounds. As was mentioned earlier in the chapter, some Arab speakers of English do not make a distinction between /b/ and /p/, and some Spanish speakers do not distinguish /v/ and /b/; therefore, this will be a good assessment activity.

- **Syllables**

  The ability to blend, segment, and delete syllables. The activity for the teaching of this concept is to ask students to clap the word parts; for example, use their names: Claudia (three claps), John (one clap). Learning about syllables is a prerequisite for ELs to put stress correctly on words. This particular activity will help Chinese speakers of English whose L1 has one syllable per character.

- **Phonemes**

  The ability to recognize problematic sounds for ELs. Chinese speakers of English have a difficult time pronouncing consonant clusters such as /spr/ and /fr/, and Spanish speakers have difficulty with /ʃ/, /j/, /dʒ/. An example activity is making digraphs useful by using crosschecking meaning. Write a sentence with /s/ words and compare that to a sentence with a word /spr/. *Chen is sad. Hua is high-spirited.* For Spanish speakers who substitute /t/ for /θ/, use the same activity—*María thinks Anna is pretty. Francisco talks a lot.*

Teachers who possess knowledge of phonology will understand and be able to anticipate the difficulties faced by ELs in producing English consonant and vowel sounds that are nonexistent in their language. They will not be overly frustrated about students' errors or insist on frequently correcting their students' mispronunciations and misspellings. Instead, they will focus on the problem sounds that ELs have by using their knowledge of the place and manner of articulation of English sounds to demonstrate to students how these sounds are produced. Sometimes the inability to self-correct will be a matter of developmental stage and they will get it when they are ready. However, self-correction is done when ELs are monitoring their own production. First, they have to know what the right pronunciation is, be able to produce the correct sound, and then remember to say it correctly, which is difficult when people are thinking about what they are going to say, instead of how they are going to say it.

POINTS TO REMEMBER

✔ Phonology is the study of the sound system of a language. It deals with the rules that govern pronunciation.

✔ Children growing up in their first language environment have formed only the connections in the brain for their native sounds.

✔ In phonology, it is important to note that each language has permissible ways in which phonemes can be arranged. This permissible arrangement is called phonemic sequence.

✔ Phonemes can be classified into two main categories: consonants and vowels.

✔ Pitch and stress are important in distinguishing meaning within a sentence in English.

✔ Tonal languages use pitch as individual syllables to contrast meaning.

✔ Speakers of any language have different styles of speaking: from formal, to informal, to casual. In English, casual or relaxed speech takes three forms in the pronunciation of words: (a) contractions, (b) "dropping" of sounds, and (c) changing of sounds.

ACTIVITIES

1. Generate a list of English words, paying attention to consonant clusters at initial and final positions. Based on this list, which may be difficult for Spanish speakers to produce? What are some ways of making these words easier for them to pronounce?

2. List five sets of words in English that have the same sound but different meanings, for example, *their, they're, there*. (1 set)

3. Write three identical sentences. In each sentence, place the stress mark on different words. How does the meaning of the sentence change with each change in stress? For example, *Whére are you going?* and *Wheré are you going?*

4. a. The *k* sound can be represented by different letters. Provide at least six different examples. Underline the part of the word that represents the k sound. For example: cup, kick, and quick.

   b. The combination of the letters *ough* can be pronounced in at least eight different ways. Provide a minimum of six different examples.
      Pair up each word you list with a word that has the same sound(s) represented by *ough*, but is spelled differently. Underline the parts of each pair that represent the same sound. For example:
      Enough, paired with fl*uff*
      Thr*ough* paired with *you*

5. Pronounce these sentences as you would in your normal speech and notice the changes in how /d/, /t/, and /z/ sound next to the /y/.
   What is the new sound?
   a. You made your blouse, didn't you?

b. Pat's usually early.

c. Carla told Yule to go home.

d. Is that what you've accomplished?

WEB RESOURCES

Fantastic Websites About Sounds of Speech. http://soundsofspeech.uiowa.edu/index. html#english, https://www.youtube.com/watch?v=16b2M-YwgKs

The Hows and Whys of Teaching Pronunciation. https://www.teachingenglishgames. com/Articles/Teaching_Pronunciation.htm

Improving English Pronunciation Using Chinese Characters. https://www.youtube. com/watch?v=E66oIgegbv0

Integrating Pronunciation into Classroom Activities. https://www.teachingenglish.org. uk/article/integrating-pronunciation-classroom-activities

Phonetic Chart Poster for Children. http://www.cambridgeenglishonline.com/ Phonetics_Focus/pdf/poster.pdf

The Phonetics Interactive 3D Models of Oral Visualization. http://d3492jnbjg00z1. cloudfront.net/

Phonology in the Classroom. https://linguisticsforteachersofells.weebly.com/phonology-in-the-classroom.html

Speaking English Activities. http://www.spokenskills.com/index.cfm?type=15& content=studentactivities

Support ELLs in the Mainstream Classroom: Language Tips. http://www. colorincolorado.org/article/supporting-ells-mainstream-classroom-language-tips

Tongue Twisters for Pronunciation Practice. http://learnenglishkids.britishcouncil.org/ en/tongue-twisters

Word Match—A Minimal Pairs Game for Teaching Pronunciation. http://eslgames. com/minimal-pairs-game/

Words and Pictures to Help Children Master Phonics. http://www.bbc.co.uk/schools/ wordsandpictures

REFERENCES

Abdelaal, N. M. (2017). Instrumental analysis of the English stops produced by Arabic speakers of English. *International Journal of Education and Literacy Studies, 5*(3), 8. doi:10.7575/aiac.ijels.v.5n.3p.8

Cao, L., Xu, K., & Ariza, E. N. W. (2018). Chinese, Japanese, South Korean, and Indian. In *Not for ESOL teachers* (3rd ed., pp. 1–36). Dubuque, IA: Kendall Hunt.

Iverson, P., & Evans, B. (2009). Learning English vowels with different first-language vowel systems II: Auditory training for native Spanish and German speakers. *Journal of the Acoustical Society of America, 126*(2), 866–877. doi:10.1121/1.3148196

Ploquin, M. (2013). Prosodic transfer: From Chinese Lexical tone to English pitch accent. *Advances in Language and Literary Studies, 4*(1), 68–77. doi:10.7575/aiac.alls.v.4n.1p.68

Reed, M., & Levis, J. M. (2015). *The handbook of English pronunciation*. Chichester, UK: Wiley-Blackwell.

Ryder, J. F., Tunmer, W. E., & Greaney, K. T. (2008). Explicit instruction in phonemic awareness and phonemically based decoding skills as an intervention strategy for struggling readers in whole language classrooms. *Reading and Writing, 21*(4), 349–369. doi:10.1007/s11145-007-9080-z

Stockall, N. (2007). Time well spent: Phonemic awareness training or paired associate learning for children with language impairments? *Forum on Public Policy: A Journal of the Oxford Round Table, 1*, 1–44.

Wade-Woolley, L. (2016). Prosodic and phonemic awareness in children's reading of long and short words. *Reading and Writing, 29*(3), 371–382. doi:10.1007/s11145-015-9600-1

Zeng, F. (2012). Tonal language processing. *Acoustics Today, 8*(2), 26–28. doi:10.1121/1.4729576

Morphology

LEARNING OBJECTIVES

Readers will be able to

- ❖ Recognize the internal structures of words
- ❖ Distinguish word categories: function and lexical
- ❖ Define free and bound morphemes
- ❖ Define word formation: derivation and inflection
- ❖ Recognize morphemes across languages

The following scenario involves the conversational exchange between a Spanish speaker and a preservice teacher:

Teacher: *Where did you go, Alberto?*
Student: *I wented to Disney World.*
Teacher: *Oh, you went to Disney World.*
Student: *Jeah.*
Teacher: *Who did you go with?*
Student: *The brother of my father taked—tooked—me dere.*
Teacher: *Oh, you mean your uncle?*
Student: *Jeah.*
Teacher: *Which rides do you like best?*
Student: *I like two ride. I like the Espace Mountin more better than the Esplash Mountin because it is the more long.*

What errors do you notice in the student's production?

WHAT IS MORPHOLOGY?

The above scenario illustrates that words have internal structures that non-native speakers have to learn. *Morphology*, a study of word formation, deals with the internal structure of words within a language. Before we go further in the study of morphology, let us begin by looking at what we know about the structure of words in English.

a. Words like *strongest* can be divided into two parts (i.e., *strong -est*), each of which has a meaning.
b. The word *female* has a meaning in and of itself; the word *in* does not. Rather, *in* indicates a relationship between two meaningful expressions (e.g., *The female in the room*).
c. The form *milk* can stand alone as a word; the form *-es* cannot.
d. *Sickly* is a word; *sickestly* is not.
e. *E-mail* is a shortened form of *electronic mail*.

In any language, words can be divided into two broad categories: *function* and *lexical*. Function words include pronouns, such as *you, he*, and *she;* conjunctions such as *and, if*, and *because;* determiners such as *a, the*, and *an*. The lexical category includes nouns (N), such as *table, chalk, iron*, and *flower;* verbs (V), such as *write, draw, drink*, and *sit;* adjectives (Adj.), such as *yellow, beautiful, skinny*, and *hand-crafted*; and finally adverbs (Adv.), such as *slowly, smoothly, fast*, and *greedily*.

The minimal meaningful units in a language are called *morphemes*. Morphemes, more traditionally referred to as linguistic signs, are arbitrary. This means that the connection between the sign and its meaning is purely conventional; it does not originate in some property of the object it stands for. For instance, there is nothing about the sound of the word *hair* that has anything to do with hair. It is just as appropriate to use the word *riah* to refer to this entity, or in French, *cheveux*, or in Spanish, *pelo*. The minimal meaningful units of language are not words but arbitrary signs or morphemes.

FREE AND BOUND MORPHEMES

Let us look at the word *players*. This word has three meaningful units: *play*, *-er*, and *-s*. The word *players* is a free form morpheme because it can stand on its own and can occur in different positions in a sentence. In contrast, the units *-er* and *-s* do not count as words because they cannot stand on their own, nor are their positions flexible. These are called bound morphemes.

There are two basic types of words in human language: simple and complex. Simple words cannot be broken down into smaller meaningful units, whereas complex words can be broken down to identifiable and meaningful components. The word *frogs* is made up of the form *frog* and the plural marker *-s*, neither of which can be divided into smaller morphemes. While many English words consist of only one morpheme, others can contain two, three, or more (see Table 7.1).

Table 7.1: Words Consisting of One or More Morphemes

One Morpheme	Two	Three	More than Three
Or			
Girl	Girl-s		
Play	Play-er	Play-er-s	
Hospital	Hospital-ize	Hospital-iz-ation	Hospital-iz-ation-s
Gentle	Gentle-man	Gentle-man-ly	Gentle-man-li-ness

Complex words, like sentences, have internal structure. Let us take the word *industrialization*; the word *industry* is a free morpheme because it can stand on its own, whereas the other morphemes (*-ion, -al, -iz, -ation*) are bound morphemes, that is, they have to be attached to free morphemes.

WORD FORMATION

New words are continuously being created in human languages. The lexical category is open in the sense that other words can be formed from lexical words. The two most common word formations are derivation and inflection. Derivation is the process by which another word is formed from a root word, usually through the addition of an affix. Derivation creates a new word by changing the category and/or the meaning of the base to which it applies. The derivational affix -er, for instance, in the word *waiter* combines with a verb (*wait*) to create a noun with the meaning *"one who does the action."*

Virtually all languages have contrasts such as singular and plural, and past and present. These contrasts are often marked by a morphological process called inflection. Inflection modifies a word's form to mark the grammatical categories to which it belongs. For instance, the inflectional affix -s in *boys* does not change the grammatical category (N) to which it belongs, and the inflectional -ed in the word *worked* does not change the grammatical category (V) to which the word *work* belongs. Refer Tables 7.1A, B, and C.

Regular and Irregular Inflectional Morphology

More ways inflection can be irregular: Suppletion (instead of a suffix, the whole word changes):

be—am—are—is—was—were—been
Go—went—gone
Good—better—best
bad—worse—worst
some—more—most

Table 7.1A: Inflectional Categories and Affixes of English

Word Class to Which Inflection Applies	Inflectional Category	Regular Affix Used to Express Category
Nouns	Number Possessive	-*s*, -*es*: table/tables, box/box*es* -'*s*, -': the dog'*s* paw, James' bag
Verbs	Third person singular present Past tense Perfect aspect Progressive or continuous aspect	-*s*, -*es*: it hails, Karen dance*s*, the river gurg*les* -*ed*: walk/walk*ed* -*ed*: paint/paint*ed* (has paint*ed*) (past participle) -*ing*: jump/jump*ing*, write/writ*ing* (present participle)
Adjectives	Comparative (comparing two items) Superlative (comparing three or more items)	-*er*: short/short*er* -*est*: tall/tall*est*

Source: http://www.cla.calpoly.edu

Table 7.1B: Irregular Inflectional Morphology

Type of Irregularity	Noun Plurals	Verbs: Past Tense	Verbs: Past Participle
Unusual suffix	oxen, syllabi, antennae		tak*en*, see*n*, fall*en*, eat*en*
Change of stem vowel	foot/feet, mouse/mice	run/r*a*n, come/c*a*me, flee/fl*e*d, meet/m*e*t, fly/flew, stick/stuck, get/got, break/broke	swim/sw*u*m, sing/s*u*ng
Change of stem vowel with unusual suffix	brother/brethren	feel/f*e*lt, kneel/kn*e*lt	write/wr*itt*en, do/d*one*, break/br*oken*, fly/fl*own*
Change in base/stem form (sometimes with unusual suffix)		send/sen*t*, bend/ben*t*, think/th*ought*, teach/t*aught*, buy/b*ought*	send/sen*t*, bend/ben*t*, think/th*ought*, teach/t*aught*, buy/
Zero-marking (no suffix, no stem change)	deer, sheep, moose, fish	hit, beat	hit, beaten, come

Syntactic marking (added meanings are indicated by a separate word rather than marking with a suffix or change to the base).

Future of verbs: *will* go, *will* eat, *will* fight, and so on.
Comparative/superlative of adjectives: *more* intelligent, *more* expensive, and so on; *most* intelligent, *most* expensive, and so on.

English Derivational Morphology

Below is a sample of some English derivational *affixes*. This is only a sample; there are far more affixes than are presented here.

In forming derivational morphemes in English, some words follow a hierarchical order. An example is the word *systematic*: the suffix *ic* is added to the root word *system*, yielding the meaning *having a system*, and when the prefix *un* is added to *systematic*, it means *not having a system*. However, the suffix *un* cannot be added to the root word, *system*, first because *unsystem* is a nonsense word. On the other hand, there are some derivational morphemes that do not follow this order. Either the prefix or the suffix can be added to the root word first. For instance, examine the word *unhappiness*, which

Table 7.1C: Some Derivational Affixes of English

Affix	Class(es) of word to Which Affix Applies	Nature of Change in Meaning	Examples
Prefix "non-"	Noun Adjective	Negation/opposite	Noun: *non*-starter Adjective: *non* partisan
Suffix "-ity"	Adjective	Changes to noun	electric/electric*ity* obese/obes*ity*
Prefix "un-"	Verb Adjective	Reverses action Opposite quality	tie/*un*tie, fasten/*un*fasten clear/*un*clear, safe/*un*safe
Suffix "-ous"	Noun	Changes to adjective	fame/fam*ous*, glamor/glamor*ous*
Prefix "re-"	Verb	Repeat action	tie/*re*tie, write/*re*write
Suffix "-able"	Verb	Changes to adjective; means "can undergo action of verb"	print/print*able*, drink/drink*able*

Source: http://www.cla.calpoly.edu

has three morphemes: *un, happy, ness*. Adding *un* first to the base word *happy* yields the meaning *not happy*, then adding the suffix *ness* to *unhappy* yields this meaning—*the state of not being happy*. This same meaning can be attained by building the word in another way. Adding the suffix *ness* to the base word, *happy*, will produce the meaning, *the state of being happy*. Now add the prefix *un* to the word *happiness*. This will produce the antonym of the word *happiness* and produce the meaning *the state of not being happy*.

As Table 7.2 illustrates, the English plural has three distinct pronunciations. The plurals of the first column are pronounced with the /s/ of sew, whereas those of the second column have the sound /z/ in zoo. The plurals of the third column are pronounced with a vowel followed by a /z/. This vowel is called a "schwa" and is written as /ə/. Therefore the three alternative pronunciations of the plural are /-s/, /-z/, and /-ə z/.

English speakers are not free to select any form of plural that they happen to fancy, but must make their choice according to the final sound of the word to which it is attached. Words that end in "voiceless" consonants, including /p, t, k/ and some others, require /-s/ as their plural. Words that end in vowels or in "voiced" consonants, including / b, d, g, r/ and some others, require /-z/. Words ending in /s/, the /tʃ/ sound of church, and a few other

Table 7.2: Allomorphs

Taps	Cobs	Hisses
Mitts	Lids	Buzzes
Backs + /s/	Lads + /z/	Crutches + /əz/
Baths	Lathes	Judges
Puffs	Doves	Wishes

consonants, require /-əz/. These three forms of the plural suffix differ in pronunciation, but they are all varieties of the "same" suffix. The individual forms /s/, /z/, and /-əz/ are said to constitute three allomorphs of the plural morpheme.

Selection among the forms of English verb suffixes follows a principle that is similar to those of selection among plural forms. Let us look at some of the past tense forms.

Present	Past
Walk	Walked /-t/
Beg	Begged /-d/
Chat	Chatted /-əd/

Can you predict the rule for the use of the three allomorphs above?

Other word formations are:

Term	Process	Examples
Compounding	Combine two words	blackbird, doghouse, mailbox
Clipping	Shortening of word	bike, condo, prep
Acronyms	Coining a new word from the first letters of other words	AIDS, NASA, FAU
Blends	Mixing two words and creating a new word	brunch, telethon, hangry
Onomatopoeia	Sound-like words	bow-wow, cock-a-doodle-doo
Backformation	A cutoff suffix with the base used as root	resurrect, enthuse
Brand names	Brand names become common words	Xerox, Kleenex, Hoover
Borrowing	A word is taken from another language	hummus, wok, macho, kimono

In some languages other than English, free and bound morphemes do not have the same status. For instance, in Hare (an Athapascan language spoken in Canada's Northwest Territories), words that indicate body parts are always bound to a morpheme designating a possessor. The word *sefi* (which means *my head)* is made up of two units connected together; it can never be broken up into two morphemes: *se, *fi. Likewise, the word *nebe*, meaning *your belly*, is never spoken or written as just *be (Sánchez-Gutiérrez & Rastle, 2013.)

Just as there are free forms in English that are bound in other languages, there are bound forms in English that are free in other languages. Past tense, for example, is expressed by a bound morpheme in English (usually -ed), but in Mandarin Chinese it is expressed by a free form *le*. Consider the following sentences:

1. *Ta haek le cha.*
   He drank past tea. (He drank tea.)
2. *Ta haek cha le.*
   He drank tea.

The past tense marker in Mandarin, /le/, is not attached to the verb *haek* because it can be separated from it by the direct object. The knowledge teachers acquire about morphology can help them understand why certain errors are made by non-native speakers of English.

In Spanish, the plural ending must show gender and article agreement, for example, *amiga* (feminine) and *amigo* (masculine). In contrast, English as a neutral article (the).

la amiga	las amigas
el amigo	los amigos
el amigo mío	la amiga mía
los amigos míos	las amigas mías

Another morphological problem for Spanish speakers has to do with the use of morphemes -er and -est. In Spanish, the comparatives and the superlatives are formed with words that are the equivalent of *more* and *the most*. For example, *prettier* will be *more pretty*. Hence, Spanish speakers who are English learners (ELs) might translate the superlative directly into English, making them sound "incorrect."

Spanish speakers may also experience difficulty in using prepositions such as *in, on*, and *at*, because in Spanish these three prepositions are collapsed into one (*en*). So, Spanish speakers may say *The book is in the floor* instead of *The book is on the floor*. Another form of "interference," which we now know are natural grammatical transfer issues, in English that Spanish speakers encounter is the *be* verb to express state of being or age. In Spanish, the verb *have* is utilized to express these concepts. For example, *I have ten years* instead of *I am ten years old*.

In Spanish, nouns are gender marked. For example, *table* is *mesa*, a feminine noun, and *book* is *libro*, a masculine noun. Articles preceding and adjectives following these noun forms must also agree in gender and number with the nouns, as in the following examples:

1. *El libro rojo está en la mesa pequeña.*
   The book red is on the table small.
2. *Los libros rojos están en la mesa pequeña.*
   The books red are on the table small.

What changes do you notice in sentence two, above?

Spanish, by contrast, inflects its nouns for number and gender, but not for possession (which is signaled by placing the particle *de* between the possessed item and the possessor, as in *la casa **de** mi madre, the house **of** my mother*. Spanish has far more inflectional categories—and affixes to mark them—for verbs than does English. Refer to Table 7.3 for Spanish inflectional morphemes.

Haitian speakers of English may leave out the plural *-s* marker in English because in Haitian Creole the plural is marked by a free morpheme, *yo*. The definite article in Haitian Creole appears after the noun, and it takes on different forms according to the noun that precedes it. It can also occur at the end of a string of words, so Haitian children, when speaking English, may leave the definite article out altogether. Pronouns in Haitian Creole are invariant. The same form is used for I/me/my, they/them/their, and so on. Meaning in this case is determined by word order; if it occurs before the verb, it is the subject. If it occurs after the verb, it is an object. Moreover, the Haitian Creole pronouns do not denote gender. One form is used for he/she/it and the corresponding forms. For this reason, Haitian children may tend to use the pronoun *he* when referring to females or inanimate objects. Another interference problem that Haitian children learning English may encounter is the use of the morpheme *be*. In sentences that describe states of being or location, no verb is utilized in Haitian Creole where the verb *be* would be used in English. For example, *I sick* instead of *I am sick*.

Another interesting difference between English and Haitian morphemes is in the verb tenses. In Haitian Creole, verb forms are invariant. Tense is indicated by particles

Table 7.3: Spanish Inflectional Categories and Affixes

Word Class to Which Inflection	Inflectional Category	Regular Affix Used to Applies Express Category
Nouns	Number	"*-s*" mano/mano*s* "hand/ hand*s*"
	Gender	"*-a*" Fem., "*-o*" Masc. hermana/hermano "sister/ brother"

Source: http://www.cla.calpoly.edu

(morphemes) placed before the verb. For instance, examine the following forms of the verb *speak*:

map pale—I am speaking
pale—spoke
a pale—will speak
te pale—have spoken

MORPHOLOGY APPLICATION IN THE CLASSROOM

Teachers may use the knowledge of morphology in this chapter to teach common suffixes, prefixes, and root words. A sample activity to teach a common prefix *re-* follows (Ebbers, 2017):

Write nine words that begin with *re-* on index cards. Use three words in which *re* means back, three words in which *re* means again, and three words in which *re* is just the first syllable and has no apparent mean- ing. Examples of words are:

rebound	redo	record
return	replay	refuse
replace	rework	reveal

Words are placed randomly on the board using magnets. Ask students what they notice about these words. Once students notice that these words begin with *re*, ask them to categorize these words under these labels: *re* for again, *re* for back, and *re* for just the first syllable.

A similar activity can be used for teaching suffixes. On the board, draw three columns and write different suffixes such as *-er, -able*, and *-ation* in each column. Ask students to do the same on a piece of paper. Model the activity by demonstrating the sample word, *import*. The root word *import* becomes *importer, importable*, and *importation*. Explain that the root word, which is a verb, becomes a noun when *-er* is added—the person that imports items; *import* (v) becomes *importable*, an adjective—things that can be imported; and *importation* is a noun, the act of importing. Then list other root words such as *present, adore, invite, restore, quote*, and *interpret* and ask students to fill in the columns.

A third activity that utilizes spelling skills also involves knowledge of morphemes. It is a hands-on activity. Choose 10–15 letters, vowels, and consonants and write them on a sheet of paper. For example, the letters are a, a, o, o, i, i, m, n, l, s, y, t, p, h, k. Students are asked to cut these letters and manipulate them to make words and write them on a piece of paper. Rules such as letters can only be used once or as many times as needed can be given to the students.

This can be a game played in teams. Teachers with the linguistic knowledge of morphemes will find the teaching of digraphs, prefixes, suffixes, and parts of speech much easier.

CONCLUSION

Morphemes are the smallest unit of meaning in a language, and morphology is the study of word formation. Not all languages use morphemes in the same way, so what can sometimes appear as language learning "errors" among ELs are actually natural areas of language transfer. Teachers can learn about their students' languages and how they function in order to understand their ELs and to facilitate their learning by teaching and working with the grammatical structure of English.

POINTS TO REMEMBER

✔ Morphology is the study of word formation that deals with the internal structure of words within a language.
✔ There are two types of morphemes: free and bound.
✔ In English, free morphemes are flexible in terms of their word order positions in a sentence, whereas bound morphemes cannot stand alone as an intelligible word.
✔ Teachers with knowledge of morphemes across languages will better understand non-native speakers of English when they make errors in speech and writing.

REFLECTION QUESTIONS AND DISCUSSION

1. What is morphology and why is it essential to know in order to facilitate ELs' English language acquisition.

2. What is the difference between derivational and inflectional morphemes? Free and bound morphemes? Provide four examples of each.

1. Study the tables below and answer the following questions:

Table 4: Nouns

Singular Nouns	Plural Nouns	Pronunciation of -s
bough		
city		
bribe		
match		
attribute		
avenue		
basque		
filet		
pot		
hero		
face		

Table 5: Verbs

Present Tense Verbs	Past Tense Verbs	Pronunciation of -ed
wash	washed	
kick	kicked	
laugh	laughed	
drag	dragged	
move	move	
tune	tuned	
need	needed	
want	wanted	

    a. For Tables 4 and 5, can you predict the rule for the plural -s and past tense -ed in English?

    b. For Table 4, can you predict how the plural -s is spelled in English? Spell out each word in the table.

    c. What are the bound morphemes in Tables 4 and 5? Are they inflectional or derivational morphemes?

    d. What problems do you anticipate that learners of English may have in learning the English plurals or the past tense?

2. Examine the following word pairs:

    communicate—communication

    verbal—verbalize

    dirt—dirty

    pure—purity

    slow—slowly

What function does the new word in each pair of words have?

3. Look at the following list of words. Which are compound words and which are not? Explain the difference in meaning between each pair of words.

    Greenhouse   green house

    Whitehouse   white house

    Blackboard   black board

    Wetsuit   wet suit

Is there a phonological change in each pair of words? Explain.

4. Below are some words from Merepekland, a language spoken only at parties.

galpur	"attractive girl"	mondep	"polite host"
galdep	"attractive host"	galdepu	"attractive hosts"

    a. List the five morphemes in these words and assign a meaning to each one.

    b. Based on these data, how would you say "polite girls," "polite, attractive hosts"?

WEB RESOURCES

How Words Work: Morphological Strategies. http://www.webfronter.com/towerhamlets/supportforlearning/other/Teaching%20morphology%20prefixes%20and%20suffixes%20etc.pdf

Morphological Awareness in the Classroom. https://www.youtube.com/watch?v=FnRzmI4zK_Q

A Morphological Approach for English Language Learners. https://www.vocablog-plc.blogspot.com/2010/08/morphological-approach-for-english.html

Morphology in the Classroom. https://www.linguisticsforteachersofells.weebly.com/morphology-in-the-classroom.html

The Power of Morphology. http://www.dyslexiahelp.umich.edu/professionals/dyslexia-school/morphological-awareness

Why Morphemes Are Useful in Primary School Literacy? http://www.education.ox.ac.uk/wordpress/wp-content/uploads/2011/04/Morphemes-research-briefing.pdf

Morpheme Match Up. http://www.readwritethink.org/files/resources/lesson_images/lesson880/match.pdf

Mouth Morphemes. https://www.youtube.com/watch?time_continue=1&v=akvVqb_3yyQ

Activities in Morphology. http://www.phillipsspeechtherapy.com/pdfs/Activities%20in%20Morphology.pdf

How Can Teachers Increase Classroom Use of Academic Vocabulary? http://www.ncte.org/library/NCTEFiles/Resources/Journals/VM/0204-may2013/VM0204How.pdf

REFERENCES

Ebbers, S. M. (2017). Morphological awareness strategies for the general and special education classroom: A vehicle for vocabulary enhancement. *Perspectives on Language and Literacy, 43*(2), 29.

Sánchez-Gutiérrez, C., & Rastle, K. (2013). Letter transpositions within and across morphemic boundaries: Is there a cross-language difference? *Psychonomic Bulletin & Review, 20*(5), 988–996.

Syntax

LEARNING OBJECTIVES

Readers will be able to

- ❖ Recognize word order in a language
- ❖ Differentiate lexical categories, linearity, and constituents
- ❖ Define the differences between lexical and syntactical ambiguity
- ❖ Compare and contrast word order across languages to support English learners' (ELs) learning

SCENARIO

The following dialogue takes place between a teacher and her student, who meet while shopping.

Teacher: *Hi, Amir. What are you doing here?*
Amir: *Hello, Mrs. Thomas. I come to get another soccer shoe.*
Teacher: *Are you playing on the school team?*
Amir: *No, I just like to play soccer. If we practice sports, we will enjoy together.*
Teacher: *Yes, exercise is good. Do you have a favorite team?*
Amir: *Yes, I like very much Brazil team. In Brazil, have good methods to train their players.*

What do you observe about the student's sentences? Do they follow the pattern of English sentences? Why or why not?

Syntax refers to the allowed order of words in a language. Native language speakers (children) may say the wrong word in a sentence, but they naturally use the correct order of the words, because they have acquired the rules of the language through its use (Krashen, 1982). Children's brains are hardwired to acquire the language that is used around them (Chomsky, 2015).

Before we further discuss the concepts related to *syntax*, let us examine the following sentences and make some observations about the structure of phrases, clauses, and sentences:

1. The phrase *the smallest car* is acceptable English; *the est small car* is not.
2. The phrase *the small car* is acceptable English; the phrase *small the car* is not.
3. The phrase *chocolate cakes and pies* has two possible interpretations.
4. The interrogative *What is she doing?* is acceptable English; *What she is doing?* is not.
5. The sentence *The palace was built in 1856* is acceptable English; *The palace has built in 1856* is not.
6. The sentence *I do not have any money* is acceptable English; *I not have any money* is not.
7. The sentence *Mary is planning to swim* is acceptable English; *Mary is planning will swim* is not.

Sentence 1 illustrates that words in a language are divided into parts of speech.
Sentence 2 illustrates that words in phrases move from left to right.
Sentence 3 illustrates that words in phrases are grouped into coherent and meaningful units (hierarchical structure).
Sentences 4–6 illustrate that sentence structures are related by transformations.
Sentence 7 illustrates that there are constraints that limit transformation of sentences.

LEXICAL CATEGORIES, LINEARITY, AND CONSTITUENTS

Words within a language are organized into different categories according to their behavior (what they do and what role they play in the language). The four major lexical categories are: noun (N), verb (V), adjective (Adj.), and adverb (Adv.). Minor lexical categories include determiner (Det.), auxiliary verb (Aux.), preposition (P.), pronoun (Pro.), and conjunction (C). Words also belong to phrasal categories. These categories include noun phrases (NP), verb phrases (VP), adjective phrases, and adverb phrases. Each of the phrasal categories contains at least one lexical category of the same basic type—in other words, a NP contains at least one noun, and a VP contains at least one verb. For example, the phrase *the cowardly attacker fled* contains the NP *the cowardly attacker*, which in turn contains the N *attacker*.

Words in English cannot appear in a random order. Phrase structure (PS) rules involve the codification of principles by which words are arranged. What is the word order pattern in the following sentence?

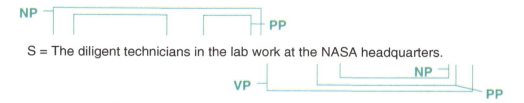

S = The diligent technicians in the lab work at the NASA headquarters.

In the above sentence there is a linear order in which words are strung. There are three large *constituents* (coherent groupings of morphemes): NP, VP, and prepositional phrase (PP). In the above sentence, the NP is *The diligent technicians in the lab*. But within the large NP, there is a smaller constituent, the PP *in the lab*. Similarly, the PP *at the NASA headquarters* contains another smaller constituent, that is, the NP *the NASA headquarters*. Constituents are, therefore, the building blocks of a sentence. The ways to test for constituents are:

1. Ability to stand as an answer to a question—Who works at the NASA headquarters? Where do they work?
2. Substitute pronoun form—They.
3. Movement—At the NASA headquarters, the diligent technicians work.

Constituency is observed in the early language acquisition stage by both first and second language speakers. Teachers generally should not ask students to answer in complete sentences unless there is a specific reason for them using the complete structure. What is more significant is teaching students to string words into coherent groupings.

SYNTACTICAL AND LEXICAL AMBIGUITY

Constituents are extremely important in interpreting ambiguous sentences, that is, sentences which contain two or more possible meanings. For instance, consider the phrase *Japanese culinary professor*. Any native English speaker may find this phrase ambiguous: it can mean either a professor of Japanese culinary arts or a culinary arts professor who is Japanese. This ambiguity is not caused by the lexical items, because none of the words contains more than one meaning. In examining the phrase *Japanese culinary professor*, we can group the words in two different constituents: (a) Japanese culinary; (b) culinary professor. In (a), the adjective Japanese describes culinary, whereas in (b), culinary professor is a constituent modified by the adjective Japanese. In other words, the professor who teaches culinary arts is from Japan.

Another example of a syntactically ambiguous sentence is *They are baking apples*. If the constituent has *baking* as a modifier that modifies apples, the sentence means the apples are specially for baking or cooking, but if the constituent includes *they are baking*, in which *are baking*, is a verb (present continuous tense), the sentence means some people are in the act of baking apples.

Another form of ambiguity arises when a word has two or more possible meanings. This is called lexical ambiguity. Consider these sentences:

Juan is sitting on a trunk.
Claudia is waiting for Juan at the bank.
Ms. Jimenez caught the bat.

The word *trunk* has several meanings: trunk of a car, tree trunk, elephant's trunk, or storage trunk; the word *bank* has more than one meaning—financial institution, river bank; the word *bat* means baseball bat or an animal.

In school, students are taught to differentiate between active and passive sentences. From the linguistic perspective, an active sentence such as *The pitcher threw the ball in the field* has one meaning and one deep structure but can be represented by several surface structures—Who threw the ball in the field? or The ball was thrown by the pitcher in the field. Whichever way the sentences are formed, the meaning of the sentence remains unambiguous: *The pitcher threw the ball in the field.* When a sentence has more than one meaning or deep structure, such as the sentence *He is a Japanese culinary professor*, it is said to be an ambiguous sentence. The sentences *He is a Japanese culinary professor* and *Juan is sitting on a trunk* have one surface structure and two deep structures because both sentences have more than one meaning.

In English, several processes are involved in transforming sentences. Examine the following sentences and identify the general rule for the sentence transformation:

Affirmative	Negative
1. She was sleepy.	She wasn't sleepy.
2. John can play the piano.	John can't play the piano.
3. Mr. Tan has two cars.	Mr. Tan does not have two cars.
4. Helen borrowed Kathy's book.	Helen did not borrow Kathy's book.

In sentences 1 and 2, negation can be made by inserting *not* next to the auxiliary verbs (was and can). However, the above step cannot be used to negate the third and fourth sentences. In 3, *Mr. Tan has not two* cars is ungrammatical and so is 4, *Helen borrowed not Kathy's book*. To negate both sentences, several steps have to be taken. First, the verb *do* has to be used, and then we need to ensure that the verb agrees with the subject. In 3, *does* is used because it is a singular verb form which agrees with the singular subject—Mr. Tan. Next, *not* is then attached to *does*. In 4, *do* takes the past tense form and becomes *did*, because the affirmative sentence is in past tense.

A common difficulty non-native speakers of English encounter is the transformation of sentences to question forms. Examine the following questions:

1. Has the boy talked to the girl?
2. Is the girl talking to the boy?
3. Does the boy like the girl?

4. Did that lady chase those boys?
5. Didn't the manager fire the clerk?

Sentence 1 can be easily accounted for by moving the first word of the auxiliary to the beginning of the sentence, in front of the initial NP. Thus *Has the boy talked to the girl* seems to be derived from *The boy has talked to the girl* by the movement of *has*. Similarly, sentence 2 is derived by moving the auxiliary *is* to the beginning of the sentence, in front of the NP. Thus, *Is the girl talking to the boy* is derived from *The girl is talking to the boy* by the movement of *is*.

A more difficult transformation is the one that involves no auxiliary at all. The sentence *The boy likes the girl* has no auxiliary, and so it has nothing to move to the front in order to make a question. If a sentence like this is to be transformed into a question, *do, does,* or *did* as a kind of dummy auxiliary must be added. It seems that English questions need some sort of auxiliary to move to the front of the sentence, and if nothing else is available, a form of *do* will have to be supplied. There are several steps that must be considered in selecting the forms of *do*. First, the form of *do* must agree with the verb tense; second, it has to agree with the subject. Therefore, in the transformation of the sentence *The boy likes the girl* to the question *Does the boy like the girl?*, these steps must be followed:

1. Choosing *does* over *did* or *do* because of its singular subject (*the boy*) and present verb tense (*likes*).
2. Insert *does* at the beginning of the sentence.
3. Use the root form of the verb in the question (*like*).

Passive sentences involve even more radical movements than questions. Consider a sentence such as *The mouse is chased by the cat*. This sentence can be derived from the active sentence *The cat chases the mouse*, but to get from the active to the passive, several changes are needed:

1. The old object (*the mouse*) moves to the beginning of the sentence.
2. The old subject (*the cat*) moves to the end of the sentence, picks up the preposition *by*, and forms a PP. This PP can be dropped.
3. Another word (*is* in this example) has to be added to the auxiliary.
4. The verb (*chase*) takes an *-ed* suffix.

WORD ORDER ACROSS LANGUAGES

Examine the set of sentences in each language and determine the dominant word order pattern in each. Is it Subject, Verb, Object (SVO); Subject, Object, Verb (SOV); or Verb, Subject, Object (VSO)?

Korean

Chun ku chayt poata.
Chun that book see (Chun sees that book).
Chun Bob-hako malhata.
Chun Bob with speak (Chun speaks with Bob).

Selayarese (a language of Indonesia)

Laallei doe Injo I Baso
Take money the Baso (Baso took the money).
Lataroi doe Injo ri lamari injo I Baso
Put money the in cupboard the Baso (Baso put the money in a cupboard).
Unlike English, in Selayarese VP begins the sentence.

French

Marie a mangé une orange.
Marie ate an orange.
Henri a une fleur rose.
Henri has a flower pink.

Irish (Gaelic)

Is drafur Sean.
Hit brother Sean (Sean's brother hit him).

What difficulties would these speakers have in learning English syntax?

Spanish has a different form of negation than does English. In Spanish, the word no is placed before the first verb in the sentence. For example:

Juan tiene un televisor.	*Juan no tiene un televisor.*
(Juan has a television.)	(Juan no has a television.)

In Spanish, the adjectives usually follow nouns and always agree in gender and number. For example, *He lives in a house yellow* instead of *He lives in a yellow house*. Questions in Spanish have an upside down question mark at the beginning to indicate the interrogative to a reader. They also have a right side-up question mark at the end. Some examples are *¿Dónde vives? (Where do you live?)* and *¿Cómo te llamas? (What is your name?)*. The same declarative sentence can be used for question forms in Spanish. The question mark at the beginning and voice inflection will signal to the readers and/or speakers that it is a question.

In French/Haitian Creole, questions are formed by simply inserting the question phrase before the affirmative statement. For example:

Elizabeth is on vacation. *¿Est-que Elisabeth est en vacances?*

How can teachers use knowledge about syntax to help their students learn the English language?

Such knowledge gives teachers insight into how words are ordered in other languages. While English is an SVO, languages like Korean and Japanese are SOV, and Irish is VSO. Teachers who understand this will not dismiss syntactic errors made by non-native learners of English as mere errors, but will understand that these errors result from a systematic application of their native language system when functioning in English. These teachers will then, for instance, focus more on the teaching of adjectives in context to reinforce students' visualization of the position of adjectives in English sentences. They will also recognize the need to teach step-by-step transformation of English sentences and focus on structures that are unavailable in the students' native language.

The following is a sample activity on teaching English syntax that teachers could use with students. Remember that these grammar-based activities should be part of an overall approach to teaching English that emphasizes actual opportunities to engage with speakers, use the language, and read/write the language for communicative purposes.

Students work with word cards to build sentences. Words cards are divided into part of speech categories: nouns (he, she, John, school); verbs (is, are, likes, jumps, walks), adjectives (pretty, short, big, fat), prepositions (in, on, to, under), and articles (a, the). Teachers stack these word cards in their categories and students choose these word cards and arrange them in a correct English sentence order. For instance, from the above word card list, students can make sentences: *John is big. She likes school. He walks to school.* Students can work in groups in this activity. This is a good way for teachers to assess and observe English learners (Els)' comprehension and application of English syntactic rules. What other sentence making activities can you think of?

POINTS TO REMEMBER

✔ Syntax is the study of how words are ordered within a sentence.
✔ There is a linear order in which words are strung in a sentence. Constituents are coherent groupings of morphemes, the building blocks in a sentence.
✔ There are two types of ambiguity: structural and lexical. A sentence that has one surface structure and two deep structures is an ambiguous sentence.
✔ Not all languages have the same word order as English (SVO)—Korean is SOV and Irish is VSO.

REFLECTION QUESTIONS AND DISCUSSION

1. What is syntax? Why is syntax an important aspect for ELs to learn?

2. What are some ways that teachers can learn about their ELs' languages and syntactic structures and use that information to support their ELs' learning?

3. Why might a Spanish speaking EL state the sentence, "mother goes to house little in the corner"? How does this sentence demonstrate the EL's knowledge of syntax in English and in the first language?

4. What is the difference between syntactical ambiguity and lexical ambiguity? Provide three examples of each.

ACTIVITIES

1. Explain to EL students how to change the following statements into question forms:
   a. The dentist likes working overtime.

   b. Gloria and Britney love dancing to a rap song.

   c. Peter walked home after the concert was over last night.

2. The following are actual newspaper headlines. Which of these are structurally ambiguous sentences and which are lexically ambiguous?
   Explain why L2 learners may find these headlines difficult to understand.

a. Police Begin to Run Down Jaywalkers

b. Safety Experts Say School Bus Passengers Should Be Belted

c. Iraqi Head Seeks Arms

d. Eye Drops-Off Shelf

e. Teacher Strikes Idle Kids

f. Panda Mating Fails; Veterinarian Takes Over

g. Some pieces of Rock Hudson Sold at Auction

h. Enraged Cow Injures Farmer With Ax

3. a. Read the sentences below. Explain the steps in changing them from declarative to interrogative sentences, and active to passive sentences.

Declarative	Interrogative
1. Karim is on the golf course.	Is Karim on the golf course?
2. Katrina has gone to the market.	Has Katrina gone to the market?
3. The doctor knows best.	Does the doctor know best?
4. Tracy could ride home with Jane.	Could Tracy ride home with Jane?

Active	Passive
1. John cleaned the yard.	The yard was cleaned by John.
2. Daisy took care of the baby.	The baby was taken care of by Daisy.
3. We will rewrite the essay.	The essay will be rewritten by us.
4. They have drunk all of the soda.	All of the soda was drunk by them.

b. What possible problems will Spanish and Haitian speakers have in producing sentences like the above?

4. Examine the sentence patterns of these languages. How are they different from English?
   a. *Saya pakai baju biru.* (Malay) *I wear dress blue.*

   b. *Ta puk hau.* (Mandarin) *He/she no good.*

   c. *Anta manitan mavatt-ai settinan.* (Tamil) *That man tree cut.*

   d. *Le gusta bailar.* (Spanish) *To him/to her likes to dance (He or she likes to dance).*

   e. *Me haces falta.* (Spanish) *To me you make lack (I miss you).*

WEB RESOURCES

Collaborative Learning: Creating Syntax. www.linkedin.com/pulse/sample-classroom-activity-i-designed-creating-inventing-monica-fox
English Language Learner Teacher Resources—Syntax. www.ellinfobcps.weebly.com/syntax.html

ESL Lesson 1—Syntax. www.youtube.com/watch?v=J8Lj2G4FfS0&t=465s

How to Teach Syntax to Kids. www.classroom.synonym.com/teach-syntax-kids-8538531.html

Parts of Speech. www.layers-of-learning.com/parts-of-speech

Seuss Syntax! Learn Syntax with Dr. Seuss! www.youtube.com/watch?v=1igmgxc4s-o

A Simple Guide to Teaching Young ESL Students About Syntax. www.fluentu.com/blog/educator-english/esl-syntax/b

Syntax in the Classroom. https://www.linguisticsforteachersofells.weebly.com/syntax-in-the-classroom.html

Syntax Surgery. https://www.youtube.com/watch?v=Wo4rrkyozAA

Teaching Syntax to English Language Learners and Native Speakers. https://www.prezi.com/uqderxk7b1ih/teaching-syntax-to-english-language-learners-and-native-spea

REFERENCES

Chomsky, N. (2015). *Aspects of the theory of syntax*. Cambridge, MA: The MIT Press.

Krashen, S. (1982). *Principles and practice in second language acquisition*. Oxford, UK: Pergamon Press.

Semantics

Readers will be able to

❖ Explain semantic concepts that show relationships in meaning between words
❖ Explain semantics concepts that show differences in meaning between sentences
❖ Identify cross-cultural differences in expressions and meaning
❖ Describe how word meanings affect English learners' (ELs) comprehension

Read the following passage and determine what you need to know in order to comprehend it (Kovalyuk, 2014).

Death of Piggo

The girl sat looking at her piggy bank. "Old friend," she thought, "this hurts me." A tear rolled down her cheek. She hesitated, then picked up her tap shoe by the toe and raised her arm. Crash! Pieces of Piggo—that was the bank's name—rained in all directions. She closed her eyes for a moment to block out the sight. Then she began to do what she had to do.

The previous passage seems like a fairly simple narrative containing simple sentence constructions and common vocabulary; it centers around a topic familiar to most of us— piggy banks. So, let us start with what we know about piggy banks. We know that piggy banks may have the following characteristics:

1. Representations of pigs
2. A place to put money (coins) in
3. Smaller than real pigs
4. Made of plastic or material that can be shattered by dropping or a direct blow

Now, the list of piggy bank characteristics may be longer, but the point is that there is nothing in the passage that gives an overall description of a piggy bank. Nevertheless, we know how it looks, its size, and value, by drawing from our life experience. In addition, other words in the passage add to our mental representation of the piggy bank. For example, we know that a tap shoe can cause the piggy bank to break, thereby suggesting its brittle composition. Once the bank is shattered in small pieces, it can no longer take its original form; hence, the implied death imagery, which sets the tone of the passage and allows the reader to understand the emotions experienced by the girl.

It seems that understanding the passage requires more than just knowing the meaning of specific words. In fact, we must fill in some information from our world knowledge (background and experiences) and understanding of the relationship between words in a single discourse to fully comprehend the passage. You will also notice that words like death and rained are used in a figurative sense, a sense other than their usual meanings. In short, words may have emotive or connotative meanings.

What this passage reveals is that the meaning of words involves drawing upon various kinds of knowledge, including the literal and figurative sense of words, real-world knowledge, and the relationship between words. Even a short and fairly simple passage, such as the piggy bank story, may be difficult for first language learners who have not yet developed an awareness of the special connotative meanings of words and the real world knowledge necessary to comprehend what they read. Comprehension breakdown can be more serious for second language learners, who do not have proficiency in the new language, or the cultural knowledge necessary for text interpretation.

WHAT IS MEANING?

Before we probe further into the specifics of each contribution to meaning, let us consider the following examples and discuss how we determine meaning for each.

1. The word *bank* has more than one meaning in English. The word *seashore* does not.
2. The word *bachelor* can mean both single and unmarried.
3. The words *sofa* and *chair* seem to be closer in meaning than the words *sofa* and *ottoman*.
4. In the sentence *Rachael Ray is the mogul of home cooking in under 30 minutes*, and the phrase *Rachael Ray and the mogul of home cooking in under 30 minutes* refer to the same person, but do not mean the same thing at all.

5. If someone were to ask you to name a mammal, would you think of a whale before a dog or a cat?

6. The statement *The trash isn't out yet, dear* can mean more than one thing, depending on the context of its utterance.

7. The statements *A diamond is a semi-precious stone* and *Limestone is a semi-precious stone* are both false for different reasons.

8. The sentence *The dog chased the mouse* is more plausible than the reverse, *The mouse chased the dog.*

Our observations in sentences 1–8 indicate that there are certain facts that an explanation of meaning must address. Assuming that these phenomena are rule-governed like many other linguistic instances, we will present some concepts and principles that partially explain these phenomena, based on the current research in the field.

Semantics is the study of the meaning of words, phrases, and sentences. Two sources that have contributed to the study of meaning are linguistics and philosophy. While linguistics primarily addresses the core meaning or sense of individual linguistic expressions, philosophy looks at how we derive meaning from sentences by examining the references and truth conditions of each. Unfortunately, meaning is a highly complex and multifaceted phenomenon which must take into account a vast array of different facts. However, it is possible to highlight some of the key theories and principles that have been developed to account for meaning. In our discussion, we will divide the study of semantics into three areas:

1. The semantic relationship between words,
2. The semantic relationship between words and syntactic structures,
3. Language as an expression of culture and worldview.

SEMANTIC RELATIONSHIPS BETWEEN WORDS

One method linguists have used to determine the sense or meaning of words involves analyzing the semantic features that comprise words. This method of analysis is called lexical decomposition. Let us consider the words *man, woman, boy*, and *girl*. How do we know that man and boy or woman and girl are more closely related than boy and girl? We know this because man and boy are similar in that they both refer to males whereas woman and girl refer to females. Similarly, we know that asleep and awake constitute a contradiction.

Other types of semantic relationships between words are *synonymy, antonymy, entailment, referent, extension*, and *prototype*. Synonymy involves different words bearing the same meaning. For example, the words *sofa* and *couch* or *attack* and *charge* share similar meanings, although these words do not have exactly the same meaning in all cases. However, we consider these words to be synonymous because of the degree of overlap between them, as illustrated in Figure 9.1.

Antonyms, on the contrary, are words that are opposite in meaning. Pairs of words such as *complete* and *incomplete, dead* and *alive, open* and *closed* are examples of words that have contradictory relationships and share no middle ground. On the other hand, gradable antonyms are pairs of words that stand on the opposite ends of a continuum; for example, *hot* and *cold, big* and *small*, and *tall* and *short* are opposites on a scale. Liquids can be warm instead of hot or cold; a person can be either tall or short, and so forth. Words like *above* and *under, doctor* and *patient* are examples of converse antonyms which do not represent extremes on a physical dimension, but rather two items in a symmetrical relationship.

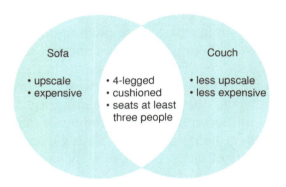

Figure 9.1: Entailment

Source: Eileen Ariza

Entailment is when the meaning of a word is logically related to previous meanings. For example, a piglet must also have the properties of a pig. On the other hand, if it is not a pig, it cannot be a piglet. The partial semantic breakdown of piglet could be illustrated as follows:

  piglet
  pig
  young

Meanings can also be determined by the reference of the linguistic expression. For example, if you point to a particular bus and say "That bus is taking the children to the zoo," then the referent for the expression *That bus* refers to the bus you are pointing to. When a child includes kittens, cats, tigers, lions, and leopards as examples of cats, the child is extending the referring expression to refer to entities that can be considered the set of all cats. This semantic process is known as *extension* and is similar to overgeneralization. When a child names a cat or a dog as an example of a pet, the child is including a prototype or a typical member of the set of all potential referents that refer to pets. Consider the following riddle: What has a face with numbers and makes a ticking sound? If you answer a watch or clock, your answer is based on a list of characteristics of a prototype clock or watch.

Another area that semantics investigates is whether the sum of word meanings helps us get the meaning of the whole. In other words, can we derive meaning by stringing word meanings together? Consider the following sentences:

1. The little boy ate a cookie.
2. The cookie a little boy ate.
3. The teacher read the book to the children.
4. The children read the book to the teacher.
5. The book was read to the children by the teacher.

Sentence 1 makes sense to us, but sentence 2 has no meaning at all, although the same words are used. Meanwhile, sentences 3 and 4 are not exactly the same, although they are formed from the same words. These sentences demonstrate that word order in a phrase provides meaning in a sentence; however, word order alone cannot help determine the meaning of a phrase, as exemplified in sentence 5. Although sentence 5 does not have the same word order or the exact same words found in sentence 3, we know that these two sentences have identical meanings. In other words, sentences 3 and 5 have identical deep structures. These examples illustrate that word order and syntactic structures help determine word meanings and the meaning of a sentence.

The relationship between grammatical structure and semantics can also be seen in sentences where words and phrases can be combined in two different ways, giving rise to two possible meanings; this is known as structural ambiguity (refer to section on syntax). Take the sentence *We need more humorous Bill Maher episodes.* If *more* modifies the phrase *humorous Bill Maher episodes*, then the sentence refers to a need for more Bill Maher episodes that are funny. But if the adjective phrase *more humorous* modifies the noun phrase *Bill Maher episodes*, then the sentence suggests that the episodes must include more humor.

Another form of ambiguity arises when a word has more than one meaning that can only be determined by its context. This can be seen in homonyms that are common in terms of pronunciation, and sometimes have the same spelling, but are different in terms of meaning. For example, the sentence *The coach is full* is lexically ambiguous because the word *coach* can refer to a *carriage* or a *person*. Other examples include *bank* /bænk/ which could mean *a financial institution* or *the river bank, pot* /pat/ could refer to *drugs* or *a flowerpot*, and *bear* and *bare* could refer to *giving birth* or *without covering or protection.*

Heteronyms, which are words that are spelled the same but pronounced differently and have different meanings, can potentially be lexically ambiguous. Without hearing the oral word and knowing the context, English learners (ELs) may have difficulty figuring out the exact meaning for the word. Some examples of heteronyms which may pose difficulties for ELs are *sow*, which could refer to *a female pig* or to *plant seeds*, and *bow*, which could refer to *bow and arrow, bending your head* or *body*, or *the front end of the boat*. Second language learners may find words with multiple denotative meanings difficult to process and understand without sufficient context and the opportunity to hear and see the words visually.

We also determine meaning based on the truth conditions of the words in a sentence, as in the following examples:

1. Pearl S. Buck, the famous American author, was 10 years old when she went to West Virginia and realized that she belonged to two worlds: China and the United States.
2. Ruth did not return the books to the library.

In sentences 1 and 2, truth or falsity cannot be determined by simply inspecting the words in the sentences. Rather, the truth or falsity of these statements depends on our knowledge of Pearl Buck from previous encounters or our consulting of reliable sources to verify the information.

LANGUAGE AS AN EXPRESSION OF CULTURE AND WORLDVIEW

Just as word order and syntactic structures are important to meaning, word meanings are also defined by individual and cultural experiences. Since word meanings often represent a speaker's reality, there is a degree to which these meanings are culturally bound. This is reflected in words that contain connotative or nonliteral meanings, an area that is sometimes most challenging for the fluent, non-native speaker. Let us consider the following two sentences: *The lady is leaving the store* and *The chick is leaving the store*. Although the subject in both these sentences refers to a female adult, the second sentence runs the risk of sounding overly informal, sexist, and discriminatory.

Other examples such as *She is slim* versus *She is thin*, and *He is obstinate* versus *He is stubborn* demonstrate the emotive connotation embedded in words considered to be synonyms. Although they share similar meaning, some words are less commonly used and more academic, as in the previous example with the word *obstinate*. Moreover, even though the pair of words share similar meanings, *slim* and *stubborn* are generally considered to be more acceptable than their counterparts. Emotional meanings can also be found in words used to refer to groups of people. For example, the word *Inuit (people)*, the plural form of Inuk meaning "person," is preferred over the word "Eskimo" because the word Eskimo has been used derogatively and was thought to mean "eaters of raw fish." This term is considered insulting and racist (see NPR.org, 2017). Hence, you can see that no two words can mean exactly the same thing in all cases. Connotative meanings convey our attitudes toward others, as well as how we think about ourselves and our worldview. Second language learners not only have to process and translate meanings already familiar to another language, but also make new associations of these meanings with the correct context (Haslam, Loughnan, & Sun, 2011).

Another case that demonstrates how language is an integral part of culture is the use of idioms. Idioms or idiomatic phrases have a fixed meaning that cannot be inferred from the meanings of the individual words. While all languages contain many such expressions, speakers must learn the meanings and use specified by the culture from which they originate. Some examples of English idioms are as follows:

Knock it off
Bite your tongue
Give you a piece of my mind
Life is not a bed of roses
(to) build castles in the air
The lion's share
Raining cats and dogs
(to) give someone a cold shoulder

How will the second language learner interpret the preceding and other idiomatic expressions such as *birds of a feather flock together*, the *iron curtain*, the *Cold War, the early bird catches the worm, he kicked the bucket, it is raining cats and dogs*, and many other idiomatic expressions? To interpret idioms successfully, the student has to learn the special meanings of these expressions as if learning a new word. Often, success in acquiring idioms requires both exposure to and contact with native speakers of the language over an extended period of time, extensive reading in the language, as well as an understanding of how words are sometimes used metaphorically to mean something beyond the linguistic expression.

By extension, subtle differences in meanings that we attach to words are directly related to our experience. Residents of Florida and those who live along the Atlantic coast of the United States have a rich vocabulary for describing hurricane conditions, just as Inuits and skiers have many words for different kinds of snow. These rich vocabularies involve concepts important to the particular speaker. To residents of geographical areas of the United States and parts of the world where hurricanes are not a naturally occurring phenomenon, the word hurricane may simply suggest an intense tropical storm that has the potential to cause massive destruction. The Nuu-Chah-Nulth people of the west coast of Vancouver Island, Canada, have an enormous trove of words relating to salmon, because they not only make a living from the sea, but they have salmon as a diet staple. Some of these words are displayed in Table 9.1.

As you can see from Table 9.1, the Nuu-Chah-Nulth not only have different words for different types of salmon, but also words describing the age of salmon because the life stage of the fish indicates characteristics such as where the fish are located, how available they are, and how they taste (Rodd, Gaskell, & Marslen-Wilson, 2002). The average person would not make this degree of distinction among salmon other than to recognize that there are probably Atlantic salmon, farm-raised salmon, and Pacific salmon.

Table 9.1: Cross-language semantics

Words for Types of Salmon	
cuw' it	"coho salmon"
hink´u·ʔas	"dog salmon"
hu-pin	"salmon trout"
kѡiḥ Nin	"old salmon"
sa-cin	"young spring salmon"
Salmon-Related Activities	
Camuqѡa	"salmon roe boiling"
ḥuqstim	"salmon-drying pole"
λlḥAta	"salmon jump as in spawning"
ʕaḥ A	"salmon go upstream"
Words for Salmon Parts	
cu.p' i	"fatback cut of salmon"
c'ipuk	"salmon eggs"
ʕawin	"salmon head"

Source: Comrie, Matthews, and Polinsky (1996, p. 141).

Other examples of culturally bound meanings are demonstrated in the way speakers use metaphors (Caballero & Diaz-Vera, 2013; Casasanto, 2014). Metaphors, broadly defined, involve a process of looking for similarities in otherwise dissimilar things for the purpose of being critical, creative, or analytical. In other words, metaphors help us analyze, categorize, and make sense of our world in order to re-create, extend, and provide new meanings for our experiences. Whorf and Veretennikov (2016) propose that cultures differ in the way they categorize and assign significance and that metaphors assist us in understanding how a culture represents a concept. For example, in American culture, time words are found in many expressions, such as the following:

Time is money.
Time is a valuable commodity.
Time is gold.
Time waits for no man, so make hay while the sun shines.
Time heals all wounds.
You're running out of time.
Use your time wisely while it is in your hand.
Time is on our side.

Although some of these expressions may sound cliché now, we continue to use them because we attach personal meanings to them. More importantly, the kinds of language used to represent specific concepts also reveal something about what is important or unimportant to a culture. If we look at the time expressions above, we sense that humanity's relationship with time is a complex one. While time is perceived as a conduit for our success, it can also be perceived as working against us, as indicated in expressions such as *time is running out, time is not on our side, time waits for no man*, and so forth.

Can you think of other expressions about time found in English and other languages? Compare the meanings for each. Are there differences in the way Americans and speakers of other languages view time?

Another example that illustrates a rich distinction between languages is the use of formal and informal second person pronouns. The *vous* / *tu* contrast in French and Haitian Creole, the Spanish *usted* / *tú*, and the *anda* / *awak* contrast in Malay are ways in which speakers show politeness. The Korean and Japanese languages, however, show politeness by adding a prefix to the verb. The following Japanese sentence illustrates how the prefix *masu* is added to the verb to show politeness (Liu & Allen, 2014).

Taroo-ga	sono	tegami-o	yomu-masu.
SUBJ	that	OBJ	reads

Taroo reads that letter.

Changes such as placement of words in a sentence, adding prefixes and suffixes, and using nouns as verbs have the power to change meanings drastically (Akmajian, Farmer, Bickmore, Demers, & Harnish, 2017), as noted in Chapter 8 of this book.

On the contrary, Spanish speakers display respect for authority and people of higher social status than themselves by using specific titles preceding a man or a woman's first name, such as Doña Carmen and Don Charlie. There are also cultures that use honorific terms such as uncle/auntie and brother/sister with the addressee's name to address acquaintances, close friends, or relatives older than the speaker in order to be polite. For example, in Malay it is not unusual for a speaker to say *Kak nak pergi ke mana?* (Older sister, where do you want to go?) when asking directions of a complete stranger on the street, if the speaker perceives the addressee to be older than he or she is. This is not to suggest that politeness is not an issue for English speakers. Rather, the examples above underscore the importance of the age of speaker and addressee in accordance with religious and cultural principles of respect for elders and the different ways in which speakers would use language to express their cultural values.

To be a fully proficient language user in the target language, ELs must understand words, sentences, and their meanings. This can be quite a daunting process when they do not know the meaning of words and the morphemes that compose them, and how the meanings of words combine into phrase and sentence meanings in the target language. The process can become even more difficult when the meaning of an expression in the target language is not very obvious or requires special knowledge that is not available to them.

Here are some instructional strategies that classroom teachers may find useful in helping ELs improve their comprehension:

- Highlight and explain cultural meanings behind words and idiomatic expressions used by English speakers.

- Teach ELs how to make inferences about the meanings of words by looking at other words surrounding the word in question. In addition, present the oral and visual form of lexically ambiguous homonyms and heteronyms to help them make more accurate predictions of word meanings.

- Refrain from using unfamiliar and/or uncommon idiomatic expressions in English when speaking with new or beginner level ELs. This will help learners to focus their attention on words that carry important messages they need to know before they can produce a reasonably intelligible response.

- Invite learners to share cultural expressions from their native language. English-speaking students will gain insights about the newcomer, develop an understanding of the struggles associated in learning a new culture and language, and acquire an appreciation of another culture and language.

- Encourage students to talk about words they hear, read, say, and write in English. This may help teachers to correct any misperception that their students may have about the new words. Additionally, teachers may learn about the different symbols and responses that influence how their ELs think and comprehend English words. In the meantime, students also gain a better understanding of the appropriate forms of language used in the American mainstream culture and ultimately heighten their confidence in communicating with other English speakers.

- Use graphic organizers such as Venn diagrams, semantic webs, and semantic feature analysis tables to help students create associations between words and concepts.

- Activate prior knowledge of words and concepts by inviting ELs to brainstorm English words familiar to them that are associated with a topic of study. In doing so, teachers may be able to determine whether their students have a similar or relevant experience needed for comprehension, sending, and receiving messages. In addition, teachers could fill in any vocabulary gaps by using role-playing, concrete manipulatives, or physical demonstration activities to build the relevant experiences that learners will need.

- Use paraphrasing as a strategy to facilitate and monitor learners' comprehension of word and sentence meanings. Show new ELs how to paraphrase, and encourage them to paraphrase sentences they find interesting and/or unusual as they are expanding their English vocabulary. At the same time, they improve their skills in writing a variety of sentences—a hallmark of good writing.

- Teach students how to use the dictionary to find meanings of English words, phrases, and sentences that illustrate how words are used. Using sentences from the dictionary as a model, encourage students to develop their own sentences by using new words they have learned.

✔ The study of semantics reveals that the nature of meaning is a highly complex and multifaceted phenomenon. To give a satisfactory account of meaning, a wide variety of facts must be considered.

✔ Concepts such as synonymy, antonymy, entailment, referent, extension, and prototype enable native speakers of a language to recognize that certain meanings follow from certain other meanings and to infer and extend new meanings to a finite set of words.

✔ Word order and syntactic structures also help speakers determine the meaning of a phrase or sentence. This close relationship between grammatical structure and semantics is evident in structurally ambiguous sentences. Lexical ambiguity arises when words have multiple denotative or connotative meanings depending on the situational context. The truth or falsity of a sentence is also determined by some extralinguistic factors—in this case, background knowledge.

✔ Native speakers of a language recognize that words reflect concepts that are important in a culture, as we have seen in considering idioms and metaphors. Words hold special meanings for specific individuals as a result of their experience.

✔ ELs must have the appropriate cultural knowledge to process language that contains special connotative meanings, idiomatic expressions, and ambiguous sentences, as well as the relevant real-world knowledge to comprehend messages in a second language.

✔ Teachers must carefully review materials and their oral instructions for any special or nonliteral use of words that require special knowledge of the target culture part of the beginning EL.

REFLECTION QUESTIONS AND DISCUSSION

1. In your own words, describe semantics. Why is semantics an essential aspect of the language learning process for ELs? Why is semantics difficult for new or beginning level ELs in particular?

2. What is the relationship between semantics and background knowledge?

3. Differentiate the semantic relationship between words, including synonymy, antonymy, entailment, referent, extension, and prototype. Note three ways that teachers can support ELs' understanding of word relationships.

4. In an episode of *Ally McBeal*, Ally enlisted the aid of her secretary, Elaine, to help her get rid of a persistent suitor. The dialogue between Elaine and Ally is as follows:

    Ally: *I tried to send him the signal, but he kept saying that sometimes we need to 'boost' the love between two people.*
    Elaine: *Then why don't you 'boost' him down the stairs?*

    What concept from semantics would help you, as a teacher, account for the word *boost*?

5. A 2-year-old boy is looking at the pictures of various birds on a box of tissues. The boy acknowledges that every item is a bird except for one: the owl. Instead of saying "bird," the child responds, "It's a cat."
   Explain the child's interpretation from a semantic viewpoint.

6. In the movie, *Analyze This*, the mobster asks the psychiatrist if there are bugs in his room. The psychiatrist responds, "What do you mean?"
   Taking a semantic viewpoint, explain why the psychiatrist is puzzled by the question.

7. Identify some prototypes and nontypical examples for the following words:
   a. *birds*

   b. *art*

ACTIVITIES

1. Research and brainstorm ideas about color metaphors used to indicate feelings, disposition, or symbolism across cultures. List your findings in two columns as follows:

Feelings/disposition/implied meaning	Color symbolism

Her face turned white as a ghost.
 White as the driven snow.
	In Western cultures:
	 White: pale
	   State of purity
	   Traditional color for brides in Western cultures
	 In India:
	   Death or funeral

Which color metaphors are universal across cultures and which are not? Are they all linked to mood? What do these metaphors say about our society or other cultures?

2. Read the short excerpt below (Anderson, Reynolds, Schallert, & Goetz, 1977) and answer the questions that follow.

   Tony got up slowly from the mat, planning his escape. He hesitated a moment and thought. Things were not going well. What bothered him most was being held, especially since the charge against him had been weak. He considered his present situation. The lock that held him was strong, but he thought he could break it. Tony was aware that it was because of his early roughness that he had been penalized so severely—much too severely from his point of view. The situation was becoming frustrating; the pressure had been grinding on him for too long. He was being ridden unmercifully. Tony was getting angry now. He felt he was ready to make his move. He knew that his success or failure would depend on what he did in the next few seconds.

   a. Who or what is Tony? What words help you determine Tony's identity?

   b. Are there alternative interpretations? Explain what semantic concepts you draw upon to arrive at various interpretations of the text.

   c. How would you help ELs develop vocabulary knowledge? List some suggestions.

3. List all the *kinship terms* found in English and another language. (Try and find a non-European language.) Compare your findings with a colleague. What concepts or values are reflected in these expressions?

WEB RESOURCES

Connecting Word Meanings Through Semantic Mapping Lesson Plan. www.readingrockets. org/article/connecting-word-meanings-through-semantic-mapping

English Language Learner Teacher Resources: Semantics. www.ellinfobcps.weebly.com/ semantics.html

The Importance of Semantics in ESL Instruction. http://exclusive.multibriefs.com/content/the-importance-of-semantics-in-esl-instruction/education

Instructional Resources for Semantics Activities. www.sedl.org/cgi-bin/mysql/framework1.cgi?andor=and&element=semantics&sortby=element&source

Reading Rockets. http://www.readingrockets.org/article/connecting-word-meanings-through-semantic-mapping

Semantics—An Overview eLecture. www.youtube.com/watch?v=8QZWx_XAO1w

Semantic Relationships Packet on Teachers Pay Teachers. www.teacherspayteachers.com/Product/Semantic-Relationships-Speech-and-Language-Therapy-2924257

Syntax in the Classroom. https://www.linguisticsforteachersofells.weebly.com/semantics-in-the-classroom.html

Using Sematic Gradients in Action. https://www.youtube.com/watch?v=zTaYuYw8GNc

REFERENCES

Akmajian, A., Farmer, A. K., Bickmore, L., Demers, R. A., & Harnish, R. M. (2017). *Linguistics: An introduction to language and communication*. Cambridge, MA: MIT Press.

Anderson, R. C., Reynolds, R. E., Schallert, D. L., & Goetz, E. T. (1977). Frameworks for comprehending discourse. *American Educational Research Journal, 14*(4), 367–381.

Caballero, R., & Diaz-Vera, J. E. (2013). Metaphor and culture: A relationship at a crossroads? *Intercultural Pragmatics, 10*(2), 205. doi:10.1515/ip-2013-0009

Casasanto, D. (2014). *Experiential origins of mental metaphors: Language, culture, and the body. The power of metaphor. Examining its influence on social life*, 249–268.

Comrie, B., Matthews, S., & Polinsky, M. (Eds.). (1996). *The atlas of languages: The origins and development of languages throughout the world*. London: Quatro Publishing PLC.

Haslam, N., Loughnan, S., & Sun, P. (2011). Beastly: What makes animal metaphors offensive? *Journal of Language and Social Psychology, 30*(3), 311–325. doi:10.1177/0261927X11407168

Kovalyuk, Y. (2014). American English idioms: Semantics and culture. *British and American Studies, 20*, 137.

Liu, X., & Allen, T. J. (2014). A study of linguistic politeness in Japanese. *Open Journal of Modern Linguistics, 4*(05), 651.

NPR.org. (2017). *Why you probably shouldn't say "Eskimo"*. Retrieved from www.npr.org/sections/goatsandsoda/2016/04/24/475129558/why-you-probably-shouldnt-say-eskimo

Rodd, J., Gaskell, G., & Marslen-Wilson, W. (2002). Making sense of semantic ambiguity: Semantic competition in lexical access. *Journal of Memory and Language, 46*(2), 245–266.

Spradley, J. P. (2016). *The ethnographic interview*. Long Grove, IL: Waveland Press.

Whorf, B. L., & Veretennikov, A. (2016). Language, mind, and reality. *Epistemology & Philosophy of Science, 50*(4), 220–243.

Pragmatics

Readers will be able to

- ❖ Determine how context influences language use
- ❖ Explain how speech acts perform functions
- ❖ Describe direct and indirect speech acts
- ❖ Apply social rules in conversation: Grice's cooperative principles
- ❖ Apply cross-cultural pragmatic rules

SCENARIO

Consider the following scenario described in Harste, Burke, and Wood, *Language Stories and Literacy Lessons* (1984):

A pastor called all the children in his Congregational church and began his sermon as part of a regular worship service:

"Children, I'm thinking of something that is about five or six inches high; that scampers across the ground; that can climb trees; that lives in either a nest in the tree or makes its home in a hollowed-out portion of a tree's trunk. The thing I'm thinking about gathers nuts and stores them in winter; it is sometimes brown and sometimes gray; it has a big bushy tail. Who can tell me what I'm thinking of?"

Robert replied: "Well, ordinarily I'd think it was a squirrel, but I suppose you want me to say it was Jesus."

Do you think Robert's response is appropriate?

In Chapter 9, we defined semantics as the study of the meanings of words and sentences by examining their individual meanings and how they are combined to make larger meanings. We also included grammar as a component of semantics; however, to fully understand the meaning of an utterance we must also understand the context in which it is uttered. *Pragmatics is the study of how people use language within a context and why people use language in a particular way.*

In the previous scenario, the children knew they were in church and must display proper church behavior. For a moment, they remained silent, until Robert, age six, finally raised his hand. The pastor was relieved and asked Robert if he knew what he was describing. Although Robert appeared unsure, his response was not entirely inappropriate—rather it underscores the point that meaning is more than just a semantic interpretation of an utterance. In fact, Robert demonstrates sensitivity to his surroundings and the person he is addressing; he knows that context affects the way he responds.

What exactly is context? In pragmatics, context can be divided into four subparts: physical, epistemic, linguistic, and social. *Physical context* refers to where the conversation takes place, what objects are present, and what actions are taking place. *Epistemic context* refers to background knowledge shared by the speakers and the listeners. *Linguistic context* refers to things that were said previous to the utterances under consideration. And, finally, *social context* refers to the social relationship and setting of the speakers and listeners.

Now let us consider how these concepts apply in Robert's situation. Robert realizes that squirrels are not the sort of thing normally talked about in a church setting (physical context), although he knows the pastor is describing a squirrel (linguistic context). He thus concludes that the pastor is expecting him to say "Jesus" since they are in church (epistemic context). He also knows that he has to behave and show proper respect for the pastor (social context); hence, he phrases his response politely (linguistic context).

Do you think Robert would adjust his response under a different set of circumstances? How would he respond to the same question if it were asked at school or by his friends or family?

DIRECT AND INDIRECT SPEECH ACTS

We will begin our discussion by describing some of the fundamental patterns of human interaction, and then proceed to how these patterns of interaction vary from culture to culture.

Speech Acts

We can use language not only to say things, but to perform an act, which makes language useful to us (Petrey, 2016). This act is referred to as a *speech act*. Each speech act or event involves a locutionary act (i.e., the act of saying something) and illocutionary act (the act of doing something). For example, if a mother says to her child, *"You have to get up early tomorrow,"* the locutionary act provides a description of what is said, which in this case is the referring expression *you* and the proposition *have to get up early tomorrow.*

On the other hand, the illocutionary force of that statement tells us what the speaker does with that statement. In this case, the mother's statement could be interpreted as an order or as an assertion. We can use language to perform a variety of functions: to convey or request information, to give orders, to make requests, to give a warning or advise, to deny a claim, and so on. Speech acts that perform their functions in a direct and literal manner are called direct speech acts. Examine the following sentences:

1. *Little John has a red truck.*
2. *Who switched off the light?*
3. *Stand there.*
4. *Please stand in line.*
5. *Stop talking or you'll have to go in time out.*
6. *Be careful, the plate is hot.*
7. *You should go to bed early if you don't want to miss the bus tomorrow morning.*
8. *I did not let the cat in the house.*

These sentences suggest that we can do many things with language. The types of speech acts in Table 10.1 are significant because of the special syntactic structures used in marking them.

To identify speech acts, we must also consider whether the action to be performed is situationally appropriate. Consider the following scenario: if a young child says to an adult, *"I'm going to drive you to work,"* we would not expect the child to perform the action, because we know the child is below legal driving age. In other words, for a speech act to be correctly performed, it must satisfy the felicity conditions associated with the act. Felicity conditions are based on (a) the participant's beliefs about the speaker's and listener's state of mind and capacities to carry out the action, and (b) whether speakers and listeners recognize the speech act to be appropriate, given the context and purpose.

It is easier for a listener to interpret a speaker's message if the speech acts are performed directly. However, this is not typically the case, as speakers may be indirect for face-saving purposes, to show politeness to other participants, to maintain secrecy, and so forth. Indirect speech acts are not performed in a direct, literal manner; that is,

Table 10.1: Speech Acts and Functions

Sentence Type	Speech Act	Function
Declarative	Assertion Denial	Conveys information Claims information is true or false
Interrogative	Question	Elicits information
Imperative	Orders	Gets others to behave in certain ways

Source: Mihalicek and Wilson (2011).

what the speaker intends is quite different from what is literally said. If a mother says to a child, *"It's quite late for you to watch television right now,"* we know that the mother's statement cannot be literally interpreted to mean that the child can do something else but watch television, or that it is getting late. Rather, we interpret the mother's message as an indirect order to go to bed. Therefore, her statement is not a direct speech act of assertion, but an indirect speech act of ordering. We can also identify indirect speech acts by considering the responses they arouse. Indirect speech acts evoke a response to an utterance different from the response the literal meaning would arouse, as the following question suggests: *Could you pass me the salt?* If the question is directed at a hearer having a meal with the speaker, the response *"yes"* or *"no"* would be inappropriate. To assume this, the hearer must interpret the speaker's utterance as more of a request than a question.

GRICE'S CONVERSATIONAL MAXIMS

Indirect speech acts perform an action in an indirect, nonliteral manner. In his article "Logic and Conversation," the philosopher H. P. Grice (1989) and Chapman (2013) refer to this implied statement or proposition as implicature. For example, a student asks a teacher, *"Mrs. Smith, can we bring one favorite toy with us on the trip to the zoo?"* and the teacher responds, *"Not if you don't want to get it dirty."* The teacher's utterance raises an implicature that there is a risk that the toy may be damaged, since the group will be outdoors and moving about. Although the teacher's implicature is not part of her utterance, we can nevertheless draw the inference that this is why the teacher believes bringing a toy is a bad idea. In other words, implicatures are contextually dependent.

To understand how speakers and listeners use and interpret implicatures, we need to examine how they are used in conversations. Just as there are phonological and grammatical rules that govern language use, there are social rules that govern conversations. These rules inform participants about what to expect in a conversation and determine whether or not the conversation will serve the participants' goals. Grice proposes that participants in a conversation generally agree to cooperate with one another. He maintains that conversations are governed by four cooperative principles or conversational maxims. When speakers intentionally violate the maxims to convey an unstated proposition, they are, in Grice's terms, *flouting the maxim*. Speakers may flout for various reasons. The four maxims that regulate conversations are discussed in the following.

Maxim of Quantity

1. Make your contribution as informative as is required.
2. Do not make your contribution more informative than is required.

Consider the following scenarios:
Jane asks her roommate, Sarah, when she walks into the kitchen of their apartment:

Jane: *What are you cooking?*
Sarah: *Lunch.*
Jane: *Something smells good. What are you making?*

In Jane's view, Sarah's response violates the maxim of quantity because what is implied in the question that she asked is what food is being prepared. If Sarah does not give a specific answer that satisfies Jane, Jane may come to the conclusion that her roommate may not be in the mood to talk or that she is more concerned about having food and not what food they will have for lunch. When speakers violate a maxim intentionally, they are flouting. The listener, on the other hand, must interpret the speaker's flout by inferring a reason for the response.

Another example of when a speaker might be obeying this maxim of quantity is illustrated in the following dialogue:

Jorge: *So what do you think of Sherman?*
Jacob: *Well, I call Sherman a "Jack of all trades." You see, in high school he spent his summers working as a lifeguard at a youth camp. He didn't really like the job, though. So when he finished high school, he worked part-time at a zoo. He . . .*
Jorge: *Hey, too much over share! I just want to know if we should hire him.*

Notice that Jorge was obeying the maxim of quantity. Obviously, he wanted Jacob to supply him information that he didn't know already about Sherman. On the contrary, Jacob's long answer may serve the purpose of ironing out any doubts that he felt Jorge might have about Sherman's ability. Contrary to what Sarah did in Scenario 1, Jacob has provided too much information. While both Sarah and Jacob flouted for different reasons, their responses have violated the principles embedded in the maxim of quantity.

Maxim of Quality

1. Say what you believe to be true.
2. Make a claim based on sufficient evidence.

The principles behind the maxim of quality provide us with some degree of confidence in the messages we deliver and receive. If people did not adhere to these two rules, we would have no knowledge as to whether someone is telling the truth or lying, and language would be useless to us. Of course, people have differing views on what they consider to be good evidence for their views. Nevertheless, we often assume that speakers are obeying this maxim and evaluate what others say based on this assumption. When the expectation for truthfulness is violated, a speaker in a conversation may flout this expectation in order to avoid sounding too confrontational or sarcastic, as the following conversation between two teenagers will illustrate:

Kim: *Hey, guess what? I received an email from the President of the United States yesterday.*
Jenny: *Oh yeah, and the First Lady sent me an invitation to her daughter's wedding.*

Do you think Jenny and Kim are telling the truth? What reasons might Jenny have for saying something that might be patently false? From the above dialogue, the implicature raised by Jenny's remark indicates that she did not believe that Kim was telling the truth. Instead of telling Kim directly that the information she has given is false, Jenny chose to say it indirectly by making a statement that is quite unbelievable. In this case, Jenny has flouted the maxim of quality as a way to express sarcasm or disbelief.

Consider another example:

Rishel: *I need someone who can make a chocolate cake for our picnic.*
JoAnn: *I can make my mom's famous chocolate cake.*

Later at the picnic, Rishel was disappointed with the result as illustrated in the following exchange:

Rishel: *I thought you said you could make a chocolate cake.*
JoAnn: *I thought I could.*

Why was Rishel disappointed? It is evident that Rishel may have inferred that JoAnn can make a chocolate cake because she had made it before. This inference may be invalid because JoAnn may have said this based on the fact that she has seen her mother bake her wonderful chocolate cake so many times in the past and assumed that she knew all she needed to know to make it. Rishel's disappointment illustrates her assumption (that JoAnn was telling the truth as conveyed in the *can*) was not met.

Maxim of Relevance

1. Be relevant.

This maxim assumes that speakers will obey the orderliness of conversations and refrain from making random topic shifts. Consider the first conversation between a mother and her 3-year-old son:

Mother: *Finish your food, Sam.*
Sam: *I want to play with my car.*
Mother: *Yes, you can play with your car after you finish your food.*
Sam: *I have [a] yellow car, green car, blue car, red car . . .*

Sam flouts the maxim of relevance because what he says is not relevant to what his mother has said. His statement raises an implicature. His mother would likely draw the inference that Sam is no longer interested in his food.

The importance of orderliness of conversation is again illustrated in the second example (Richards & Seedhouse, 2016).

Hayam: *Do you think Suher is dating that new kid, Jack?*
Marwan: *Well, she walks to school with him and sits with him during school lunch every day. She also appears at every school function that Jack attends.*
Hayam: *Aha . . . I thought so!*

Hayam may assume that what Marwan has said is relevant if she infers that Suher is dating Jack. But, if Marwan knew that Suher is frequently seen to be with Jack because she is returning a favor to an old friend, who happens to be Jack's best friend, then what Marwan said would have been misleading. Despite what Marwan knows or does not know, it is clear that speakers generally assume that people will not make random topic shifts as a way to maintain orderliness in communication.

Maxim of Manner

1. Avoid vague expressions.
2. Avoid ambiguous expressions.
3. Do not be excessively wordy.

These maxims are especially important for teachers to note because they concern the way we regulate conversations by expecting that speakers will avoid using jargon or expressions listeners cannot be expected to know. This maxim also stresses the need for messages to be delivered in a clear and concise manner. Consider the following statement:

Campbell's soup is the best because it has one-third less salt.

To challenge this claim, one might ask if this brand of soup is better because it has one-third less salt than what it used to have or because it has less salt than the soups of its competitors. We challenge this claim because it tends to implicate a lot using open-ended comparatives that imply multiple meanings, thereby making it ambiguous. Designed to convey the superiority of a product, these types of open-ended comparatives are abundant in the language of advertising. Here are a few examples (Schrank, n.d.):

"Anacin: Twice as much of the pain reliever doctors recommend most." (Twice as much of what pain reliever?)
"Supergloss does it with more color, more shine, more sizzle, more!"
"Coffee-mate gives coffee more body, more flavor."
"You can be sure if it's Westinghouse." (Be sure of what?)
"Scott makes it better for you."

Equally important to consider is how this maxim of manner may be applied in the way different cultures use language. Consider the following conversation between two friends:

Larry: *Did you like the movie, Hiroshi?*
Hiroshi: *Yeah, it was interesting. I liked the music a lot.*

Hiroshi's response might be considered vague and confusing by North Americans because no comment is made about the movie other than to comment on the music. The speaker may intentionally flout to avoid hurting a friend who has a high opinion of the movie. His indirectness reflects an attempt to preserve the dignity, feelings, and "face" of his friend, which is an important style of interaction of most East Asian cultures, such as Japanese, Korean, Thai, Chinese, and Malaysian, as well as Mexican culture (Samovar & Porter, 2004). While most Americans try to avoid vagueness and ambiguity and get directly to the point, Asians' and Mexicans' indirect approach to communication reflects the emphasis on protecting and maintaining the social harmony of the collective group. For many Americans, the immediate effect (the intended message) is a major goal of communication, whereas Asians generally do not want to be responsible for causing someone to feel shame. Even when negative messages are intended, Asians prefer the use of indirect language. In the Chinese culture, the most powerful insult is delivered when the words have the power to affect the conscience of the person being insulted or causing one to lose sleep. These differences make one thing very clear, though. North Americans' use of direct language may be viewed by most Asians and Mexicans as harsh and rude.

CROSS-CULTURAL PRAGMATICS

Pragmatics maintains that language is embedded in a cultural context; social rules governing language use may vary from culture to culture. For example, the Western or American greeting *"How are you?"* may be misconstrued by listeners from a different culture as a question which obligates the listener to impart extensive information, when, in fact, a simple response such as *"fine, thanks,"* *"good,"* or *"okay"* would suffice. In some cultures, greetings may be signaled by the use of words that may be viewed as irrelevant, inappropriate, or meaningless by speakers of other languages. One form of Chinese greeting, *"Have you eaten?"* which is commonly used as a conversational opener, may strike Anglo speakers as odd, but, for a culture whose traditional history dates back to times when famine was common due to natural disasters, pestilence, and overpopulation, the priority given to food consumption in this greeting is a sign of prosperity. Hence, when one is greeted by a question related to whether one has eaten, the implicature of the question is that the speaker hopes that the person being addressed will have a prosperous life.

Similarly, the Malay language *"Where are you from?"* or *"Where are you going?"* is a socially appropriate conversational opener, particularly among young, urban Malaysians. The question may raise several implicatures depending on the context. One implicature is that time is a valuable commodity in the increasingly fast-paced life of upwardly mobile

Malaysians; the evoked response will help speakers and listeners gauge how much time should be invested in the conversation. Another implicature is that mobility is a sign of economic prosperity.

Another example of culture being manifested through language can be seen in how speakers vary in their strategies of responding to compliments. Those from Asian cultures, which tend to emphasize group over individual strength or success, may not know how to behave in an appropriate way in response to an English-speaker's compliment. Observe how the non-native speaker of Chinese background responds to a compliment given by a native speaker:

Native speaker: *That was the best roast duck I've ever tasted.*
Non-native speaker: *Thank you, but my mother and grandmother make more delicious roast duck.*

As you may conclude, *thank you* would have been a sufficient response. But in cultures that value group and team effort as being instrumental to individual success, it is not surprising to hear speakers respond to compliments in the same way as in the above dialogue. When speakers transfer social rules from their native language to another language, the result may be confusion and misunderstanding on the listeners' part. Second language learners must learn these pragmatic rules if they want to communicate effectively with native speakers. This process may take time.

Just as larger social contexts have bearing on how speakers use language to serve their purpose, there are also many social conventions that govern language behaviors in any classroom. For example, a student new to an American classroom would interpret the teacher's question *"What do you think?"* differently from his or her American counterparts. American students would generally interpret the teacher's question as one that seeks individual opinion. However, the new language learner may interpret the question as seeking confirmation of the teacher's opinions or views as a mark of respect for elders or for those in authority. This may lead the teacher to believe that the new student is unable to think or reason well. Diaz-Rico (2013) illustrates that when an American teacher asks a student who is sitting at her seat, *"Are you finished with your work?"* the implicature of the question is that the student should be self-directed and not waste time doing nothing once she is finished. However, in some cultures, students may expect the teacher to praise them for completing their work early. Differences in cultural values and how they are displayed may be sources of difficulties for second language learners who are new to American classrooms.

It goes without saying that the rules and uses of language reflect the values of a culture. As the previous examples illustrate, certain rules in a foreign language that appear to be arbitrary and meaningless to non-native speakers may appear to be quite logical to native speakers. Because language reflects many of the deep structure values of a culture, teachers of new English learners (ELs) must not simply assume that their students speak and think in the same way as those in the mainstream English culture and that the only thing needed is to teach them labels and expressions in English. To help new ELs understand English language expressions, teachers must present the rules and symbols of language in context and make culture a component of their English language instruction as much as possible.

Here are some tips that teachers may find useful when teaching new ELs about English pragmatics:

- Use scenarios, case studies, cultural capsules in reading, writing, and discussions to highlight how speakers use language within a context and how culture may influence why speakers use language in particular ways.
- Use direct and literal statements as much as possible to avoid confusion.
- Provide models of different forms of classroom discourse and turn them into lessons on language and culture. Teachers could model how students should address their American teachers, what they would say to greet their peers and teachers, how to request information and permission from their teachers, how to express disagreements in class, and so on.
- Suspend making negative judgments about the new ELs when they appear to say something that seemed confusing or awkward to you at first. Chances are that these learners may be transferring their cultural norms and native language patterns when communicating in English. Teachers should try to find out what they are trying to say by probing and asking confirmation questions such as "Do you mean to say . . . or . . . ?" or ask them to elaborate, or explain by examples or acting out.
- Encourage new ELs to interact with their peers and teachers as much as possible. This allows them to learn the meanings of current words and expressions frequently used by native speakers in everyday communication.

POINTS TO REMEMBER

✔ Pragmatics is the study of how people use language within a context and why people use language in a particular way.
✔ In pragmatics, context can be divided into four subparts: physical, epistemic, linguistic, and social.
✔ We can use language not only to say things (locutionary act), but also to perform an act (illocutionary act). This is referred to as a speech act.
✔ Speech acts that perform their functions in a direct and literal manner are called direct speech acts. For example, Heidi has a ball.
✔ Indirect speech acts are not performed in a direct, literal manner, that is, what the speaker intends is quite different from what is literally said. For example, the statement *"It is cold"* in here raises an implicature; it could be interpreted as a request to turn up the thermostat.
✔ There are four conversational maxims that regulate conversation and help us understand how speakers and listeners use and interpret implicatures. These four maxims relate to quantity, quality, relevance, and manner of utterance. When speakers violate (flout) one or more of these maxims, their utterance raises an implicature. Because ELs may have a tougher time interpreting indirect or implied statements, teachers must be clear and concise in giving instructions or making statements to the students.

✔ Since language is embedded in a cultural context, social rules governing its use vary from culture to culture. For example, cultures may use different sets of social rules for the act of greeting or complimenting. When ELs transfer social rules from their first to their second language, the result may be a communication breakdown. They must learn the pragmatic rules of the target culture if they are to communicate well with native speakers.

✔ There are also many social conventions that govern language behaviors in any classroom. ELs who are new to a U.S. classroom need to learn the appropriate rules for doing things or risk being misunderstood or misjudged by their English-speaking peers.

✔ Teachers can teach ELs culturally acceptable classroom behaviors through simulated role-plays and by going over classroom routines with new learners of English.

REFLECTION QUESTIONS AND DISCUSSION

1. What is pragmatics and why is it important for ELs' language learning?

2. Why is pragmatics an often overlooked aspect of language teaching and learning for ELs?

3. Explain how cultural differences in pragmatic rules may affect their behavior and perception of them?

ACTIVITIES

1. Interview two students of English and find out what speakers of their native language would say in the following situations:
   a. to compliment someone on work well done
   b. to disagree with someone's ideas in class or other public settings
   c. to ask for permission to leave the classroom

   What pragmatic rules do speakers of the students' culture observe in the previous situations?

2. Consider the following conversation between a child and a parent:

   Parent: *What are you doing?*
   Child: *Nothing.*

   Which maxim does the child's reply appear to violate? Explain the implicature of the child's response.

3. Examine the conversation between an English-speaking teacher and her Samoan student:

   Teacher: *What a beautiful necklace!*
   Student: *Thank you. (She proceeds to remove her necklace.) Please take this necklace. It is yours.*
   Teacher: *Oh no, I can't. You should keep something as beautiful as this.*

   What implicature does the student draw from the teacher's question? What can you say about the pragmatics of complimenting someone in American and Samoan cultures?

4. Examine and discuss how a speaker could be using the statements below in both a direct and indirect manner. Consider the contexts in which these statements could be uttered. How does context affect their function?

   a. *I can't believe it!*
   b. *Have fun!*
   c. *I'm really hungry.*
   d. *Are you done yet?*
   e. *Me?*

5. Consider the following scenario involving Juan, an English as a second language (ESL) learner of Mexican background, and his friend Joe, a native-speaker of English.

   Juan: *I've got to go home now.*
   Joe: *O.K. See you later.*
   Juan: *When?*

   Based on your knowledge of speech acts, what function does Joe's utterance perform? Explain why Juan's question may seem odd to a native English speaker.

6. A parent says to a child, *"If you don't march up to bed right now, you'll be sorry."* What felicity condition does a child assume in order to interpret the parent's remark as a felicitous threat?

7. For each of the following utterances, determine (a) which of Grice's maxims does the second utterance appear to flout and (b) the implicature raised by the second utterance.
   a. Jane: *What are you reading?*
      Sue: *A book.*
   b. Bob: *Are you going out tonight?*
      Ray: *Do birds have wings?*
   c. Kathy: *Do you like the dress I got you?*
      Joan: *Yes, I feel like a disco queen.*
   d. Tim: *Isn't our new coach cool?*
      Joe: *Yeah, he gets my vote for Coach of the Year!*

8. Cazden (1986) cites the following exchange between a teacher and a Puerto Rican student:

   Student (sitting at his desk): *"Teacher, teacher, come here."*

   Teacher (who is on the other side of the room helping other children): *"There is no one by that name here. We all have names!"*

   Student looks at the teacher quite puzzled, then looks down and continues his work and does not attempt to seek the teacher's attention again.

   What cultural pragmatics does the student observe? In what way does this contrast with the teacher's perspective?

WEB RESOURCES

American English—Teaching Pragmatics. https://www.americanenglish.state.gov/resources/teaching-pragmatics

"In Your Shoes" Pragmatic Language Activity. www.thespeechroomnews.com/2012/07/in-your-shoes-pragmatic-language.html

Pragmatics in the Classroom. www.linguisticsforteachersofells.weebly.com/pragmatics-in-the-classroom.html

Pragmatics Lesson Plans. www.slplessonplans.com/pragmatics

Speech Act Activity—Pragmatics. https://www.coerll.utexas.edu/methods/modules/pragmatics/06

Teaching Pragmatics in Conversation. www.busyteacher.org/9191-how-to-teach-pragmatics-esl-conversation-classroom.html

The Role of Pragmatics in Second Language Teaching. http://www.digitalcollections.sit.edu/cgi/viewcontent.cgi?article=1479&context=ipp_collection

REFERENCES

Cazden, C. B. (1986). Classroom discourse. In Wittrock, M. C. (Ed.), *Handbook of research on teaching* (3rd ed., pp. 432–463). New York, NY: Macmillan.

Chapman, S. (2013). Grice, conversational implicature and philosophy. In *Perspectives on pragmatics and philosophy* (pp. 153–188). New York, NY: Springer.

Diaz-Rico, L. T. (2013). *The crosscultural, language, and academic development handbook: A complete K-12 reference guide*. New York, NY: Pearson Higher Ed.

Grice, H. P. (1989). *Studies in the way of words*. Cambridge, MA: Harvard University Press.

Mihalicek, V., & Wilson, C. (2011). *Language files: Materials for an introduction to language* (11th ed.). Columbus, OH: Ohio State University Press.

Petrey, S. (2016). *Speech acts and literary theory*. London, UK: Routledge.

Richards, K., & Seedhouse, P. (Eds.). (2016). *Applying conversation analysis*. Basingstoke, UK: Springer.

Samovar, L., & Porter, R. (2004). *Communication between cultures* (5th ed.). Belmont, CA: Wadsworth.

Schrank, J. (n.d.). *The language of advertising claims*. Sunset.backbone.olemiss.edu. Retrieved http://home.olemiss.edu/~egjbp/comp/ad-claims.html

Nonverbal Communication

Readers will be able to

- Distinguish different aspects of "silent language"
- Recognize cross-cultural differences in gestures, eye contact, space, and touch
- Identify misunderstandings that are due to differences in nonverbal communication

Read the following scenarios and try to identify what is the source of the cross-cultural misunderstanding.

1. A mainstream, US teacher wanted to praise a Thai student for the good work she produced. When the teacher reached out to touch her head, the student moved away from the teacher.
2. An English as a Foreign Language (EFL) teacher teaching in Saudi Arabia was passing out assignments to the students with her left hand. The students were not pleased with the teacher and showed their displeasure by frowning. Why?
3. A teacher asked a newcomer English learner (EL) student a question in class. The student did not understand the question and thus barely looked at the teacher when responding. The teacher then retorted, "José, you need to pay attention in class." Why do you think the teacher said this?
4. An elementary EL student eager to answer a teacher's question ran up to the teacher and held her hand. The teacher took a step back and asked, "What do you want to tell me, Lim?" Lim suddenly looked disappointed and replied, "Uh . . . it is not important."

What do you think might be a source for the cross-cultural misunderstandings between the participants in each scenario?

NONVERBAL COMMUNICATION STRATEGIES

So far we have explored how language allows us to express our ideas and readily communicate information to one another, but in some types of communication, a great deal of information is conveyed nonverbally by using our faces, our bodies (gestures), and our sense of personal space. *Nonverbal communication is the way of expressing feelings or meaning without using words.*

In this chapter, we discuss the various aspects of nonverbal communication and point out how they vary from culture to culture, just as verbal language varies. Oftentimes, these nonverbal differences can be a source of confusion for individuals new to a culture. For example, looking someone in the eye may be acceptable in one culture but inappropriate in another. To accurately interpret each culture's particular style of communication, we need to understand the various aspects of the culture's "silent language."

Gestures

Every language and culture employs gestures or body movements that carry meaning. Just as there are verbal labels that convey different meanings across languages, there are also gestures that are not universal in meaning. Some gestures may convey meanings considered inappropriate or taboo in some cultures or languages. For example, the U.S. hitchhiking signal is considered taboo in New Zealand and Australia. The hand signal with the arm outstretched to the side and the palm facing down to show the height of a child is considered insulting in Colombia, as it is used only to show the height of an animal. The height of a person will be shown with the hand flipped up. The American gesture for "O.K." is a symbol for money in Japan and is considered obscene in several Latin American cultures. Latin American newspapers took delight in publishing a picture of President Nixon giving the O.K. symbol with both hands, which is a vulgar symbol of infidelity in Latin American cultures (Hasler, Salomon, Tuchman, Lev-Tov, & Friedman, 2017). The goodbye gesture (open hand raised, shake from left to right and vice versa) is considered insulting in Turkey, as it signals that someone is mentally unstable. While signs made with crossed fingers often signal a close bond between two people in the United States, the same signal is considered insulting in Paraguay and some Latin American cultures. In many countries, throwing a shoe at a person is a gesture of grave insult or protest. For example, an Iraqi journalist threw shoes at President George W. Bush, calling him a dog. Posters of Bush with shoes around his face were placed everywhere to show the disdain for him. These are the worst gestures to show someone in many countries because the shoes are dirty.

Space

In "high contact" cultures such as Latin American and Greek, people are usually comfortable standing closer together than are Americans when talking. However, in "low-contact" cultures such as those found in Northern Europe and North America, people usually stand farther apart when talking. Typically, the distance between people in North America should be at least an arm's length or up to 6 ft, depending on the social relationship between the speakers and the situational context. For many mainstream Americans, this area of personal space may only be violated if speakers are close friends or family members. A stranger who violates this personal space could be considered confrontational and aggressive. Even in a crowded elevator, Americans generally signal the boundaries of their personal space by maintaining minimal eye contact or positioning themselves so they are not facing each other. A sensitive teacher must understand how students use personal space in their respective cultures and try to help them understand how these norms are displayed in the American culture context.

It is also important to note that individual personalities and gender differences may influence people's use of personal space. Individuals who are more introverted may prefer to maintain a greater distance than those who are extroverted. Generally, individuals of the same gender will tolerate less distance between them than they will allow a person of the opposite sex. Whether personalities, culture, or context determine the messages we send nonverbally through the use of bodily space, it is clear that a violation of the proxemics rule can cause discomfort to certain individuals. Proxemics is the amount of space that people feel is needed between them when communicating.

Every country has its own definition of appropriate space between each other. Some people stand intimately close to each other, even sharing breath as a sign of closeness. Other people, like in the United States, feel violated if people stand too close to them. Also, men may touch,hug, kiss (cheeks or lips) and hold hands with each other with no homosexual intentions, but are not allowed to show affection to girls in public. Additionally, the girls will act affectionately with each other while being totally heterosexual.

Eye Contact

It is commonly accepted that, in certain situations, insufficient or excessive eye contact may cause cross-cultural misunderstanding. In North America, speakers must maintain some eye contact—sometimes accompanied by a smile—to show a level of interest in and attention to a speaker or listener. Failure to maintain sufficient eye contact may have negative consequences; speakers may be viewed as being inattentive, uninterested, or sometimes dishonest.

Speakers from east Asia, Mexico, and Latin American countries, however, will view some eye contact as a sign of disrespect for older and authority figures. This is also true with teachers, who are considered authority figures and should be respected. In Latino culture, for example, children are discouraged from looking at the adult in the eye when being reprimanded. In fact, children are expected to display shame or remorse by bowing their head when they are punished for misbehaving. Children from Spanish and Asian backgrounds may be given corporal punishment if they look at the adult in the eye.

Teachers who are not aware of this fact sometimes make false assumptions about nonnative speakers who do not maintain eye contact. Unfortunately, the expression "Never trust a person who can't look you in the eye" resonates all too clearly in some teachers' impressions of new ELs. Moreover, asking an EL to "look at me when I talk to you," may be inappropriate.

Touch

Interestingly, every culture sets out rules for when touching is tolerable or intolerable. While individual preference should be considered, the right to touch depends on various factors, such as the person's gender, social hierarchy, and the relationship between individuals. But how these rules are carried out varies from culture to culture, as well as from subculture to subculture. Although it is not possible to generalize across large groups of people, some trends in behavior across groups can be observed. For example, African Americans may be more prone to touching than White Americans; however, Americans of any race generally find opposite-sex touch more tolerable in certain circumstances than people from the Mediterranean or the Far East. In some cultures, the right to touch increases as one moves up the social ladder; typically, a person of higher rank may touch a subordinate. Individuals who wish to interact with members of a different culture must learn to observe these rules or risk offending the other parties involved.

Importantly, teachers must be sensitive to how their body language may demonstrate their attitudes toward diverse learners and toward EL students and their families. Teachers who learn and employ cross-cultural skills will be able to build a classroom climate of respect and value for all students, regardless of their native origins—a climate which will have a great impact on student success.

POINTS TO REMEMBER

✔ Just as we use language to communicate, we also convey meaning through nonverbal means.

✔ Different aspects of nonverbal communication include how speakers use space, gestures, touch, and eye contact.

✔ Meanings assigned to gestures are not always universal across cultures. Some gestures are considered taboo in one culture, but not in another. Moreover, cross-cultural variations exist among people within cultures.

✔ High-contact cultures allow more bodily contact between speakers, whereas low-contact cultures define certain boundaries for personal and public space, depending on the level of intimacy, familiarity, gender differences between speakers, and the formality of the setting.

✔ In some cultures, eye contact between speakers must be maintained, whereas in others, eye contact is considered rude and confrontational, especially if displayed by a younger speaker toward an older authority figure.

✔ Different cultures also have specific rules about what is permissible touching and what is not. These rules depend on various factors such as gender, social hierarchy, and the relationship between individuals.

✔ A sensitive teacher will employ appropriate cross-cultural skills that signal respect toward their students of different cultural backgrounds. Once students feel respected and comfortable in their classrooms, they will be able to learn.

REFLECTION QUESTIONS AND DISCUSSION

1. Consider the following scenarios:
   - A teacher calling on a student in class
   - A parent talking to a child at home
   a. What body language is considered acceptable in American culture for the participants in each scenario?

   b. What are some areas in which an EL's cultural rules for interaction might violate American nonverbal communication strategies?

   c. How can you help ELs understand nonverbal communication strategies in American culture?

2. Provide examples of nonverbal communication strategies that may be acceptable in one culture, but shocking or confusing in another.

ACTIVITIES

1. Investigate how other cultures use gestures, space, touch, eye contact, and other nonverbal means to communicate with people. List some nonverbal communication strategies that are different from those in the mainstream American culture. Discuss their implications for the classroom.

WEB RESOURCES

Helpful Nonverbal Communication Activities. www.thoughtco.com/nonverbal-communication-activities-1857230

Non-verbal Teaching Techniques of Successful Foreign Language Educators. www.fluentu.com/blog/educator/language-teaching-techniques

Tips on Nonverbal Communication in the Classroom. www.teaching.monster.com/benefits/articles/9350-9-tips-on-nonverbal-communication-in-the-classroom

Body Language and Gestures Vocabulary Matching Exercise. www.eslflow.com/Body-language---gestures-vocabulary.html

Good Body Language Improves Classroom Management. www.nea.org/tools/52227.htm

Non-verbal Communication. https://www.teachingenglish.org.uk/article/non-verbal-communication

Non-Verbal Communication. www.youtube.com/watch?v=SKhsavlvuao

Nonverbal Communication Exercises. www.theatrefolk.com/blog/nonverbal-communication-exercises

Non-verbal Communication—TEDxBritishSchoolofBrussels. https://www.youtube.com/watch?v=E6NTM793zvo

Non-Verbal Signals. http://www.theteachertoolkit.com/index.php/tool/non-verbal-signals

REFERENCE

Hasler, B. S., Salomon, O., Tuchman, P., Lev-Tov, A., & Friedman, D. (2017). Real-time gesture translation in intercultural communication. *Ai & Society, 32*(1), 25–35. doi:10.1007/s00146-014-0573-4

Discourse

Readers will be able to

- ❖ Understand and describe of discourse
- ❖ Define and categorize organization patterns of conversations and written texts
- ❖ Decipher cross-cultural conversational and rhetorical patterns
- ❖ Recognize that English learners' (ELs) communicative ability depends on understanding the discourse rules of the target language

1 The following conversation takes place between a teacher (T) and her EL student (S):

> T: *Can you tell me about the picture you drew?*
> S: *It's my dog, Sam.*
> T: *What kind of a dog is he?*
> S: *She a poodle. She got beautiful hair.*
> T: *What do you like to do with your dog?*
> S: *I like to play ball with her. I kick the ball, she run and catch it.*
> T: *It sounds like fun. Does your dog also sleep with you?*
> S: *Yeah, she sleep on my bed, near my feets. She like to make . . . (scratches his head in search for the right word, and hesitates for a moment, then makes the sound of a dog snoring.) She make noise.*
> T: *Oh, you mean she snores?*
> S: *Yes, she like to do that.*

Do you think there is conversational flow in this dialogue? Why or why not? How does the teacher help the student to stay within the topic and keep the conversation going?

WHAT IS DISCOURSE?

Much of what we have studied so far has focused on how we process language at the sentence level, not on how humans process larger units of discourse. In this section, we focus mainly on conversational and rhetorical patterns and compare how these styles may vary across languages.

Discourse: Cross-Cultural Conversational Patterns

Maintaining a conversation in any language requires a set of skills. Some skills are generally employed in many languages, but the way in which each is carried out in real time communication may vary from language to language. Research suggests that the ability to maintain a conversation in a second language requires the following:

a. **Turn-taking.** To have successful oral interaction, participants must understand the implicit rules governing when and how long a person speaks, when and how long a person should remain silent, who can nominate topic shifts, and so forth. These rules may be different from one language to another, and may cause misunderstandings that can affect student's ability to succeed in school. For example, native speakers of English accept the notion that only one person speaks at a time, whereas in Hawaiian and other languages that have a longstanding tradition of didactic storytelling, overlapping talk is permissible (referred to as "talk story"). This is because Hawaii is a culture of group storytelling rather than passing stories through the generations by reading. Intergenerational interaction through talk is more important that reading stories. Additionally, not many stories are written in the common "pidgen" way of speaking. This is particularly problematic when learners encounter classroom discussions that require students to respond individually.

SCENARIO

2 The following conversation is between two teachers (T1 and T2) who have been observing a group of English learner (EL) children learning to write in English.

T1: *Did you notice Maria's* (a Spanish speaking girl) *story had a beginning, a middle, and an end?*

T2: *Yes, I think she's making a lot of progress in writing. What did you think of Hoang's story?*

T1: *Well, I didn't like it as much as Maria's. Hoang tends to move away from his topic quite often; instead of talking about his hobby, he sometimes includes information about what other family members like to do that has nothing to do with him or the topic. I don't know . . . it's too distracting, I suppose.*

What assumptions do these English-speaking teachers make about what makes good writing? What inferences can you draw about how writing is organized in different languages?

b. **Topic selection and relevance.** One of Grice's conversational maxims, reviewed in Chapter 10, (Kleinke, 2010) is that participants generally try to cooperate by exploring and maintaining topics of interests to all participants. Other factors in determining topic selection are based on the context of the interaction, social relationships between the participants, and the purpose of the communication. For example, cultures may have different views about the meanings of words such as freedom, sexuality, leadership, democracy, or security and have different levels of comfort in speaking openly about these topics in the public arena. While AIDS (acquired immune deficiency syndrome) and LGBTQ (lesbian, gay, bisexual, transgender, and queer) issues may largely be accepted for public discussion in the United States, traditional cultures may frown upon their members who speak about these issues publicly, because they run counter to the cultural, religious, or moral principles of the group. Hence, members may shy away from certain topics to save face of the collective group. "Saving face" means to avoid embarrassing or shaming someone.

c. **Conversational repair.** When communication breakdown occurs, participants use various techniques of self-correction and clarification to eliminate misunderstandings. For example, speakers repeat or paraphrase their message (*Uh . . . what I mean to say is . . ., As I've said earlier . . ., Can you say that again?, What* *do you mean?*, and so on). These strategies enable learners to overcome some of the difficulties they experience in sending and receiving messages.

d. **Appropriateness.** The varieties or styles of speech that native speakers adopt depend on various factors such as age, gender, and cultural backgrounds. Native speakers of a language learn to employ *speech register, a term used to describe the varieties of speech styles that are appropriate for individual contexts.* Casual conversations between two close friends may feature slang and spontaneous speech that may not be used in a formal speech register, such as when a student makes an oral presentation on an academic topic to her teacher and peers. It should also be noted that what is an appropriate topic in one cultural context may be considered taboo in another. For example, in American culture, it is generally not appropriate to ask personal questions related to age, salary, and weight; the freedom to ask these questions depends on how close the relationship is between participants, the context, and the cultural norm in which these questions may be asked. Some topics that are innocuous in the American culture are offensive in other cultures. For example, in the Arab culture a person would never ask a man about his wife, or a woman about her husband. This question exceeds the boundaries of benign conversation.

WRITING ACROSS CULTURES

Just as there are rules of language use in oral discourse, there are similar rules in written discourse. In the middle 1960s, research in contrastive rhetoric suggested that culture affects second language writers' preference of rhetorical and organizational patterns. Investigation of expository paragraphs written in English by ELs Kaplan (1988) and Vahidi (2008) from various linguistic backgrounds found four different discourse structures that contrasted with English linearity, as shown in Figure 12.1.

First, let us examine a sample passage written by an English-speaking student:

PASSAGE 1

(a) Underage drinking is becoming a problem in our community. (b) Every Monday and Tuesday I hear kids telling each other about last weekend and how they went out and got "plastered" or "wasted" and how stupid their parents are for not noticing. (c) For the rest of the week they go around planning what they are going to do next weekend. (d) When I hear them talking I just think to myself, "If they only knew." (e) I know. (f) I am a teenage alcoholic. (g) All through my junior high and high school years I thought I was cool because I drank. (h) Little did I know that the situation was getting out of hand. (i) By the time I was a freshman in high school it was getting so I needed a shot of whiskey just to get me out of bed. (j) It got worse. (k) Next I started taking drinks to school and drinking them at lunch. (l) I had to have a drink just to feel "normal." (m) My grades went down and my athletic ability, which had always been excellent, also went down (Connor, 1987, p. 70).

If you consider that one's culture is reflected in writing, how would you describe the organization of ideas in Passage 1? How would you describe the organization of ideas in Passage 1? Looking at Passage 1 carefully, notice that the initial sentence introduces the topic of discourse, and the subsequent sentences develop the topic by supporting examples. Although not all English texts are linear, native speakers of English generally expect written texts to have minimal digressions or repetitions, unlike the patterns classified as Semitic, Asian Romance, and Russian. Contrastive rhetoric has expanded its focus by investigating specific differences in overall organizational structures and other rhetorical devices in writings across languages. While some scholars note that there is tremendous variation within language and writing, there are some trends that have been discerned over time, especially as writing usually reflects the culture of the society.

Kaplan (1988) visualized constrastive rhetoric with the illustrations below. He took into consideration that social contexts of writing would be reflected in the writing styles of different learners from different cultures. (Connor-Connor, 1996).

Figure 12.1: Cultural Contrasts in Writing (Connor-Connor, 1988, Kaplan, 1988 and Vahidi, 2008)

As studies on contrastive rhetoric have noted, cultures vary in the rhetorical devices they use to present words, sentences, and paragraphs to their readers. These studies argue that these rhetorical differences do not illustrate that one language is better than the other; rather, they simply reflect how languages adhere to their own particular patterns of thought. These rhetorical devices have significant effect when writers transfer the rhetorical form of their first language that does not conform fully with the rhetorical form of the target language. The result may raise problems for the target language reader.

To illustrate how cultures vary in the rhetorical devices they use to present words, sentences, and paragraphs to their readers, read Passage 2. Passage 2 has been translated from Korean.

How would you describe the organization of ideas in Passage 2? Unlike Passage 1, the writer in Passage 2 introduces the topic in the initial sentence, then moves away from the topic in sentences b and c, then back to the subject in sentence d. Later, the subject is further developed by what it is not, rather than what it is, as demonstrated in sentences e–i. It appears that Korean discourse approaches the subject indirectly and has a looser style of development than English rhetoric, where a main idea is introduced and subsequent ideas must be directly connected to the main theme. A similar rhetorical pattern has been noted for Japanese and Chinese. Texts in Korean follow a four-part structure—*Ki-Sung-Chon-Kyul*—which is similar to the Japanese *Ki-Shoo-Ten-Ketsu* framework, which has origins in classical Chinese poetry. This framework follows the pattern shown below:

introduction and loose development
↓
statement of the main idea
↓
concepts indirectly related to the argument
↓
conclusion of the main idea

PASSAGE 2

(a) Foreigners who reside in Korea, as well as those who study the Korean language in foreign countries are, despite their deep interest, ignorant of the basis on which the Korean alphabet, Hangul, was formulated. (b) The Korean alphabet, composed of combinations of lines and curves, at first seems more difficult than Japanese Kana for those who use the Roman alphabet, and as the combination of vowels and consonants multiplies, it appears more difficult to memorize all the combinations.

(c) This seemingly complicated combination of vowels and consonants can, on the contrary, be mastered with no more effort than is needed to learn the Roman alphabet or Japanese Kana, for one must merely memorize two dozen vowels and consonants, the principal letters of the Korean alphabet.

(d) The sounds of these five words are of the same kind as k, t, p, s, ch; however, they are named hard sounds because the sounds are harder than k, t, p, s, ch. (e) Some people think these sounds are the same as g, d, b, z, j, because st, sp, ps, sch which are used with g, d, b, as sounds today are combination words. (f) And some people say, "The words which mark hard sounds are sk, st, sp." (g) They say, "g, d, b are not Korean. (h) These were made to mark Chinese." (i) So they wanted to take g, d, b out of Korean (Eggington, 1987, p. 154; Ramsay, 2000).

From an English perspective, the Korean text may appear poorly focused, when in fact it is the preferred rhetorical pattern in Korean academic discourse.

Differences in rhetorical patterns between Arabic and English have also highlighted that patterns of thinking vary across languages. One rhetorical difference between Arabic and English is found in the use of paragraphing in writing. Paragraphs are segments in a text that have distinct units of meanings and serve to help readers follow writer's divisions of thought with relative ease. A paragraph has to contain a series of sentences that convey a specific theme or unit of meaning. In other words, paragraphs must have unity and coherence. Hence, paragraphing is a type of visual signal to help readers move from one point to another. Passage 3 is a translation of an Arabic newspaper article (Shiyab, 2017) that reflects Arabic paragraphing style.

PASSAGE 3

It must be understood that the national administration of this country must go in line with the armed forces because both of them aim at protecting the country and maintaining its security and stability.

Along this kind of understanding, His Highness, Jabir Al-Ahmad, clearly spelt out the importance of strengthening the armed forces, and reexamining the capabilities of these forces in such a way that they become the protecting armour of Kuwait.

And at the same time, affirming Kuwait's commitment toward its (sister) Arab countries.

However, these matters are only a small part of Kuwait's worries, which include third-world countries, the nonaligned states, the Islamic and Arab countries, and Palestine at the center of all this.

How many paragraphs are found in Passage 3? Does each paragraph express a specific theme or unit of meaning? After examining the passage closely, you will find that the passage contains four paragraphs with three themes—one in paragraph 1, another in paragraphs 2 and 3, and the third in paragraph 4. To the English writer, Passage 3 may appear somewhat confusing because there is no specific theme or idea expressed in each paragraph, which forces readers to supply their own visual to the writing. Plus, the illogical division of paragraphs 2 and 3 may add more confusion to an English reader. This lack of visual signal may pose genuine problems for English readers who expect writers to make everything as clear as possible to the reader. Shiyab concludes that Passage 3 reflects a pattern of Arabic paragraphing used for aesthetic purposes typically found in Arabic journalistic texts. Other rhetorical devices have also been noted in the English texts translated from Arabic and other languages. Additional discourse patterns found in Arabic and other languages are as follows:

Arabic: English texts written by Arab students are characterized by repetition, emphasis, and parallelism, where the first idea is completed in the second part, as well as the use of more oral features heavily influenced by classical Arabic which reflects oral traditions (Bohas, Guillaume, & Kouloughli, 2016; Rabab'ah, 2005; Tahaineh, 2014). They stress that these differences reflect a preference for the "aural style," a mode that reflects solidarity and shared cultural beliefs. He argues that Arabic writers may also write in a "visual" style just as English writers do, but this style is generally not preferred by Arabic writers because the writing appears distant and noninteractive to them. Similar patterns have been found in comparisons of Hebrew and English (Bick, Goelman, & Frost 2011; Zellermeyer, 1988).
Spanish: Spanish speaking EL writers tend to write longer sentences (Almehmadi, 2012) and use many coordinating and subordinating clauses (Almehmadi, 2012; Reppen & Grabe, 1993).
Thai: Studies have found that Thai writers tend to use more repetition (Chakorn, 2006) and prefer narrative structures that employ a high frequency of figurative language, for example, metaphors, similes, and personification. These preferences may reflect the fact that narrative plays a greater role in Thai culture and instruction than it does in English (BBC, 2014).

These differences in rhetorical styles affect the ability of non-native speakers to communicate in the English-speaking discourse community. However, these differences do *not* in any way indicate that there is something deficient or inferior about a language or the cognitive abilities of non-native speakers. Rather, these differences must be considered differences in cognitive styles (Kubota & Lehner, 2004).

Beginning EL writers must learn the rhetorical conventions in English discourse to write well in their second language. Classroom activities and tasks must provide ample opportunities for children to experiment with language in written communication. Free writing activities and shared or independent reading activities are ways in which ESL writers can learn the conventions in written communication. These must be included in any training program for ESL learners and should not be delayed until ESL writers have developed good oral and listening skills in English.

POINTS TO REMEMBER

✔ The study of discourse examines how humans process units of conversational and written discourse beyond the sentence level.

✔ Studies have shown that conversational and rhetorical patterns vary across languages.

✔ Maintaining a conversation in any language requires a set of skills, including turn-taking ability, topic selection and relevance, conversational repair ability, and determining the appropriateness of topic and speech style within a specific context.

✔ While these conversational skills are required in all languages, the way each subset is carried out may vary from culture to culture. Cultures have various sets of social norms governing when and how long a person speaks or remains silent, who can nominate topics, how males and females address each other, and so forth.

✔ Just as there are rules for language use in oral discourse, similar principles apply in written discourse. Research in contrastive rhetoric suggests that culture affects second language writers' preferences for rhetorical and organizational patterns.

✔ These cross-cultural preferences in rhetorical and organizational patterns should not be interpreted as deficiencies in a language or in a student's cognitive abilities.

✔ Teachers should not prematurely judge students' social and written skills as deficient, as students may already be competent in their first language. Instead, teachers must be prepared to help ELs understand discourse patterns in English by providing modeling and samples of English discourse, and by reading and writing activities, even if the learner is not yet proficient in English.

REFLECTION QUESTIONS AND DISCUSSION

1. What is discourse? Provide a definition in your own words with three examples. Share your definition and examples with a colleague.

2. What is contrastive rhetoric? Why is this important in teaching ELs?

ACTIVITIES

1. Observe patterns of classroom interaction in a class. Does the teacher primarily interact with all students as a group or with each student individually? Do students respond voluntarily or only when they are called on? How does the teacher extend the children's use of language in small groups? In one-on-one interaction with the student?

2. Read the passage below, which was written by an EL student.

My grandfather has lived in the end of the nineteenth and the beginning of the twentieth century. I never saw him but I know much about his life and his time and I know enough about his behavior and habits because my father is like him. My grandfather was born, raised, and died in the mountain village which lack anything of modern society. He had to work hard early and to faith against nature for surviving and this way of life leads generally to wisdom, friendship, and peace of health and spirit. Now, this kind of life is called traditional, archaic, and sometimes miserable but I don't know if it is right or wrong.

What language elements make the passage seem "foreign"? Consider the grammatical and vocabulary errors, spoken language features, and other expectations you have as a reader. Note your observations below for each:

   a. Grammatical/vocabulary transfer (from knowledge of first language to English)

   b. Spoken language features

   c. Other expectations you have as a reader

3. Asking a person's age is considered taboo in the United States.
   a. Name five other taboo topics in U.S. culture. Discuss possible reasons for their inappropriateness.

   b. Next find out if these topics are also taboo in a specific foreign culture.

   c. How should teachers address this issue of appropriateness so that they do not offend their ESL learners or vice versa?

WEB RESOURCES

Academic Discourse: Supporting English Language Learners with Rigor. https://www.youtube.com/watch?v=8vsDao5SXMY

The Cultural Divide of Discourse: Understanding How English-Language Learners' Primary Discourse Influences Acquisition of Literacy. http://www.grdg620.pbworks.com/f/mays%2Bell.pdf

Discourse and ELLs Blog. https://www.sites.google.com/site/ecet2parabolas/discourse-and-ells

ELL Strategies for Discourse. www.prezi.com/cvkbjjedxid7/ell-strategies-for-discourse

Teaching Channel: Academic Conversations with ELLs Series. https://www.teachingchannel.org/videos/improve-conversation-skills-ells-ousd

Using Response Protocol. http://www.colorincolorado.org/article/extending-english-language-learners-classroom-interactions-using-response-protocol

REFERENCES

Almehmadi, M. M. (2012). A contrastive rhetorical analysis of factual texts in English and Arabic. *Frontiers of Language and Teaching, 3*, 68–76.

BBC. (2014). *A guide to Thai.* Retrieved from http://www.bbc.co.uk/languages/other/thai/guide/alphabet.shtml

Bick, A., Goelman, G., & Frost, R. (2011). Hebrew brain vs. English brain: Language modulates the way it is processed. *Journal of Cognitive Neuroscience, 23*(9), 2280–2290. doi:10.1162/jocn.2010.21583

Bohas, G., Guillaume, J. P., & Kouloughli, D. E. (2016). *The Arabic linguistic tradition*. New York, NY: Routledge.

Chakorn, O. O. (2006). Persuasive and politeness strategies in cross-cultural letters of request in the Thai business context. *Journal of Asian Pacific Communication, 16*(1), 103–146.

Connor, U. (1987). Argumentative patterns in student essays: Cross-cultural differences. In U. Connor & R. B. Kaplan (Eds.), *Writing across languages: Analysis of L2 text*. Reading, MA: Addison-Wesley.

Connor, U., & Connor, U. M. (1996). *Contrastive rhetoric: Cross-cultural aspects of second language writing*. Cambridge, UK:Cambridge University Press.

Eggington, W. G. (1987). Written academic discourse in Korean: Implications for effective communication. In U. Connor & R. B. Kaplan (Eds.), *Writing across languages: Analysis of L2 text*. Reading, MA: Addison-Wesley.

Kaplan, R. B. (1988). Contrastive rhetoric and second language learning: Notes toward a theory of contrastive rhetoric. In A. Purves (Ed.), *Writing across languages and cultures: Issues in contrastive rhetoric* (pp. 275-304). Newbury Park, CA: Sage.

Kleinke, S. (2010). Speaker activity and Grice's maxims of conversation at the interface of pragmatics and cognitive linguistics. *Journal of Pragmatics, 42*(12), 3345–3366.

Kubota, R., & Lehner, A. (2004). Toward critical contrastive rhetoric. *Journal of Second Language Writing, 13*(1), 7–27.

Rabab'ah, G. (2005). Communication problems facing Arab learners of English. *Grazer linguistische Studien, 3*(63), 63–75.

Ramsay, G. (2000). Linearity in rhetorical organisation: A comparative cross-cultural analysis of newstext from the People's Republic of China and Australia. *International Journal of Applied Linguistics, 10*(2), 241–256.

Reppen, R., & Grabe, W. (1993). Spanish transfer effects in the English writing of elementary students. *Lenguas Modernas, 20*, 113–128.

Shiyab, S. (2017). *Patterns of Thinking Across Languages*. Translation Directory.com. Retrieved from http://www.translationdirectory.com/article619.htm

Tahaineh, Y. (2014). A review of EFL Arab learners' language: Pitfalls and pedagogical implications. *International Journal of English Linguistics, 4*(1), 84–102. doi:10.5539/ijel.v4n1p84

Vahidi, S. (2008). The impact of EFL learners' rhetorical organization. awareness on English academic/expository text comprehension. *Pazhuhesh-. e Zabanha-ye khareji, 41*, 145–158. Journal of Language, Culture, and Translation (LCT), 1(2) (2012), 49–67.

Zellermeyer, M. (1988). An analysis of oral and literate texts: Two types of reader-writer relationships in Hebrew and English. In B. Rafoth & D. Rubin (Eds.), *The social construction of written communication*. Norwood, NJ: Ablex.

Dialectal Variations

LEARNING OBJECTIVES

Readers will be able to

- ❖ Distinguish differences in regional dialects
- ❖ Distinguish differences between standard and nonstandard language varieties
- ❖ Describe features of different varieties of World Englishes
- ❖ Describe the process of English language acculturation
- ❖ Define and explain attitudes toward World Englishes

Ms. White's first-grade classroom consists of 18 students. Although most of her students are originally from Florida, several of the students come from the Northeast and the Midwest. In one of her vocabulary lessons, Ms. White showed students pictures of a tap, a water fountain, a boy carrying a bag, a bottle of Sprite, and a pail. She asked her students to name these items.

> Ms. White: *Johnny, what's this?* (pointing to the picture of a tap) Johnny: *It is a faucet.*
> Anna: *No, it is a spigot.*
> Mary-Lou: *No, it is a tap.*
> Ms. White: *All of your answers are correct. People in different parts of America use different words for the same item.*

Can you guess which regions of the United States Johnny, Anna, and Mary-Lou are from? Can you guess the term people from Wisconsin use for water fountain? What do people from Iowa call a bottle of Sprite and a bucket? How about the New Yorkers; what word would they use to describe someone carrying something?

REGIONAL DIALECTS

In Pennsylvania one often hears the words *youse* and *youns*. This may sound funny to the ears of those who are familiar with only the standard dialect of the English language; nevertheless, such differences do not hinder communication. *Dialects are variations within a language that may be intelligible to the speakers of that language*; for instance, a Bostonian English speaker may not have difficulty understanding a Texan English speaker. On the other hand, languages that are mutually unintelligible are languages that have separate systems, such as Chinese and Swahili.

A dialect atlas contains maps that exhibit regional variations in a language. Isoglosses are lines on the map that represent the boundaries between dialects, demarcating regions that use particular features (usually phonological or lexical). For instance, people in the northern and eastern parts of Pennsylvania use *pail* and *curtains* instead of *bucket* and *blinds*. There are several major regional dialects in the United States. The main dialect areas in the eastern United States are the Northern, Midland, and Southern regions. Refer to Table 13.1 for lexical features of U.S. regional dialects.

Lexical Variation

Tables 13.2 and 13.3 show lexical differences between American, Canadian, and British English.

Table 13.1: American Regional Dialects

Northeast	South	Midwestern	West
brook	branch	creek	creek
faucet	spigot/spicket	tap	hydrant
johnnycake	corn pone	corn bread	corn bread
pail	bucket	pail	bucket/pail
tonic	coke/cold drink	soda/pop	pop
string beans		snap beans	
quarter of five			quarter till five
bag			sack
sick to my stomach			sick at my stomach
(cherry) pit			(cherry) seed

Source: (Hamilton, 2018)

Table 13.2: Canadian English and American English

Canadian English	American English
chesterfield	sofa
serviette	napkin
eh?	huh?
faucet	tap

Source: (Hamilton, 2018)

Table 13.3: British and American English

Food		Clothing		Motor Vehicles	
British English	American English	British English	American English	British English	American English
bangers	sausages	grip	hairpin	bonnet	hood
chips	french fries	jumper	sweater	boot	trunk
cooker	stove, range	knickers	underpants	drop top	convertible
prawn	shrimp	nappy	(women's)	dynamo	generator
fizzy drink	soda	rousers	diaper	lorry	truck
			pants		

Source: (Hamilton, 2018)

Phonological Variation

Examples of phonological variation in regional dialect are: in eastern New England, postvocalic /r/ is not heard in words such as *barn, four, daughter*, and /a/ is used for /ae/ in words such as *aunt, bath*, and *half* (O'Grady, Dobrovolsky, & Aronoff, 1989). Also in this region the linking /r/ is a phonological variation. For instance, in the sentence *The boys who play the tuba are in the school band*, note that for speakers who have linking /r/ in their phonological rule, *tuba* will be pronounced with /r/ at the end. The phonological rule for this is to insert an /r/ between a word ending in a vowel and another word beginning with a vowel. In the middle regions of the United States, the postvocalic /r/ is retained, as in car, as opposed to eastern New England and Southern English. In Southern English, the /s/ assimilates the voicing of the adjacent vowels to yield /z/ in words such as *greasy.*

Morphological Features

Tables 13.4 and 13.5 list some morphological differences between Appalachian, African American, and standard American English.

Syntactic Variation

Tables 13.6 and 13.7 list some syntactic differences between Appalachian (AE), African American (AAE), and standard American English (SE).

What do you notice about the differences between these dialects and Standard English?

Table 13.4: Appalachian English (AE) Versus Standard English (SE)

Appalachian English	Standard English
clumb	climbed
het	heated
ruck	raked
drug	dragged

Table 13.5: African American English (AAE) Versus Standard English (SE)

African American English	SE
He need to get a book from the shelf.	He needs . . .
She want us to pass the papers to the front.	She wants . . .

Table 13.6: Appalachian English (AE) Versus Standard English (SE)

Appalachian English	SE
He might could make one up.	He could make one up.
I useta couldn't count.	I used to not be able to count.
He ain't never done no work to speak of.	He has never done anything to speak of.

Table 13.7: African American English (AAE) Versus Standard English (SE)

African American English	SE
I didn't have no lunch.	I did not have any lunch.
The tea always be cold.	The tea is always cold.

STANDARD VERSUS NONSTANDARD

Read the following statements:

1. He come a-running.
2. He must didn't hear me.
3. I didn't have no lunch.
4. She be late every day.
5. He does not have anything.
6. She don't know nothing.
7. I think /th´k/ Jill is a nice person.
8. His cigar smells bad.

Which of the previous statements do you consider standard speech? What makes a dialect standard or nonstandard? Is standard dialect more correct than nonstandard? Does it have more grammatical rules than nonstandard?

A dialect is considered standard or nonstandard on the basis of these three factors:

1. Prestige—prestige corresponds to the *social status* of the speakers of the dialect. (The language spoken by the wealthy and the educated is usually more standard or more prestigious (higher social status) than that spoken by the working class.)
2. Ethnicity—the speakers' race (the Spanish spoken in Spain is considered more standard than Guatemalan Spanish.)
3. Region—the parts of the country in which the dialect is spoken. In the United States, the Midwestern dialect is considered more standard than the Southern.

Within a speech community, there may exist a standard speech variety perceived by speakers as higher in status. Some teachers reprimand their students when they do not speak "proper" English—"proper" meaning Standard English. What is "proper" or Standard English? It is a dialect perceived by the members of the speech community as being prestigious because it has been defined as such by the community. Standard English has formal and informal levels. The formal standard appears mainly in writing, public speeches, and television news scripts. It is taught in schools and is characterized by restrained vocabulary and strict adherence to grammatical elements, such as subject–verb agreement and tenses. The informal standard takes into account the context in which it is used and is flexible and subjective. Examples are conversations at parties and talk around an office break area.

Most teachers are obligated to enforce the use of Standard English in their classrooms. Diaz-Rico (2013) suggests that they often choose one of the three following philosophical positions on the teaching of Standard English:

- Replacive or eradicationism: Standard English supplants the dialect of vernacular-speaking students. Teachers see their roles as correcting students' "errors."
- Additive or bidialectism: Maintains both the standard and the vernacular variety for use in different social situations. Teachers may encourage students to use colloquialisms to lend flavor to creative writing or dialogue, while reserving Standard English for formal classroom contexts.
- Dialect rights: Rejects the necessity to learn and practice standard spoken English. Teachers do not teach Standard English.

Teachers who subscribe to any one of the above positions need to understand the consequences of this decision and its implications for students and families. Teachers who subscribe to the first position may be sending a message to students who speak other dialects of English that their dialect is inferior. In some cases, in which students who speak a vernacular language have been enrolled in English as a second language (ESL) classes without their parents requesting the classes, parents have shown anger and disapproval. Parents may find such placement insulting and inappropriate because their children already speak English as their native language. Teachers who take the replacive eradicationism stance should understand and address the social functions that dialects serve.

Teachers who choose the second position (additive or bidialectism) realize that they are preserving their students' civil rights; they are helping to combat the myth that anything other than Standard English is deficient. Teachers who have studied dialect variation are more likely to respect their students' respective dialects of English and convey information about English variation within the United States.

Teachers who choose the third position (dialect rights) may be preventing students from developing a second variety of English that may benefit them in a society that harbors language prejudice against nonstandard varieties of English. Teachers who show students how Standard English currently plays a role in their lives, and how their own dialect is different from other systems, give students a knowledge base for developing a second variety. Moreover, language awareness instruction is crucial in examining dialect prejudice. Such instruction is beneficial not only to vernacular speakers but to all students.

SCENARIOS

1	Joe: *Hey, Hamid! What are you up to? Do you have any plans next week?*
	Hamid: *Well, Joe, my sister is getting married next week. So I've got to go back to my kampung.*
2	Sally: *The movie is boring, eh?*
	Nancy: *Well, I like it actually.*

WORLD ENGLISHES

Are there any words in the preceding scenarios that you do not recognize as belonging to standard American English? Can you tell from what language backgrounds the speakers might be? In the first scenario, the second speaker used the Malay word *kampung* to mean hometown or village. In the second scenario, the first speaker used a Canadian question tag *eh* as a confirmation check. There are a number of studies that have documented a growing number of Englishes used internationally (Crystal, 2007; Pennycook, 2017).

Many nations in the world not only use English extensively at the social level, but also adopt English as an official language—meaning that official government business is conducted in English. In the early 1980s, Kachru (1985) described these as three groups: the inner circle of native English speakers; the outer circle where English is used as a language of communication (lingua franca) among linguistically diverse groups of people; and an expanding circle where the use of English continues to grow (see Figure 13.1). Today, it is not uncommon to learn that young children in many countries such as China or Ukraine are learning English and using it as a medium of instruction in school. Hence, Kachru's concentric circles may continue to change and reflect new uses of English into the near future.

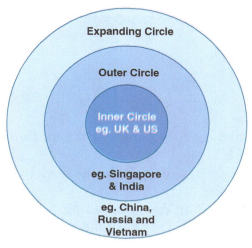

Figure 13.1: Kachru's Concentric Circles of English

© Kendall Hunt Publishing Company

Examine the following Englishes and their variation:

Canada

- "The *bill* please." (bill = check)
- I drove 50 *clicks* last week. (clicks = kilometers)
- My *hoase* (house) is *oat* (out) in the country.
- It's really cold out, *eh*?
- *Washing powder* = laundry soap
- *Washing up liquid* = dishwashing liquid

(For more examples see www.//canadian.demon.co.uk/lang.htm.)

Australian English

- *arvo* = afternoon
- *dinkie die* = the whole truth
- *egg nishner* = air conditioner
- *Whyne chevva cold share* = Why don't you have a cold shower?
- *billabong* = river pool
- *kookabura* (a native bird)

New Zealand English

- *big sitter* = sleeper sofa
- *eketahuna* = a small town devoid of basic amenities and remote from the outside world, similar to the American usage of Timbuktu
- *home and hosed* = safe, completed successfully
- *hottie* = hot water bottle
- *anklebiter* = toddler, kids

Singapore/Malaysia

- Ginger tea is good for your sore throat—it is very *heaty*.
- I got *presen* from *dem*.
- They *chop* your ticket when you go in (to the fair). (Singapore)
- She doesn't like any fruit, *la*.
- You want a *rubber*, *isn't it*? or You speak English, *is it*?
- Alamak, he is a *lawyer buruk*! (My gosh, he has the sharp-tongued wit of a lawyer. Typically used in a negative sense.)

(Platt & Weber, 1980)

Caribbean English

- *Gimme wat me wan lemme gwan* (Give me what I want, let me go home). (Jamaican Patois)
- "Urmilla: Girl, I in big trouble. Big, big trouble. If you know what tiger go and do! He go and invite two Americans he does work with to come for Indian food tonight.
- Rita: *Is wat happen to him at all? He crack? He is a damn fool in truth. He bringing wite people to eat in dat hut? Tiger must be really going out of he head, yes. . . ."* (*excerpt from Samuel Selvon's novel, A Brighter Sun, Trinidad, 1971*).

(Comrie et al., 1996, pp. 153, 156)

Nigerian English

- I like her. *She's a nice fellow.*
- *One pig big pass all we pigs came into our yard* (A pig bigger than all our pigs come into our yard).

(Comrie et al., 1996, p. 153)

Indian English

- There will be *kirtan* and *ardasa* for the peace of the departed soul.
- His *soyem* Fateha will be solemnised on . . . and all the friends and relatives are requested to attend the Fateha prayers.
- *police wala* = policeman
- *lathicharge* = to attack with a baton

(Galloway & Rose, 2015)

What linguistic features contribute to such different varieties of English? And what purpose do they serve for the speakers who use them? English has spread to linguistically and culturally pluralistic societies, and the variety of English that emerges in a particular area reflects the locality and needs of the speakers within that community. Studies of World Englishes (Galloway & Rose, 2015) have documented features of the many varieties of English and have raised questions about how these features meet the needs of speakers' sociocultural contexts.

Also notice that the English language as spoken around the world has gone through phonological, morphological, and lexical innovations. These innovations involve the borrowing of local words and the redefinition of English words in new contexts, in simplifying of sounds to fit the phonology of the local language, and the simplifying of grammar. Differences among these varieties of English may be reflected at one or more linguistic level, as described below.

A. Lexical

1. Contextual redefinition of English lexical items:

For example, the word *heaty* as shown in the earlier example refers to foods that make the body hot, whereas the opposite concept—*cooling*—refers to the reverse effect. These concepts are based on long-established Chinese beliefs (Chu, Yao, & Tan, 2017). The word *chop* in Singaporean/ Malaysian English means to stamp something. *Fellow* in Nigerian English refers to both males and females. The word *crack* in Trinidad English means "crazy" and "craic" pronounced similarly in Irish English means "fun."

2. Local word borrowings:

These lexical items give flavor to different varieties of English. They may carry cultural content and punch not found in another English language variety. For example, Indian English samples reflect lexical items that are culturally specific to death announcements; these words reveal the religious and cultural backgrounds of the deceased. The Singaporean/Malaysian expression *lawyer buruk* literally translates into "razorsharp and manipulative wit," which can be good or bad depending on the context of its utterance. Just as many Native American words have entered the American English lexicon, Australian and New Zealand English have words that come from the Aboriginal languages. Words like *eketahuna*, *kookaburra*, and *billabong* have been borrowed for plants, animals, or landscapes that were unknown in Europe or anywhere outside of Australia and New Zealand.

New words are also created by combining words from two different languages, such as *lathicharge* and *police wala*, which mean "an attack with a baton" and "a policeman," respectively, in Indian English.

B. Phonological

The following are phonological innovations of different varieties of English:

1. Deletion of final consonants, such as /s/ in *presents* in Singaporean and Malaysian English.
2. Sound substitution, such as consonants /d/ for /th/ as in *them* or *that* in Singaporean/Malaysian and Caribbean English, vowels /o/ for /aw/ as in *house*, and /oa/ for *out* in Canadian English.
3. Sentence intonation that employs a rhythmic pattern not found in many native varieties; for example, in the sentence *I wanted a bicycle*, there will be more frequent breaks between syllables in Singaporean English, producing an overall staccato effect.
4. Combination of syllable reduction and sound substitution such as the /ay/ for /ey/ in *g'dye, myte* for "good day, mate" and /ah/ for /r/ as in *egg nisher* for "air conditioner" in Australian English.

C. Grammar

Some of the differences in grammatical features that make one variety of English distinct from another are as follows:

1. Omission of auxiliary verbs such as the *be* verbs in Caribbean and Singaporean/ Malaysian English: *I in big trouble.*

2. Use of different tag questions such as *is it* or *isn't it* in Malaysian or Singapore English to signal confirmation of a previously mentioned or implied fact or a question that requires a yes or no answer. A similar phenomenon is evident in Canadian English, where *eh* is used at the end of a question to signal "don't you think?"

3. The use of extra particles at the end of a word to show solidarity, rapport, or informality such as *la* in Singapore and Malaysian English.

4. The use of different words to denote grammatical function, for example, *pass* in Caribbean English expresses comparison.

Now you may consider some of these varieties of English to be "broken English"; however, studies have shown that these non-English features are typical and systematic within a particular variety and thus should be viewed as different from the linguistic norm of the native speaker's variety. Similar phenomena can also be observed in the speech of native English speakers. Take for example Appalachian English constructions: *I was a-washing one day* and *I can't hardly read it* (Montgomery, Reed, Anderson, & Bernstein, 2016). Although many native speakers may label the use of prefix *a-*in verbs and double negation as ungrammatical, these constructions are systematic and regular in Appalachian English.

Like any regional dialect of native speakers' English, different varieties of World English also fall within a continuum of standard versus nonstandard, depending on notions associated with the social prestige of the speakers who use a particular variety. Thus, dialect is accorded power because the speakers are in a position of political, economic, and educational power, not because the dialect itself is superior. In addition, some varieties of English such as those spoken in Singapore, Malaysia, Nigeria, India, and the Caribbean have been nativized, a phenomenon found when a speech variety is acquired in a non-English culture or context, resulting in the birth of a new variety of English.

Teachers working with ELs must be aware that some of their students may be using a different variety of English from their own. In some cases, English may be the students' primary language, and hence make them native speakers of English in their own countries of origin. However, upon arrival in the American classroom, these students will immediately realize that their variety of English may not be readily understood by teachers who speak another standard model of English. This experience can frustrate learners who have seen themselves as competent English speakers.

Teachers must handle this delicate situation in a sensitive manner to avoid increasing students' anxiety levels and thus impeding learning. Although it is important that students communicate intelligible messages, teachers must not cast judgments based on a student's variety of English or the accent the student employs. Teachers should also refrain from disparaging students' English because a student's home language or dialect is, on the social level, an important identity marker. By not respecting a student's dialect, teachers are indirectly disparaging the student's family, friends, and values, a practice which can be detrimental to the student's development and positive self-concept. Teachers should not try to replace the learner's home dialect or variety with the language of the school; instead, they should empower students by allowing them to maintain their home dialect while learning a new variety of English and showing how these speech registers are appropriate for various contexts. Students must be encouraged to speak and write in their home language or dialect and, at the same time, learn to master the language of the normative culture in their society if they are to succeed in school.

✔ Dialects are variations within a language that may be intelligible to other speakers of that language.

✔ A dialect atlas contains maps that exhibit regional variation in a language.

✔ Isoglosses are lines drawn on the map representing boundaries between dialects. These lines also demarcate the region that uses a particular feature (usually phonological or lexical).

✔ The main dialect areas in the eastern United States are the Northern, Midland, and Southern regions.

✔ A dialect is considered standard or nonstandard on the basis of prestige, ethnicity, and region.

✔ Within a speech community there exists a standard speech variety perceived by speakers as higher in status than other speech varieties.

✔ Teachers who are obligated to enforce the use of Standard English in their classrooms should be aware of three possible philosophical positions: replacive or eradicationism, additive or bidialectism, and dialect rights.

✔ As English language use has become internationally widespread, new varieties of English have emerged.

✔ The differences between varieties of English are reflected on one or more linguistic level: phonology, grammar, and lexical.

✔ The linguistic features of varieties of English also convey social, emotional, and cultural meanings that make them distinct from one another.

✔ Teachers can empower students by validating the EL's home variety of English and allowing them to use their home language whenever appropriate; however, teachers must also help learners master the language or dialect of the dominant culture to help them excel in school and in the culture at large.

REFLECTION QUESTIONS AND DISCUSSION

1. What are dialects of language? Why is the term "variety" a more neutral term to use when referring to languages?

2. Define and describe World Englishes and provide three examples of how they differ? How are they similar?

3. Discuss how social status among speakers relates to language varieties and particularly among different varieties of English both in the United States and internationally. How can teachers address social status and language variation in their classrooms?

ACTIVITIES

1. The left column contains terms used in the United States, and the right column contains terms used in other English-speaking countries, for example, England, Australia, and Canada. Match each American term with its non-American counterpart.

United States	Other English-Speaking Countries
_____biscuit	a. tomato sauce
_____cookie	b. chips
_____ketchup	c. biscuit
_____french fries	d. essence
_____flavoring	e. scone
_____shrimp	f. fag
_____stroller	g. handbag
_____scotch tape	h. lift
_____corn	i. jumper
_____raincoat	j. lemonade
_____Elevator	k. gearbox
_____Sprite, 7 Up	l. prawn
_____set a table	m. mac (macintosh)
_____sweater	n. maize
_____mailbox	o. pushchair
_____newsstand	p. lay a table

United States	Other English-Speaking Countries
_____to vacuum	q. letter box
_____popsicle	r. kiosk
_____purse	s. lolly
_____broil	t. hoover
_____transmission	u. grill
_____cigarette	v. cellophane tape

2. Compile a list of standard and nonstandard expressions in English.

3. Watch a segment of any Disney movie (e.g., The Lion King, The Little Mermaid).
   a. What kind of dialect do the "good" or "bad" characters typically employ?

   b. Does the use of different speech styles reflect attitudes toward different groups of speakers who speak a particular dialect? Explain.

   c. As a teacher, what would you do to promote students' awareness of the functions of dialects and dispel negative stereotypes about dialects and their speakers?

4. Examine the excerpts below written by a non-native author and the short dialogue that follows. How do these writers convey social, emotional, and cultural content through their English? What linguistic features do you notice in these samples that give them a non-native flavor?
   a. Dilchain had, in the meantime, discovered a small earthern doll buried under the oven when she was cleaning it one day. She went and showed it to Begam Habib.

   "It is the effect of witchcraft," she said, "which is responsible for Mian's illness."
   The tender hearts of women were filled with dread. They sent Dilchain to Aakhoonji Saheb, who wrote verses from the Koran on seven snow white plates in saffron water. The plates were to be washed with a little water, and the water from one plate was to be taken for three days, a drop in the morning . . .
   But a strange thing happened inside the senana. A pot full of ill-omened things came flying in the air and struck against the bare trunk of the date palm whose

leaves had all fallen. Another day some cooked cereal was found lying under the henna tree . . .

Poor women from the neighbourhood came, fluttering their burqas and dragging their slippers under them, and sympathized . . .

Thus they came and sympathized and suggested cures and medicines. One said to Begam Habib: "You must go to the tomb of Hazzrat Mahboob Elahi and pray . . .

"You must give him water from the well at Hazarat Nizamuddin's tomb," another suggested. "It has magical qualities and has worked miracles . . .(Ahmed Ali, pp. 278–279 in Tremblay, Darwill, & McCarthy, 2018)

b. The following dialogue is between two Singaporean females who are close friends. They are eating lunch at the school cafetaria:

Ah Mei: *Aiya, Chan. Why are you eating so little only?*
Soo Chan: *Nolah! Cannot grow fat one. I must lose some weight.*
Ah Mei: Soo Chan. *If you go on a diet, you will soon disappear one.*
Soo Chan: Nolah . . . *All my clothes are tight already. I got nothing to wear any more. Also no money to buy more clothes.*
Ah Mei: *Where got one? You look nice in your cheongsam that night. No need to worry anymore about your weight.*

5. Search the Internet and compile a list of linguistic differences in varieties of English spoken outside the United States. Explain the linguistic features that mark each variety of English.

WEB RESOURCES

Dialect Blog. http://www.dialectblog.com
Do You Speak American?. http://www.pbs.org/speak/seatosea/americanvarieties
English Language Learning Tips- Varieties of English. www.youtube.com/watch?v=YvbEODnJVTc
Everyone Has an Accent. https://www.tolerance.org/magazine/fall-2000/everyone-has-an-accent

International Association for World Englishes. www.iaweworks.org

Issues and Implications of World Englishes for Teachers. https://www.slideshare.net/NotMelanie/issues-and-implications-of-world-englishes-for-teachers

Teaching About Dialects. ERIC Digest. www.ericdigests.org/2002-2/dialects.htm

REFERENCES

Chu, N. H. S., Yao, C. K., & Tan, V. P. Y. (2017). Food therapy in Sinosphere Asia. *Journal of Clinical Gastroenterology, 52*, 105–113.

Comrie, B., Matthews, S., & Polinsky, M. (Eds.). (1996). *The atlas of languages: The origins and development of languages throughout the world.* London, UK: Quatro Publishing PLC.

Crystal, D. (2007). *English as a global language.* Cambridge, UK: Cambridge University Press.

Diaz-Rico, L. T. (2013). *The crosscultural, language, and academic development handbook: A complete K-12 reference guide.* Boston, MA: Pearson Higher Ed.

Galloway, N., & Rose, H. (2015). *Introducing global Englishes.* New York, NY: Routledge.

Hamilton, V. (2018). International English: A Guide to Varieties of English around the World. Reference Reviews, 32(2), 16-17.

Kachru, B. (1985). *Standards, codifications, and sociolinguistic realism: The English language in the outer circle.* Cambridge, UK: Cambridge University Press.

Montgomery, M., Reed, P. E., Anderson, B., & Bernstein, J. B. (2016). *The archive of traditional Appalachian speech and culture.* Columbia, SC: University of South Carolina.

O'Grady, W., Dobrovolsky, M., & Aronoff, M. (1989). *Contemporary linguistics: An introduction.* New York, NY: St. Martin's Press.

Pennycook, A. (2017). *The cultural politics of English as an international language.* New York, NY: Taylor & Francis.

Platt, J., & Weber, H. (1980). *English in Singapore and Malaysia: Status, features, functions.* Kuala Lumpur: Oxford University Press.

Tremblay, P., Darwill, B., & McCarthy, J. (2018). *The exorcist tradition in Islam: Exorcism; Hadith* [Online]. Retrieved from https://www.scribd.com/document/369954376/The-Exorcist-Tradition-In-Islam-pdf

Development of the English Language

Readers will be able to

- ❖ Demonstrate how a language tree traces the relationship between various languages
- ❖ Describe how English originates from the Indo–European language family
- ❖ Chart historical events that influenced the evolution of the English language
- ❖ Cite examples of lexical borrowings found in English
- ❖ Describe the language origins of word borrowings in English
- ❖ Explain the changing nature of word meanings over time

SCENARIO

Ms. Duncan noticed that her Spanish-and French-speaking students did much better in comprehending a passage reading in class than did her Thai students. She found that her Spanish and French speakers recognized some English words such as *vigilante*, *incommunicado*, and *assault* in their reading passage because these words are similar in form and meaning (or "cognates") to the words in their native language. Because these words are central to the overall meaning of the text, they were able to use their word knowledge to make good predictions about the main ideas of the text. In contrast, her Thai students struggled because there were too many unfamiliar words.

What knowledge did Ms. Duncan's Spanish- and French-speaking students rely on for comprehending the reading passage in English? What generalizations can you make about Spanish, French, and English? What generalizations can you make about English and Thai?

LANGUAGE FAMILIES

Just as we have a family tree to trace the genealogy of our ancestors, there are language trees that trace the relationships among languages that have contributed to the makeup of the English language. The diagram in Figure 14.1 displays a partial family tree of the Indo–European languages, showing how some words in English are similar to those in German, French, and Italian. For instance, English *mother*, is similar to German *mutter*, French *mere*, and Italian *madre*. English and German are "sister" languages, with a common parent, whereas English and French are "cousins," sharing a common ancestor (Indo–European), but with distinct parent languages.

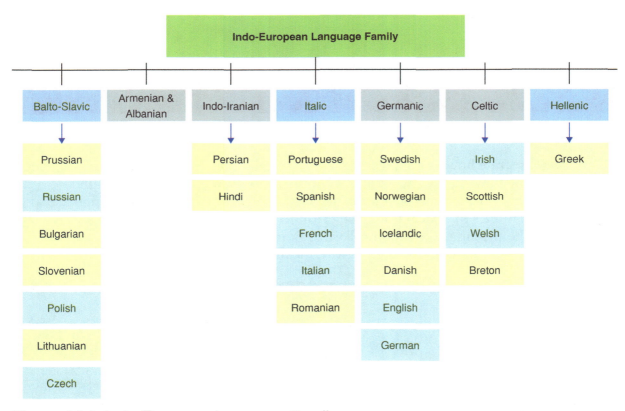

Figure 14.1: Indo-European Language Family

HISTORY OF THE ENGLISH LANGUAGE

The evolution of the English language has been influenced by many historical events, such as the conquest of English speakers by speakers of other languages like those from Scandinavia and France. In addition, through trade and colonialism, English speakers have come into contact with other language groups, such as Chinese, Japanese, Swahili, and Spanish. Dramatic changes in the English language also reflect intellectual attitudes toward languages, as well as social, political, and religious influences in history. For example, Latin was the language of the Church in the early era of Christianity, as well as the language of the upper social class and of intellectuals. As such, many religious words with Latin roots have been incorporated into English. Similarly, at the height of Greek civilization, the Greek language was perceived as a language associated with intellectuals and the upper social class, thereby bringing numerous Greek borrowings in the English language.

Word Families								
English	*Mother*	German	*mutter*	French	*mére*	Italian	*madre*
English	*mosquito*	Spanish	*mosca (fly)*					Italian	*mesea (fly)*
English	*alligator*	Spanish	*lagarto (lizard)*					
English	*delicatessen*	German	*delikatesse*	French	*delicatessen*	Italian	*delicatessen*
English	*housewife*	German	*hausfrau*					
English	*stove*	Latin	*extufa*				Italian	*stufa*
English	*hospital*	Latin	*hospes*				Italian	*ospedale*
English	*massage*	French	*masser*	Portuguese	*amassar (to knead)*	Italian	*massaggio*
English	*savvy*	Spanish	*saber (to know)*				Italian	*sapere*
English	*two*	Italian	*due*	Russian	*dva*	Italian	*(to know)*
English	*three*	Italian	*tre*	Russian	*tri*		
English	*sister*	Italian	*sorella*	Russian	*sestra*		

Table 14.1 provides a chronological account of the historical events that influenced and shaped the English language.

Table 14.1: A Chronological Table of the History of English—External History

Dates	Events	Language Influence	Stages
ca. 900–700 B.C.	Settlement of British Isles by Celts	Celtic—in London, Dover, Avon, Cornwall	Pre-English
55 B.C.	Beginning of Roman raids	Latin—preserved in a few forms: -chester < *castra* "camp"	

(Continued)

Table 14.1: A Chronological Table of the History of English—External History (*Continued*)

Dates	Events	Language Influence	Stages
43 A.D.	Roman occupation of "Brittania"		
Early 5th century	Romans leave British Isles		
449 A.D.	Germanic tribes defeat the Celts	Germanic—Anglo-Saxon	Old English (450–1100)
ca. 600 A.D.	England converted to Christianity (Borrowings: *abbot, altar, cap, chalice, hymn, relic, sock, beet, pear, cook, rue, school, verse*)	Latin, via the Christian Church	
ca. 750 A.D.	*Beowulf* writings are composed (only extant manuscript written ca. 1000 A.D.)		
9th–11th century	Invasions by Scandinavians (Borrowings: *birth, sky, trust, take, skirt, disk, dike; simplified pronoun system*)	Scandinavian	
1066 A.D.	Battle of Hastings—Norman Conquest (Borrowings: *court, enemy, battle, nation, crime, justice, beef, pork, veal, mutton, charity, miracle*)	Norman French, Latin via Norman French for learned vocabulary	
ca. 1200 A.D.	Normandy and England are separated		Middle English (1100–1450)
13th–14th century	Growing sense of Englishness		
1337–1450	Hundred Years' War		
1340–1450	Chaucer		

(*Continued*)

Table 14.1: A Chronological Table of the History of English—External History (*Continued*)

Dates	Events	Language Influence	Stages
1476	First English book is published; spelling standardized		Early Modern English (1450–1700)
1564–1616	Shakespeare (Greek and Latin borrowings: *anachronism, allusion, atmosphere, capsule, dexterity, halo, agile, external, insane, adapt, erupt, exist, extinguish*)	Latin and Greek, via the influence of printing and the Renaissance in Europe	
16th–19th century	Imperialism (Borrowings: *mogul, rajah, safari, loot, bandana, pajama*)	Swahili, Hindi, Tamil, Chinese, etc., via the various colonies	Modern English (1700–present)
19th–20th century	Development of North American, Australian, African, Caribbean, and South Asian varieties of English; Scientific and Industrial Revolution	Technical and regional vocabularies	

Source: Language Files (2017, p. 335).

Read the following list of words now considered to be mainstream English. Have you noticed any words in another language that are similar to these? What are they? In what languages do you think these words originated? (Hint: check a dictionary or word etymology online (https://www.etymonline.com/))

chaperone	Florida	cuisine	zero
mustang	succotash	cinnamon	papaya

Like all languages, English has been influenced by other languages throughout its development and has borrowed a huge number of vocabulary items from many languages. Table 14.2 includes samples of borrowed items. Some of these words may still appear foreign, whereas others have been partially naturalized to sound like English. Teachers may use this knowledge to their advantage by drawing on word cognates to help English learners (ELs) make the connection between their first and second language. It may also make ELs learners beam with pride when they see how their culture or native language has influenced the English language they hear today, and may thereby increase their motivation to learn the new language.

Table 14.2: Samples of English Borrowings

	Food-Related	Health and Fitness	Fighting/Crime Words	Arts/Pop Culture
Spanish	Empanadas Tostadas Nachos Potato Chili Cafeteria Barbecue		Federal (officer) (detective) Vigilante (jail) Incommunicado Guerrilla	Tango Cha cha Conga
Greek	Oleo margarine (Latin and Greek) Gyros	Biopsy Carcinogen Leukemia Oncology Panacea Euthanasia Gymnasium Sarcoma Isotonic (exercises)	Helicopter Periscope Genocide	Drama Theater Tragedy Dialogue Episode Comedy
Dutch	Crullers Waffles		Bazooka	
Chinese	Bok choy Mandarin Tea Chow time Ketchup	T'ai chi	Gung ho Snorkel	
French	Hash Dessert Hors d'oeuvres Baguette Praline Frappes Filet Bisque Stew Boil	Hospice Polyp Massage Masseur Masseuse	Sabotage Assault Barricade Commandant Lieutenant Soldier Enemy Troops Parachute	Vaudeville Shows Disco

(Continued)

Table 14.2: Samples of English Borrowings (*Continued*)

	Food-Related	Health and Fitness	Fighting/Crime Words	Arts/Pop Culture
Arabic and Yiddish	Sherbet Candy Kebab Bagel Challah Nosh Couscous Knish Matzoh ball			
German	Bratwurst Delicatessen Frankfurter Noodle Pretzel Pumpernickel Schnitzel Hamburger		Flame throwers	
Latin		PenicillinSurgeon Diet Tumor	Torpedo	

	Food-Related	Animals	Dwellings	Arts/Pop Culture
Native American	Shawnee cake (Johnny cake) Journey Succotash	Caribou Moose Opossum	Igloo Wigwam	
African/African American vernacular	Yams Okra Gumbo		Crib (house)	Wannabe (wanna be) Bust out, chat, cut, break (synonyms for rap)

A young boy wants to praise his mom.

Son: *Mom, you're a beast.*
Mother: *I'm a what? You want to be grounded, young man?*
Son: *No, you don't understand, Mom. I'm saying you're cool.*

LEXICAL AND SEMANTIC CHANGE

What do you think is happening in this situation? You probably noticed that both mother and son have different expectations of what the word *beast* connotes. This example illustrates how words, like grammar and other aspects of language, change over time and how meanings are determined by the speakers' needs—linguistic or social. Evidently, the word *beast* is now being used in a positive sense, unlike its original meaning. Such semantic changes occur in several forms: (a) by extending new meaning to the original word meaning, (b) by reducing the referent of the original word, (c) by expressing opposite connotations from its original, and (d) by creating a new hybrid.

Table 14.3 illustrates several types of lexical and semantic changes in the English language over time (Youn et al., 2016). The arrows indicate the lexical and semantic changes that each word has undergone. Can you think of new words that have changed meaning over time?

As teachers, it is important to realize that language is not a set of formulaic rules for learners to master. Although teachers must help learners in developing standard forms of English, especially in written format, they cannot be overly prescriptive in their approach to how speakers actually use language. As you have probably noticed, many of the words in Table 14.3 are obsolete and may not be a part of the mainstream English we hear today. On the other hand, there are also some words that were introduced in specific domains that have now entered mainstream English. For example, words like "texting," "google," and "screenshot" are all relatively new words. Because language use is socially and contextually bound, it is not surprising to find young learners picking up terms and using them for expressive functions.

Teachers can be open and allow students to use these words to express themselves, while also teaching students the appropriate speech registers for a variety of contexts. As we have noted, some words may require cultural information not readily available in the English learners' (ELs) schemata, and thus may require explanations from the teacher.

Table 14.3: Examples of Lexical and Semantic Change in the English Language

Domains	Sample Words	Time
Holidays	Carol (Ring Dance) → Christmas Carols (Choral Singing)	Before 18th century
	Pudding in the belly → Stuffing	
	St. Nicolas → Santa → Santa Claus (clipping from Dutch Sinterklaas)	18th–19th century
	All Saints Day (All Hallows day) → Halloween	
	Rockets → Firecrackers	
	Armistice Day → Veterans Day	20th century
Sports	Kicking the bladder (A.D. 43) → Fut balle (12th century) → Football (which includes soccer, rugby, and American football)	Before 18th century
	Rounders (South England) → Baseball	
	The number of cats → The number of bases in baseball	18th–19th century
	Game plan (specific to sports) → A general term for advance strategy → Plan	
	Scramble (mixing foods as in eggs) → War terms (in World War II to connote speed and disorganization) → In football (to refer to quarterback's efforts to stop onrushing offense)	
	Slapping five → High five → Gimme five → Gimme some skin	20th century
Health	Stress (4th century—emotional and physical exhaustion) → Burnout (cessation of jet engine operation)	Before 18th century
	Quacks (1600s; persons who sell medicine door to door) → Snake-oil Salesman (1920s) Spawns Words Like Alternative Medicine (1990s)	20th century–present
	ARC (AIDS-related complex)	
	AIDS virus → HIV (human immunodeficiency virus)	

(Continued)

Table 14.3: Examples of Lexical and Semantic Change in the English Language (*Continued*)

Domains	Sample Words	Time
Pop Culture/ Rap	Blue devils (meaning depression) → Blues (music) Hillbilly music → Country music Cowboy movie → Gun opera → Horse opera → Western movie Picture show → Motion picture → Flick (slang term) 10 (a 1979 movie title) → She's a 10 (a beautiful woman) Gump (popularized by the movie Forrest Gump) → Gump our way to Bosnia (to refer to military strategy) Beat → Kick (the beat in RAP music) → Scratch extends to mean "to move a record back and forth for percussion effect in rap music"	18th–19th century 20th century–present 20th century–present
Cyberspace	Information + superhighway = Computer communication systems Hacker (an expert programmer) → An expert programmer who performs illegal activities Surf + net = Surf the net (navigating the Internet) Bogus (1960s; silly or stupid) → Bogotify ("make bogus") and bogue but ("act bogus")	20th century–present

POINTS TO REMEMBER

✔ A language family tree traces the relationship between languages.
✔ English and German are sister languages, sharing the same parent language (Germanic), whereas English and French are "cousins," sharing a common ancestor, the Indo–European language.
✔ Many historical events, such as the conquest of English-speaking countries by speakers of other languages, have influenced the evolution of the English language.
✔ Attitudes toward languages, as well as social, political, and religious influences, reflect the dramatic change in the English language.

- English has been influenced by many languages over time and has borrowed many vocabulary items.
- Some of these words have been adapted to fit the phonology of the English language, while others may still appear foreign in sound and spelling.
- Teachers can help ELs by drawing their attention to word cognates.
- Word meanings are not static and new words are created based on speakers' linguistic and social needs.
- Changes in word meanings occur in different forms. A word may extend meanings of the original word or narrow the referent of the original word.

REFLECTION QUESTIONS AND DISCUSSION

1. Describe word trees. Why are they useful?

2. How do languages change over time? Why do languages change over time?

3. Should teachers teach ELs informal English such as slang and jargon? Why or why not?

ACTIVITIES

1. The following words are a small sample of English borrowings from other languages. Use your knowledge of languages and the dictionary to discover the languages of origin for these words. (Hint: The words are grouped into language groups.)
   a. adobe, alfalfa, canyon, cargo, rodeo, lasso, ranch

   b. kindergarten, hausfrau, spiel, sauerbraten

   c. balcony, stanza, studio, torso

d. botany, climax, psychiatry, zoology

e. affidavit, agenda, monk, veto

f. algorithm, emir, giraffe, harem, sultan

g. commodore, cruise, dock, scum, spool, yacht

h. apparel, chemise, fork, napkin, suppr

i. chipmunk, kayak, raccoon, skunk, squash, pecan, podunk

j. bonsai, hara-kiri, tycoon, soy bean

2. Look up the etymology of the following words in a dictionary.

ancient	hunt	menial
esteem	prejudice	reins
fatal	subtraction	zodiac

3. Watch children's television programs and commercials to collect samples of children's language.
    a. List the linguistic expressions that you find different from your own speech. Explain the meanings of each.

b. How can teachers use this knowledge to make their instruction and daily communication more appealing to young students?

4. Read the following excerpt from a newspaper article from *La Jornada*. Underline any English cognates that you can find in the text.
Publicado el 1 diciembre 2017
Washington, DC

MICHAEL FLYNN SE DECLARA CULPABLE DE MENTIR AL FBI

Washington. El ex asesor de seguridad nacional de la Casa Blanca Michael Flynn se declaró culpable hoy de hacer declaraciones falsas al FBI en relación con las investigaciones de una presunta intromisión rusa en las elecciones presidenciales estadunidenses, informaron los medios en Washington. Ante un tribunal federal en Washington, Flynn admitió haber mentido a los investigadores en enero sobre su conversación con el entonces embajador ruso en Washington, Serguei Kisliak, el 29 de diciembre de 2016.

a. Make predictions about the contents of the text.

b. Explain how cognates can facilitate some level of comprehension.

WEB RESOURCES

American Federation for Teachers—English Language Development. https://www.aft.org/periodical/american-educator/summer-2013/english-language-development

English Language Resources for Teachers. http://www.englishteacherwebsites.com/resource-te.html

English Words Are Most Borrowed by and Lent From Other Languages. https://www.youtube.com/watch?v=wuIJYMb42Fg

Linguistic Borrowing. https://www.youtube.com/watch?v=Hgt0yLkHGxU

The Linguistics Roadshow—Language Families. https://www.lingroadshow.com/resources/languages-of-the-world/language-families

Role of the Teacher—English Language Development. http://www.tkcalifornia.org/teaching-tools/english-language-development/teaching-strategies

Think CERCA—English Language Development. https://www.thinkcerca.com/eld

REFERENCES

Language Files. (2017). *Skaau.com*. Retrieved from http://www.skaau.com/vb/showthread.php?t=694370

Youn, H., Sutton, L., Smith, E., Moore, C., Wilkins, J. F., Maddieson, I., & Bhattacharya, T. (2016). On the universal structure of human lexical semantics. *Proceedings of the National Academy of Sciences, 113*(7), 1766–1771.

A Knowledge Base for Language Theories and Applications

PART

III

First and Second Language Acquisition

Readers will be able to

- ❖ Recognize the stages of first and second language acquisition
- ❖ Recognize an English learners (EL) student's internal system of grammar
- ❖ Discern and address developmental sequence in second language acquisition

The following are some samples of children's first language productions:

1	Child:	*Nobody don't like me.*
	Mother:	*No, say "Nobody likes me."*
	Child:	*Nobody don't like me.* (repeated eight times)
	Mother:	*Now listen carefully, say "Nobody likes me."*
	Child:	*Oh, nobody don't likes me.*
2	Adult:	*Whose toy is that?*
	Child:	*That dog toy.*
	Adult:	*Oh . . . That's the dog's toy.*
	Child:	*Aha . . . That dog toy.*
3	Child:	*Mommy, Daddy goed to work.*
	Mother:	*Yes, your daddy went to work.*

FIRST LANGUAGE ACQUISITION

In the first scenario the child does not simply imitate or repeat an adult's utterances, even though the adult has given the child the correct form. In the second scenario the child may try to imitate an adult, but may not yet be able to do so accurately. In the third scenario the child develops a personal system of grammar and produces novel utterances he or she has never heard from an adult. If language learning is simply a process of imitation and memorizing rules and words, how do children learn these rules when most are not explicitly given to them?

The scenarios above demonstrate that children often attempt to figure out these rules on their own. The study of language acquisition aims to determine how children acquire linguistic grammar, or rules of a language, which provides a foundation for their ability to speak and interpret verbal messages.

OTHER EXAMPLES

1. A child says, [næna] for banana, [dedo] for potato, [wio] for wheels
2. A child may say "take" first, then "took," and then "taked," and finally say "took" consistently.
3. A child may acquire the -ing verb forms as in "she going" before the past or third person present, as in "she went" or "she goes."

(Continued)

As shown in the first example above, children will simplify a word by deleting the first syllable. A syllable is a structure consisting of one consonant or a consonant cluster followed by a vowel. The deletion of initial consonant or consonant clusters in these words may be attributed to the fact that the first syllable is an unstressed syllable and is thus not a perceptually salient or prominent sound. The ability of children to dissect the syllabic structure of a word depends on whether the stressed syllable is generally longer and louder than the unstressed syllable. In examples 2 and 3, certain inflectional morphemes are acquired in stages before they become more adult-like (see Chapter 7). The question, then, is how do children learn all the rules of the language they are exposed to?

The following section will discuss the developmental stages of first language acquisition regardless of what the first language may be.

DEVELOPMENTAL MILESTONES IN LANGUAGE LEARNING

Crying, Cooing, and Babbling Stage

During the first year of life, an infant's cooing, crying, and babbling reveal early signs of language-like behaviors. Although the child's strings of consonant- and vowel-like sounds do not have any intelligible meaning to an adult, some psychologists and linguists have argued that these behaviors carry specific functions. One function is to provide practice for later speech. Another is to provide a means for socialization between the child and others in his or her environment. When adults talk to infants, they often encourage them to babble by nodding and rewarding them with a big smile. This experience is socially rewarding for children and provides incentives for continuing their efforts to develop speech.

However, there are also those who have suggested that babbling is related to biological maturation, an early sign of when a child's brain reaches a critical level of development that predisposes the child to language. Whatever the reasons, it is apparent that children are able to process complex linguistic input early on in life and continue to proceed at a relatively fast pace.

In the following sections the different linguistic stages for language acquisition will be discussed. However, these stages are simply averages, and do not, in any way, suggest that all learners in a specific age group are similar. Despite variability within an age range, all learners go through similar stages, no matter what their first language may be. In the following section, the linguistic stages in the acquisition of phonology, morphology, syntax, and semantics will be discussed. Although the examples are drawn from children learning English as a first language, the general principles are relevant to other first languages. It is important to note that since the study of first language acquisition deals with very young informants, interpretations of children's language samples are often based on an adult's perspective, not on the child's own understanding of his or her system of grammar.

Acquisition of Phonology

At a very early age, children must learn to distinguish and master the phonemes in their language(s). Recall that even at a very young age, infants can discern sounds across different languages. In fact, many children around the world have access to more than one linguistic system from birth and are bi- and multilingual.

Since there are infinite numbers of words to learn in a language, it would be impossible for children to simply memorize individual words. Instead, they learn to break words into smaller units of sounds and sound combinations that they can manage and use to create new words. Table 15.1 summarizes the consonants, vowels, and syllable structures that are acquired in stages.

Table 15.1: Early Stages of Children's L1 Phonological Productions

	Stages	Examples
1. Consonants	**Early stage:**	/ba/ for *bottle*
	/p, b, m, w/ acquired first.	*telebision* (with a /b/ instead of /v/)
	Labial before alveolars, palatals, and velars	/da/ for *daddy*
	Stops and nasals	/ma/ for *mommy*
		/du/ for *juice*
	Later:	
	Liquids /l/	/wio/ for *wheel*
	Fricatives /f, v, θ, ð, s, z, š, ž, h/	/wuv/ for *love*
2. Vowels	**Early stage:**	/dada/ for *daddy*
	Vowels /a, i, u/	/si/ for *see*
	These are universal vowels, i.e., they occur in many languages and tend to be acquired before rare ones. Also, they are very distinct from each other along the front-to-back and vertical dimensions.	/pun/ for *spoon*
3. Syllable structure	**Early stage:**	/tu/ for *Matthew*
	(C) V (initial C may be dropped)	/su/ for *shoe*

(Continued)

Table 15.1: Early Stages of Children's L1 Phonological Productions (*Continued*)

	Stages	Examples
	CV structure preferred first	/gagi/ for *doggie*
	(*Reduplication of syllable structure is common.*)	/gud/ for *good*
		/top/ for *stop*
		/mama/ for *mommy*
		/baba/ for *bottle*
	Later:	/buh/ for *bird*
	CVC	/boken/ for *broken*
	CCVC (initial cluster)	/kwɪk/ for *quick*
	CVCC (final cluster)	/dæns/ for *Janet's*

As children are learning new words, they begin to understand that words have sounds and meaning. In their attempt to learn their first words, they will show many variations in pronunciation. Some may be able to approximate adults' productions, whereas others may produce a very distorted production that is not very comprehensible to anyone. As can be seen in Table 15.1, in the early stages, children tend to treat entire words as if they were single sounds and are unaware of the changes in meaning induced by variations in sounds. In other words, they treat the entire word as a single unit, paying less attention to the parts of the word. However, in order to learn more words, they must learn to break down words and use different sound combinations to produce new words. Several sound patterns are developed early in life.

Initially, children tend to acquire sounds that are maximally different from one another. It is no surprise that children acquire /pa/, /ba/, /ma/ first because these labial sounds /p, b, m/ are distinct from the vowel /a/ and thus the CV-syllable structure seems to be the preferred structure in many young children's productions. Earlier in Chapter 6, you learned that bilabials are produced by a complete obstruction of the airstream, whereas the vowel /a/ is produced by a wide opening in the vocal tract. Later, they will produce consonant clusters such as /tr/ in *tree* and /kw/ as in *quick*. Consonants that share similar properties like /l/ and /r/ are mastered last.

In addition, children may sometimes delete consonant or vowel sequences in multisyllabic words. Consider this: the first syllable of words such as *banana* or *potato* may sometimes be deleted because they are not as loud and prominent as the other syllables in a word. Hence, linguistically novice children may not pay attention to parts of words that are unstressed. Once children learn to distinguish between stressed and unstressed syllables, they will learn to dissect continuous strings of speech more easily.

In summary, children acquire the phonological system of their native language(s) in developmental stages. They must learn to master fine motor coordination. Receiving significant language input and encouragement from people around them will support their language development.

Table 15.2: Early Stages of Children's L1 Morphological Productions

	Stages	Examples
1. Inflectional/ grammatical morphemes	Early stage: (ages 2–5) -ing acquired first, followed by: past -ed, plural -s and -es, possessive 's, third person present -s	*She playing* *She wented / goed* *Feets* for *feet, ducks, dogs, horses,* /dæns su/ for *Janet's shoe*
2. Derivational morphemes	Productive morphemes like -er, -ly, un- tend to be acquired first before morphemes such as -hood, -ize	*Un-* + happy Farm + -er Careful + -ly

Acquisition of Morphology

Children also exhibit predictable stages in acquiring morphemes in their first language. (See Table 15.2 and also Chapter 7.) Words that are acquired first typically have concrete referents and relate directly to the immediate environment.

In addition, morphemes and words that carry important semantic information tend to be produced before functional morphemes. For example, children acquire the -*ing* morpheme as in *walking* before the third person present marker -*s* as in *walks*, because -*ing* indicates "action in progress," whereas the -*s* present tense morpheme seems redundant to the child because it does not affect meaning, except to show subject agreement. Children tend to acquire plurals quite early, but they may not have complete mastery of this form until a later stage of development. For example, children may not produce any plurals at first. Later, when children discover the plural -*s*, they may apply -*s* to irregular nouns like *feet* and *men*, producing *feets* and *mens*, respectively. This misapplication of rules is known as *overgeneralization*. Children will outgrow these deviant forms with time and practice.

Only eight inflectional morphemes exist in English, whereas derivational morphemes are much more extensive. Because of this, less is known about the acquisition of derivational morphemes as opposed to inflectional morphemes. Nevertheless, evidence suggests that the acquisition is somewhat systematic and predictable. The more productive the morphemes are (i.e., if they can be attached to many free morphemes), the greater the chances are that the morphemes will be acquired first. This explains why *un-* and -*ly* are acquired before -*hood* and -*ize*.

Acquisition of Syntax

Children's first signs of syntactic knowledge do not begin until about the age of one. From Table 15.3, you can see how children begin by producing single-word utterances that consist of words like nouns and verbs. Although children are limited to one-word production in the early stages, they can understand and possibly intend to convey more meaning in their production. This is evident from how children are able to understand other's speech consisting of more than one word. As their vocabularies expand, they

Table 15.3: Early Stages of Children's L1 Acquisition of Syntax

	Stages	Examples
1. Length of utterance	Holophrastic stage (one word)	/gek/ for *bug* /bet/ for *bed* /dak/ for *sock* /ge/ for *crayon*
	Two-word stage (telegraphic speech; i.e., function words are omitted as focus is given to semantic content)	/weo go/ for *wheel go* *Mommy book* (possesser + possession) *this shoe* (demonstrative + entity) *Katie eat* (agent + action) *Baby there* (object + location) *Kick ball* (action + object)
	Multiword stage (some telegraphic speech still evident)	*Janet eat cookie.* *Throw red ball.* *Mummy no go.*
2. Plurals	Initially, no plural marker is used	*Man, toy*
	Then plural *-s* acquired first, followed by irregular plurals	*Mans, feets, dogs, toys* *Mens, footses* *Men, feet*
3. Negatives	Put *no* in front of sentence	*No milk, no go.*
	Then insert a negative word (*no, can't, don't, not*) in between the subject and the verb or adjective. (*Be* verb is often omitted.)	*Baby no sleep.* *I not break doll.* *I not thirsty.*
	Use negation with *somebody* or *something*	*I don't see something instead of* *I don't see anything.*
	Then replaced with nobody or nothing and later with anybody or anything	*I don't see nothing.* *I don't see anything.*
4. Questions	Use rising intonation followed by:	*Mommy cup? More juice?* *Daddy going?*
	(Around age 3) Use can, *will* and other auxiliary verbs in yes/no questions; auxiliary verbs precede subject	*Are you sad?* *Is he going?*

(Continued)

Table 15.3: Early Stages of Children's L1 Acquisition of Syntax (*Continued*)

	Stages	Examples
	Do not invert subject and verb in *wh-* questions	*Why I can't go?* *Why you are sad?* *Where he is going?*
	Invert subject and verb in *wh-* questions	*Where's Daddy going?*

will produce two-word utterances that reflect a consistent set of word orders or semantic relation. For example, the phrase *Mommy go* shows agent–action relationship, whereas *baby there* shows object–location relationship. Later, children will learn to combine and expand their two-word utterances to form utterances consisting of three or more words.

Children also go through various stages in their development of negatives. At first, they will simply put *no* at the beginning of a sentence to show negation, such as the phrase *no toy*. Then, the *no* or *not* is inserted in between the subject and the verb, producing sentences such as *baby no sleep* or *I not thirsty*. They will tend to use somebody and something in negated sentences such as *I don't see something*. As children are continuously exposed to adult grammar, their speech will become more adult-like by using *anybody* or *anything* in negated sentences.

Children also show creativity in learning the rules of question formation. Initially, children produce questions by using a rising intonation, such as *Mommy cup?* Later, they will place auxiliary verbs in the front of a question. At this time, they do not know how to use *wh-* words to form questions. Once they can produce *wh-* words, they will insert *wh-* words in declarative sentences, producing an utterance such as *Why I can't go?* It takes a while before they finally figure out the subject and verb inversion in questions. It is clear that children do not simply imitate speech that they hear around them, nor do they make random errors all the time. In fact, for the most part, children's productions reveal the active construction of rule learning and application that evolves over time, resulting in finely tuned adult grammar. Table 15.3 summarizes salient syntactic structures that children acquire over time.

Acquisition of Semantics

Although semantics is the least understood field of all linguistics areas, there are some generalizations that can be made about how children learn vocabulary in their own languages. The acquisition of vocabulary words does not occur in set stages, but there is evidence that children develop vocabulary in two systematic ways. Table 15.4 summarizes the process.

Earlier, in Chapter 9, we stated that one way of determining word meanings is by analyzing their semantic features that single out classes of words with shared properties. For example, the word *table* can be used with *dining table*, *bistro table*, *study table*, and

Table 15.4: Early Stages of Children's L1 Acquisition of Semantics

	Examples
Lexical Semantics 1. *Overgeneralization:* Unlike adults, children use a word to label items that typically do not belong to the same class	A child may use *ticktock* to refer to clocks, parking meters, and the dial on a set of scales. A child may use *doggie* to refer to furry things, slippers, other animals that move, such as ducks, toads, and etc.
2. *Narrowing:* Applying a word to a smaller set of referents than is done in adults' lexicon	A child may not consider an *olive* a fruit or *whales* mammals as these are quite far removed from the other members of the same class.
Sentence Semantics 3. Interpreting passive sentences as if they were active (ages 4–5)	*She pushed him* (active) and *She was pushed by him* (passive) may be interpreted as *She pushed him.*
4. Difficulty interpreting bare infinitives: subordinate clause comprising an infinitive verb without a subject	*I told you where to sit* is correctly interpreted as *I told you where you should sit.* But *I ask you where to sit* is incorrectly interpreted as *I ask you where you should sit* instead of *where I should sit.*
5. Principle of order of mention	A child may correctly interpret the sentence *He came home before he ate lunch* as *First he came home, then he ate lunch.* But a child may incorrectly interpret *Before he ate lunch, he came home* as *First he ate lunch and then he came home.*

Source: Linguistics 001 (2017) and Parker and Riley (2005).

end table because all of these things are objects to put things on. However, this semantic concept has to be learned by children. This process is not always easy because many words may shift meaning from one occasion to the next. Thus, it is natural that in the early stages, children will learn to link words they hear to their own experiences and their primitive conception of word meaning, resulting in productions such as *ticktock* to mean "anything that ticks," and *doggie* to refer to "any animal that moves." Likewise, children may narrow a class of noun based on the same process and thereby conclude that a tomato is a vegetable and not a fruit. Linguists have claimed that children's overgeneralizations and narrowing of words reflect their incomplete definitions of word meanings that are different from what adults possess.

A child's acquisition of semantics is inextricably bound to syntax. For example, linguists have learned that some children may not fully acquire passive structure until much later (at about 6–10 years old). Thus it is not unusual to hear children interpreting passive sentences, such as *She pushed him* and *She was pushed by him* as if they were active sentences. It appears, in this case, that meaning is determined by the order of constituents; this phenomenon is also observed in children's interpretations of sentences with main and subordinate clauses. For example, the sentence *Before he ate lunch, he came home* may be interpreted as "he ate lunch first, followed by the act of coming home." Like the passives, the bare infinitives in English are acquired relatively late. *Bare infinitives are structures that do not have an overt subject*, for example *I told you where to sit.* Children may interpret the sentence *I told you where to sit* as "I told you where you should sit" because native speakers interpret the subject of *where to sit* by determining the closest noun phrase to the left. However, there are exceptions. Many native speakers will interpret *I ask you where to sit* to mean "I ask you where I should sit" and not "where you should sit," even though *you* is the closest noun phrase to the left.

You will notice that the first language acquisition process is rule governed and develops in predictable stages. As noted earlier, children do not simply parrot adults' speech. In fact, children produce errors in their speech that reflect an active process of rule testing through trial and error. As they acquire more knowledge and confidence in using a language, these errors disappear and their language becomes more target-like over time. Words that are acquired first are usually words related to the immediate linguistic environment; they are grounded in the "here and now" principle.

SCENARIO

The following is a retelling of Little Red Riding Hood by Chen, a 5-year-old Chinese-speaking girl.

> Teacher: *Have you read this book, Chen? Do you know the story?*
> Chen: *Yes. I know.*
> T: *Will you tell me?*
> C: *Yep. There was a girl and she was—she wented to her grandma house and then she see animal.*
> T: *Wolf.*
> C: *Yep. Wolf. The wolf want to eat her and . . . (hesitates) eh . . . I don't know.*
> T: *Yes? And so what did she do?*
> C: *(Chen thinks for a moment.) She ranned home and she see a man with gun.*

SECOND LANGUAGE ACQUISITION

In this scenario, Chen, a second language learner of English, does not just reproduce words and sentences that she has heard uttered by native speakers but experiments with English language rules and produces novel words such as *ranned*, *wented*, and *grandma house* as well as omitting the article before a noun.

Some of the patterns of "errors" made by second language learners are similar to those of children acquiring English as their first language. Although second language learners vary greatly in their acquisition of a second language, they progress through similar second language developmental stages. The following sections discuss the patterns in second language acquisition.

DEVELOPMENTAL MILESTONES IN SECOND LANGUAGE LEARNING

Silent Period

In the comprehension stage, also known as the silent period or preproduction stage, the learner simply listens and absorbs the sounds and rhythms of the new language. As listeners become familiar with the flow of the speech sounds of the new language, they also start to pick up on isolated specific words in the perceived strings of new and unfamiliar sounds. They are also internalizing knowledge of what makes an acceptable sentence in a new language. During this stage, learners may appear anxious when asked to produce speech. Therefore, teachers with second language learners at this stage of their second language learning process should not force them to speak. They should not feel frustrated when students do not respond to them; this is a normal, initial stage that second language learners go through in learning a new language. During this stage, teachers can provide a lot of comprehensible input by using visuals, manipulatives, gestures, and context clues and modeling expected behavior and encouraging students to join in group chants and songs. Teachers should not overtly correct errors, as this heightens learners' anxiety levels and does not guarantee they will internalize the rules. Teachers can provide learners with a rich language environment and modeling where they can use the input to the best of their abilities.

After the silent period, learners will go through early production (one- or two-word stage), speech emergence (phrases and short sentences), and intermediate fluency (begin to engage in discourse). All of these stages involve linguistic elements such as phonology, morphology, syntax, semantics, and pragmatics.

LINGUISTIC STAGES

Acquisition of Phonology

There are several reasons why second language learners may not initially produce the sounds of the target language correctly. This may be attributed to the concept of transfer, a process whereby language learners use their knowledge of the first language in the second language:

A. Speakers may transfer the segmental structure of L1 to L2. An example is the L2 phonemic distinction that L1 lacks. Japanese has one phoneme /r/ with allophones l and r; thus they do not make a distinction between /l/ and /r/, whereas in English there is a phonemic distinction between the two. Therefore, Japanese or Chinese speakers may experience difficulty in producing /r/.

B. Speakers may also transfer phonological rules from L1 to L2. German speakers devoice the word-final obstruents when learning English, yielding both *back* and *bag* as /baek/, because in German the word-final obstruents must be voiceless.

C. Speakers may also transfer phonotactic constraints (i.e., conditions for a permissible sequence of segments) from L1 to L2. For example, in English it is permissible to string three consonants in the syllable-initial cluster such as *straight* and *splendid*. Speakers whose native languages do not permit this will put in a vowel to break up the cluster. For instance, Spanish speakers will say /estop/ for *stop* and /especial/ for *special*, and Arab Egyptian speakers will say /fired/ for *Fred* and /c̆ildirUn/ for *children*.

Acquisition of Morphology

Second language learners go through predictable stages in acquiring morphemes in their second language. These stages are similar to the stages children go through in acquiring English as their native language. The plural morphemes (PLU) (*boy / boys*) are acquired before the present (PRES) (*He eat / eats pizza*) and possessive (POSS) (*girl bag / girl's bag*) morphemes. Morphemes are also acquired according to their morphological function rather than their phonological form.

The examples in Table 15.5 show the order of grammatical morphemes acquired by children learning English as a second language. In their seminal work, Dulay and Burt (1983) reported that children from different first language backgrounds seem to have a similar order of acquiring the English morphemes. For instance, the (PLU) morpheme as in *boy / boys* and (progressive) as in *cry / crying* are acquired earlier than (third person singular) as in *like / likes* and (POSS) as in *Mom cup / Mom's cup*. Studies have found that non-native English speakers in their acquisition of the (PLU) forms seem to have misanalysed the irregular plural form as a root form and thus inflect it again with the regular plural suffix, as in *sheep / sheeps*.

Table 15.5: Early Stages of Children's L2 Acquisition of Morphemes

	Stages	**Examples**
1. Inflectional/ grammatical morphemes	Early stage: (3–5 years old) -s, -es -ing followed by third person singular pres -s past -ed and possessive -'s,	*boys and girls, sheeps, feets, noses, cause them hungry and crying* Many like pizza. *She boughted it at the store.* Mom *kuh* (cup)
2. Derivational morphemes	Productive morphemes such as -er, -ly, un- tend to be acquired before morphemes like -hood, -ize.	*longer, lovely, untidy neighborhood, familiarize*

As for the derivational morphemes, *-er*, *-ly*, *un-* in words such as *longer*, *lovely*, *untidy* are acquired sooner than morphemes such as *-hood*, *-ize* in words such as *brotherhood* and *familiarize*.

Acquisition of Syntax

Second language children produce these syntactic structures during their second language acquisition process, as shown in Table 15.6.

Table 15.6 shows three components of the acquisition process of syntactic structures by ELs: length of utterance, negation, and questions.

Length of utterance: English language learners (ELs) go through the holophrastic stage (*cup*) to the telegraphic stage (*He cry*) and the multiword stage (*I not cry*).

Table 15.6: Early Stages of Children's L2 Acquisition of Syntax

	Stages	Examples
1. Length of utterance	Holophrastic stage	kuh (cup)
	Two-word stage (telegraphic speech; i.e., function words are omitted as focus is on meaning)	He cry; Hims back
	Multiword stage (some telegraphic speech still exists)	I not cry; Tran nots here. She boughted it at the store. Mary didn't wanted it.
2. Negatives	Put no in front of sentences by: inserting a negative word *no* or *not* between the subject and the verb or adjective (*Be* verb is often omitted)	*I not cry.* *Tran nots here.*
	Use negation with the incorrect auxiliary	*Lucy doesn't gots the glue.*
3. Questions	Use rising intonation followed by:	*Tan is reading?*
	The production of *wh-* questions begins	*What you study?* *What the time?*
	Auxiliaries such as *is, are,* was appear, but are not yet inverted systematically with the subject	*Why I can't color?* *What she is singing?* *Why you don't draw?*

Negation: Regardless of native language background, ELs' most common first attempt at negating in English is to place the negative particle *no* (or occasionally *not*) before the phrase to be negated, as in *I not cry* and *no eat*.

Questions: In the initial stage of forming questions, ELs tend to add rising intonation to their sentence structures, such as *Tan is reading?* Then the attempt at *wh-* questions begins; however, the auxiliary is usually omitted, such as *What you study?* Another stage in forming questions is when the auxiliaries are not yet inverted systematically, as in *What she is singing?*

Acquisition of Semantics

In acquiring semantics, second language learners go through stages similar to the stages first language children go through in learning words. Studies have documented several generalizations about these stages. Table 15.7 displays the stages in which ELs acquire meanings. The common developmental strategy that children learning English as a second language employ is the overgeneralization of the superordinates due to their limited vocabulary (*animal* instead of *dog*). Other developmental strategies are the inappropriate use of synonyms (*long* instead of *tall*) and the use of circumlocutions which involve substituting a descriptive phrase for a word that the learner has not yet acquired (*a lady who is carrying a baby* instead of *a pregnant lady*). Perhaps the most common difficulty that ELs face in the semantic domain is the acquisition of idioms (*break a leg*) and with words that have one form but many meanings (*diamond, bank*).

In sum, learners of a language follow a developmental sequence of stages. Some stages of second language learning appear similar to stages of first language, including acquisition of specific morphemes and overgeneralization of linguistic rules. Importantly, ELs already have knowledge of a first language system. When they use that knowledge in acquiring the

Table 15.7: Early Stages of Children's L2 Acquisition of Semantics

Lexical Semantics	Examples
1. Overgeneralization: Using superordinates due to limited vocabulary	*animal* instead of *dog; small* instead of *little (I have small money); boys and girls* instead of *children*
2. Inappropriate use of synonyms	*My brother is long and thin* instead of *tall I will borrow you the book* instead of *lend*
3. Use of circumlocutions in place of an exact word	*A lady who is carrying a baby* instead of *a pregnant lady*
4. Acquisition of idiomatic expressions, *polysemes* (one form with related meaning) and *homonyms* (one form with unrelated meaning) takes longer	*Break a leg, run up, run down, run out; mouth* used for eating, opening of river; diamond (baseball, stone)

second language, the process is referred to as language transfer. Teachers can support ELs' learning of English by supporting ongoing development of the first language in schools and at home.

First Language Acquisition

✔ Cooing, babbling, and crying are precursors to true language development. They not only enable infants to experiment and practice different sounds for later speech, they also provide a means for infants to communicate their needs to others. All of this motivates infants to continue developing their language-learning potential.

✔ Children's first language acquisition occurs in developmental stages. At the phonological level, sounds that are easy to produce will be acquired first, that is, labial consonants are acquired before alveolars, palatals, and velars. Universal vowels and vowels that are distinctive from one another will be acquired first. Syllable structures consisting of consonants and vowels are acquired first, followed by two- or three-consonant clusters in the initial or final positions of a word.

✔ Grammatical morphemes are acquired in a predictable order. Inflectional morphemes such as -*ing*, past -*ed*, and plural -*s* are acquired before possessives -*'s* and third person -*s*.

✔ Syntactic structures are acquired in a predictable order from one- to two-word stage to multiple-word stage. Sentence types such as negatives and questions are also acquired in stages.

✔ Children do not simply imitate adults' speech or memorize the rules and words of a language.

✔ Children develop their own internal system of grammar by testing the rules themselves, applying the rules, and later modifying their grammar to match that of adults. During this process, children may make overgeneralization errors that are produced by misapplying rules to instances where they do not apply.

✔ Children may not correct their overgeneralized productions even if they are corrected by adults because their own system of grammar may not be developed enough to accommodate such changes.

✔ Children's early vocabulary is centered in the "here and now"; they relate to their immediate experiences.

Second Language Acquisition

✔ Some patterns of "errors" are normal developmental language learning.

✔ Some second language learners will go through a silent period at the initial stage of their second language acquisition process.

✔ The stages that learners go through in learning their second language are:
  • Silent period/preproduction stage
  • Early production (one- or two-word stage)

- Speech emergence (phrases and short sentences)
- Intermediate fluency (begin to engage in discourse)

✔ Second language learners go through a predictable order of acquiring grammatical morphemes and syntactic structures in English, just like children learning their first language.

✔ "Errors" made by second language learners may be attributed to transfer of L1 rules to L2.

✔ Second language learners also demonstrate some similarities to first language learners in their acquisition of word meanings. They may overgeneralize the meaning of a word. Second language learners, due to their limited vocabulary, may also substitute words or phrases.

REFLECTION QUESTIONS AND DISCUSSION

1. Describe the developmental stages of a child's acquisition of syntax. How do these stages compare to second language learning acquisition?

2. How would a teacher use his or her study of second language acquisition process in teaching ELs?

3. Why might an EL's learning of English appear have "errors?"

ACTIVITIES

1. Which construction in the following sets a–d would a child acquire first when learning English?

a.	/a/ heart	/æ/ bat	/e/ bay
b.	/b/ boot	/k/ back	/v/ van
c.	VC (oh!)	CV (go)	CVC (bat)
d.	/ð/ (that)	/m/ my	/t/ toy

2. Consider the following exchange between a mother and her 3-year-old son about a book they are reading together:

> Mother: *What is this story about?*
> Son: *The very hungry caterpitar.*
> Mother: *Yes, it's a hungry caterpillar.*
> Son: *Aha hungry caterpitar.*

What does this exchange illustrate about why the child pronounced the word *caterpillar* as *caterpitar?*

3. List some examples of children's productions that illustrate the phonological process of reduplication.

4. Why does a child acquire *-ing* before the *-ed* and *-s* or *es-* marker for plurals? (Hint: See previous section on morphology.)

5. For each set of constructions below, state which forms a child acquiring English would be expected to acquire first, second, and third?

   a. *I no sleep, I not sleep, No sleep, I don't sleep*

   b. *Are you sleeping?, You sleeping?, You are sleeping?*

6. A child refers to dump trucks, bulldozers, trailers, tractors, and steam rollers as trucks, but does not refer to cars as trucks. Later on, the child might refer to the dump trucks and trailers as trucks. How would you explain the child's rules for processing word meanings?

7. Examine this dialogue between Thomas, an English-speaking child, and Victor, a Spanish-speaking child.

   > Thomas: *What did you do yesterday, Victor?*
   > Victor: *I go to my uncle house and I play with Marie and Juan—my cousins.*
   > Thomas: *I stayed home because my mom got sick and she couldn't take me out.*

Victor: *Oh . . . my aunt, she sick too. So, my uncle tell us we make no noise. So, we play in yard. You want play soccer now?*
Thomas: *Let's go!*

a. Examine Victor's utterances and list the morphological and syntactical errors that he makes.

b. Refer to Table 15.5 and the above dialogue to comment on the stages of the acquisition of morphology that Victor goes through.

8. Why do Chinese speakers of English say /pray/ instead of /play/ and /flied/ instead of/ fried/? (Hint: Refer to earlier section on phonology.)

WEB RESOURCES

The Birth of a Word. attribute to Deb Roy https://www.ted.com/talks/deb_roy_the_birth_of_a_word

Child Language Acquisition: Key Theories. https://www.youtube.com/watch?v=jr_hK2Owq8o

First Language Acquisition. https://www.prezi.com/bzysbgea11dy/first-language-acquisition

Language Learning Success Stories: People Who Have Learned Languages in a Limited Amount of Time. http://ikindalikelanguages.com/blog/language-success-stories-people-who-have-learnt-languages-in-a-limited-amount-of-time

Learning English Through Stories. http://www.cambridgeenglish.org/learning-english/parents-and-children/information-for-parents/tips-and-advice/008-learning-english-through-stories

The Linguistic Genius of Babies. https://www.ted.com/talks/patricia_kuhl_the_linguistic_genius_of_babies

Second Language Acquisition. https://www.prezi.com/0daxj4uvmymq/second-language-acquisition-l2

Stages of Second Language Acquisition: ESL, ELL, LEP & Bilingual. https://www.youtube.com/watch?v=Hk7_lBaFC5w

Stephen Krashen on Language Acquisition. https://www.youtube.com/watch?v=NiTsduRreug

William O'Grady: What Makes Hangul Great. https://www.youtube.com/watch?v=gJ5ABpTycZs&t=19s

REFERENCES

Dulay, H., Burt, M., & Krashen, S. (1983). *Language two*. New York, NY: Oxford University Press.

Parker, F., & Riley, K. L. (2005). *Linguistics for non-linguists: A primer with exercises*. Boston, MA: Pearson/Allyn and Bacon.

Nonlinguistic Factors That Influence Second Language Acquisition

LEARNING OBJECTIVES

Readers will be able to

- ❖ Describe the relationship between age and length of exposure to second language acquisition
- ❖ Differentiate distinctions in cognitive styles and their influence on second language acquisition
- ❖ Distinguish differences in personality traits and their influence on second language acquisition
- ❖ Categorize types of motivation and success in language acquisition
- ❖ Connect the relationship between social distance and language acquisition

SCENARIO

Examine the following comments about second language learners:

I don't understand why Rosa is not showing that much progress in her English. She has been in the United States for 7 years and she gets to hear English all the time. Her parents want her to do well in school and believe that her future will be better here than in Mexico. On top of that, she gets a lot of English everywhere. So what's preventing her from learning English well?

I notice that many English learner (EL) children are very fluent in English, but their parents may not be as fluent, even though they have been in America for the same length of time. Children are like sponges, always absorbing information.

The only way to learn is to speak and use the language constantly. But how will these EL children learn if they refuse to speak in class or answer our questions? They must learn to participate in class if they want to do well here.

Look at Hoang. He has been here for only 2 years but his English is improving every minute. He likes to talk in class, participates in every class discussion, and is not afraid to ask questions when he doesn't understand. I think he will pick up the language very quickly.

Do you think the views expressed are justified? Why or why not? Can you offer alternative explanations for why individuals have different levels of success in learning a second language?

In earlier chapters, the role of linguistic variables in second language acquisition was discussed but other factors also affect second language learning. Some of those include age, cognitive style, and personality.

AGE

There is a prevailing assumption that children learn a second language more readily than adults. This view is largely influenced by an earlier language learning theory by Lennenberg (1967) called the "critical period hypothesis" (Alghizzi, 2014), which states that children must have exposure to language in an age range, in order to build critical left brain structures. Those structures enable them to gain native-like competence in language. Lennenberg found that the age range is between birth and puberty.

While researchers may have differing views about the implications of the critical period hypothesis in second language learning, it is generally accepted that children who are exposed to another language at a very early age have a greater chance of producing native-like fluency and accent. Length of exposure to the language (i.e., time exposed to its use) has also shown to correlate positively with language proficiency. It is not unusual to expect that those who begin learning a second language at an early age may simply have longer exposure to the language and ultimately achieve greater proficiency. Moreover, young children are typically less self-conscious about learning a second language; they are not expected to perform at a cognitively higher level than adults and thus experience less anxiety. All of these factors may promote acquisition.

On the other hand, adults may be more efficient at learning a new language because they bring with them extensive knowledge, mature cognitive skills, and strategies for problem-solving, which may facilitate second language acquisition. Adults, however, may not be able to produce accent-free speech if they acquire the second language after puberty (Kupisch et al., 2014). Moreover, non-native adult learners of a language may also choose to speak English with an accent to maintain or project their personal or cultural identity through their speech, or modify the degree of accent in their speech, depending on the context.

COGNITIVE STYLES

Cognitive styles refer to the way learners approach problem-solving tasks, conceptualize, and organize information. Cognitive styles may mediate between emotion and cognition; for example, one's emotional state may elicit tendencies toward reflectivity or toward impulsivity. In other words, if a student is in an impulsive mood, the student may demonstrate an impulsive style of learning. And if the student is in a reflective mood, she may be more likely to exhibit a reflective learning style. These distinctions may have several implications for language acquisition. Researchers have found that children who are more reflective tend to make fewer mistakes in reading than impulsive children (Das, Janzen, & Georgiou, 2007). Conversely, children who are more impulsive tend to be faster readers; they adopt a strategy of reading for understanding by guessing from context and they are not overly concerned with errors. Such a style could have positive effects on language learning.

What important considerations for second language learning can we draw from these differences in cognitive styles? Knowing that learners exhibit these differences, teachers must be mindful not to judge errors made by impulsive learners who may be taking more risks with language. But then again, the reflective learner must be given time to react and respond to instructional material and other activities done in the classroom.

Additional cognitive styles are *field independence* and *field dependence*. Field independent and field dependent are an analytical ability that enables learners to distinguish and analyze the parts from the whole. Field dependence, however, means a person analyzes information in a holistic way and does not easily distinguish the parts from the whole (Grey, Williams, & Rebuschat, 2015).

How does this information relate to second language learning? It appears that classrooms that focus on structure drills and other activities involving analysis and attention to specific details and explicit rules may work well for field-independent learners. Field-dependent learners may do better when instruction does not focus explicitly on rule learning but introduces language structures through contextually embedded whole language activities such as story reading, oral discussions, group work, and so on.

It is important that teachers view these cognitive styles as general tendencies, which may be exercised in varying degrees by learners, depending on the context. Teachers should thus refrain from labeling students as either specific type. More importantly, teachers must be cognizant that each individual is unique and should help learners develop flexibility in the way that they learn.

PERSONALITY TRAITS

There are certain personality traits that appear to correlate with good second language acquisition, although supporting empirical studies are somewhat inconclusive. Impulsivity and risk-taking behaviors appear to be important to successful learning of a second language. Good language learners who have fewer inhibitions will be more willing to take a calculated risk and will try to figure out the language as much as they possibly can. Dehbozorgi (2012) found that Puerto Rican children learning English displayed significantly greater risk-taking behaviors with an English-speaking interviewer than with an English-speaking bilingual. They reason that ELs will unconsciously adjust their speech for the interlocutor (the speaker)—in this case making more elaborations and explanations for the English-speaking interviewer and thereby demonstrating more risk-taking behaviors. Such a learner may be well-suited for the less formal learning environment.

It is often accepted that extroverted learners will acquire language at a faster rate than introverted learners. This is because extroverts, by nature, are generally considered to be more assertive, adventurous, responsive, talkative, and, consequently, more inclined to continue learning the language. However, Ockey (2011), and Zafar and Meenakshi (2012) found that extroversion has no relation to pronunciation but correlates with length of exposure to English. They also found that introversion affects performance on language tasks involving grammar and reading. These disparate findings suggest two things: (a) the effect of personality on language acquisition may be inversely related. It is possible that learners who have long exposure to the second language may become more extroverted and (b) extroversion may enhance communicative language ability more than knowledge of linguistic rules or academic language learning.

Stephen Krashen (1981), a prominent figure in the field of English language learning, Chakrabarti and Sengupta (2012), and Zen and Apriana (2015) all stress the negative effects that anxiety plays in language learning. Learners who generally have a high global self-esteem (overall self-assessment) or specific self-esteem (such as self-evaluation on specific tasks such as writing a paper or driving a car) and low inhibitions may have a better chance at achieving successful language learning than those with a lower sense of self and many anxieties. Thus it is important that teachers help learners become comfortable by providing instruction that is clear, authentic, meaningful, and appealing, while offering support in the form of encouragement so that students remain interested in their own learning.

SOCIAL PSYCHOLOGICAL FACTORS

EL learners' motivation and attitude may also influence the degree of success in second language acquisition. Moskovsky, Alrabai, Paolini, and Ratcheva (2013) carried out significant studies on motivational factors affecting second language acquisition identified two basic types of motivation: instrumental and integrative. Their work follows the seminal contributions of Gardner and Lambert (1972) in second language motivation. *Instrumental motivation* refers to motivation for learning a language based on instrumental reasons, such as getting promoted to a higher grade, gaining admission to a good program of study, competing for scholarships, doing well in classroom tasks and tests, and so forth. *Integrative motivation* refers to the learner's desire to identify with the members of the target culture and to understand and appreciate the values and knowledge of the target culture and its speakers. A learner who is integratively motivated may not have to "lose oneself" in that process. An integratively motivated language learner is one who desires to learn the new language so they will be able to get to know the native speakers of that language (Dörnyei, 2014).

It is also important to note that the degree of success achieved by learners may be motivated by attitudes that are both instrumental and integrative. For example, EL children in the United States may wish to learn English to do well in school and to "fit in" with the mainstream student population; however, because young learners may not have the fully developed attitudes of their adult counterparts, their attitudes toward a culture may have little or no effect on their second language acquisition.

In addition, Maslow's (1970) hierarchy of needs points to equally important forms of motivation: intrinsic and extrinsic (Williams, Mercer, & Ryan, 2016). Intrinsic motivation refers to the learner's internal desire and self-determination to learn. For example, ELs in the United States may recognize that English is an important tool of communication in their classrooms, and thus may work hard to acquire fluency. If the learners are studying a second language to fulfil a parent's wish, then the motivation is extrinsic.

In what way do these forms of motivation affect language learning? Learners who are instrumentally and intrinsically motivated may do equally well in acquiring another language. But the former may lack the persistence for learning the target language once a specific task is accomplished, or when the external reward or punishment related to the behavior is removed. Learners who begin to appreciate and value target language speakers and to achieve a sense of self-satisfaction may do well in the long run, as they are more likely to persist in learning and increasing their abilities in the language.

Another sociopsychological factor focuses on attitudes of second language learners. Because second language learning involves the integration of the cultural skills, values, and ideas of the new culture, second language learners' attitudes toward the target language culture and its members may either contribute to or hamper language acquisition. Schumann's (1978) acculturation model (see also Pourkalhor & Esfandiari, 2017) hypothesizes that success in second language acquisition requires learners to adapt to the target culture. How well the learners adapt to the new culture depends on the *social distance* between the learner and the target language group. Social distance is determined by the differences in size between groups, the ethnicity, and the political and social status of the second language group. The more learners perceive themselves to be politically or socially inferior to the target language group, or perceive their cultural values or ideas to be in conflict with those of the target language and culture, the greater the social distance (Chizzo, 2002).

Equally important is how teacher and peer attitudes can influence learning ability. Teachers and mainstream peers must display respect for second language learners and their cultures and language groups, and be willing to accept them for who they are and not judge them through the lens of their own culture. These orientations toward EL students will support their language learning process and experiences.

POINTS TO REMEMBER

✔ Age correlates with second language acquisition. Younger children are more likely than adults to acquire native-like pronunciation. However, adults are cognitively more advanced in acquiring grammar and vocabulary in a second language.

✔ Cognitive style is a significant factor in language acquisition, because learners will respond to the form of instruction that matches their learning styles. Since each learner is unique, teachers must diversify language instruction as much as possible. Exposing students to different learning styles will help them become more versatile in their learning approach.

✔ The relationship between extroversion and language acquisition is not conclusive. Extroversion may not always be a factor in acquisition; rather, it may be a consequence of language acquisition. In fact, both extroverts and introverts may become successful at language acquisition. Extroversion may be a factor in promoting natural communicative ability.

✔ ELs' attitudes and motivations may also affect language acquisition. Learners with integrative motivation, a desire to identify with and appreciate the values and the members of the target culture, may be more likely to continue learning and persevere through obstacles they encounter in their learning. The motivation to succeed is increased if the learners are internally—as opposed to externally—driven to learn a language.

✔ ELs with instrumental motivation, a desire to learn a language for utilitarian purposes, may also do well in acquiring a language; but this motivation may be reduced once learners have met their target goal. Similarly, learners whose desire to learn is instrumental and intrinsic may also do as well as learners who are extrinsically and instrumentally motivated.

✔ Learner attitudes toward the target language culture and its members may also influence how well they adapt to the new culture. The greater the social distance, the more difficulties learners will have with learning the second language.

✔ Teachers must demonstrate respect for and acceptance of the values of second language learners, their families, and their cultures.

REFLECTION QUESTIONS AND DISCUSSION

1. As you learned, there are a variety of nonlinguistic factors that affect second language learners' language learning processes. What are they?

2. What is "social distance" and the various components of it? Provide three examples of social distance related to second language teaching and learning?

3. How might a teacher support an EL student in her classroom who appears to be introverted? How might a teacher support an EL who demonstrates field independence tendencies?

ACTIVITIES

1. Read the following case studies and answer the questions that follow:

CASE STUDY 1

Edward is a Haitian-Creole speaker who is attending fifth grade in a public school in America. He has a younger brother in second grade. His parents only speak Creole at home. Both Edward and his younger brother have limited English because they have only been studying English for 1 year. Unlike his younger brother, Edward tends to shy away from talking to other people outside his family. He is afraid that his classmates will make fun of his English.

But Edward knows that he must improve his English to do well in school. He also wants to improve his English to get along with his peers. His parents try to encourage him to read, write, and speak more English at home. Unfortunately, he sometimes gets frustrated with things that occur in his school life. He likes learning about the customs of many other groups of people in the United States, but he feels that no one is interested in knowing about his. Stories read in class tend to show role models from the mainstream group. In other words, he feels that he has been silenced, and this has affected his self-esteem. He sometimes feels embarrassed about his cultural origin.

To make matters worse, most class work requires students to work out problems independently, leaving Edward to struggle on his own. He wishes he could ask his classmates for help with his homework because he believes he learns best by sharing his ideas with other people.

CASE STUDY 2

Stephanie arrives in the United States from Brazil at age 5. She is placed in kindergarten at a public school. Stephanie is an only child and her parents have migrated to the United States to seek a better life. Both her parents are educated and hold college degrees; her dad is an engineer and her mom is a nurse. Stephanie speaks Portuguese at home. She loves to read and write stories in Portuguese.

(Continued)

Her parents have some working knowledge of English, but speak very little English at home. They want Stephanie to continue using her Portuguese so that she will not forget her cultural heritage. They are confident that Stephanie's English language learning will not be affected, since she will be getting plenty of opportunities to use English in and outside of school.

In class, Stephanie tends to be quiet. She normally takes her time to do her work in class. In Brazil, she was praised by her teacher for being very careful in her work and producing work superior to that of her peers. But things are different in America. Sometimes she gets into trouble for not finishing her in-class work on time. Her teacher wants her to stay more focused on her tasks. Although she has a lot of ideas, she does not feel comfortable sharing her opinions in class. She is concerned that her teachers and peers may think she is not intelligent enough, and this makes her even more frustrated.

a. What nonlinguistic factors affect Edward and Stephanie's second language acquisition?

b. What changes in instruction would you make to accommodate Edward and Stephanie's learning needs?

2. You are 18 years old and for the first time are taking a foreign language course in Spanish. You live in a multilingual community where Spanish is a dominant language. What are your chances of acquiring Spanish as a second language? What would you predict to be factors promoting your success in Spanish?

3. Recall your experiences in learning another language. In what ways did your personality and cognitive styles contribute to or inhibit your general success in learning that language?

WEB RESOURCES

2 Types of Motivation to Get Your ESL Students to Love Learning English. https://www .fluentu.com/blog/educator-english/how-to-motivate-esl-students

9 Factors That Influence Language Learning. https://www.google.com/search?q=9+ Factors+That+Influence+Language+Learning&rlz=1C1GGRV_enUS751US751&o

q=9+Factors+That+Influence+Language+Learning&aqs=chrome..69i57.3390j0j8&sourceid=chrome&ie=UTF-8

Cognitive Learning Styles in the Student-Centered Classroom. https://www.scilearn.com/blog/cognitive-learning-styles-student-centered-classroom

How to Motivate ESL Students. https://www.busyteacher.org/3644-how-to-motivate-esl-students.html

How to Motivate Your Students & Be a Better ESL Teacher. https://www.oxfordseminars.com/blog/5-ways-to-motivate-your-students-become-a-better-esl-teacher

How You Would Differentiate Between Linguistics and Non-Linguistics Communication?. http://www.masscommunicationtalk.com/how-you-would-differentiate-between-linguistics-and-non-linguistics-communication.html

The Roles of Styles and Strategies in Second Language Learning. ERIC Digest. https://www.ericdigests.org/pre-9214/styles.htm

Social Factors in Second Language Acquisition. https://www.omjaeducation.wordpress.com/2012/02/20/social-factors-in-second-language-acquisition

Ways of Motivating EFL/ESL Students in the Classroom. https://www.teachingenglish.org.uk/blogs/alexenoamen/ways-motivating-efl-esl-students-classroom

What Teachers Need to Know About Language. https://www.people.ucsc.edu/~ktellez/wong-fill-snow.html

REFERENCES

Alghizzi, T. M. (2014). Critical period hypothesis. *Language in India, 14*(1), 15–22.

Chakrabarti, A., & Sengupta, M. (2012). Second language learning anxiety and its effect on achievement in the language. *Language in India, 12*(8), 50–78.

Chizzo, J. (2002). Acculturation and language acquisition: A look at Schumann's acculturation model. Retrieved from http://gse.gmu.edu/assets/docs/lmtip/vol3/J.Chizzo.pdf

Das, J. P., Janzen, T., & Georgiou, G. K. (2007). Correlates of Canadian native children's reading performance: From cognitive styles to cognitive processes. *Journal of School Psychology, 45*(6), 589–602. doi:10.1016/j.jsp.2007.06.004

Dehbozorgi, E. (2012). Effects of attitude towards language learning and risk-taking on EFL student's proficiency. *International Journal of English Linguistics, 2*(2), 41–48.

Dörnyei, Z. (2014). *The psychology of the language learner: Individual differences in second language acquisition*. Mahwah, NJ: Routledge.

Gardner, R. C., & Lambert, W. E. (1972). *Attitudes and motivation in second language learning*. Rowley, MA: Newbury House.

Grey, S., Williams, J. N., & Rebuschat, P. (2015). Individual differences in incidental language learning: Phonological working memory, learning styles, and personality. *Learning and Individual Differences, 38*, 44–53.

Krashen, S. (1981). *Second language acquisition and second language learning*. Oxford, UK: Pergamon Press.

Kupisch, T., Barton, D., Hailer, K., Stangen, I., Lein, T., & van de Weijer, J. (2014). Foreign accent in adult simultaneous bilinguals. *Heritage Language Journal, 11*(2), 123–150.

Lennenberg, E. (1967). *Biological foundations of language*. New York, NY: John Wiley & Sons.

Maslow, A. (1970). *Motivation and personality* (2nd ed.). New York, NY: Harper & Row.

Moskovsky, C., Alrabai, F., Paolini, S., & Ratcheva, S. (2013). The effects of teachers' motivational strategies on learners' motivation: A controlled investigation of second language acquisition: The effects of teachers' motivational strategies. *Language Learning, 63*(1), 34–62. doi:10.1111/j.1467-9922.2012.00717.x

Ockey, G. (2011). Self-consciousness and assertiveness as explanatory variables of L2 oral ability: A latent variable approach. *Language Learning, 61*(3), 968–989. doi:10.1111/j.1467-9922.2010.00625.x

Pourkalhor, O., & Esfandiari, N. (2017). Culture in language learning: Background, issues and implications. *Language, 5*(1), 23–32.

Schumann, J. (1978). Social and psychological factors in second language acquisition. In J. Richards (Ed.), *Understanding second and foreign language learning: Issues and approaches*. Rowley, MA: Newbury House.

Williams, M., Mercer, S., & Ryan, S. (2016). *Exploring psychology in language learning and teaching*. Oxford, UK: Oxford University Press.

Zafar, S., & Meenakshi, K. (2012). A study on the relationship between extroversion–introversion and risk-taking in the context of second language acquisition. *International Journal of Research Studies in Language Learning, 1*(1), 33–40. doi:10.5861/ijrsll.2012. v1i1.42

Zen, E. L., & Apriana, A. (2015). Contributing factors toward first and second language acquisition: A manifestation of Krashen's affective filter hypothesis. *Engaging Linguistics and Literature: Perspectives and Insights Beyond the Curriculum*, 256–264.

CHAPTER

Seventeen

First and Second Language Acquisition Theories and Models

LEARNING OBJECTIVES

Readers will be able to

- ❖ Name and describe the theoretical perspectives of language acquisition
- ❖ List the stages when a child develops his or her own system of grammar
- ❖ List and recognize the theories of Krashen's Monitor Model
- ❖ Distinguish the differences between social language and academic language and how they relate to Cummins' theories of second language acquisition
- ❖ Recognize the stages of McLaughlin's model of language processing: controlled and automatic
- ❖ Recognize Bialystok's model of language processing: implicit versus explicit knowledge
- ❖ Apply Bialystok's and McLaughlin's models: focal versus peripheral levels
- ❖ Recognize stages of interlanguage within Selinker's Interlanguage Theory

Kayla: *I can't believe your sweet little Ginger is already talking! How old is she? What were her first words?*

Consuela: *She's 18 months. Her first words took me by surprise. She said "Mo," the nickname we gave to the lost and hungry little puppy we found under the bridge near our house. 10 months later, she was saying "Mo, go cookie."*

Having read the previous scenario, can you explain how children, who have no knowledge of language at birth, acquire language?

FIRST LANGUAGE ACQUISITION THEORIES

We have already established that language involves a complex and rule-governed system that humans use to communicate. How, then, do children, who at birth have no knowledge of language, suddenly develop the ability to use sounds, morphology, and syntactic and lexical rules to produce sentences they may never have heard before by the time they turn 5? Do children simply imitate what they hear from adults and other children around them? Or do they actually seek out patterns, hypothesize, and test rules of the language they hear around them? Do children pick up their first language through intensive teaching? These are the fundamental questions that a theory of first language acquisition attempts to answer. The following section will discuss several theoretical perspectives on language acquisition.

Behaviorism

A major influence on the behaviorist perspective originally came from B.F. Skinner (1957) and later Pena-Correall and Robayo-Castro (2007), who argued that language learning is a culturally determined and learned behavior. Behaviorist proponents claimed that learners learn by undergoing training and practice through a series of stimulus and response chains and operant conditioning, all reinforcers that motivate the formation of a language habit. In other words, a person's utterance becomes a stimulus which, in turn, will initiate a response. This response will then act as a stimulus and the cycle continues. Language learning, like learning how to walk, requires effort and training. Behaviorists also claimed that learning how to write is not universal across cultures because some cultures do not have a history of written or scripted language. Learning how to write, then, involves a conscious effort and specific training, as well as culturally based knowledge and a willingness to learn by trial and error. Thus, this perspective emphasized the importance of *environmental factors* which shape what the learner will eventually know and learn.

However, this perspective fails to account for how children can produce novel utterances they have never heard before (such as, "I hate you, Mommy.") It also fails to explain instances of regression evident when children are developing their own system of grammar. The fact that children may initially be able to orally produce the word [top] for *stop*, later regress to [stop] and eventually sound more adult-like, is evidence of language regression, a natural phenomenon in the acquisition process. In addition, children are sometimes impervious to adult error correction at various levels, indicating that they do more than simply imitate and repeat adults' utterances.

Nativist Perspective

Unlike the behaviorist view, the nativist believes that language learning is biologically determined. In other words, each person is endowed with an innate ability to learn language. Linguist Noam Chomsky, a major influence on this paradigm, refers to our basic innate language learning capacities as the Language Acquisition Device (LAD) (Chomsky, 2000). This LAD contains general knowledge about the basic properties common to all languages, including phonology and phonological rules, distinctive features, and so forth. Since human beings are already born with this "grammar" in place, less emphasis is given to how environment affects the acquisition process. This view asserts that environment only serves to trigger the LAD, which determines what children will acquire, such as the precise language, for example, Spanish, Swahili or Sepedi, she will learn.

Nativists also contend that children actively construct grammar for themselves by actively listening to the language around them and trying to determine the patterns in the utterances. For example, a child's initial hypothesis on how to form past tense verbs is to add /-ed/ to all verbs, thus producing forms such as *wented*, *holded*, and *eated*. When they discover that the rule no longer matches the adult form, they will modify or add another rule which will eventually match the adult form. It is for this reason that the nativist perspective is sometimes referred to as the mentalist view.

Another compelling reason for the innate theory is the effect that error correction has on children. As we saw in the first scenario in Chapter 15, a child progresses through language in predictable stages. The child will not respond to error correction if the child is not developmentally ready. Similarly, the child acquires much of his or her language ability before coming to school, thereby supporting the innate structures argument.

Even though nativists and behaviorists differ fundamentally on how much language is innate, they agree that some innate structures are necessary at the initial stages of learning. While the nativist perspective credits children as active learners and recognizes the complexities of the acquisition process, it fails to account for the fact that adults and caregivers do provide children with negative feedback or correction on their production. Several studies have documented that adults correct their children's utterances covertly (Ambridge, 2013), as the following example suggests:

Teacher: *What did you see, Maria?*
Maria: *I see baby ducks.*
Teacher: *At the park? You saw baby ducks at the park? How wonderful!*

The theory that children simply figure out the rules on their own may lack sufficient support. In addition, recent neurological findings have revealed the importance of mental stimulation through social interaction in stimulating proper brain development, which strengthens other pathways for learning in young children (Leisman, Mualem, & Mughrabi, 2015). Children who are not given adequate mental stimulation and opportunities for interaction with adults and peers before puberty may "wire their brains" differently than their counterparts who have rich socialization experiences.

Social Interactionist

Social interactionists believe that human language emerged from the social role that language plays in human interaction. Like behaviorists, they believe that environment plays a key role and those adults in the child's linguistic environment are instrumental in language acquisition. However, there is a fundamental difference in how the behaviorists and social interactionists view that process. While the behaviorists view learners as empty vessels into which information must be poured, the social interactionists view learners as participants who are actively negotiating meaning with those with whom they interact.

Speech between a mother and child or between a native and non-native speaker reveals conversational strategies that focus on the meaningful and intentional use of language, all of which foster language acquisition in young children. One influential advocate of this perspective was the Soviet psychologist Lev Vygotsky (1978). He believed that learners bring two levels of development to their learning: an actual developmental level and a potential developmental level. These two levels are referred to as the *Zone of Proximal Development*. Through social interaction, adults and peers can assist learners to move from their zone of actual development to the zone of potential development, by using simplified language, choosing topics that are concrete in the learner's immediate environment, and providing elaboration and clarification so that learners can understand input provided to them (Wertsch, 2008).

Figure 17.1 summarizes the basic similarities and differences between the behaviorist, nativist, and social interactionist perspectives.

Brain-Based Principles

Studies have revealed that the human brain is made up of thousands of nerve cells or neurons that form a communication network in the brain. These connections in the brain enable us to process and interpret different kinds of information from many different stimuli, including visual, tactile, oral, auditory, and olfactory (smell). The human brain also has areas that specialize in different cognitive functions. The left brain hemisphere is responsible for analytical reasoning, temporal ordering, and arithmetic and language processing, whereas the right brain hemisphere is in charge of processing nonlinguistic sounds, including music and information requiring visual and spatial skills.

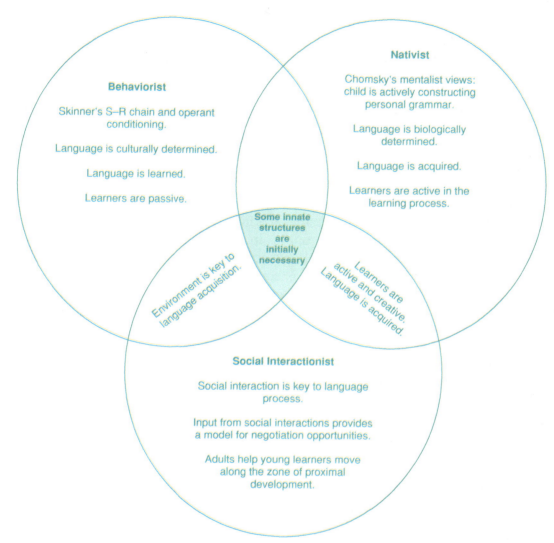

Figure 17.1: Venn Diagram That Summarizes the Salient Characteristics of the Three Language Theories

Scientists have also found that the specialization of cognitive functions in the brain can be reversed at an early age if there is injury to one part of the brain. For example, if a young child suffers an injury to the part of the brain responsible for language processing, the right brain hemisphere can develop that function to compensate for the loss in the left hemisphere. However, individuals who have completed the "hard wiring," or specialization of functions, in the brain cannot reverse the functions, regardless of the severity of the brain damage.

Recent discoveries about the brain reveal a profound insight about new windows of opportunity. While important discoveries are being made about the brain as we write, there are sufficient insights about the brain available today to benefit teachers in their efforts to enhance classroom instruction. A study conducted by neuroscientists Joy Hirsch and Karl

Kim at the Memorial Sloan-Kettering Cancer Center in New York shed light on how children and adults use different parts of their brains when learning a second language (Hirsch, Moreno, & Smith, 2001). Using an MRI scanner, brain scans of individuals learning a second language during their adult life and their childhood years, were taken as they thought aloud about what they had done the day before—first in their first language and then in the second language. Results showed that those who were learning a second language as adults used a distinct region of the brain (Broca's area) for their first language, which is the region of the learning process center of the brain that manages speech production. Those who were learning a second language as children made use of the same area to produce speech. Both groups, however, showed similarities in their use of Wernicke's area, the region in the brain that is the language processing zone for understanding and interpreting information.

Hirsch explains that the difference between adults and children can be attributed to the way the brain is hard wired. In the bilingual brain, those who learn another language when they are young may intertwine sounds and structures from all languages into the same area (Hernandez, 2013). Once this hard wiring is complete, new sounds and structures must be processed by a different area of the brain. Researchers also agree that these differences might be caused by the differences in the way young children learn another language as compared to adults.

Findings from brain studies also provide useful information for how teachers can enhance learning by improving their delivery of instruction, by improving student's levels of motivation and active participation, and by eliminating potential barriers to learning. Above all, they underscore the fact that all students have the ability to learn. Caine and Caine (1997, 1991) list several major principles of brain-based knowledge and their applications for language teaching, which are summarized in Table 17.1 (Lombardi, 2008).

PARALLEL DISTRIBUTED PROCESSING (PDP)

Over the past several decades, cognitive scientists have compared the human brain's information processing capabilities to those of a computer. Earlier computer metaphors of the brain presuppose that information is taken in, processed in a single central processor in the working memory, and then stored in the long-term memory for future retrieval. This model of a computer-like human brain also assumes that the brain processes information in a sequential or serial manner. However, a group of cognitivists (McClelland, Rumelhart, & Hinton, 1986; Rogers & McLleland, 2014) has proposed that the human brain is capable of processing many kinds of "messy" cognitive tasks on a daily basis and hence developed a model called parallel distributed processing (PDP), a processing system which is similar to the workings of the brain.

In the PDP model, the processing units are compared to the connections between neurons in the brain. When stimulated by the environment, the connections between neurons will be activated, forming a web of association. The PDP proponents reason that humans are far better than computers when considering many pieces of information simultaneously. They contend that processing occurs in parallel forms and proceeds simultaneously along many different dimensions. For example, the reading process does not move from simple decoding to holistic processing for comprehension. Instead, the processes move at many different levels simultaneously. As we read, we also attend to the lines, curves, and angles in letters, the meaning of words, the syntactic structures, our knowledge of the content, our reading purpose, and our attempt to integrate the meanings of new words with the constructed meaning in our memory. In other words, top-down (holistic), bottom-up (decoding), and a combination of top-down and bottom-up processing can occur in chorus in a single act of reading. While little is known about whether the PDP model will be the "wave of the future" in the cognitive sciences, its strong resemblance to certain aspects of human cognition may offer insights into human learning. Refer to Table 17.1 for the principle of brain-based principles of language acquisition and their pedagogical implications for teachers.

Table 17.1: Brain-Based Principles and Their Pedagogical Implications

Principle	Pedagogical Implications
1. The brain is a complex adaptive system. It can simultaneously process many pieces of information.	Instruction that provides a variety of experiences and uses different methods and approaches can activate many different aspects of the brain, thereby increasing learning potential.
2. The brain is a social brain. Learning is influenced by the levels of social interaction with others.	Instruction should include cooperative techniques that encourage student–student interaction and provide opportunities for learners to take more control, work more democratically and cooperatively, and become independent thinkers and explorers.
3. The search for meaning is innate.	Activities and materials presented in a meaningful, relevant, and interesting manner allow students to make the emotional connection which enhances long-term memory. Learning is also enhanced by familiarity with routines and schemes already present in the learners.
4. The brain searches for and generates patterns on any incoming messages.	Instruction that is fun and contains an emotional "hook" will allow the brain to search and create meaning more so than activities that require learners to react passively.
5. Emotions are crucial to memory.	Instruction should not make learners feel physically or emotionally threatened. It should support and validate the abilities, talents, and backgrounds of learners.
6. The brain processes parts and wholes simultaneously.	Language structures and vocabulary are best learned when they are embedded in meaningful contexts of problem-solving and activities using natural language.

(Continued)

Table 17.1: Brain-Based Principles and Their Pedagogical Implications (*Continued*)

Principle	Pedagogical Implications
7. Learning involves both peripheral and focused attention.	Music, art, and other kinds of rich environmental stimuli can support natural language acquisition. Teachers' enthusiasm, acceptance, and sensitivity to learner needs can also send subtle signals that support learner growth.
8. Learning involves both conscious and subconscious processes.	Instruction must allow learners to experience and do something with language, as well as to review what they have learned so that they can reflect, take charge, and negotiate personal meanings.
9. There are at least two types of memory: spatial and rote learning systems. The spatial system is analogous to episodic memory, which stores personal, autobiographical experiences in long-term memory. The rote learning system is akin to memorization of discrete, unrelated bits of information and is motivated by rewards.	Instruction must involve novel experiences that tap into the spatial system and not focus on memorizing language structures. Structures must be contextually introduced through demonstrations, drama, pantomimes, story reading, retelling activities, etc.
10. Learning is enhanced by challenging and stimulating instruction. High levels of stress and anxiety may inhibit learning.	Teachers must create a low anxiety classroom by praising learners for their accomplishments and by utilizing learners' values, knowledge, and background experiences to further learning. They must also maintain reasonably high expectations of their students. Introducing sensory activities can help students tap into their physical abilities as well as their intellectual strengths and can raise the comfort levels of students.
11. Each brain is unique. Different environments and experiences give individuals their own unique characteristics.	Instruction must include all learners' learning styles and encourage expression of understanding through all senses.

SECOND LANGUAGE ACQUISITION THEORIES AND MODELS

So far you have read about the factors and conditions that influence first language acquisition. Do you think that these theories can adequately explain the second language acquisition process? Consider these questions: Why do children acquire second language oral fluency better than adults? Do children learning their first language and children learning their second language go through the same acquisition process? Are the circumstances surrounding children and adults learning a second language the same? Even though first language acquisition theories may also apply to the second language acquisition process, they may not be able to fully capture the complexity of a second language acquisition process. First language acquisition theories are not sufficiently equipped to explain the degrees of levels of success that second language learners achieve. The following section offers other models and theories that examine factors and circumstances which can influence second language acquisition.

Krashen's Monitor Model

One of the leading scholars of second language acquisition theory is Stephen Krashen. In his Monitor Model, Krashen outlines five hypotheses related to second language acquisition: (a) Acquisition versus Learning Hypothesis, (b) The Natural Order Hypothesis, (c) The Monitor Hypothesis, (d) The Input Hypothesis, and (e) The Affective Filter Hypothesis. There are many implications for the classroom that can be drawn from Krashen's Monitor Model. For instance, Krashen uses the metaphor of a filter that facilitates or hinders learning. When students are placed in a safe, secure, and caring environment that challenges them to learn, the affective filter will be lowered and, according to Krashen, learning will take place. But when the learning environment is threatening, full of anxiety, and is not challenging enough, the affective filter will be raised and learning will be blocked. Refer Table 17.2 for explanations and applications of Krashen's Monitor Model (Krashen, 1981).

Essentially, Krashen hypothesizes that languages are acquired (a more Natural Approach than "learning," which takes place with direct attention to the forms and functions of language) when students have reduced anxiety or a lower "affective filter" during the process, are provided language input at a supported level slightly beyond what they can achieve alone ("comprehensible input"), and monitor their production. One of the cornerstones of Krashen's theory that frequently guides teachers' instructional decision-making with English learner (EL) students is ensuring that there is language input that is comprehensible for their students and that the level of support is appropriate for reaching the next stage of language proficiency.

Cummins' Second Language Framework

Jim Cummins (1981, 2016), among others (Bunch, 2010; Greenfader & Brouillette, 2017) makes a distinction between social language and academic language. *Social language*

Table 17.2: Krashen's Monitor Model

Hypotheses	Applications
The Affective Filter	
Emotional variables such as anxiety, motivation, and self-confidence play a part in language acquisition.	A safe and secure environment Cooperative learning, mutual respect, and high expectations.
The Input Hypothesis	
Language is acquired when learners understand messages (comprehensible input). They must be exposed to messages slightly beyond their level of proficiency, i.e., i +1.	Teachers should provide comprehensible input in many forms, e.g., use of visuals, less complex structures, paraphrases, slower and more enunciated speech. For example, students understand messages with "unacquired" grammar with the help of context.
The Monitor	
An error-detecting mechanism that is responsible for accuracy. It is an editor that confirms or repairs student utterances. There are three types: optimal, overusers, and underusers. Overusers refer to conscious grammar all the time. Underusers do not refer to their conscious grammar at all, and optimal users monitor when to focus on form.	Students may not internalize teachers' explicit corrections because of their developing grammatical system. Therefore, a teacher's modeling of correct sentences provides a rich input for students to use later in developing and monitoring accuracy in speech and writing. In addition, students should be given time to detect and self-correct their errors. Hence, teachers should focus more on correcting students' errors in writing by giving ample time for students to review their written productions and maximize their use of the monitor for error correction.
The Natural Order Hypothesis	
Certain rules within a language are acquired before others. Correct usage of grammatical structures is acquired gradually by children acquiring their first and/or second language.	Grammatical structures need not be the center of curriculum organization. Problem-solving structures will promote acquiring of rules.
Acquisition vs. Learning	
Learning = formal knowledge of a language (rules). Acquisition = language acquired at the subconscious level (child's acquiring his first language).	Communicating meaning is more important than drill and practice. Learners are given time to internalize language before they respond. Partial and incomplete utterances are acceptable.

refers to everyday conversational language which is context embedded—supported by the use of illustrations, realia, demonstrations, and so forth. Studies have shown that second language learners acquire social language in approximately 2 years and academic language in 5–7 years. Since social language deals with the here-and-now language, second language speakers tend to acquire it faster than they acquire *academic language*, the language of school tasks which is often more abstract and decontextualized. Communication involving academic language may be more difficult because it is context-reduced (little or no context clues).

Teachers may find it puzzling that ELs who maintain fluent spoken English have difficulties in reading and writing. This can be explained by Cummins' second language framework that differentiated students' social language and academic language. Refer to Cummins' four quadrants for appropriate tasks and strategies to help ELs at varying proficiency levels move from social language (Quadrant A) to academic language (Quadrant D) (Figure 17.2). In Figure 17.2, several examples of specific strategies at different stages of language proficiency are listed. In Quadrant A, strategies such as developing survival vocabulary and following demonstrated directions are cognitively undemanding (easy) and

Cognitively Undemanding (Easy)	
A Developing survival vocabulary Following demonstrated directions Playing simple games Engaging in face-to-face interactions Participating in art, music, and physical education	**C** Engaging in telephone conversations Reading and writing for personal purposes: notes, lists, sketches, etc.
B Participating in hands-on science and mathematics activities Making maps, models, charts, and graphs Solving math computational problems Making brief oral presentations Understanding academic presentations through the use of visuals, demonstrations, active participation, realia, etc. Understanding written texts through discussion, illustrations, and visuals Writing academic reports with the aid of outlines, structures, etc.	**D** Understanding academic presentations without visuals or demonstrations: lectures Making formal oral presentations Solving math word problems without illustrations Writing compositions, essays, and research reports in content areas Reading for information in content areas Taking standardized achievement texts
Cognitively Demanding (Hard)	

Context-Embedded (Clues) — left axis; *Context-Reduced (No Clues)* — right axis

Figure 17.2: Language and Content Activities within Cummins' Quadrants

Source: Adapted from Chamot and O'Malley (1986), Cummins (1981), and Mohammadipour and Rashid (2015).

contain high contextual clues. These activities are best employed when teaching second language learners who are at the preproduction or early production stage of language acquisition. As these learners become more proficient in the target language, teachers can gradually increase the degree of task difficulty, and activities from Cummins' Quadrants B and C can be used. Activities in Quadrant D, such as understanding academic presentations without visuals or demonstrations, lectures, and making formal oral presentations, are examples of cognitively demanding tasks that are context-reduced; that is, they offer few or no clues. These types of tasks are meant for high intermediate and advanced second language learners.

Cummins also argues for the significance of *common underlying proficiency* (CUP) in second language learning as opposed to *separate underlying proficiency* (SUP). CUP refers to the underlying language system in which bilingual students' languages interact and whereby language transfer takes place (see Chapter 14). SUP assumes that languages are separate in the brain, and content and skills learned in the primary language will not transfer to the target language. Again, Cummins' theory of CUP implies that knowledge and literacy skills in a student's native language will transfer to his or her learning of a target language (Cummins & Swain, 2014). In other words, children learning to read and write Mandarin Chinese develop concepts about print and the role of literacy that make learning to read and write English easier, even though Mandarin Chinese and English do not share a similar writing system. Cummins strongly asserts that once children build a strong foundation in the native language, learning a second language, as well as learning in general, readily builds upon this foundation. Bilingual education is based on these assumptions about learning.

McLaughlin's Attention-Processing Model

McLaughlin (1980), Bialystok (1978), and Moghaddam and Araghi (2013), proponents of cognitivist theory in the second language acquisition field, have criticized Krashen for his "simplistic account" of conscious versus subconscious processes in the acquisition versus learning hypothesis. McLaughlin and Bialystok argue that for knowledge to be stored in the long-term memory, learners have to be aware of this knowledge; this idea conflicts with Krashen's notion that acquisition takes place in the subconscious mode and learning takes place in the conscious mode. Following McLaughlin's argument, learners who "acquire" as opposed to "learn" a second language must have a certain level of awareness, that is, operate at a conscious level; it cannot all be subconscious.

In their model of the second language learning process, McLaughlin and colleagues prefer the terms controlled and automatic processing mechanisms to Krashen's acquisition versus learning distinction. McLaughlin defines the controlled processing mechanism as a limited and temporary capacity, while the automatic processing mechanism is referred to as "relatively permanent" processes (McLaughlin, Rossman, & McLeod, 1983, p. 142; Neuner, 2002). An example of controlled processing is the learning of a new skill, such as soccer. When one first learns to play soccer, one can deal only with the basic elements of kicking the ball, passing the ball to another player, or defending the ball from being taken away by the opponent. Everything else about the game is far too complicated for the beginner's limited capacity.

Meanwhile, automatic processing, according to McLaughlin, is similar to what expert learners do. The expert learner can manage many types of information simultaneously because certain subskills have become automatic. However, learners with limited linguistic capacity may not be able to juggle as much linguistic information simultaneously. Learners who have developed expert skills are able to manage processing of a more "accomplished" skill where the hard drive of their brain can manage hundreds and thousands of bits of information simultaneously. For example, language-proficient learners may do several things at once while understanding and sending verbal messages in a conversation. They pay attention to selective words and try to find a match between the sounds they hear and the words in their mental lexicon; they pick up intonation cues to interpret messages, and assess a speaker's purpose, body language, and setting to fill in gaps in understanding; finally they apply appropriate discourse rules based on their knowledge of the setting in giving their responses. Because proficient language users have a more developed grammar and vocabulary system, they are able to attend to other aspects of the communication system that less proficient language learners are not. McLaughlin and others also maintain that these two types of processing skills may utilize peripheral attention (similar to inductive learning) and focal attention (similar to deductive learning).

Their view of controlled and automatic processing has several implications for the second language classroom. One implication can be demonstrated by how a child acquires language. Children generally do not pay attention to the learning of forms or grammatical rules; instead, their focus is on communication of meaning. For instance, in kindergarten and lower grade classrooms, children are exposed to a rich print environment and contextually embedded language that encourage children to internalize language naturally.

Another implication of McLaughlin's model can be seen in how adults learn a second language. Unlike young children, older second language learners may be able to articulate rules and analyze language but may not be able to transfer this knowledge to communicative situations that require the use of such knowledge. Language instruction for older children and adults tends to emphasize learning of rules and vocabulary pertinent to their program of study. This is normally expected, because older learners are cognitively more mature and have the learning experience to analyze and understand rules. As such, they may be more receptive than children to classrooms that focus on rule learning, an unnatural context for language learning. Newer proponents in the second language field maintain that language can be acquired without explicit focus on forms. They stress that language can be internalized if learners are exposed to meaningful and authentic language through engaging learner-oriented activities appropriate to the students' language developmental process. In other words, communication should be the goal of any language instruction.

Bialystok's Analysis/Automaticity Model

Bialystok's model of second language learning is similar in many ways to McLaughlin's in that they both emphasize the importance of introducing authentic and contextually embedded language through meaningful activities. But Bialystok's model goes further in accounting for how automatic processing is accomplished by second language learners.

Bialystok (1978) maintains that language processing involves the use of both explicit and implicit knowledge. Explicit knowledge refers to a person's knowledge about a language and their ability to articulate that knowledge. Implicit knowledge refers to information that is automatically and spontaneously used in language tasks. According to Bialystok, the distinction between automatic and spontaneous processing refers to the relative access the learner has to both of these forms of knowledge. This access hinges on the learner's control, defined as "the ability to intentionally focus attention on relevant parts of a problem to arrive at a solution" (Bialystok & Mitterer, 1987, p. 148; Terry, 2014). An example of how control affects language processing is demonstrated by the performance of native and highly proficient non-native speakers. Whether native speakers can or cannot provide an analysis of their explicit knowledge of their L1 grammar, all native speakers can automatically and spontaneously process and produce utterances in their L1. On the other hand, non-native speakers may be able to analyze and explain L2 grammar, but may go through a time delay in the production of L2 because they are less experienced with their second language than L1 speakers are with their first language.

In other words, second language learners need more time to process linguistic input because they have to move back and forth between explicit and implicit knowledge of the language in interpreting linguistic messages. This insight underscores the need for teachers to be patient with second language learners, giving them ample time to process verbal messages—especially those communicated orally. Teachers also need to include a variety of elicitation techniques appropriate for learners at different stages of linguistic proficiency. These include dialogue journals or reading response logs, in addition to asking students to respond orally in class.

What practical applications for the second language classroom can be drawn from McLaughlin's and Bialystok's models? Both McLaughlin and Bialystok suggest that the ultimate goal of using language is to communicate, and therefore, second language learning should focus more on meaning and not on form. While second language learners should be introduced to graded complexity of language structures, explicit teaching of forms should be done at a peripheral level. Once learners become engaged in activities that encourage them to use language in a purposeful and meaningful way, they will eventually learn the forms of the language (see Table 17.3).

It appears that McLaughlin and Bialystok see parallels between controlled/focal attention and Krashen's conscious learning of a language, in addition to similarities between peripheral/automatic cell processing and Krashen's acquisition route, a subconscious process of language acquisition.

Table 17.3: Practical Applications of McLaughlin's and Bialystok's Models

	Controlled	Automatic
	new knowledge; limited capacity	well trained, capacity is practically unlimited
Focal intentional attention	grammatical explanation word definition copy a written model "memorizing" a dialogue prefabricated patterns	scanning, editing, peer-editing advanced L2 learner focuses on models, clause formation, etc.
Peripheral incidental attention	simple greetings total physical response (TPR)/ Natural Approach new L2 learner fully completes a brief conversation	open-ended group work rapid reading, skimmingfree writes normal conversational exchanges of some length

Source: Brown (1994, p. 285).

SELINKER'S INTERLANGUAGE THEORY

Selinker's (1972) interlanguage theory maintains the separateness of a second language learner's system and gives the system a structurally intermediate status between the native and target languages. According to Selinker, second language learners are producing their own self-contained linguistic system. The system is not a native language system, nor the target language system, rather it falls between the two. It is the best system that the second language learner possesses to provide order and structure to linguistic stimuli (see Figure 17.3).

COMMON PROBLEMS OF LEARNERS OF ENGLISH

In second language acquisition, it is expected that second language learners will produce an interim language between their first and second language which is referred to as the *interlanguage* (Selinker, 1972). This interlanguage system causes second language learners to produce "errors" that may be attributed to interference from the mother tongue or difficulties of learning complex English structures. As we described earlier, these are typical developmental processes and stages of second language acquisition, and teachers are advised to consider these as such. Transfer where there appears to be "interference" from the primary language, occur most commonly between two languages that have similar but not identical systems. For example, while Spanish and English have similar consonants, their vowels and sentence stress are very different, causing pronunciation difficulties for Spanish-speaking ELs. On the other hand, learners who speak languages that are not closely related to English, like Chinese or Arabic, may make fewer transfer

Figure 17.3: Stages of Interlanguage Development

mistakes. However, many of the processes in learning English may stem from the English structures that are sometimes less predictable and regular. To cope with these, second language learners may overgeneralize or simplify the rules of the target language, which consequently leads to an interlanguage in the target language. The following list gives more examples of common linguistic problems faced by ELs of different language backgrounds to help teachers recognize some of the language issues in English by speakers from different primary language backgrounds and the reasons for these issues (Swan & Smith, 2007).

EXAMPLES OF ENGLISH LANGUAGE DEVELOPMENT FACED BY ELs

I. Spanish speakers
   A. Pronunciation/Rhythm and Stress
   1. Syllable-timed language: Generally all syllables take about the same time to pronounce. Extra length may be used for emphasis.
   2. In contrast, stressed syllables in English carry a pitch change and are pronounced more distinctly than unstressed syllables pronounced with a neutral vowel /ə/ or /ɪ/.

3. Show no contrastive stress, causing difficulty in recognizing and producing contrastive stress in sentences such as *With sugar or without **sugar?*** (The last word is more heavily stressed by Spanish speakers, whereas heavier stress given to contrasting words ***with*** and ***without*** in English.

B. **Grammar**
  1. Word order: Indirect object must have a preposition, and direct and indirect objects can go in either order (*They send to Jenny the pictures* instead of *They send Jenny the pictures*).
  2. Adverbials or object complements regularly placed before a direct object:
     * *Mr. Martinez speaks very well English.*
     * *She took to the vet her dog.*
  3. Questions: Spanish speakers have difficulty with do/does/did:
     * *Did they went?*
     * *Do they went?*
     * *Do she goes?*
     * *Does she goes?*
  4. Plurals:
     * Mass nouns can take plural forms in Spanish, which give rise to *furnitures* and *informations*.
     * No irregular plurals in Spanish, so Spanish speakers tend to make mistakes such as *childs* and *childrens*.
  5. Articles: The definite article is used with mass nouns and plural nouns used in a general sense:
     * *The food is more important than art (vs. Food is more important than art.)*
     * *Do you like the chocolate cakes? (vs. Do you like chocolate cakes?)*

C. **Vocabulary**
  1. One word in Spanish expresses different meanings in English, for example:
     * *Gastar* = wear, wear out
     * *Tirar / botar* = throw, throw away
  2. Spanish speakers have difficulty with two or three part verb phrases like *put up, put away,* and *put off*, whose meanings cannot be deduced from the meanings of the parts.
  3. Spanish avoids ordinals, giving rise to *the five of June*.
  4. False cognates: Some words in Spanish and English have similar spellings and meanings (true cognates, like *examen* [exam] and *medalla* [medal]), but some words in English and Spanish have completely different use/meaning (false cognates). Examples of false cognates:
     * *Libreria* (bookshop)
     * *Propaganda* (advertising)
     * *Sensible* (sensitive)

D. **Orthography/Punctuation**
  1. Contractions: Spanish has no contracted verb forms, thus Spanish speakers have difficulty in hearing *I'll come* or *I'd come. I'll* and *I'd* may be construed as *I.*

2. Punctuation: Spanish uses a comma to separate decimals and a stop to separate thousands (8.000 = eight thousand; 8,25 = eight point two five).

II. French speakers

A. **Pronunciation/Rhythm and Stress**

1. French often uses grammatical constructions to mark contrast, whereas English uses stress to show contrast. For example:

    Question: Didn't you go to the grocer's? English: *No, I went to the **baker's.*** (Stress on the last word).

    French: *Non, c'est à la boulangerie que je suis allée.* (No, it's to the baker's that I went.)

2. Pronounce dark /l/ as /əl/, like *terri bùll* (for *terrible*) and *lit tùll* (for *little*). Stress is on the last syllable in multisyllabic words.

B. **Grammar**

1. Verbs: Difficulty in pronouncing the –*s* ending on third person singular present tense. The –*s* ending is written but not pronounced in French.

2. No equivalent of the English progressive. French speakers may use present tense to talk about actions that began in the past and continue into the present, like *I work in Paris since August for 6 months.*

3. French uses present tense instead of present progressive tense, like *Julie can't come to the phone now. She takes a bath.*

4. Since French doesn't have the progressive tense, it may express future time using the present tense, like *I eat with Christine this evening.*

5. Word order: An adverb often comes between the verb and the direct object, giving rise to incorrect sentences like
    - *I forget always (adverb) the way to his house.*
    - *He offers never (adverb) to help.*

C. **Vocabulary**

1. False cognates: While many French and English words are derived from the same roots, there are false cognates that can lead to miscomprehension. Examples of false cognates:
    - French *avis* = opinion, *not* advice
    - French *evident* = obvious, *not* evident
    - French *sympathique* = nice, easy to get along with, *not* sympathetic

2. Verb "take": French uses the equivalent of "take" where English would use "have," giving rise to errors like *Let's take a drink.*

D. **Orthography/Punctuation**

1. Days of the week, months, languages, and national adjectives are not capitalized in French.

2. Quotation marks are written as <</>> instead of '/' or "/".

3. Commas are used in French where they are not used in English, thus leading to mistakes like *Consonants that are doubled in writing, are usually pronounced like single consonants.*

III. **Arabic speakers**
   A. **Pronunciation/Rhythm and Stress**
      1. Arabic has only vowel sounds (three short, three long, and two diphthongs) and 32 consonants, whereas English has 22 vowel sounds and diphthongs and 24 consonants. The shaded phonemes in the diagrams below show vowels and consonants that are equivalent or near equivalent in Arabic, and so they may not present articulation difficulty for Arabic learners of English. The unshaded phonemes, however, may cause some problems.

Consonants

p	b	f	v	ɵ	ð	t	d
s	z	ʃ	ʒ	tʃ	dʒ	k	g
m	n	ɳ	l	r	j	w	h

Vowels

i:	I	e	æ	eɪ	aɪ	ɔɪ
a:	ɒ	ɔ:	ʊ	aʊ	əʊ	ɪə
u:	ʌ	ɜ:	ə	əa	ʊə	aɪə/aʊə

/eə/ as in *hair*
/ʊə/ as in *tour*
/ɪə/ as in *hear*
Source: Swan and Smith (2007).

      2. The most difficult English vowels and consonants for Arabic speakers:
         • / I / and /e/ are confused (*bit* for *bet*)
         • Diphthong /eI / is confused with /e/ *(red* for *raid*).
         • Arabic /h/ is unvoiced and pronounced with a harsh aspiration.
         • /v/ and /f/ are allophonic; they are pronounced as /f/, like *It is a fery nice college.*
      3. In some Arabic dialects (that do not have the /g/), /g/ and /k/ are often confused, leading to difficulties in pronouncing words like *goat/coat* or *bag/back*.
      4. Arabic has predictable and regular word stress, whereas English word stress is unpredictable and has meaning-altering effect. Thus Arabic speakers find English contrastive stress in *con' vict* (verb) and *c'onvict* (noun) difficult.
   B. **Grammar**
      1. Word order: In Arabic writing, a sentence begins with a verb followed by the subject. This can lead to mistakes such as *Decided the minister yesterday to visit the school.*

2. Questions and auxiliaries: Arabic has no equivalent of the "do" auxiliary. To indicate a question, a rising intonation is used in place of a question word, such as *You like coffee?*
3. In Arabic, the word *where?* is *wayn?* which is often confused with *when?*
4. Negatives: Arabic uses particles (*laa* or *maa*) before the verb to show negatives, so Arabic speakers may make mistakes in English like *He not play football.*
5. Arabic has no verb "to be" in present tense (am, is, are). Thus, these are often omitted (*The boy tall*).
6. In Arabic, the past progressive is formed by using the past tense of the verb followed by the present tense of the verb (e.g., *he was he eats = he was eating*).
7. The use of reported speech in Arabic tends to use the tense of the original speech and not the past tense form. Thus, Arabic speakers may say *He said he is* (for *was*) *going to Egypt.* The present tense form is preferred, because direct speech is more common than reported speech in Arabic.
8. No future tense in Arabic. A present tense form is used to refer to future.

C. **Vocabulary**
1. Adverbs of manner are often expressed in a phrase such as *with speed* (Arabic) = quickly and *in a dangerous way* (Arabic) = dangerously.
2. There are a few Arabic loan words in English such as *radar, algorithm, television, and helicopter*. However, Arabic speakers have to learn a vast pool of English words to be able to read and write in English.

D. **Orthography/Punctuation**
1. Arabic orthography reads from right to left. Only consonants and long vowels are written.
2. No upper and lower case distinction.
3. Arabic learners of English tend to misread letters with "mirror" shapes like *p* and *q, d* and *b.*
4. Arabic writing is phonetic, so the high irregular English spelling plus completely different alphabetic system make English writing highly challenging for Arabic-speaking ELs.

IV. Chinese speakers
A. **Pronunciation/Rhythm and Stress**
1. Chinese lacks initial consonant clusters, so Chinese speakers tend to insert a slight vowel between the consonants (*spoon = sipoon*).
2. Final consonant clusters are equally difficult. Chinese speakers tend to create an extra syllable or simplify the cluster by dropping the last consonant (dogs may be pronounced as /dɔgəz/ or /dɔg/.
3. Syllables are generally more pronounced in Chinese than in English. Thus, Chinese-speaking ELs may stress too many English syllables, and make weak syllables stronger.
4. Intonation changes in Chinese are used to distinguish homonyms (words with the same pronunciation), whereas English intonation signals change sentence meaning and thus may sound funny to Chinese speakers.

B. **Grammar**

1. Sentences in Chinese usually start with a "topicalized" subject or object that is detached from the rest of sentence, as in *That boy—I'm going to talk to him one of these days*. This sentence structure will not transfer well to English.

2. Chinese does not have inflections, so its verb forms are uninflected. Instead of conjugating verbs like we do in English, Chinese expresses the concept of time by means of adverbials, word order, and context. English tenses are often confusing and cause frequent errors such as:
   - I have seen her two days ago.
   - *I found that the room is empty.*
   - *My brother left home since nine o'clock.*

3. Chinese-speaking ELs find the use of English present tense to indicate future events very puzzling and may perceive present tense to mean "present time." Therefore, the following utterances in English are confusing to these learners:
   - *There is a movie tonight.*
   - *The play we just saw tells a tragic story.*

4. English relative structures are difficult for Chinese speakers, and so they tend to omit or add pronouns and have difficulty with using *whose*. Hence, mistakes like the following are often made:
   - *There are many people have that idea.* (*who* is omitted)
   - *That's the shop that I told you about it.* (*it* is not required)
   - *I know the man his bicycle is stolen.* (avoided using *whose* to show possession)

5. Chinese uses the same word order for questions and statements. Therefore, inversion in English interrogatives may be ignored, giving rise to mistakes such as:
   - *You and your family last summer visited where?*
   - *When she will be back?*
   - *What was called the movie?*

6. Noun modifiers in Chinese come before the noun they modify, so English postmodifiers may cause confusion and generate errors like the following:
   - *This is important something.*
   - *This is a very difficult to solve problem.*

C. **Vocabulary**

1. There are no equivalents for the English phrasal and prepositional verbs (such as *take off, take up, gave in,* or *gave up*) in the Chinese language. Because of this, Chinese speakers may say *Please continue with your work* instead of *Please get on with your work*. Sometimes, confusion with phrasal verbs can lead to errors in statements such as: *The plane takes up easily* (for *takes off*) or *They've worked forward this plan.* (for *worked out*).

2. Idiomatic expressions are difficult for Chinese speakers as well as for any other language learners. Three common Chinese greetings employ different expressions from those used in English greetings that sound odd to the English speaker when they are translated into English:
   - *Where are you going?*
   - *You have come.*

3. Other expressions frequently used by Chinese speakers which may confuse English speakers are:
   * *Did you play very happy?* (for *Did you have a good time?*)
   * *Don't be polite* (for *Make yourself at home.*)
   * *Please eat more.* (for *Would you like a little more?*)

D. **Orthography/Punctuation**
   1. Chinese is a logographic language written with characters known as hànzi. Each character represents a syllable, and many characters are made up of two or more characters, which help speakers to distinguish between many Chinese homonyms.
   2. Chinese learners find English spelling difficult because the letter-sound correspondence in English is quite unpredictable. Spelling errors may also arise from incorrect pronunciations (*anser* for *answer, docter* for *doctor*) or omission of syllables (*determing* for *determining*).

   Recent work in the field of second (multilingual) language acquisition emphasizes the importance of supporting, developing, and using students' multiple languages in schools, following a practice of *translanguaging* (García & Wei, 2013; Makalela, 2015). Translanguaging refers to the dynamic process of using a student's full linguistic repertoire as an integrated communication system for learning. The implications for translanguaging are numerous for teachers, who can provide resources for multilinguals in schools, such as texts, online materials, and grouping for language learning and support.

   In sum, first and second language acquisition occurs in developmental stages. Several key scholars have proposed theories related to how this process occurs and how knowledge of the first language supports and influences acquisition of the second (English). It is important for teachers to remember that EL students are bi- and multilingual, and the more support teachers can provide for the development of the first language(s), the more those skills and knowledge will transfer. Hence, ongoing first language development supports the development of English and additional languages.

POINTS TO REMEMBER

✔ Children's first language acquisition occurs in developmental stages. At the phonological level, sounds that are easier to produce will be acquired first. Grammatical morphemes and syntactic structures are acquired in a predictable order.

✔ Children do not simply imitate adults' speech or memorize rules or vocabulary. They develop their own internal system of grammar by testing the rules out themselves, applying them, and later modifying their grammar to match that of adults.

✔ Several main theories of language acquisition include behaviorist, nativist, and social interactionist. These theories differ in the ways the role of the internal language learning process and the role of the environment (practice, training, reinforcement).

✔ Brain-based theories stress that language learning is more than just a cognitive function. These highlight how factors such as affective filters, comprehensible input embedded in meaningful contexts, background experience, and learning approaches influence language acquisition.

✔ Krashen and Cummins offer frameworks and models for second language learning, including the Monitor Model, academic versus social language, and CUP and SUP.

✔ It is important for teachers to understand that second language learners who have good conversational skills (basic interpersonal communication skills [BICS]) may still have difficulties in performing their school-related tasks because of the specific academic language required to perform those tasks.

✔ Teachers can use activities within Cummins' four quadrants to advance students from the level of language proficiency they are in (e.g., for preproduction and early production, use activities such as developing survival vocabulary, playing simple games, and engaging in face-to-face interactions before asking students to write or orally present on topics containing complex concepts and language).

✔ Both McLaughlin's and Bialystok's models suggest that because the ultimate goal in using language is to communicate, learning, or acquiring a language should emphasize meaning instead of form.

✔ Selinker's Interlanguage Theory proposes that second language learners produce their own self-contained system that falls somewhere between the L1 and the L2 systems.

REFLECTION QUESTIONS AND DISCUSSION

1. a. Behaviorist proponents claim that children develop their grammar based on the language they hear spoken around them. Nativists and social interactionists say that this view is not entirely correct. What arguments do the nativists provide to explain what the child brings to the task of acquiring a language? What would the nativists and social interactionists disagree on?

   b. Discuss how brain-based theories support the claims made by the social interactionist perspectives?

2. Discuss how brain-based theories support the claims made by the social interactionists and the PDP proponents.

3. Forms such as *I going, I no go,* I wented, *my foots* are common examples of children's productions. How would the behaviorist, nativist, and social interactionist perspectives view these forms of language production?

4. Which of the following individuals would have the greatest chance of success in acquiring a language? Explain your reasons by drawing support from various theories of language acquisition.
   a. A 9-year-old child who is being raised by hearing impaired parents, and who has been isolated from other people, first learns language at age 9

   b. An English as a second language (ESL) learner who begins learning a second language at the age of 7

   c. An ESL learner who begins learning a second language at the age of 15

5. Select three brain-based principles and develop instructional activities that reflect each principle. Include suggestions that have not been mentioned in the text.

6. Read the following case study and do the following tasks: (a) Identify Krashen's hypotheses that are reflected in the case study and (b) Which of Krashen's hypotheses in the Monitor Model are not addressed by the teacher in the case study? (c) What other classroom applications can the teacher use to reflect (b)?

The bland exterior of the portable building would not invite a second glance, but opening the door reveals an explosion of colors, stimulating materials, and a roomful of smiles. This is Mrs. Mitchell's self-contained EL classroom at Indian Groves Elementary School. Mrs. Mitchell's EL program schedules different grade levels of EL students, for daily 1-hour classes, focusing on language arts, spelling, and writing.

Mrs. Mitchell starts her lesson by allowing the children to chat with each other as the day's materials are distributed. She asks students about their weekends and other short, personal, welcoming interjections. Then the children are asked to sit on the reading carpet. She is about to read them a book called "The Cloud Book." Before reading the book, Mrs. Mitchell asks the children, "How many of you have looked up in the sky and seen clouds made of different shapes?" As she asks the question, she points to the picture of the clouds. Several students raise their hands and tell about clouds they have seen. Mrs. Mitchell then tells her students that they are going to learn the names of the clouds. As Mrs. Mitchell reads the book, she uses hand gestures when referring to "sky," "clouds," "low to the ground," "flat," and other words in the story. The actual names of the clouds are repeated by Mrs. Mitchell four times to ensure the students understand. After she finishes reading the book, Mrs. Mitchell writes the names of the clouds on the board for students to copy. The children draw and write the names of the clouds in their own journal. The teacher also shows the children an example of the completed project so they are clear on what they are to do. While the students are doing the project, Mrs. Mitchell circulates, gives encouragement to them, and helps certain students remember what the different clouds looked like.

ACTIVITIES

1. Identify a bi- or multilingual person in your community. Conduct an informal "interview" with this person and ask about his or her experiences learning a second language? What aspects of the process emerge and how do they relate to behaviorism, nativism, and/or social interactionism? Was that person able to acquire academic language and academic literacy in the second (or additional language)?

2. Observe a classroom for one full class period. How is language used? What kinds of language do you notice? Can you identify examples of social language? Academic language?

WEB RESOURCES

B. F. Skinner—Focus on Verbal Behavior (1988). https://www.youtube.com/watch?v=-Iz6uOkk_Kk

Bilingualism Good for the Brain, Researchers Say. http://www.latimes.com/health/la-he-bilingual-brain-20110227-story.html

CALLA—Cognitive Academic Language Learning Approach. https://www.youtube.com/watch?v=BFtOu87ZLVM

Distinct Cortical Areas Associated with Native and Second Languages. https://www.prezi.com/a_6shudeuf8q/distinct-cortical-areas-associated-with-native-and-second-la

Learning a Second Language at Any Age May Slow the Brain's Decline. http://www.latimes.com/science/sciencenow/la-sci-sn-bilingual-language-speaker-cognitive-decline-20140602-story.html

Parallel Distributed Processing (PDP). https://www.youtube.com/watch?v=MjubRN6yL_g

PECS and Skinner's Verbal Behavior. https://www.youtube.com/watch?v=5JHI4caDrQU

Vygotsky Sociocultural Development Individuals and Society. https://www.youtube.com/watch?v=-p_-0n2f35o

REFERENCES

Ambridge, B. (2013). How do children restrict their linguistic generalizations? An (un) grammaticality judgment study. *Cognitive Science, 37*(3), 508–543. doi:10.1111/cogs.12018

Bialystok, E. (1978). A theoretical model of second language learning. *Language Learning, 28*, 69–84.

Bialystok, E., & Mitterer, J. (1987). Metalinguistic differences among three kinds of readers. *Journal of Educational Psychology, 79*(2), 147–153. doi:10.1037/0022-0663.79.2.147

Brown, D. (1994). *Principles of language learning and teaching*. Upper Saddle River, NJ: Prentice Hall.

Bunch, G. C. (2010). Preparing mainstream secondary content-area teachers to facilitate English language learners' development of academic language. *Yearbook of the National Society for the Study of Education, 109*(2), 351–383.

Caine, G., & Caine, R. (1991). *Making connections: Teaching and the human brain*. Alexandria, VA: Association of Supervision and Curriculum Development.

Caine, G., & Caine, R. (1997). *Mind/brain learning principles*. Retrieved from http://www.newhorizons.orgofc_21clicaine.html

Chamot, A. U., & O'Malley, J. M. (1986). *A cognitive academic language learning approach: An ESL content-based curriculum*. Washington, DC: National Clearinghouse for Bilingual Education.

Chomsky, N. (2000). Linguistics and brain science. In A. Marantz, Y. Miyashita, & W. O'Neil (Eds.), *Image, language, brain: Papers from the first mind articulation project symposium* (pp. 13–28). Cambridge, MA: The MIT Press.

Cummins, J. (1981). The role of primary language development in promoting educational success for language minority students. In California State Department of Education (Ed.), *Schooling and language minority students: A theoretical framework*. Los Angeles, CA: Evaluation, Dissemination and Assessment Center, California State University.

Cummins, J. (2016). Reflections on Cummins (1980), "The cross-lingual dimensions of language proficiency: Implications for bilingual education and the optimal age issue." *TESOL Quarterly, 50*(4), 940–944.

Cummins, J., & Swain, M. (2014). *Bilingualism in education: Aspects of theory, research and practice*. New York, NY: Routledge.

García, O., & Wei, L. (2013). *Translanguaging: Language, bilingualism, and education*. New York, NY: Palgrave.

Hernandez, A. E. (2013). *The bilingual brain*. New York, NY: Oxford University Press.

Hirsch, J., Moreno, D. R., & Kim, K. H. S. (2001). Interconnected large-scale systems for three fundamental cognitive tasks revealed by functional MRI. *Journal of Cognitive Neuroscience, 13*(3), 389–405. doi:10.1162/08989290015113742

Krashen, S. D. (1981). *Second language acquisition and second language learning*. Oxford, UK: Oxford University Press.

Leisman, G., Maulem, R., & Mughrabi, S. K. (2015). The neurological development of the child with the educational enrichment in mind. *Educational Psychology, 21*, 79–96. doi:10.1016/j.pse.2015.08.006

Lombardi, J. (2008). Beyond learning styles: Brain-based research and English language learners. *The Clearing House: A Journal of Educational Strategies, Issues and Ideas, 81*(5), 219–222.

Makalela, L. (2015). Bilingualism in South Africa: Reconnecting with *Ubuntu* translanguaging. In O. García & A. Lin (Eds.), *Encyclopedia of bilingualism and bilingual education*. New York, NY: Springer.

McClelland, J. L., Rumelhart, D. E., & Hinton, G. E. (1986). The appeal of parallel distributed processing. In D. E. Rumelhart, J. L. McClelland, & PDP Research Group (Eds.), *Parallel distributed processing: Explorations in the microstructures of cognition Vol. 1: Foundations*. Cambridge, MA: MIT Press.

McLaughlin, B. (1980). On the use of miniature artificial languages in second-language research. *Applied Psycholinguistics, 1*, 357–369.

McLaughlin, B., Rossman, T., & McLeod, B. (1983). Second language learning: An information-processing perspective. *Language Learning, 33*, 135–158.

Moghaddam, A. N., & Araghi, S. M. (2013). Brain-based aspects of cognitive learning approaches in second language learning. *English Language Teaching, 6*(5), 55.

Mohammadipour, M., & Rashid, S. M. (2015). The impact of task-based instruction program on fostering ESL learners' speaking ability: A cognitive approach. *Advances in Language and Literary Studies, 6*(2), 113–126. doi:10.7575/aiac.alls.v.6n.2p.113

Neuner, S. (2002). Learning as information processing: Reflections on cognitive theory in second language instruction. *Babylonia, 10*(4), 35–39.

Pena-Correall, T., & Robayo-Castro, B. (2007). B.F. Skinner's verbal behavior: 1957–2007. *Revista Latinoamericana De Psicologia, 39*(3), 653–661.

Rogers, T. T., & McClelland, J. L. (2014). Parallel distributed processing at 25: Further explorations in the microstructure of cognition. *Cognitive Science, 38*(6), 1024–1077. doi:10.1111/cogs.12148

Selinker, L. (1972). Interlanguage. *IRAL-International Review of Applied Linguistics in Language Teaching, 10*(1–4), 209–232.

Skinner, B. F. (1957). *Verbal behavior*. New York, NY: Appleton-Century-Crofts.

Swan, M., & Smith, B. (2007). *Learner English—A teacher's guide to interference and other problems*. Cambridge, NY: Cambridge University Press.

Terry, N. (2014). Dialect variation and phonological knowledge: Phonological representations and metalinguistic awareness among beginning readers who speak nonmainstream American English. *Applied Psycholinguistics, 35*(1), 155–176. doi:10.1017/S0142716412000276

Wertsch, J. (2008). From social interaction to higher psychological processes. A clarification and application of Vygotsky's theory. *Human Development, 51*(1), 66–79. doi:10.1159/000112532

Meeting the Needs of English Learners

LEARNING OBJECTIVES

Readers will be able to

❖ Address the challenges that 21st century teachers face in meeting the needs of English learners (ELs)

❖ Determine and use appropriate approaches for attaining and organizing background information to help meet the needs of ELs

❖ Acquire academic preparation to use appropriate strategies for successful achievement of ELs in classrooms

SCENARIO

On a bright sunny morning, the school secretary walked into Ms. Garcia's first grade class with a new student. She said: "This is Ika, Ms. Garcia. She's been assigned to your class. She doesn't speak any English. Her parents just arrived from Russia this week." "Welcome, Ika!" said Ms. Garcia, taking Ika by the hand and making a place for her on the floor next to herself. Ika became the eighth EL in Ms. Garica's class of 28. Unfortunately, none of the other ELs speak Russian, though Ms. Garcia has four other languages represented in her class and she speaks only English and Spanish.

Meeting the needs of a multilingual population is not an easy task for any teacher. Because diversity seems to be the norm rather than the exception in today's society, teachers are continuously challenged to find ways to be effective in their everyday teaching.

BEST PRACTICES FOR ENGLISH FOR SPEAKERS OF OTHER LANGUAGES INSTRUCTION

Previous chapters in this textbook outlined and discussed best practices for EL instruction. The following points have been stressed throughout the chapters:

- Providing comprehensible input (using visuals, charts, graphs, etc.)
- Providing a supportive environment
- Providing dual language instruction
- Respecting the stages of oral language development
- Employing simple language, slower speech when warranted, rephrasing, and repeating
- Providing meaningful practice
- Establishing a link between the home and the school
- Providing opportunities for ELs to engage in lessons by responding nonverbally
- Providing instruction addressing varied cognitive styles
- Utilizing translanguaging (use of the multiple languages) to integrate students' systems of communication (García & Wei, 2014)

In addition to these practices listed, teachers must provide a meaningfully based context-rich and cognitively demanding curriculum. The American Educational Research Association (2004) published a piece on boosting academic achievement of ELs in terms of literacy. The following critical components are provided: (a) explicit instruction in word recognition through phonological awareness, practice reading, phonics, and frequent in-class assessment and (b) explicit instruction in skills that are needed to comprehend the text, such as vocabulary building in context, strategies to aid comprehension, and academic oral language development. Further, the push for academic achievement for ELs has been recognized across the country and strategies and objectives can be found through WIDA (World Class Instruction; wida.us), CAL (Center for Applied Linguistics, n.d.; cal.org), TESOL International, and through ESSA (Every Student Succeeds Act, n.d. [ed.gov/ESSA], formerly known as NCLB, or No Child Left Behind).

One of the major understandings that practitioners and scholars have reached is that ELs cannot be provided special assistance only in the English language. Other assistance such as bilingual education, richer and more sustained collaboration between content area teachers and English language specialists, specifically designed academic instruction in English (SDAIE), and/or sheltered English instruction must also be considered

(Coady et al., 2007; Varghese, 2005; Varghese & Park, 2010). Other best practices found in the literature include:

- Integrating language and content instruction
- Developing lessons and units that foster concept development, practice, and application
- Building background knowledge by providing concrete experiences
- Ensuring that textbooks and trade books are at the students' instructional level
- Balanced literacy instruction
- Cooperative/interactive learning
- Providing a caring and trusting environment
- Addressing learning styles and multiple intelligences (Wilson, Fang, Rollins, & Valadez, 2016).

Getting Set

In a review of the literature (Freeman & Freeman, 2007; Lamar & Dixon, 2008; Verplaetse & Migliacci, 2008) on characteristics and optimal conditions in schools and classrooms for ELs, the following best practices are among the ones most commonly identified and discussed:

1. Know the students in the classrooms.
   - Where are they from?
   - What is their L1 (native language)?
   - How long have they been in the United States?
   - How much prior schooling have they had?
   - How have they performed during prior schooling?
2. Teach language through academic content.
   - Students learn language via varied academic content, subjects, and experiences.
   - Language is kept in its natural context.
   - Students have real purposes to use language.
   - Students acquire academic vocabulary, language structures, and meaning within the content areas.
3. Employ thematic instruction.
   - Language is taught in meaningful contexts.
   - More exposure to the "same" language for an extended period of time provides ample opportunities for language acquisition.
   - Instruction is organized through "Big Question" themes.
   - Integration of themes through other content subjects aids in building academic concepts and vocabulary more easily.
   - Through themes, instruction can be connected to ELs' lives and backgrounds.

4. Draw on ELs' language and culture by previewing, viewing, and reviewing in the students' L1.
   - The preview in L1 makes input more comprehensible and allows for students to connect this input with prior knowledge they may have on the particular subject/theme.
   - Provide an oral summary by reading a book on the theme in the first language(s).
   - Ask key questions and allow ELs to work in same language groups to brainstorm what they know about the theme.
   - Ensure the use of comprehensible input by employing all necessary techniques.
5. Emphasize meaningful reading.
   - Instruction should focus on text level skills to engage ELs in reading for comprehension.
   - Effective instruction follows a sequence in which responsibility for reading gradually shifts from the teacher to the student.
   - Employing varied teaching reading approaches, such as "read-alouds," shared reading, guided reading, and independent reading, which leads to more successful readers.
6. Maintain high expectations.
   - Students will perform at higher levels when expectations are high and teachers project the attitude that "ELs can achieve at higher levels."
   - Provide scaffolding to aid in achievement of higher expectations.
   - Employ real language plentifully; watering down the curriculum is ineffective and leads to lower achievement levels.
7. Demonstrate concepts and ideas.
   - Use manipulatives and realia (real life items and artifacts), role-play, and nonverbal gestures assisted by visuals to help in the clarification of concepts.
8. Emphasize critical information.
   - Use bold letters, underlining, and highlighting important facts and information to call attention to critical points.
   - *Always* use materials with pictures, charts, and graphs to assist in grasping main points of lessons and visual aids that support comprehensible input (see Chapter 17).
   - Allow and encourage ELs to draw pictures of main ideas.

Other Ways to Provide for ELs

The following are other ways to provide for ELs:

- Engage students in many activity-oriented and hands-on experiences to provide concrete experiences that make input much more comprehensible for ELs.
- Emphasize small group work and teamwork to allow all students to contribute at their own levels. Small group activities also encourage ELs to share in a less threatening environment. Teams/small groups must be balanced, taking into consideration EL's English language development.

- Provide a "print rich" environment, but ensure that it is comprehensible to the students. Labeling everything in the classrooms is an excellent way to provide this "comprehensible input." Word lists (with pictures) of vocabulary/concepts are also helpful in providing a print rich environment.
- Set time aside to read to the students, making sure numerous pictures and objects are used to introduce and clarify new vocabulary/concepts. Big books, predictable books, and pattern books are particularly effective for ELs.
- Welcome the richness of cultural diversity in the classroom. Using ELs' places of origin as part of social studies units gives geography, for example, a new meaning. It is a golden opportunity for native speakers to learn about different parts of the world in a more meaningful way.
- Study the art, music, cuisine, customs, and language(s) of the cultures represented in the classroom. Examining many cultures is a way to help students recognize and value similarities and differences among cultural groups.
- Read multicultural versions of the same fairy tale, which is a great way to learn about these cultures, as it helps students to realize the common elements as well as the differences.
- Use charts and graphs to help new ELs understand new concepts while acquiring the English language. Charts and graphs help make the input comprehensible because they are less dependent on language.

Diversity in the classroom provides rich opportunities for intercultural learning and sharing. The traditional teacher role of imparting knowledge to a homogeneous group of students is a thing of the past. All teachers today are language teachers. The teaching of all subjects, whether social studies, science, or mathematics, is attached to the need to develop language while students acquire historical, scientific, and mathematical knowledge and concepts.

As mentioned in Chapter 17, ELs progress through similar second language developmental stages, although they vary greatly in their acquisition of the new language. This places tremendous demands on teachers who teach ELs. To meet these demands, teachers must develop a greater understanding of the complexity of second language acquisition and be cognizant of specific strategies needed to effectively meet the needs of ELs.

SECOND LANGUAGE ACQUISITION

Krashen and Terrell (1983) noted four stages in oral language development:

1. **Silent, preproduction, or comprehension stage**
   a. This stage is similar to the period of time that infants (from birth to approximately 9 or 10 months) are listening and interacting with those around them in a nonverbal fashion.
   b. Preproduction is used to describe the phase similar to that of the period when infants do not yet produce language.

c. Comprehension equates with the fact that infants and toddlers initially comprehend much more language than they are able to produce; comprehension precedes production.

2. **Early speech emergence**
Language begins to emerge slowly; one-word sentences, then two-word sentences, and then simple grammatical structures are employed.

3. **Speech emergence**
Language continues to evolve; phrases and short sentences are employed.

4. **Intermediate fluency**
More complex language is employed; the learner engages in discourse. The use of more complex sentences is evident.

Other renditions of these stages include beginning fluency and advanced fluency.

Over the past 15 years, the WIDA consortium developed a set of standards, guidelines, and model performance indicators that teachers of ELs can use to identify, gauge, and support their students. As of today (2018), WIDA is currently being used in 38 states and D.C. across the United States. The WIDA framework encompasses various language proficiency levels with grade-level clusters of what students are able to do across the four language areas of listening, speaking, reading, and writing (these are referred to as the "Can Do" Descriptors; Figure 18.1). WIDA classifies language proficiency using six levels as follows:

1. Entering
2. Beginning
3. Developing
4. Expanding
5. Bridging
6. Reaching

Although there are general trends in terms of the order in which students progress in their English language learning, from listening to speaking, reading, and then writing, it is important to note that these are just trends. Critical is EL students' knowledge of their first language and how that supports (transfers) their acquisition of English. What implications does this theoretical knowledge have for classroom teachers in the 21st century?

Some extensive research and instructional strategies have been written regarding effective teaching with ELs (see Diaz-Rico, 2017; Herrera & Kavimandan, 2017; Herrera & Murray, 2015), below we offer a summary of some early teaching strategies for teachers of ELs.

1. Teachers will have students in their classrooms who are in the "silent period." Though these students are not speaking English yet, they are being exposed to the language constantly while at school. However, this language needs to be made "comprehensible" for them to begin to understand what is being said. There are a series of language modifications teachers can employ to make their input "comprehensible." The English

	Level 1 Entering	Level 2 Beginning	Level 3 Developing	Level 4 Expanding	Level 5 Bridging	Level 6 - Reaching
READING	• Match icons or diagrams with words/concepts • Identify cognates from first language, as applicable • Make sound/symbol/word relations • Match illustrated words/ phrases in differing contexts (e.g., on the board, in a book)	• Identify facts and explicit message from illustrated text • Find changes to root words in context • Indentify elements of story grammer (e.g., characters, setting) • Follow visually supported writter directions (e.g., "Draw a star in the sky.")	• Interpret information or data from charts and graphs • Identify main ideas and some details • Sequence events in stories or content-based processes • Use context clues and illustrations to determine meaning of words/phrases	• Classify features of various genres of text (e.g., "and they lived happily ever after" –fairly tales) • Match graphic organizers to different texts(e.g., compare/contrast with Venn diagram) • Find details that support main ideas • Differentiate between fact and opinion in narrative and expository text	• Summarize information from multiple related sources • Answer analytical questions about grade-level text • Identify, explain, and give examples of figures of speech • Draw conclusions from explicit and implicit text at or sear grade level	
WRITING	• Label objects, picture, or diagrams from word/phrase banks • Communicate ideas by drawing • Copy words, phrase, and short sentences • Answer oral questions with single words	• Make lists from labels or with peers • Complete/produce sentences from word/ phrase banks or walls • Fill in graphic organizers, charts, and tables • Make comparisons using real-life or visually- supported materials	• Produce simple expository or narrative text • Seeing related sentences together • Compare/contrast content- based information • Describe events, people, processes, procedures	• Take notes using graphic organiseres • Summarize content-based information • Author multiple forms of writing (e.g., expository, narrative, persurasive) from models • Explain strategies or use of information in solving problems	• Produce extended responses of original text approaching grade level • Apply content-based information to new contexts • Connect or integrate personal experience with liteneatural/content • Create grade-level stories or reports	

Figure 18.1: Is a sample of the WIDA reading and writing "Can Do" descriptors for grade cluster 3–5.

Source: From *WIDA Consortium* by Margo Gottlieb, M. Elizabeth Cranley, and Andrea Cammilleri. Copyright © 2007 by Board of Regents of the University of Wisconsin System. Reprinted by permission

for speakers of other languages (ESOL) literature refers to these as caregiver speech because they are associated with what mothers or caregivers do when communicating with babies. These include:

- Use of simple language
- Use of gestures, facial expressions
- Slowing down
- Enunciating clearly
- Repeating
- Rephrasing

In addition to the use of caregiver speech, teachers must use visuals such as pictures, objects, realia, charts, and graphs to ensure that the input they are providing non-English speakers is comprehensible.

2. During the silent period, ELs can and should be involved in all classroom activities and lessons. Although they are not yet speaking, they can use their first languages to learn English and academic content, they can respond nonverbally, such as through the use of total physical response (TPR). In this technique, students respond nonverbally to commands given by the teacher.

In addition, the use of pictures, objects, and realia are excellent ways to get students involved in learning. The teacher may ask students to sort pictures, arrange objects, or select specific pictures/objects to ascertain their comprehension of the lesson presented.

For example, the teacher may ask students to select pictures of the famous monuments in Washington, DC, described in the lesson, or to select pictures that show the House of Representatives and the Senate after studying U.S. government. In this way students can participate in lessons before they speak any English. This helps develop a positive self-concept because students feel successful when they are able to be involved in the lessons, even though their oral language may be emerging.

3. Using pictures, objects, and realia is also necessary when introducing new vocabulary in context, since there is much vocabulary students will need to acquire knowledge and concepts. Visuals help students attach meaning to what is being said. They make "input comprehensible" (Krashen, 1981; Latifi, Ketabi, & Mohammadi, 2013). Another way of encouraging comprehensible input is by simplifying the language and language structures employed in instruction. Repeating key points in different contexts is very effective, as is rephrasing what has been said. Some teachers have a tendency to speak fast; slowing down is essential. These "sheltering" techniques are essential when teaching second language learners.

The following are effective strategies for involving students who are in the "early speech emergence stage":

- Asking questions that require only a yes/no, or pointing to the answer:
  Is this a high plains or mountain?
  Is this precipitation or evaporation
- Asking either/or type questions:
  Is this the Washington Monument or the Lincoln Monument?
  Asking short answer questions that can be answered with one or two words

As ELs develop more language, teachers can continue to involve them in activities that require more complex language and language structures.

Meeting the needs of the students in today's classrooms requires teachers to modify their teaching strategies by incorporating second language acquisition techniques. Modifying the language employed to conduct lessons, using visuals, and involving students in lessons by allowing them to respond nonverbally while in the silent stage are effective strategies. By employing these strategies in their classrooms, teachers will begin to make a positive impact in meeting the needs of their diverse student population.

POINTS TO REMEMBER

✔ Background information teachers acquire about their students is necessary and helpful in providing for their needs, particularly knowledge of ELs' first language and literacy levels, which should continue to be supported and developed.
✔ ELs progress through similar second language developmental stages.
✔ Krashen and Terrell classify oral development into several stages: preproduction, early speech emergence, speech emergence, and intermediate fluency.
✔ The WIDA consortium identifies six language proficiency levels in their framework for teaching EL students: entering, beginning, developing, expanding, bridging, and reaching.

✔ Using visuals, modifying the language employed to teach lessons, and involving students by having them respond nonverbally in the initial stages of second language development are all excellent ways of meeting the needs of second language learners.

✔ Caregiver language or modified language includes: use of simple language, gestures, and facial expression to convey meaning; slowing down speech; enunciating clearly; repeating; and rephrasing.

✔ There are numerous modifications teachers must make to provide the optimum learning environment for ELs.

REFLECTION QUESTIONS AND DISCUSSION

1. List specific ways that teachers can attain background information about their ELs.

2. List strategies teachers can employ to help ELs better adjust to their new environments.

3. Describe four classroom activities that are effective in the second (new) language acquisition process.

4. Give examples of activities teachers may employ to engage ELs at each of the four stages of oral language development.

5. Explain the term "caregiver speech." How does it relate to "motherese?"

ACTIVITIES

1. Complete the following chart by drawing a parallel between the four stages in second language acquisition and the oral language development of infants/toddlers. Use the knowledge acquired from this chapter, your own experiences with children, and your own knowledge.

Stage of Second Language Acquisition	Infant/Toddler Language Interactions
1. Silent/preproduction stage; EL listens, interacts nonverbally. May smile, show visual interest, etc. Child listens and absorbs the sounds and rhythms of the language.	1. Infant does not speak; cries, coos, babbles. smiles, which make for practice for future speech. Child listens and absorbs the sounds and rhythm of the language.
2. Comprehension stage. Comprehension precedes production. Child may be able to understand and/or respond physically to commands or requests.	2. Infant/toddler does not speak but comprehends much more than he or she produces.Comprehension precedes production. Child may be able to respond physically to commands or requests.
3. Early preproduction (one or two word stages). Then speech emergence stage- phrases and short sentences are uttered. Children acquire L2 in developmental stages.	3. Sounds are produced with variations in pronunciation. Children acquire the phonological system of their native language in developmental states. Holophrastic stage (one word). Telegraphic speech (function words are omitted and focus is on semantics.
4. Intermediate fluency-they begin to engage in discourse through words they are learning to use. Predictable order of acquiring grammatical morphemes and syntactic structures, just like L1 children. Often errors can be attributed due to the incorrect transfer from the L1 to L2. Errors are developmental, just as are errors in L1 children.	4. Multiword stage (some telegraphic speech still evident.) First no plural marker is used (eg. man, toy). Then plurals, followed by irregular plurals. (mans, feets, dogs,, mens, footses, feet.) Negatives: No go. No milk. Finally, two word questions with uplifting voice. More juice? Mommy go?

WEB RESOURCES

6 Strategies to Meet English Language Learners (ELL) Needs. https://www.resumes-for-teachers.com/blog/english-second-language/six-strategies-meeting-needs-english-language-learners-ell

10 Tips for Meeting the Needs of Diverse Learners. https://www.teachingchannel.org/blog/2016/02/10/10-tips-diverse-learners-gbt

Delicate Balance: Meeting the Needs of ELL Students. https://www.education.com/reference/article/balance-manage-needs-ell-student

ESL Struggles and Strategies. https://www.youtube.com/watch?v=-bWU238PymM

Extending English Language Learners' Classroom Interactions Using the Response Protocol. http://www.readingrockets.org/article/extending-english-language-learners-classroom-interactions-using-response-protocol

Helping ESL and ELL Students. https://www.youtube.com/watch?v=lARm7Otokzs

Integrating ELL Students in General Education Classes. https://www.edutopia.org/blog/integrating-ells-general-education-classes-dorit-sasson

Meeting the Needs of Language Learners. https://www.buncee.com/blog/edubuncee-for-meeting-the-needs-of-english-language-learners

Preparing All Teachers to Meet the Needs of English Language Learners. https://www.americanprogress.org/issues/education/reports/2012/04/30/11372/preparing-all-teachers-to-meet-the-needs-of-english-language-learners

Strategies for Teaching English Language Learners. https://www.scholastic.com/teachers/articles/teaching-content/strategies-teaching-english-language-learners

REFERENCES

American Educational Research Association. (2004). *English Language Learners: Boosting Academic Achievement. Essential Information for Education Policy* (Vol. 2(1)). Washington, DC: Author.

Center for Applied Linguistics. (n.d.). Retrieved from http://www.cal.org

Coady, M., Hamann, E. T., Harrington, M., Pacheco, M., Pho, S., & Yedlin, J. (2007). Successful schooling for ELLs: Principles for building responsive learning environments. In L. S. Verplaetse & N. Migliacci (Eds.), *Inclusive pedagogy for English language learners: A handbook of research-informed practices* (pp. 245–255). New York, NY: Lawrence Erlbaum Associates.

Diaz-Rico, L. T. (2017). *The cross cultural, language, and academic development handbook: A complete K-12 reference guide* (6th ed.). New York, NY: Pearson.

Every Student Succeeds Act (ESSA). (n.d.). Retrieved from https://www.ed.gov/ESSA

Freeman, D., & Freeman, Y. (2007). *English language learners: The essential guide*. New York, NY: Scholastic.

García O., & Wei, L. (2014). Translanguaging and education. *In Translanguaging: language, bilingualism and education*. London, UK: Palgrave Macmillan.

Herrera, S. G., & Kavimandan, S. K. (2017). *Accelerating literacy for diverse learners: Classroom strategies that integrate social engagement and academic achievement, K-8* (2nd ed.). Boston, MA: Pearson.

Herrera, S. G., & Murray, K. G. (2015). *Mastering ESL/EFL methods: Differentiated instruction for culturally and linguistically diverse students* (3rd ed.). New York, NY: Pearson.

Krashen, S. D. (1981). *Second language acquisition and second language learning*. Oxford, UK: Oxford University Press.

Krashen, S. D., & Terrell, T. D. (1983). *The natural approach: Language acquisition in the classroom.* Hayward, CA: Alemany Press.

Lamar, D., & Dixon, R. (2008). SETESOL 2008: A baker's dozen: 13 sweet treats for content teachers. In *Session presented at SETESOL 2008*, Birmingham, AL.

Latifi, M., Ketabi, S., & Mohammadi, E. (2013). The comprehension hypothesis today: An interview with Stephen Krashen. *E-FLT: Electronic Journal of Foreign Language Teaching, 10*(2), 221–233.

Varghese, M. M. (2005). An introduction to meeting the needs of English language learners. Retrieved from http://www.newhorizons.org/spneeds/ell/varghese.htm

Varghese, M. M., & Park, C. (2010). Going global: Can dual-language programs save bilingual education? *Journal of Latinos and Education, 9*(1), 72–80. doi:10.1080/15348430903253092

Verplaetse, L. S., & Migliacci, N. (Eds.). (2008). *Inclusive pedagogy for English language learners: A handbook for research-informed practices.* New York, NY: Lawrence Erlbaum,

WIDA. (n.d.). Retrieved from https://www.wida.us

Wilson, J., Fang, C., Rollins, J., & Valadez, D. (2016). An urgent challenge: Enhancing academic speaking opportunities for English learners. *Multicultural Education, 23*(2), 52.

TESOL STANDARDS, PRE-K-GRADE 12

The standards publication presents five language proficiency standards. They include both social and academic uses of the language students must acquire for success in and beyond the classroom.

The English language proficiency standards are as follows:

Standard 1: English language learners (ELs) communicate for social, intercultural, and instructional purposes within the school setting.

Standard 2: ELs communicate information, ideas, and concepts necessary for academic success in the area of language arts.

Standard 3: ELs communicate information, ideas, and concepts necessary for academic success in the area of mathematics.

Standard 4: ELs communicate information, ideas, and concepts necessary for academic success in the area of science.

Standard 5: ELs communicate information, ideas, and concepts necessary for academic success in the area of social studies.

Source: tesol.org http://www.tesol.org/docs/books/bk_prek-12elpstandards_framework_318.pdf?sfvrsn=2

Strategies and Styles

Readers will be able to

- ❖ Determine differences between learning strategies and styles
- ❖ Identify strategies and styles in language acquisition
- ❖ Identify appropriate communication strategies for English learner (EL) students
- ❖ Describe the cognitive academic language learning approach (CALLA) and its benefits to EL students
- ❖ Relate Gardner's multiple intelligences (MI) to EL students' learning needs

A teacher is doing a shared/modeled writing activity with a group of second graders in a mainstream classroom. There are some ELs in the class. Today, the teacher, Mrs. Abrams (T), will demonstrate to the students (S1, S2, etc.) how she composes writing by thinking aloud about the steps she takes and the decisions she makes as she writes.

> T: *Children, last week we read a story about a little boy's favorite person, who happens to be his hero. We also discussed what makes a person a hero and why. Well, today we are going to write about our own personal hero. Let's write this together.*
>
> *Now where do I begin?*
>
> *Maybe we should name one person whom we admire most. Then we will list some reasons why we like the person. OK, whom do you admire most?*
>
> (Students shout several answers: Michael Jordan, Pokémon Pikachu, grandfather, etc. Since there are many suggestions, the students are asked to vote on someone they all agree to be a hero. Finally everyone agrees on Michael Jordan as their hero.)
>
> T: *What makes Michael Jordan a hero?*
> S1: *He plays good basketball. He can jump very high.*
> T: *OK. I will draw a circle and write "Plays basketball well," and "He can jump," in each circle. Does anyone know if "basketball" is one word or two words?*
> S2: *Two words.*
> S1: *No, it is one word.*
> T: *Maybe, we will write it as two words now. Later, we will check to see if we are correct. Now, what else do we like about Michael Jordan?*
> S3: *He is very funny. I like his movie* Space Jam.
> S4: *I laughed so hard when I watch this movie.*
> T: *OK, we will draw another circle, and inside it we will write, "funny."*

What observations did you make while reading this scenario?

What are some general approaches the class is learning to use to process information before they begin to write? The teacher is highlighting several different strategies for organizing and generating ideas before writing. She also will demonstrate the use of a "word web," a graphic organizer to help students focus, generate, and organize ideas, instead of concentrating on grammar and mechanics. In other words, the teacher is modeling brainstorming strategies in the prewriting stage. Does this influence how learners process and understand information? What type of learners would benefit most from the teacher's use of a word web and verbal explanations?

Now reflect on the strategies you have used or still use when learning to read and write in your first language and in another language. Do you apply the same strategies in all learning situations? What type of a learner are you? What kind of instruction inhibits or promotes your ability to learn effectively?

What Are Learning Strategies?

Second and foreign language educators have been seeking ways to help learners in their efforts to be successful in learning and communicating in their target language. These efforts have brought about much discussion regarding how learning strategies can provide positive support to students in their attempts to learn a new language. First of all, there are several definitions of learning strategies (Oxford, 2016). Language learning strategies help learners improve their knowledge and understanding of a target language. They are the conscious behaviors students can incorporate to facilitate language learning tasks and help them to recognize their individual language learning process. Oxford (2016) describes what strategies are and how to use them appropriately with individual learners, since each student learns differently. Operationally defined, *learning strategies* are strategic techniques used by language learners to comprehend and process new information, to recall prior knowledge, and to apply knowledge and skills to facilitate learning (Knowles, Holton, & Swanson, 2014; Nyikos, 1991). They are the tools we use to make learning more effective, engaging, and rapid. According to Stern (1992, p. 261), "the concept of learning strategy is dependent on the assumption that learners consciously engage in activities to achieve certain goals and learning strategies can be regarded as broadly conceived intentional directions and learning techniques." Benson and Voller (2014) maintain that students who find their own learning styles and strategies can develop techniques to become autonomous learners.

Schmidt (1994) and Cohen (1996a, 2014) further explain that all language learners use language learning strategies either consciously or unconsciously when processing new information and performing tasks in the language classroom. However, if learners are unable to identify any strategies associated with the task at hand, then the behavior would simply be referred to as a process, not a strategy. For example, a learner may use the behavior of skimming the title, headings, and subheadings of a text or previewing pictures to get an overall idea before doing a close reading of a text. If the learner is at all conscious (even if peripherally) as to why the previewing is taking place, then it would be a strategy. Since a language classroom is like a problem-solving environment in which language learners are likely to face new input and difficult tasks given by their instructors, learners' attempts to find the quickest or easiest way to do what is required, that is, using language learning strategies, is inescapable. Many research studies in the field of learning strategies for foreign language and second language learning (Cohen, 1990; Cook, 2013; Nyikos, 1991; O'Malley & Chamot, 1990; Oxford & Carmen, 2017) have underscored the fact that language learning is a very complex cognitive skill and have linked the use of appropriate strategies to successful language performance. In order for students to become competent in a new language, they must be given the tools needed for effective learning.

What are Communication Strategies?

While learning strategies are typically strategies we use for processing input, communication strategies are verbal and nonverbal strategies for producing clear messages in the second language. As we know, language processing may involve both comprehension and production simultaneously (Chater, McCauley, & Christiansen, 2016; Tarone, 1981) thus making it difficult to separate the two. However, these distinctions illuminate the nature of communication. Figures 19.1 to 19.4 provide taxonomies for the two types of strategies: learning and communication strategies.

Few studies have looked at the explicit relationship between strategy instruction and second learners' performance in the target language. In his study of the effects of strategy instruction on high school students in Hungary who were learning English as a foreign language, Dörnyei (1995, 2014) found that explicit instruction on three communication strategies (topic avoidance and replacement, circumlocution, and fillers and hesitation devices) "provides these learners with a sense of security in the L2 by allowing them room to maneuver in times of difficulty. Rather than giving up their message, learners may decide to try and remain in the conversation and achieve their communicative goal" (Dörnyei, 1995, p. 80). Cohen (1996b, 2014) went beyond the limited number of specific communication strategies used in Dörnyei's study in 2014 and found that instruction in communication strategy was beneficial when learners are engaged in discussions of speaking strategies, given the opportunity to review checklists of possible strategies, and practice those strategies in class. He added that learners should work on developing their own list of strategies that they will use in different language learning and using situations (Baytar, 2014).

How can understanding learning and communication strategies be helpful in second language classroom learning? One of our most important goals is to train learners to become autonomous by showing them the "how to" of learning a language in the most efficient and productive way. Because ELs have varied experiences, training, and linguistic proficiencies, teachers are in a better position to help them if they understand a myriad of effective strategies and apply them in their teaching techniques and materials. Of course teachers should not force learners to adopt specific strategies and cannot expect all learners to immediately embrace all strategies; some students may bring preconceived ideas about what instruction should be like, based on their previous training (Bialystok, 1985; Moeller, & Nugent, 2014). In addition, learners may forget the effective strategies they use consciously or unconsciously or be unsure of strategies they used when learning their L1 that can be transferred to L2. Consequently, they may not be able to make the transfer. It is vital, then, that these strategies be revived through instruction and guided practice. Ultimately, strategic instruction will offer students opportunities to practice an array of effective strategies from which to choose when they encounter different classroom tasks and life situations. The instructional strategy CALLA was developed for the sole purpose of providing learners with tools to learn.

CALLA LEARNING STRATEGIES

While the Natural Approach and total physical response (TPR) promote the acquisition of social language, CALLA is a strategy that promotes the acquisition of academic language. Chamot and O'Malley (1994) and Chamot (2014), the creators of CALLA, intended it to help second language learners become autonomous learners by empowering them to achieve academically. CALLA integrates content (the core curriculum's key concepts and ideas), language (the language needed to access the content), and strategies (students' own use of special techniques to help them learn).

CALLA learning strategies are divided into three strategic categories: metacognitive, cognitive, and social affective.

A. Metacognitive Strategies

There are five subcategories of metacognitive strategies: advanced organization, advanced preparation, organizational planning, selective attention, and self-evaluation. Figure 19.1 outlines each metacognitive strategy.

B. Cognitive Strategies

There are nine subcategories of cognitive strategies: contexualization, elaboration, grouping, imagery, inferencing, note-taking, resourcing, summarizing, and transfer.

Figure 19.2 illustrates the subcategories of cognitive strategies.

C. Social Affective Strategies

There are three subcategories of social affective strategies: cooperation, questioning for clarification, and self-talk.

Can you identify the social affective strategies in the following scenario?

- Advanced Organization
  (Preview main ideas and concepts of the material to be learned by skimming the text for organization)
- Advanced Preparation
  (Rehearse the language needed for oral and written tasks)
- Organizational Planning
  (Plan the parts, sequence, and main ideas to be expressed orally or in writing)
- Selective Attention
  (Attend to or scan key words, phrases, linguistic markers, sentences, or types of information)
- Self-Evaluation
  (Judge how well one has accomplished a learning activity after it has been completed)

Metacognitive Strategies

1 Application of Metacognitive Strategies

Ms. Lott's second grade class has been reading a series of stories on a related theme—geographical locations. The students have read "Buffy's Orange Leash," which takes place in the United States; "Soccer Sam," which takes place in Mexico; and "Nessa's Fish," which takes place in the Arctic. Today they will be reading the story "Slippery Ice," which takes place in Antarctica. Before the students read the story, Ms. Lott previews main ideas and concepts by reviewing the locations of past stories on a world map, using an overhead transparency. Student volunteers locate Antarctica on the world map. Then Ms. Lott rehearses the language needed for oral and written tasks by displaying a pocket chart consisting of words that describe penguin actions (taken from the story). Students will act out the actions as they read the story. Next, they will create a song to the "Twinkle, Twinkle Little Star" tune, using all the words they have learned about penguins. Ms. Lott helps students select key words and phrases by displaying a penguin poster and distributing cards in the shape of a fish to help students concretize concepts related to penguins. On this card, each student writes a word that retells the story he or she has read. Students will then organize the word cards on the poster around the penguin, creating a word web. After students have read the story and related activities have been completed, Ms. Lott asks students what they have learned from the story. She also asks what learning activities they liked best and why.

The teacher in the previous scenario used all five subcategories of metacognitive strategies. Can you locate them?

SCENARIO

2 Application of Cognitive Strategies

Ms. Lott's class is reading another story, "Tacky the Penguin" by Helen Lester. She asks students to examine the cover, then has them discuss why the penguin on the cover might be considered tacky. Students are encouraged to respond freely, using their word knowledge and the picture. She also asks students to tell her in what part of the world they think the story might take place. After students do choral reading, Ms. Lott shows them a word web with the word *tacky* in the center. They are asked to brainstorm for other words that are similar in meaning. As the students provide the words, Ms. Lott puts them in the smaller circles that extend from the big circle containing the word *tacky*. Once students have finished with the reading activity, Ms. Lott tells them to act out scenes from the story as she reads the story again. She specifically asks them to act out the words describing the actions of the penguin. She selects several lines in the story and assigns students specific roles in the story to act out. Students wear teacher-made costumes when

(Continued)

- Contextualization
  (Place a word or phrase in a meaningful sentence or category)
- Elaboration
  (Relate new information to what is already known)
- Grouping
  (Classify words, terminology, or concepts according to their attributes)
- Imagery
  (Use visual images—mental or actual—to understand and remember new information)
- Inferencing
  (Guess meanings of new items from text, predict outcomes, or complete missing parts)
- Note-Taking
  (Write down key words and concepts during reading or listening activities)
- Resourcing
  (Use reference materials such as dictionaries, encyclopedias, or textbooks)
- Summarizing
  (Make a mental or written summary of information gained through listening or reading)
- Transfer
  (Use what is already known to facilitate a learning task)

Cognitive Strategies

- Cooperation
  (Work together with peers to solve a problem, gather information, check a learning task, or get feedback on oral and written performance)
- Questioning for Clarification
  (Ask a teacher or peer to clarify or explain, rephrase, or give examples)
- Self-Talk
  (Use mental techniques to boost one's own confidence and reduce anxiety when completing a task)

Social Affective Strategies

3 Social Affective Strategies

Ms. Lott's lesson objectives are for students to identify the adjectives and verbs used in the two stories ("Tacky the Penguin" and "Slippery Ice") and for them to describe the events in proper sequence when retelling the stories. For this lesson, she uses the cooperative learning structure—jigsaw reading. First, she groups students in fours. These groups are the home groups.

Each member of a home group is assigned a number, 1, 2, 3, or 4. Students must learn about the others on their team and look out for one another. Then, Ms. Lott assembles an "expert" team, consisting of students who have the same number; for instance, all number ones form a group, number twos get together and form another group, and so on. Each "expert" group is given a task to do. The tasks for this lesson are:

Group #1: Locate, color, and label the geographical areas in which each story is set.
Group #2: Identify three verbs and three adjectives in the stories and draw or act them out.
Group #3: Using a Venn diagram, compare and contrast the characters in the two stories.
Group #4: Retell the stories using the excitement map—an extension of a simple retelling.

Ms. Lott gives each "expert" group 15 minutes to complete its task. Then, she reassembles the home groups and asks each member to teach his or her assignment to the others in their group. Every member in the "home" group must have the information that covers all of the given tasks. Then, Ms. Lott tells the students they are going to play a game called "Jeopardy." She writes comprehension questions about the two stories and puts them in a hat. She will draw one question at a time and pick a number (1–4) to answer the question. Because students do not know whom she will pick to answer the question, everyone must know the answer, so they have to work together and teach one another to answer the question correctly. In this game, students not only help one another, but they must boost each other's confidence and cheer each other on. Each member must convince other members that they can provide the correct answer. After a series of questions, the winning team receives a prize. The game is competitive, yet fun.

COMMUNICATION STRATEGIES

It is not enough for second language learners to be able to read, write, and understand basic knowledge in their L2; they must also be able to communicate and get things done.

Del Hymes (1974, 2013) developed a term called *communicative competence,* which he defines as one's ability to use the language appropriately in a variety of contexts. This means knowledge of grammar alone is not enough to guarantee second language learners the ability to use the language appropriately in social contexts. Canale (1983) and Kern and Kramsch (2014) identify four elements of communicative competence: grammatical, sociolinguistic, discourse, and strategic competence.

Grammatical competence focuses on the accuracy of the language "code," that is, vocabulary, grammar, pronunciation, and spelling.

Sociolinguistic competence involves the appropriate use of language in varied social settings, that is, requesting information, refusing assistance, and other social etiquette.

Discourse competence is the learners' ability to appropriately engage in conversation. Learners need to know the skills of combining and connecting phrases and sentences. They also need to know conversational rules, such as giving and taking of the floor while talking, and written discourse rules, such as using appropriate address for different audiences.

Strategic competence pertains to the way language is used, both verbally and nonverbally, to achieve communication goals. Strategic competence is used for two main reasons: (a) to make meaning clear in communication and (b) to embellish communication. The subcategories of strategic competence are illustrated by the following scenario.

SCENARIO

4 Strategic Competence—A Yellow Ribbon

It is sharing time in the classroom. Miguel has brought in an Easter basket. Although he is relatively inexperienced in communicating in English, he is anxious to share his basket with the class. Miguel communicates in English with Spanish intrusion, relying on his Spanish to fill in for words not yet part of his limited English vocabulary. Miguel tells the class about his basket with smiles and gestures; then the teacher encourages the class to raise their hands and question him about his basket.

Miguel: *This basket. I'm got little candy for … for … dia de Pascua [Easter]. I'm got huevos de colores [colored eggs] blue, green, yellow. I'm got little pollitos [chicks]. Me sit and eat chocolate con mi hermana [with my sister].*

Teacher: *Girls and boys, now you may ask Miguel questions about his basket. Remember to raise your hands!*

Adeleine: (Raising hand.) *What color is the ribbon?*

Miguel: *Ribbon?* (Taken aback by the unfamiliar word "ribbon," looks around the classroom as if searching for a cue to the meaning. Finally, his gaze rests on Maria. Maria points to the ribbon in Adeleine's hair; Miguel has found his cue.

(Continued)

Miguel:	*A yellow ribbon!* (Look to Adeleine for confirmation. Adeleine nods yes. Miguel is elated.)
Carlos:	*Can I have a green egg you have in your Easter basket?*
Miguel:	*What?* (Looks puzzled.)
Carlos:	*Can I have the green egg? Look—Look—Look.* (Forms an egg shape with his hands).
Miguel:	(Stares in basket.)
Carlos:	*Green egg.* (Gets up and points to the green egg in basket.)
Miguel:	(Smiling) *O.K. Here green egg!*

Source: Ventriglia (19829, pp. 69–70).

This scenario illustrates how a brief conversational exchange between native speakers and beginning non-native speakers can be a complex and laborious task. Here, we will focus on what Canale calls second language learners' strategic competence. In *strategic competence*, communication goals are achieved by the manipulation of language, both verbal and nonverbal (Cohen, 2014). Researchers such as Tarone (1981) and Gass and Selinker (2008) provide a taxonomy of strategic or communication strategies, as shown in Figure 19.4. This taxonomy has stood the test of time and is still useful today.

Now that we know the different strategies second language learners use in their target language communication, let us analyze the strategies that Miguel used in the yellow ribbon scenario. Notice that Miguel uses the language switch strategy in reverting to chunks of Spanish. He appeals for assistance by repeating or imitating the word ribbon to show signs of uncertainty about what the word means. Here, he did not ask a question, but used nonverbal gestures (looking at Maria and staring in the basket). Carlos also uses mime to explain his question to Miguel (forms an egg shape with his hands).

As teachers of second language learners, we need to understand the communication strategies our students use. It is important that teachers complement students' communication and learning strategies with instructional strategies appropriate to their level of linguistic proficiency. For example, when second language learners use the circumlocution strategy, teachers should understand that they have not acquired the appropriate term and will try to explain the concept using related terms available to them. At this point, the teacher may supply the word in context and restate the word for the learner. A teacher who understands the basic elements of communication strategy will focus on key words and use various communication strategies to facilitate their students' understanding and delivery of a message.

- Approximation
  (A substitute word that the second language learner knows is incorrect, but has semantic features similar to the desired item, e.g., points/dots, rounds/circle, pipe/water pipe)
- Word Coinage
  (Make up a new word to communicate a desired concept, e.g., water bird for duck)
- Circumlocution
  (The second language learner describes characteristics or elements of the object or action instead of using the appropriate term in the target language, *e.g., the lady who is carrying a baby in her tummy for a pregnant woman*)
- Literal Translation
  (Word-for-word translation from the native language, *e.g., Go sleep outside* referring to sleeping not in the bedroom, but in the living room)
- Language Switch
  (Use of L1 without bothering to translate, *e.g., pollitos* [chicks])
- Appeal for Assistance
  (Learner asks for the correct term, e.g., "What is this? What do you call this?" or uses nonverbal gestures)
- Mime
  (Nonverbal strategies are used instead of the term for lexical item, e.g., forms egg shape with hands)

Classification of Communication Strategies

Source: Tarone (1981).

LEARNING STYLES

While learning and communication strategies deal with specific techniques for problem-solving, learning styles refer to the general approaches to learning that may persist even though the content and nature of problem-solving changes. Learning style is thus defined as the "habitual strategies determining a person's typical modes of perceiving, thinking, and problem solving" (Messick, 1976, p. 5).

Howard Gardner's (1983, 2017) seminal work on multiple intelligences (MI) describes several distinct intelligences, all of which can be nurtured in many different ways over time. These intelligences influence the way one learns and processes new information. Gardner further states that individuals may draw upon more than one intelligence in any problem-solving task and that these intelligences may work in harmony. Table 19.1 gives an overview of several types of intelligences and applications for teaching and assessing students with regard to these forms of intelligences.

Other intelligences such as spiritual, existential, and moral intelligences have been suggested or explored by Gardner and colleagues. However, only existential intelligence (the capacity to raise and reflect on philosophical questions about life, death, and ultimate

Table 19.1: Applications of Multiple Intelligences in Instruction and Assessment

Intelligence	Characteristics	Teaching	Assessing
Linguistic	Loves to read, write, tell stories, enjoys verbal interactions	Do storytelling activities, creative writing, reports and essays, oral and silent reading, memory games	Oral/written reports Dialogue journals Reading response Thinking/learning logs Memorization
Bodily-Kinesthetic	Loves to move, touch, gesture, use body language	Do sports, dance, acting, experiments, craft projects, field trips	Physical demonstrations Role playing Mime/charade games Read aloud with finger puppets Interpret story through dance
Spatial/Visual	Loves to visualize/create a mental picture, to draw and design, or to play with things in order to understand new information	Use visuals, charts, maps, and other graphic organizers to sort information Use video and computer-assisted instruction	Posters, charts, diagrams, illustrations, model constructions
Musical	Loves listening to melodies and is sensitive to pitch and rhythm	Do singing activities and poetry readings, reader's theater, jazz chants	Write a rap/song/ballad to display understanding Create sound effects for reader's theater or skit
Logical–Mathematical	Loves to work with numbers, figure out and explore patterns and relationships, do experiments, solve puzzles	Do math games, simulation, and thinking games	Solving mathematical and logic problems Student inventions Classify ideas Show relationship and pattern between ideas

(*Continued*)

Table 19.1: Applications of Multiple Intelligences in Instruction
and Assessment (*Continued*)

Intelligence	Characteristics	Teaching	Assessing
Interpersonal	Loves to interact with people and show leadership skills. Good at communicating, negotiating, organizing	Whole and small group discussions of topics. Class debates, oral interviews, reader response to peer writing, think-pair-share reading activity, jigsaw activity, structured controversies, board games	Group summary/report of video, reading, or problem-solving activities. Group negotiates on a solution to controversial problems or dilemma
Intrapersonal	Prefers independent work and is self-directed and motivated	Independent tasks on special interest topics. Reflective journals, self-assessment journals	Student portfolios where learners make personal choices of work to be included in the portfolio. Reading or writing rubrics of individual students. Self-made multimedia projects/reports
Naturalistic	Prefers to work with nature, nurturing and relating one's natural surroundings to learned information (This intelligence was added to MI theory in 1997)	Nature walks, field trips that involve examining natural habitats, caring for animals	Collect and analyze information related to nature, e.g., writing an I-search paper on environmentally related topics such as the protection of endangered species, the conservation of the environment, dealing with global warming, etc.

realities) has been considered because it meets most of the criteria of Gardner's MI theory. In class, teachers can include this intelligence in interdisciplinary lesson plans when discussing ethical issues, addressing topics such as ways to become civic-minded and contributing citizens who benefit nation building (Altan, 2001).

What is the practical application of the MI theory/learning styles theory for second language classrooms? First and foremost, because teachers will work with diverse groups of learners, it is essential that they understand the concept of learning styles and learners' language-learning capabilities so that they can develop language-learning materials to address these differences. With this knowledge, teachers will position themselves to better help students identify their strengths and shortcomings, and to facilitate the transfer of their strong skills to new learning.

Second, EL students must learn to adapt their learning styles to the educational culture of their new environments in order to be better prepared for American classrooms. Some studies of learning styles have demonstrated differences between mainstream and minority students in American classrooms. Research in the area of learning styles of children who are native English speakers suggests that learners have four learning style preferences: visual, kinesthetic, tactile, and auditory learning (Dunn, 1983, 1984; Kamińska, 2014.

However, Backes (1993) and Wolf, David, Butler-Barnes, & Zile-Tamsen, 2017) found that Native American high school students preferred sharing and community learning environments and indirect, reflective, and experiential learning, while mainstream students preferred concrete-sequential learning, a mode of thinking that typifies logical–mathematical intelligence. Reid (1987) and Radwan (2014) found differences in learning styles between English as a second language (ESL) students in intensive English classes in the United States and their native English speaking American counterparts. Most ESL students preferred tactile and kinesthetic learning; however, those who had been in American classrooms longer had adapted their learning styles and become more auditory and less tactile. These findings suggest that students' learning style preferences or predispositions may be nurtured by their respective cultures or learning environment.

Third, EL students in elementary classrooms who had little experience in American classrooms may benefit from training that allows them to expand on their existing styles. Fourth, since learners may exhibit differences in learning styles, it is important that teachers also include methods of assessment that are balanced and reflective of different intelligence (suggestions for alternative assessment and self-assessment methods discussed further in the section on self-assessment). This does not mean all forms of intelligence must be covered in assessing student performance. What is important is that teachers provide several methods of assessment from which students can choose. For example, they might ask a student to answer guided questions about a reading passage by drawing a diagram or picture that describes the text, or by analyzing the text and drawing comparisons and contrasts to other texts, or by performing a drama that highlights the important ideas.

Planning lessons for instruction should address individual MI, and students' needs should be considered carefully so all students can be reached. Materials and exercises should be incorporated using multiple sensory systems that exploit a particular intelligence. Students can be encouraged to reflect upon their own learning styles and how their particular intelligences relate to their daily lives.

Reid (1998) and Moore (2014) offer specific ways for teachers to modify their lesson plans to match different styles.

- Include activities that allow students to do both group work (collaborative learners) and some individual work (independent learners).
- Assignments should be written (visual learners) and spoken (auditory learners); this can be achieved by including activities such as note-taking, reading–writing, and discussions.
- Include hands-on activities such as role-play and demonstrations for concrete learners and individual problem-solving tasks for abstract learners.
- Teachers should allow reflective learners to do activities that require time for examining options and present active learners opportunities for spontaneous learning experiences.

POINTS TO REMEMBER

✔ Communicative competence is defined as one's ability to use language appropriately in a variety of contexts. There are four main communicative competencies: grammatical, sociolinguistic, discourse, and strategic.

✔ Strategic competence involves paraphrasing, borrowing, appealing for assistance, mime, and avoidance.

✔ Teachers should have informed knowledge of the communication strategies second language learners employ, so that they can match instructional strategies to learning strategies.

✔ The Cognitive Academic Language Learning Approach (CALLA) integrates content, language, and strategies. It consists of three main categories of strategies: metacognitive, cognitive, and social affective.

✔ Metacognitive strategies attend to organizational skills and self-evaluation; cognitive strategies include, among others, contextualization, imagery, summary, and note-taking. Social affective strategies include cooperation, questioning, clarification, and boosting one's self-confidence.

✔ Learning styles refers to the general ways in which we process and respond to information in our environment.

✔ ELs may have already developed culturally distinct learning style preferences and must learn to adapt their learning styles to their target language classroom to function well in their new learning environment. Teachers can ease ELs' transitions into their new classroom cultures by including students' dominant learning styles in their instruction, as well as exposing them to other ways of learning. In this way, learners will expand their learning styles and have more options to choose from and apply to different kinds of problem-solving tasks.

1. Do you think students should be taught strategies for learning a language? What was missing in your previous study of a second or foreign language? What could have been done to make your learning of another language more successful?

2. Read the vignette and answer the question that follows.

   During a math lesson, Ms. Johnson puts her students in groups and asks them to solve the following word problem:

   There are two tables of different sizes in a banquet hall. One size seats five people and the other size seats eight. At tonight's banquet, 79 people will be seated at fewer than one dozen tables and there will be no empty places. How many tables of each size will there be?

   Examine the list of CALLA learning strategies. Which strategies would you use to facilitate students' ability to solve this math problem?

3. Read the following description of the classroom interaction between an EL child and his tutor:

   Ms. Jacobs showed Luis, a sixth grade EL student, a calendar for the month of April. Then she asked him: "What happens in spring?" She then wrote out the word spring *and showed pictures of flowers and hatched chicken eggs. Luis tried to answer her but could not (Luis's expression indicated that he did not have the English words he wanted). He turned to the other children in the group and spoke to them in Spanish. It appeared as if he was asking them a question. The teacher kept prompting Luis by showing him the pictures of flowers and hatched eggs and saying, "Flowers grow and eggs hatch." Luis looked at her, but kept shaking his head. He glanced back at the pictures on the calendar. He stood up and pointed to the picture of the Easter basket on the calendar. Ms. Jacobs then said: "Oh yes, Easter is in spring!"*

   a. At what level of English proficiency is Luis?

   b. What communication strategies does he use to communicate with Ms. Jacobs?

c. What other strategies can Ms. Jacobs use to facilitate communication with Luis?

4. How would you find out what your students' learning style preferences might be?

5. Do you think teaching styles should match students' learning styles? Explain why or why not.

ACTIVITIES

1. Interview a second language learner of English. What were some communication strategies used by the second language learner during the interaction? Give examples.

2. Conduct a library research on cross-cultural learning style preferences. Are there learning styles that seem to be preferred by ESL students from specific cultures? How will these differences in learning styles affect student learning?

WEB RESOURCES

7 Learning Styles: An ESL Teaching Strategy That Works. https://www.fluentu.com/blog/educator-english/esl-teaching-strategies-styles
CALLA—Cognitive Academic Language Approach Video. https://www.youtube.com/watch?v=BFtOu87ZLVM
CALLA—ESOL Strategies. https://www.esolstrategies.weebly.com/calla.html
CALLA—Monitoring Monkey. https://www.youtube.com/watch?v=eIzx2eQWwmc

Cognitive Academic Language Learning Approach. https://www.study.com/academy/lesson/cognitive-academic-language-learning-approach.html

Do's and Don'ts for Teaching English-Language Learners. https://www.edutopia.org/blog/esl-ell-tips-ferlazzo-sypnieski

REFERENCES

Alhawiti, M. M., & Abdelhamid, Y. (2017). A personalized e-learning framework. *Journal of Education and e-Learning Research, 4*(1), 15–21.

Altan, M. Z. (2001). Intelligence reframed: Multiple intelligences for the 21st century: Howard Gardner. *TESOL Quarterly, 35*(1), 204–205.

Backes, J. (1993, May). The American Indian high school dropout rate: A matter of style? *Journal of American Indian Education, 32*(3), 16–29.

Baytar, B. (2014). Implicit and explicit grammar teaching. In B. Baytar (Ed.), *Linguistics, culture and identity in foreign language education* (p. 365). Sarajevo, Bosnia: IBU.

Benson, P., & Voller, P. (2014). *Autonomy and independence in language learning*. New York, NY: Routledge.

Bialystok, E., & Sharwood Smith, M. (1985). Interlanguage is not a state of mind: An evaluation of the construct for second-language acquisition. *Applied linguistics*, *6*(2), 101–117.

Canale, M. (1983). From communicative competence to communicative language pedagogy. In J. Richards & R. W. Schmidt (Eds.), *Language and communication*. New York, NY: Longman.

Chamot, A. U. (2014, December). Developing self-regulated learning in the language classroom. Knowledge, skills and competencies in foreign language education. *Proceedings of the sixth Centre for Language Studies (CLS) international conference* (pp. 4–6). Singapore.

Chater, N., McCauley, S. M., & Christiansen, M. H. (2016). Language as skill: Intertwining comprehension and production. *Journal of Memory and Language, 89*, 244–254.

Cohen, A. D. (1990). *Second language learning: Insights for learners, teachers, and researchers*. New York, NY: Harper and Row.

Cohen, A. D. (1996a). Second language learning and use strategies: Clarifying the issues. Retrieved from http://www.carla.umn.edu:16080/ strategies/resources/SBlclarify.pdf

Cohen, A. D. (1996b). The impact of strategies-based instructions on speaking a foreign language. Retrieved from http://www.carla.umn.edu/about/profiles/CohenPapers/SBlimpact.pdf

Cohen, A. D. (2014). *Strategies in learning and using a second language*. Alexandria, VA: Routledge.

Cook, V. (2013). *Second language learning and language teaching*. New York, NY: Routledge.

Dörnyei, Z. (1995). On the teachability of communication strategies. *TESOL Quarterly, 29*(1), 55–85.

Dörnyei, Z. (2014). *The psychology of the language learner: Individual differences in second language acquisition*. New York, NY: Routledge.

Dunn, R. (1983). Learning style and its relation to exceptionality at both ends of the spectrum. *Exceptional Children, 49*, 496–506.

Dunn, R. (1984). Learning style: State of the scene. *Theory into Practice, 23*, 10–19.

Gardner, H. (1983). *Frames of mind: The theory of multiple intelligences*. New York, NY: Basic Books

Gardner, H. (2017). Taking a multiple intelligences (MI) perspective. *Behavioral and Brain Sciences, 40*, 183–184.

Gass, S., & Selinker, L. (2008). *Second language acquisition: An introductory course*. New York, NY: Routledge.

Hymes, D. (1974). *Directions in sociolinguistics*. Philadelphia, PA: University of Pennsylvania Press.

Hymes, D. (2013). Country: Toward linguistic competence in the United States. In *The sociogenesis of language and human conduct* (189–224).

Kamiñska, P. M. (2014). *Learning styles and second language education*. London, UK: Cambridge Scholars.

Kern, R., & Kramsch, C. (2014). Communicative grammar and communicative competence. In C. A. Chapelle (Ed.), *The encyclopedia of applied linguistics*. Malden, MA: Wiley.

Knowles, M. S., Holton III, E. F., & Swanson, R. A. (2014). *The adult learner: The definitive classic in adult education and human resource development*. New York, NY: Routledge.

Messick, S., & Associates (Eds.). (1976). *Individuality in learning*. San Francisco, CA: Jossey-Bass.

Moeller, A. K., & Nugent, K. (2014). *Building intercultural competence in the language classroom* (p. 161). Faculty Publications: Department of Teaching, Learning and Teacher Education. Retrieved from http://digitalcommons.unl.edu/teachlearnfacpub/161

Moore, K. D. (2014). *Effective instructional strategies: From theory to practice*. Los Angeles, CA: Sage.

Nyikos, M. (1991). Prioritizing student learning: A guide for teachers. In L. Strasheim (Ed.), *Focus on the foreign language learner*. Lincolnwood, IL: NTC.

O'Malley, J. M., & Chamot, A. U. (1990). *Learning strategies in second language acquisition*. Cambridge, UK: Cambridge University Press.

Oxford, R. L. (2016). *Teaching and researching language learning strategies: Self-regulation in context*. New York, NY: Taylor & Francis.

Oxford, R. L., & Carmen, M. A. (2017). *Language learning strategies and individual learner characteristics: Situating strategy use in diverse contexts*. London, UK: Bloomsbury.

Radwan, A. A. (2014). Gender and learning style preferences of EFL learner. *Arab World English Journal, 5*(1), 21–32.

Reid, J. (1987). The learning style preferences of ESL students. *TESOL Quarterly, 21*(1), 87–111.

Reid, J. (1998). Learning styles." In P. Byrd and J. Reid (Eds.), *Grammar in the composition class*. Boston, MA: Heinle and Heinle.

Schmidt, R. W. (1994). Deconstructing consciousness in search of useful definitions for applied linguistics. *AILA Review, 11*, 11–16.

Stern, H. H. (1992). *Issues and options in language teaching*. Oxford, UK: OUP.

Tarone, E. E. (1981). Some thoughts on the notion of communication strategy. *TESOL Quarterly, 15*, 285–295.

Ventriglia, L. (1982). *Conversations of Miguel and Maria: How children learn a second language*. Reading, MA: Addison-Wesley.

Wolf, P. S., David, A., Butler-Barnes, S. T., & Zile-Tamsen, V. (2017). American Indian/Alaskan native college dropout: Recommendations for increasing retention and graduation. *Journal on Race, Inequality, and Social Mobility in America, 1*(1), 1.

SELF-ASSESSMENT OF ORAL LANGUAGE

Name _____ Date _____

Check (✓) the box that shows what you can do. Add comments.					
What Can You Do in English	**Difficulty Level**				**Comments**
	Not Very Well	**Okay**	**Well**	**Very Well**	
1. I can ask questions in class.					
2. I can understand others when working in a group.					
3. I can understand television shows.					
4. I can speak with native speakers outside of school.					
5. I can talk on the phone.					
6. I can ask for an explanation.					

O'Malley, J. Michael; Pierce, Lorraine Valdez, *Authentic Assessment for English Language Learners*, 1st Ed., © 1996. Reprinted by permission of Pearson Education, Inc., New York, New York.

SELF-ASSESSMENT OF ACADEMIC LANGUAGE FUNCTIONS

Name _____ Date _____

Check (✓) the box that best describes how well you can use English. Add comments.					
Task	Not Very Well	Okay	Well	Very Well	Comments
1. I can describe objects and people.					
2. I can describe past events.					
3. I can listen to and understand radio programs.					
4. I can listen to and understand video and television.					
5. I can state on opinion.					
6. I can agree and disagree.					
7. I can summarize a story.					
8. I can give an oral report.					

O'Malley, J. Michael; Pierce, Lorraine Valdez, *Authentic Assessment for English Language Learners*, 1st Ed., © 1996. Reprinted by permission of Pearson Education, Inc., New York, New York.

SELF-ASSESSMENT OF READING STRATEGIES

Name _____ Date _____

Check (✓) the box that indicates how you read.			
Reading Strategies	**Often**	**Sometimes**	**Almost Never**
1. I think about what I already know on the topic.			
2. I make predictions and read to find out if I was rich.			
3. I reread the sentences before and after a word I do not know.			
4. I ask another student for help.			
5. I look for the main idea.			
6. I take notes.			
7. I discuss what I read with others.			
8. I stop and summarize.			
9. I choose books from the library on my own.			
10. I make outlines of what I read.			

O'Malley, J. Michael; Pierce, Lorraine Valdez, *Authentic Assessment for English Language Learners*, 1st Ed., © 1996. Reprinted by permission of Pearson Education, Inc., New York, New York.

CHAPTER

Twenty

Language Learning and Strategies for Error Correction

LEARNING OBJECTIVES

Readers will be able to

- ❖ Distinguish major types of learner errors
- ❖ Determine the role of error correction in language acquisition
- ❖ Prepare and plan appropriate techniques for error correction

SCENARIO

Examine the students' and teachers' comments below regarding learning errors and error correction. What do you notice about the way students and teachers view error correction in language learning?

Students' Comments:

"My teacher tells me this is very good work. But when I get my work back, my paper is full of errors. I think my teacher didn't like my work."

"I just can't say anything without making mistakes. That is why I keep quiet."

"I know I don't say it right. I want to learn. I want my teacher to correct all my mistakes."

Teachers' Comments:

"I don't understand what my students are saying, so how can I correct them?"

"My students are making the same mistakes over and over again, although I've corrected their errors many times."

"I've got to correct all their errors; otherwise, I'm not doing my job!"

Although there is no doubt that both the students and teachers above recognize that making errors is a natural part of the learning process, they have different opinions about "errors" and the language learning process. Because language learning involves emotional, psychological, and cognitive states, teachers should not ignore the effect that error correction has on language acquisition. At the same time, teachers often feel that they face a dilemma: if errors are left uncorrected, will students' language learning become fossilized and permanent? And if they do address errors, which should they correct and how? The answers to these questions will depend on students' language proficiency, educational background, and risk-taking behavior (Diaz-Rico, 2013).

LEARNER "ERRORS"

We use the word "error" in quotes because much of what teachers see and hear in English learners' (ELs) language production are issues of language transfer and developmental phases of second language acquisition (see Chapter 17). In other words, these are normal in the process of learning English. However, teachers frequently ask for guidance in addressing students' language production. We offer the following guidelines for teachers:

a. Teachers should not correct every error that learners make in speech and writing. If a learner is still at the early stages of language acquisition, teachers should encourage the student to experiment `with language and not worry too much about accuracy. If the student says, *"I wear blouse blue"* or *"I no go in there,"* the teacher can model correct forms of English and respond *"Oh, you wear a blue blouse?"* or *"You did not go in there. What did you do then?"* The important thing is to remember that learners are still getting the correct structures they need; focusing too much on their errors will cause unnecessary anxieties and raise the affective filter (Krashen, 1981), which can hamper learning.

b. As learners get more confident with their new language, teachers can focus on specific errors that interfere with communication. Research (James, 2013) suggests that there are certain types of errors that may hinder communication. These are considered *global errors*. These errors are usually characterized by incorrect word order pattern, omission or incorrect use of transitional expressions, omission or incorrect use of lexical items that carry significant information, and incorrect use of words caused by poor pronunciation. Remember that these differences based on students' knowledge, use, and transfer from her first language. Some examples of global errors are listed below:

Incorrect sentence structure:

- *The bus use many people. (Many people use the bus.)*
- *Not do homework principal will call to office. (The principal will call students to the office if they do not do their homework.)*
- *If we practice sports, we will enjoy together. (If we practice sport together, we will enjoy ourselves.)*
- *This way, can gain plenty of experience.* (missing subject: *This way, we can gain plenty of experience.*)
- *Hungry and poor drove Timoen to despair.* (missing gerund: *Being hungry and poor drove Timoen to despair.*)

On the other hand, learners may also commit errors that do not hinder communication. These are considered *local errors*; meaning can still be inferred from context. These errors are usually characterized by misuse of verb tense; incorrect use of verbs to describe conditions/state of being; incorrect use of inflectional morphemes; omission of articles such as *a*, *an*, or *the*; and so on. Examples of the different types of local errors are as follows:

Misuse of verb tenses:

- *People <u>will</u> feel sick every time they saw these.*
- *Our interviews were conducted face to face, and the time taken on each person <u>is</u> 15 minutes.*
- *I <u>knew</u> Marcella since 1970.*
- *I wish you <u>are</u> staying here with me.*

Omission of plurals and misuse of singular and plural nouns:

- *He has many <u>problem</u>.*
- *These <u>knifes</u> need to be sharpened.*
- *The <u>Chineses</u> celebrate their New Year in February.*

Misuse of count and uncountable nouns:

- *He gave me useful <u>advices</u>.*
- *He collects antique <u>furnitures</u>.*
- *She traveled with a lot of <u>luggages</u>.*

Misuse of plurals of compound nouns:

- *She bought two <u>photos</u> albums.*
- *He has two <u>son-in-laws</u>.*

Errors in comparative constructions:

- *I have <u>more big</u> toys at home.*
- *I <u>prefer</u> reading than watching films.*
- *Day after day, I felt weak <u>than</u> before.*

Errors in reported speech:

- *I don't know why <u>did</u> this happen.*
- *Marisol's friends advised her <u>don't</u> be so proud.*

Errors in subject–verb and pronoun agreement:

- *I can't work anymore; my body <u>feel</u> weak.*
- *Everybody <u>were</u> waiting to see what would happen next.*
- *Advertising <u>are</u> essential for modern businesses.*

Missing *be* verb:

- *It never easy for me to forget a good friend. (It is never …)*
- *This subject not very popular among middle school students. (This subject is …)*

Miscellaneous:

- *Maria, my best friend likes Barbie dolls (missing comma: my best friend,)*
- *I <u>have</u> eight years old (misuse verbs that describe state or conditions: I am eight years old.)*
- *I ate big apple. (Article omission: I ate a …)*

Some of these errors may sound odd to a native speaker, but they do not interfere with communication. Teachers should also bear in mind that they should not overcorrect errors rarely committed by students. Correction should consistently focus on the most frequent errors, rather than on isolated errors.

In summary, the criteria for selecting errors to correct depend on several factors: (a) the students' needs and their personal reactions to error correction, (b) the comprehensibility of the message, and (c) the frequency of particular types of errors. Depending on the cultural and training backgrounds of ELs, some students expect grammar instruction and expect their teacher to correct their error. Unless their grammar needs are met, they may not be receptive to try other indirect techniques of error correction that require learners to self-correct with some teacher assistance.

c. Teachers should not judge grammatical and lexical forms used in nonstandard or non-native varieties as errors. While these varieties may have their unique syntax, semantic system, grammar, pronunciation, and rhythm, they are not linguistically inferior. In addition, with the growth in English worldwide and World Englishes, there are many varieties of English that sound different but are perfectly correct in the context of communication. Like every other language, these varieties are fully systematic, grammatical, symbolic, and pose no barrier to abstract thought. However, as previously discussed, teachers are responsible for making sure that their ELs develop the standard form used in school. Hence, teachers must stress the importance of keeping both language systems so that their students can navigate through a variety of situations in which they are expected to use language.

STRATEGIES FOR ERROR CORRECTION

The following are some strategies for English as a second language (ESL) student error correction that, with a teacher's help, will promote self-correction.

- Identify the error.
- Rephrase (or model) the question or explanation.
- Explain a key word or grammatical rule.
- Repeat student answers with correction.
- Provide cues for students to self-correct; for example, using fingers to represent each word produced by the learner. Then tell students that the finger that is down denotes that the word is grammatically incorrect. Ask learners to correct their errors, giving further hints as necessary.
- Compile some samples of high frequency errors made by the whole class, keeping the students' identities anonymous. Circle the errors and facilitate student correction.
- Ask students to listen to their taped oral reading, and another tape produced by a more proficient peer. Then ask them to compare differences in pronunciation between the two tapes.

Because error correction may influence learners' attitude toward learning the target language, here are some "do nots" of error correction:

- Do not overly correct learners' errors, especially speech errors. This can increase their reluctance to participate in discussions and experiment with language in both oral and writing activities.
- Do not try to correct too many errors at a time, as this may put undue burden on their processing ability. The rule of thumb is to correct global errors first before local errors, or correct errors that students frequently produce first before other less frequent errors.
- Do not correct student's errors in front of the whole class, as this may make them embarrassed.
- Do not judge grammatical forms and word choice used in nonstandard varieties or non-native varieties as incorrect. When teachers do this, they are undermining the role and function of the learners' native language experience and knowledge as an important bridge to acquiring the target language.

POINTS TO REMEMBER

✔ Although errors are natural in language learning, teachers can strategically address the errors that can occur as part of the developmental process of second language acquisition.
✔ Teachers should first focus on global errors (those that hinder communication), rather than local errors (those that do not interfere with communication).
✔ Teachers should not overcorrect isolated errors that are not committed frequently. Too much emphasis on accuracy can heighten learner anxiety, which, in turn, will impede learning.
✔ Teachers must take into consideration the learners' needs, first language(s), level of linguistic proficiency, and personal reaction to error correction.

REFLECTION QUESTIONS AND DISCUSSION

1. What are global language errors? Local errors? Identify two examples of each.

2. Have you tried learning another language? If so, what tactics, tips, or tricks did you use in trying to correct your mistakes? How do you remember the correct way to say or do something?

1. Examine the following errors produced by ELs. Which do you consider to be global errors? Local errors? Why?
   a. My aunt is arrive in town last night.

   b. People in this world need a friends.

   c. Is very hot today.

   d. In Germany, have good methods to train their athletes.

   e. That boy faced a lot of problems, as having no money, friends with father, and so on.

   f. I am interesting in learning about space.

   g. When he saw the unpleasant food, he looked disgusting and called the waiter.

   h. It's dangerous to cut cars on the road.

   i. In my country isn't army, navy, and air force.

   j. Though my grandmother is old, he is very strong.

k. I like to seat in front of the class.

l. We open our shoes in the house.
Describe the approach you would use to correct some of the errors above.

2. The following writing sample was written by an elementary EL student. Are there global errors in this passage? Explain.

My Mom came from Cyoba and my dad came from Racha. My Daddy is going to take me to Racha this summr. My Mom is going to take me to Cyoba when she feels safe. Racha is cold so my daddy likes cold. Cyoba is hot so my mommy likes hot. My Mom shows me lots of magasens about Cyoba.

My dad tells me about racha. My dad's Dad was ararond in the time Anastasha was alive. My mom was varey rich intil the Bad Prasadint in Cyoba tock thar money away. Now thay are powr but Daddy gives Mommy Money.

Source: Adapted from Literacy Folder Writing Assessment K–2, Broward County Public Schools.

WEB RESOURCES

7 Ways to Error Correct. http://elt-connect.com/error-correct

Best Ways to Correct English Mistakes in Your ESL Class. https://www.youtube.com/watch?v=kt899DEd43s

Better or Worse Comic Illustrates the Danger of Error Correction. http://www.gocomics.com/forbetterorforworse/2010/05/07

Dealing With Students Errors. http://www.eslfocus.com/articles/dealing_with_student_errors-401.html

EFL Teacher Training—Error Correction. https://www.youtube.com/watch?v=AHj5lAEpih8

Errors and Strategies in Language Acquisition. https://www.ukessays.com/essays/teaching/errors-and-strategies-in-language-acquisition.php

Error Correction in the Second Language Classroom. http://www.clear.msu.edu/resources/newsletter/past-issues/error-correction

Larry Ferlazzo: ESL/EL Error Correction—Yes, No, or Maybe? http://www.teachingenglish.org.uk/blogs/paul-braddock/larry-ferlazzo-eslell-error-correction-yes-no-or-maybe

My Students' Favourite Error Correction Activity. https://jellybeanqueen.wordpress.com/2016/11/05/my-students-favourite-error-correction-activity

Response: Effective Strategies for EL Error Correction. http://blogs.edweek.org/teachers/classroom_qa_with_larry_ferlazzo/2016/04/response_effective_strategies_for_ell_error_correction.html

REFERENCES

Diaz-Rico, L. T. (2013). *The crosscultural, language, and academic development handbook: A complete K-12 reference guide*. Boston, MA: Pearson Higher Ed.

James, C. (2013). *Errors in language learning and use: Exploring error analysis*. New York, NY: Routledge.

Krashen, S. (1981). *Second language acquisition and second language learning*. Oxford, UK: Pergamon Press.

Second Language Teaching Methodologies

LEARNING OBJECTIVES

Readers will be able to:

- ❖ Determine chronological development of language methodologies
- ❖ Utilize the principles and techniques of various language teaching methodologies

SCENARIO

Students sit in a semicircle, attentively listening to the dialogue, presented on tape, of a conversation between two friends talking after class.

> Susan: *Hi Carlos! How are you today?*
> Carlos: *Fine, thanks. And you?*
> Susan: *Fine. Are you going to the cafeteria?*
> Carlos: *No, I'm going to the library.*
> Susan: *I am going to the library too. Can I walk with you?*
> Carlos: *Sure, let's go.*

The teacher asks the whole class to repeat the taped dialogue, line by line. He models the pronunciation of some of the words. Then, he asks students to work in pairs; one student assumes the role of Susan and the other Carlos. After 5 minutes of practicing the dialogue, the teacher asks students comprehension and vocabulary questions.

The previous vignette depicts one of the methodologies presented in Table 21.1. The table presents the chronological development of foreign language teaching over a period of more than a century.

Although these methodologies were first used in foreign language teaching, over the years, at times they were adopted into the teaching of English as a second language (ESL) and may even be used in the mainstream classrooms today.

The term ESOL (used interchangeably with ESOL and TESOL) methodologies have not always reflected student-centered approaches. In fact, the Grammar Translation Method (GTM) was one of the earliest methods in foreign language teaching at the start of the 20th century and was first used in the teaching of classical languages. The GTM focuses learning the grammar of the target language but not on communicative competence. This method was used in the hopes that students would be able to appreciate literary works written in the target language. However, this methodology assumed that students would already be familiar with the grammar of their native language. Since students learn the target language for the purpose of reading literary works, reading and writing skills are greatly emphasized, while speaking skills are considered less important.

The Direct Method (DM) became popular as a reaction to GTM. Since GTM failed to teach students to communicate, the DM focuses on teaching students to communicate in the target language. In this method, students are required to communicate in the target language without reverting to their native language; therefore, translation is not allowed.

During World War II, there was an urgent need in the United States to teach foreign languages to military personnel. During that era, although DM taught learners to communicate in the target language, learners were not learning the target language fast enough. At the time, descriptive linguistics and behavioral psychology were prevalent areas of study, and exciting ideas in both fields contributed to the birth of yet another method in language teaching—the Audio-Lingual Method (ALM). Like the DM, the goal of the ALM is for students to communicate in the target language. There are many similarities and differences between the principles of both methods.

Additional language teaching methodologies surfaced in the early 1980s as a lot of research was conducted in second language acquisition. Scholars such as Krashen and Terrell (Krashen & Terrell, 1983) outlined another language learning method called Natural Approach. The pendulum of language teaching shifted again. Current approaches in second language teaching emphasize students learning the additional language are similar to how young children acquire their first language. Since children acquire their first language without the imposition of grammatical rules, the Natural Approach integrates techniques drawn from other methodologies that emphasize the promotion of comprehensible and meaningful activities over the teaching of grammatical rules.

Total Physical Response (TPR), an offshoot of the Natural Approach, was developed by James Asher (Asher, 1969). He asserted that speech comprehension can be demonstrated through physical action to various commands in an informal and low anxiety learning environment (Richards & Rodgers, 2014).

Second language teaching methodologies have come a long way from GTM to current methods, such as the Whole Language and cognitive academic language learning approach (CALLA). The Whole Language approach and CALLA advocate teaching language

Table 21.1: Chronology of Language Teaching Methodologies

Time Period	Method	Explanation	Techniques	Error Treatment in Classroom	Teacher's Role	Student's Role	Current Application
Until the late 19th century	Grammar Translation	Based on the way Latin and Greek are taught. The purpose of this method is to teach the reading of literary works in the target language. There are no linguistic or learning theories to support this method.	Memorization of grammatical rules and vocabularies. Direct translations to and from another language are intellectual exercises that enhance students' comprehension of how their own language functions. Little or no emphasis on oral skills, as the focus is on reading and writing. The rules are reinforced in drills and translation exercises. Classes are taught in students' native language. Bilingual dictionary is used.	Accuracy in bilingual translation is the focus in correction and feedback. Peers or teachers correct mistakes.	Following a traditional way of teaching, the teacher is the authority figure in the class, helping students read literature in the target language. They provide translation and corrections when necessary. Input is in the form of the unidirectional lecture format.	Students follow teacher's instruction closely. They have very limited opportunity to work with their peers.	Use of dictionary. Provide translation when necessary. Label words and items in L1.
Late 19th–early 20th century	Direct	Purpose is to promote communication in target language without translating. The premise is that the second language should be learned as naturally as possible, just as children learn their native language.	The use of native language is forbidden. Grammar is taught inductively through fill-in-the-blank exercises. Contextualization of language within a situation or topic is employed.	It is very important that students produce correct pronunciation and grammar. The teacher can use a variety of means to elicit self-correction.	Teachers must have native or near-native fluency in target language, as they will be modeling and controlling the flow of "natural" input in the target language. Teachers foster environments in which students' participation is elicited.	Students are active participants, communicating their thoughts and ideas frequently. They absorb as much input as possible so that they can begin to think in the target language.	Small group work. Grammar can be provided peripherally. Use social language to teach academic language. Use topics of real interest, such as hobbies, movies, etc.

(Continued)

Table 21.1: Chronology of Language Teaching Methodologies (*Continued*)

Time Period	Method	Explanation	Techniques	Error Treatment in Classroom	Teacher's Role	Student's Role	Current Application
1940–1950	Audio-Lingual Structur-allinguist, Charles Fries popular in the 1950's.)	Language is viewed as a habit-formation process, reflecting the theory of behavioral psychology. L2 should be learned without reference to L1. Speaking and listening precede reading and writing, as language is equated to speech.	Stimulus-response drills; memorization of dialogues; exclusive use of L2; grammar rules are taught indirectly; the order of skills learned: listening, speaking, reading, and writing.	Students' responses are positively and immediately reinforced. Errors are immediately corrected to avoid the forming of bad habits. First, students are asked individually to repeat the corrected word or sentence. Later the rest of the class will do the same.	Teacher is in control of all activities in class. Provides students with a model for imitation, directs all activities, makes corrections and provides reinforcement where necessary.	Students mimic and memorize dialogues and patterns. They work in language lab with tapes to practice listening and speaking.	Initial memorization of relevant canon utterances in target language. Skits using dialogue.
Late 1970s, early 1980s	Natural Approach (Krashen and Terrell)	A second language is learned using the same process that children use to learn to speak. The method integrates Krashen's hypothesis of L2 language acquisition and observations on acquisition of L1 and L2 languages. Students need to acquire a huge inventory of vocabulary to understand and use speech. Meaning is emphasized over grammatical accuracy. The method proposes to develop students' basic interpersonal communication skills (BICS) or social language and cognitive academic language proficiency (CALP), or academic language.	The content of lessons reflects students' needs and language proficiency levels. Class activities are meaningful, and repetition of grammatically perfect sentences is avoided. Games and problem-solving tasks are used in class. Students' silent period is acknowledged.	Students are free to make errors. Corrections are made through restatement or modeling of correct utterances.	Teachers provide instruction that is comprehen-sible, by using a variety of interesting activities that meet students' needs, proficiency skills, and class objectives. Teachers' create a conducive and relaxed learning environment that does not pressure students to speak when they are not ready.	Students are encouraged to participate in communi-cative activities that promote language acquisition. They focus on context and key words to arrive at the general meaning. Inference skills are highly promoted.	Low anxiety class atmosphere where learning and acquisition of language will take place. Use communicative activities such as role-play, drama, and skits. Use realia and authentic materials, such as magazines and newspapers.

(*Continued*)

Table 21.1: Chronology of Language Teaching Methodologies (*Continued*)

Time Period	Method	Explanation	Techniques	Error Treatment in Classroom	Teacher's Role	Student's Role	Current Application
1974	Total Physical Response (TPR) (Asher) Whole Language (Goodman, 1986)	Action and speech are combined in an informal and stress-free learning environment. Comprehension precedes speech, as speech will emerge naturally. TPR syllabus is sentence based; focusing on grammar and vocabularies through meaning is the primary emphasis.	Physical action is used to teach language. Students indicate comprehension through movement and actions. Students listen and respond physically to oral commands for first 10 hours of instruction. Use target language only.	Errors are tolerated by teachers, as meaning and comprehension is the major focus. Errors are expected, and only major ones are corrected at first. Correction of errors should always be made in context and in a nonthreatening manner.	The teacher plans and directs activities. Language input is provided in the form of commands. As students become more in control of their learning, teachers guide their interaction individually, as well as on a whole-group basis.	First, students observe the behavior modelled by teachers and volunteers. Students should show comprehension through action, although they are not required to produce language until they are ready. Students should understand different combinations and sequences of commands and adapt to new situations.	Use TPR to act out difficult words. Observe students' silent period. Correct errors that hinder communication.
1970s and early 1980s	Whole Language (Goodman, 1986)	Learning proceeds from whole to part. Learning should take place in the L1 language to build concepts and facilitate the acquisition of the L2 language.	Lessons are purposeful and student centered. Cooperative learning.	Making errors is a normal process in learning. Errors are corrected meaningfully and in a contextualized manner.	Teacher makes informed decisions about teaching, learning, reading, and writing. Focuses on literacy and the process of learning, rather than the products.	Students experiment and take risks when learning the new language. They should see themselves as producers of knowledge and not be afraid to make mistakes.	Student-centered classroom. Use literature in class. Content-driven language curriculum.
1987	CALLA (Chamot and O'Malley, 1994)	See Chapter 17.					

(*Continued*)

Table 21.1: Chronology of Language Teaching Methodologies (*Continued*)

Time Period	Method	Explanation	Techniques	Error Treatment in Classroom	Teacher's Role	Student's Role	Current Application
21st century	All methods within the Communicative Approach	e.g., Problem-Based Learning.	Lessons are based on students' collaboration in solving a problem. Students identify a problem area in the theme, research, analyze data, synthesize information, and finally report findings. Promote self-learning and students' ownership toward discovering informed knowledge.	Making developmental errors is viewed as normal. Teachers address meaningful error-correction in students' final drafts.	Facilitator and guide.	Active participation and assuming responsibilities in all aspects of the learning process.	Use in inter-disciplinary thematic unit lessons.

through the use of meaningful content areas and the integration of language acquisition skills. Today, the most significant goal in language teaching is for learners to achieve communicative competence (both oral/aural and literacy) in the target language through academic content (Diaz-Rico, 2013).

A summary of the principles and techniques of the abovementioned methods are presented in Table 21.1.

POINTS TO REMEMBER

✔ The Grammar Translation Method, which originated in the late 19th century, uses techniques such as memorization of grammatical rules and vocabularies, direct translations, and drill exercises to teach the target language. The purpose of the method is to teach the reading of literary works in the target language.

✔ The Direct Method (DM), which began in the early 20th century, forbids the use of native language in the class. Grammar is taught inductively through fill-in-the-blank exercises. Language is taught in context.

✔ The Audio-Lingual Method (ALM) was first used in the 1940s. It is based on the behaviorist view of language learning. The order of skills learned are listening, speaking, reading, and writing. L2 should be learned without reference to L1.

✔ The Natural Approach emerged in the late 1970s and early 1980s. It is based on how children acquire their first language and integrates Krashen's hypotheses: affective filter, the "input hypothesis," natural order, and acquisition versus learning. Teachers should provide a comfortable, low anxiety classroom that is conducive to learning. Learners' silent period is acknowledged, and communicating meaning is emphasized over grammatical accuracy.

✔ TPR is a method that uses physical actions to teach language. Students show comprehension through movement and response to teacher commands. The learning environment is stress free. Since comprehension precedes production, learners can use nonverbal responses, by repeating the motion, nodding and pointing, or acting out the answers.

✔ Whole language was developed in the early 1980s. It centers on the idea that learning proceeds from whole to parts. Lessons in this approach are student-centered and purposeful. Curriculum is literature based, and cooperative learning is used.

REFLECTION QUESTIONS AND DISCUSSION

1. Explain how the ALM reflects the behaviorist view of language learning.

2. Using the principles behind the Natural Approach, brainstorm a list of teaching methods that teachers can use with ELs.

ACTIVITIES

1. Mrs. Groce's reading class consists of 19 EL students. She begins the class with everyone sitting on the carpet. She reviews the book "Little Red Riding Hood" which she read to the class yesterday. She explains that she is going to read them another book today: "the Chinese Red Riding Hood" called "Lon Po Po." Mrs. Groce reads this story aloud to the students, using hand gestures and facial expressions, and acting out some words in the story. After she reads the story, she tells the children that they are going to compare the two stories using a Venn diagram already drawn on chart paper. Some students need help understanding her questions, so Ms. Groce's bilingual aide clarifies the questions in their home language—Spanish.

   When Ms. Groce asks an EL student who is at early production stage of English proficiency to answer a question, she asks the bilingual aide to translate the question and offers a wait time of approximately 2 minutes. The other children are restless and shout out the answer, but Ms. Groce tells them to wait for the student to answer the question. The student answers the question and Ms. Groce continues her lesson.

Using Table 21.1, identify the approaches behind the different techniques found in the above vignette.

2. Compare and contrast these three methods: Whole Language, DM, and ALM in terms of the following:
   a. Techniques
   b. Error treatment
   c. Student's role

Based on the above, which method(s) provides the ideal environment for optimum language acquisition? Why?

WEB RESOURCES

Key Strategies for ELL Instruction. https://www.teachingchannel.org/blog/2013/10/25/strategies-for-ell-instruction

EL Strategies and Best Practices. http://www.colorincolorado.org/ell-strategies-best-practices

ESL Methods—English Language Teaching. https://www.owlcation.com/humanities/Foreign-language-teaching-methods-approaches

Language Teaching Methodologies. http://esl.fis.edu/teachers/support/method.htm

Teaching English Without Teaching English. https://www.youtube.com/watch?v=8pZa6R3rmRQ

Theories/Methods/Strategies/Research. https://www.mydigitalchalkboard.org/portal/default/Content/Viewer/Content?action=2&scId=100051&sciId=1405

Theories—Methods & Techniques of Teaching English. https://www.youtube.com/watch?v=cKm7Z9Eb16A

REFERENCES

Asher, J. J. (1969). The total physical response approach to second language learning. *The Modern Language Journal, 53*(1), 3–17.

Chamot, A. U., & O'Malley, J. M. (1994). *The CALLA handbook: Implementing the cognitive academic language learning approach.* Reading, MA: Addison-Wesley.

Diaz-Rico, L. T. (2013). *The crosscultural, language, and academic development handbook: A complete K-12 reference guide.* New York, NY: Pearson Higher Ed.

Fries, C. C. (1963). *Linguistics and reading* (Vol. 2). New York, NY: Holt Rinehart and Winston.

Goodman, K. (1986). *What's whole in whole language*. Richmond Hill, ON: Scholastic TAB.

Krashen, S. D., & Terrell, T. D. (1983). *The natural approach: Language acquisition in the classroom*. San Francisco, CA: Alemany Press.

Richards, J. C., & Rodgers, T. S. (2014). *Approaches and methods in language teaching*. New York, NY: Cambridge University Press.

A Knowledge Base for Assessment, Evaluation, and Family Engagement

Literacy Development and the English Learner

Readers will be able to

- ❖ Describe literacy development (reading and writing) for English Learner (EL) students
- ❖ Describe five areas of reading for ELs
- ❖ Determine effective scaffolding and strategies for ELs' literacy development in reading and writing

Emilio is a fifth grade EL student in Brittany's mainstream classroom. He moved from Guatemala to Florida in fourth grade. Emilio's World Class Instructional Design and Assessment (WIDA) reading level is a 2.0, his writing level is a 2.5, and his speaking level is a 4.0. Brittany has a total of three ELs, and she uses a variety of instructional strategies to build literacy for all of her students. She uses learning centers in her reading and writing block. In the centers, students work independently on either a computerized reading program, sustained silent reading, writing to prompts that she has created, or completing Frayer model for key vocabulary development (see Figure 22.1).

Emilio completes individual work at the computer and proceeds, with his small group, to the sustained silent reading center where he can choose a book to read. He quickly selects *Harry Potter and the Order of the Phoenix* by J. K. Rowling and pretends to read it by opening it the middle of the book. However, it is clear that the book is well-above his English reading ability level. Using Emilio's WIDA reading score, Brittany selects three books that seem to interest Emilio, who loves playing basketball and learning about the solar system, and that align to his ability level. One is a translated Harry Potter book, and two others relate to sports and the solar system. She also provides him a translation dictionary and a bilingual glossary that he can use while reading the books.

Literacy development—in this chapter reading and writing—is an essential part of schooling. UNESCO (2003) notes that literacy "is about more than reading and writing—it is about how we communicate in society. It is about social practices and relationships, about knowledge, language and culture. Literacy—the use of written communication—finds its place in our lives alongside other ways of communicating."

Today, students must have knowledge about multiple forms and genres of literacy, including the ability to analyze and use digital literacy, reading and writing across a broad variety of text genres, and academic content area literacies. However, as noted above in the scenario with Emilio, teachers need to ensure that EL students are fully engaged in literacy; they can do so by aligning ELs' ability levels with the texts and literacies they are using.

One of the first thing that teachers need to know to support the literacy development of EL students is their knowledge, skills, and uses of literacies across all of their languages. Can the student read in his first language? Other languages? What literacy experiences has the student had in his or her home country? This is an important consideration because literacy skills, including knowledge of sound–symbol relationships, directionality of print, authorship, and so on transfer across all of a student's language systems. For example, a student who has attended school in her home country and who has acquired first language literacy skills can transfer those skills into her English language development. In addition, for students who engage in literacy activities at home bring those knowledges to the classroom as well. Some home literacies may include print used in home meal planning and recipes, religious texts, and letter writing (Coady, 2009).

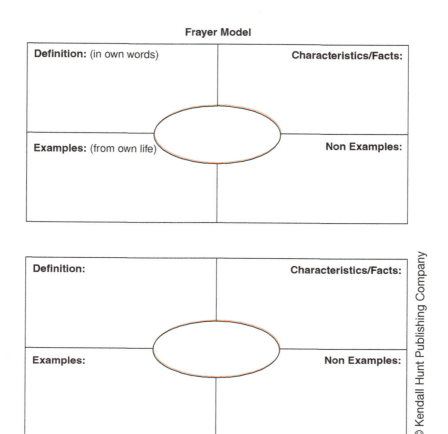

Figure 22.1: Frayer Model (Vocabulary Boxes)

Another key consideration for teachers of ELs is the student's interest area and, cultural background. Emilio, for example, enjoys specific sports and learning about the solar system, stars, and planets. During free reading times where students can explore topics in depth and enjoy using text, teachers may provide an array of materials that students can choose from and at various language ability levels. It is far more likely that students will engage in literacy activities when they relate to and enjoy the topics rather than when their selection is limited.

READING

Reading is a complex process, which may explain why many EL students struggle to read while they are learning English. In addition, English as a linguistic system has a *deep orthography*, meaning that the symbols (letters) do not regularly correspond to the same sounds (phonemes). The irregularity of the sound–symbol system may confuse beginning readers of English. In contrast, Spanish is a linguistic system with a *shallow orthography*, meaning that the letter-phoneme correspondence is regular and predictable. Hence, many EL students who speak and read Spanish may need to learn that English is less regular and has many exceptions to its linguistic, written rules.

In 2000, the National Reading Panel (2000) outlined five components of reading. The five instructional areas include phonemic awareness, phonics, vocabulary, fluency, and comprehension. However, as noted above, for EL or emergent bilingual students many literacy skills transfer from the first to subsequent languages. While the developmental process of reading for ELs is this supposed to be ELs is similar to that of monolingual, native English speakers, ELs have the added benefit and opportunity to acquire literacy in multiple languages, and teachers would do well to support literacy across all languages.

Teachers of EL students may need to instruct and support EL students in their reading ability across the five component areas of reading. We outline those areas in the following (Colorín Colorado, 2017).

Phonemic Awareness

Phonemic awareness is the ability to hear and manipulate different sounds in a language. EL students, particularly those who are at or beyond puberty, may have difficulty "hearing," recognizing, or producing new sounds. This is because over time, the brain does not recognize those sounds unless they are used repeatedly. Teachers may need to model new sounds and how to produce them, including demonstrating where in the mouth the sound is produced, where the tongue and lips are located when the sound is produced, and how air flows through the mouth when the sound is produced. Students should produce sounds/words that they know the meaning of; otherwise, sound and reading are nonsensical to the EL.

Phonics

Phonics is the relationship between a sound and its written letter (in English). Remember that not all languages are alphabetic and use letters. Some languages such as Chinese use characters that roughly correspond to a syllable. Essential to reading is the ability to understand the relationship between letters in English and the sounds of the spoken language. For EL students who have knowledge of literacy in their first language, their task is to learn how a new symbol matches its sound. Those students have an advantage in acquiring literacy in English. Nonliterate students, in contrast, will need to learn the concept of sound-symbol correspondence, new words, and new sounds. Teachers of EL students should use hands on activities to teach letter–sound relationships, including manipulatives such as sound boxes, and should always teach phonics in context. They should also use as much literature as possible, and reinforce their knowledge of sound-symbol correspondence by working with beginning and ending sounds, rhyming words, and homonyms. Like phonemic awareness, EL students should learn to decode real words that they know in English, rather than nonsensical words or sound combinations.

Vocabulary

Vocabulary is a cornerstone to language development because vocabulary is an area of language that supports listening, speaking, reading, and writing. Robertson (2017) notes that an EL student's "maximum level of reading is determined by his or her knowledge of words". Word knowledge helps students to understand text across many genres: magazines, digital sources, assessments, narrative, and academic texts.

When EL students engage in activities that build vocabulary, it supports their overall ability to read. However, vocabulary development can be challenging because the types of language used across academic content areas can differ quite a bit. For example, vocabulary encountered in a science text with scientific terminology and syntax structures differs from vocabulary encountered in a social studies text. A history text may contain many regular and irregular past tense verbs; however, a science text may use mostly present tense or conditional verbs (what would happen if . . . ?). In addition to that the same vocabulary word may have a completely different meaning in a science text or social studies text. Take, for example, the word *table*. An EL may know the word as an object in a room but may not know its relationship to the periodic table of elements or a high plains table in geography.

Some strategies that teachers can use is to ensure that EL students are reading at the appropriate reading level and preselect words that will provide the EL with the support needed to comprehend the overall meaning of the text. Using gestures, realia (actual objects), visuals, and graphic organizers are essential tools in an EL teacher's toolkit. An example of a story graphic organizer can be seen in Figure 22.2. A graphic organizer can be differentiated for ELs of different language ability levels. For example, a blank story graphic organizer may be useful for intermediate or advanced readers of English, and a graphic organizer with a bilingual glossary of words, pictures, or sentence frames may support reading development for a beginner EL student. While teachers may need to provide microscaffolding for ELs in reading by assisting them on the spot, planning ahead for vocabulary (and language) development is a more efficient approach to reading development (Coady, Harper, & de Jong, 2016).

Finally, for students whose languages share the same Greek and Latin root words of English, teachers can use cognates to support their EL students reading development. An example of a cognate is education and *educación* (Spanish) or library—a place that has and lends books—and *libro*, the word book in Spanish. In fact, students with knowledge of Spanish can increase their English language vocabulary tremendously by learning how cognates work across English and Spanish.

Fluency

Fluency is the ability to read a text quickly and with accuracy. However, before delving in to fluency as reading quickly, it is crucial for teachers to note that not all language groups share the idea that reading quickly is a skill. In fact, across African languages, reading and speaking slowly so that the recipient can discern the meaning and emotions of a message, is a positive cultural trait. Fluent readers, then, are not always fast readers. Fluency as a skill provides a connection between word recognition (site of a word) and comprehension (its meaning). Frequently, fluency in a language precedes comprehension; hence, EL students may appear fluent and appear to read well but not comprehend fully what they are reading. To build fluency, students can practice reading out loud, listening to fluent readers and follow along in the text, and learning intonation and emotion in reading a passage.

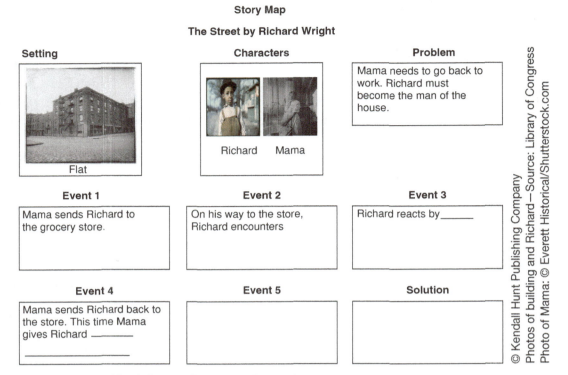

Figure 22.2: Modified Story Graphic Organizer

Comprehension

Comprehension is the ability for students to understand and interpret text. Robertson (2017) notes that comprehension is difficult to master, and it frequently takes ELs many years to gain the skills surrounding text comprehension, such as close reading, the use of context clues. She notes that ELs need to do three things to comprehend text: (a) decode what they read; (b) make connections between what they read and what they know; and (c) reflect and think deeply about what they have read. These skills take time to develop, but comprehension of text is an essential aspect of schooling. Teachers can support comprehension by learning to identify the main idea of text, supporting vocabulary development within and across text, and checking frequently for comprehension. Activities such as taking a picture walk, using outlines, connecting text to students' background knowledge, and helping students to summarize text are useful for ELs.

WRITING

Like reading, writing is a skill normally developed in the context of a child's education, and that is especially true when students are expected to write within specific academic genres. Writing is also a complex skill and typically—but not always—one of the language abilities that takes the longest to develop, following listening, speaking, and reading. Just as reading is the ability to decode symbols to discern meaning, writing is the ability to encode meaning using symbols. However, as Diaz-Rico (2013) notes, "writing is no longer an activity that can be postponed until English learners can speak English fluently" (p. 188).

Writing is arguably a series of multiple "processes" (Diaz-Rico, 2013, p. 188) that include the ability to convey meaning through text. We indicate multiple processes because it is rare for someone to write without planning to write, drafting, revising, editing, revising again, and so on until a writing selection is published. Writing, of course, goes hand in hand with reading, so teachers can think of these areas as reinforcing each other and can design literacy activities that include both of those areas of language development.

In addition, writing is a social act that includes how authors conceive and convey their message, their intended audiences, and the context in which the writer writes. Interestingly, EL students also consider whether or not their audience is biliterate and if they can convey meaning in multiple languages to an audience. For example, as Coady and Ariza (2010) found in their research with emergent biliterate students, bilinguals have the added task and intelligence of discerning whether their intended audience is bilingual or not. In their example Esteban, a high school EL student, used his knowledge of literary strategies, punctuation, and capitalization to ensure that his monolingual audience would understand his message (see Figure 22.3). Note how Esteban uses these techniques to add meaning to his response to the writing prompt, If I Could Be Someone Else for a Day.

What assumptions does Esteban make about his audience (reader) in his writing sample on page 326.

Writing for EL students is a complex process, and students will require added time and opportunities to write to develop their craft. Moreover, students who have an actual purpose for writing, such as seeking additional information on a website, as well as a real audience, such as writing a proposal to the school principal to extend the lunch time, can learn to gauge tone and message in writing. EL students who are literate in the first language in writing can also transfer many of those skills across languages. Transfer can include numeracy, punctuation, print directionality, and so on. Appendix A demonstrate the developmental stages of writing.

There are multiple ways that teachers can support the writing development of ELs. One way is through collaborative writing. *Collaborative writing* refers to projects written by more than one person. The use of peers in writing can be a helpful support for EL students, especially when they are allowed to write and collaborate with students who share their same first language in the prewriting stage. They also benefit from collaborative writing by working with strong writers who can share their work.

Like writing in general, collaborative writing takes added time for students to brainstorm and prewrite using oral language to explore and develop their ideas; draft and put onto paper some main ideas; revise and expand writing into a coherent structure; and gain feedback through peers, writing conferences, and/or teacher feedback. Other parts of the writing process include editing, grammar correction, and using computer technologies.

Recent research (García & Li Wei, 2014) has focused on bi- and multilingual students' use of multiple languages in classroom learning and literacy development in a process referred to

> "If I could be someone else for a day"
>
> If I could be someone else for a day I'll take any president in American continent and try to see how difficult is to be in that level of power and control.
>
> If that president is from a poor country, I would like to STOP all the funds from "leving", in other words people takin what they don't ern and hurting others.
>
> If I am on the president's power, I would try to focus my gol on this country, the united states, how some people have low cuality of live and other people have high cuality. I try to stop taking venatage of financial marckets on the people and focus on how the people is living in TRUTH!!
>
> I would use my control to have my people live in peace. Let some other countries live. That's how I can lead.
>
> In conclusion, I would be a president of power and help all the people in the American continent.
>
> Esteban

Figure 22.3: Esteban's Writing: If I Could Be Someone Else for a Day

as translanguaging. In those spaces, teachers in both mainstream and bilingual classrooms support students' use of multiple languages to build oral and literacy skills. Some examples of that work includes students' written stories, narratives, and academic essays using two or more languages; students' engaging in prewriting (oral) activities through the use of a common first language, with support for writing in English. These strategies hold promise for the increasing number of bi- and multilingual students in today's classrooms.

POINTS TO REMEMBER

- ✔ Literacy includes the ability to read and write.
- ✔ Multilingual students who have literacy in the first language can transfer their knowledge into English.
- ✔ Teachers can build EL students' five areas of reading by building background knowledge, helping students to connect new information to prior knowledge, and ensuring that students use real words.
- ✔ Writing is a process that includes multiple steps and stages. EL students can engage in collaborative writing for authentic purposes.

REFLECTION QUESTIONS AND DISCUSSION

1. In your own words, define literacy. What literacy activities are common in today's global and digital environment?

2. What are the five areas of reading, identified by the National Reading Panel, and how can teachers support those five areas of reading for ELs?

3. Why is comprehension difficult for ELs?

4. What are some ways that teachers can support bilingual students in process writing?

ACTIVITIES

1. Read Esteban's writing sample in the chapter. Identify places in the writing sample where Esteban conveys meaning in the writing by using punctuation, capitalization, and areas of language that "transfer" from Spanish, his first language, into English. Share your findings with a colleague.

2. Scan your local community for environmental print by visiting businesses, stores, local community centers, and so on. What kinds of print do you encounter? In what ways does that print convey messages? (include symbols in addition to words)

WEB RESOURCES

Colorín Colorado. Fostering literacy development in English language learners. http://www .colorincolorado.org/article/fostering-literacy-development-english-language-learners

Reading Rockets. English language learners and the five essential components of reading instruction. http://www.readingrockets.org/article/english-language-learners-and-five-essential-components-reading-instruction

REFERENCES

Coady, M. (2009). "*Solamente libros importantes*": Literacy practices and ideologies of migrant farmworking families in north central Florida. In G. Li (Ed.), *Multicultural families, home literacies and mainstream schooling* (pp. 113–128). Charlotte, NC: New Age.

Coady, M., & Ariza, E. (2010). Struggling for meaning and identity (and a passing grade): High-stakes writing in English as a second language. *MEXTESOL, 34*(1), 11–27.

Coady, M., Harper, C., & de Jong, E. (2016). Aiming for equity: Preparing mainstream teachers for inclusion or inclusive classrooms? *TESOL Quarterly, 50*(2), 340–368. doi:10.1002/tesq.223

Colorín Colorado. (2017). Reading comprehension strategies for English language learners. Retrieved from http://www.colorincolorado.org/article/reading-comprehension-skills-english-language-learners

Diaz-Rico, L. T. (2013). *The crosscultural, language, and academic development handbook: A complete K-12 reference guide*. Boston:Pearson Higher Ed.

García, O., & Wei, L. (2014). *Translanguaging: Language, bilingualism, and education*. Basingstoke, UK: Palgrave.

Eunice Kennedy Shriver National Institute of Child Health and Human Development, NIH, DHHS. (2000). Report of the national reading panel: Teaching children to read: Reports of the subgroups (00-4754). Washington, DC: U.S. Government Printing Office.National Reading Panel Publications—NIC

O'Malley J. M., & Pierce, L. V. (1996). *Authentic assessment for English language learners*: *Practical approaches for teachers* Boston, MA: Addison-Wesley.

Robertson, K. (2017). *Reading 101 for English language learners*. Colorín Colorado. Retrieved from http://www.colorincolorado.org/article/reading-101-english-language-learners

UNESCO. (2003). *Perspective on literacy*. Retrieved from http://unesdoc.unesco.org/images/0013/001318/131817eo.pdf

APPENDIX A: DEVELOPMENTAL STAGES OF WRITING

Many students will illustrate—then write—illustrate—then write—which is a process of revision. This enhances the writing process and is necessary for writing.

Stage 1: Random Illustration
- Scattered and no sense of story.
- Kindergarten students spend a lot of time in this phase.
- A Readiness Stage—to get to the product you are looking for.

Stage 2: Picture Grounded in One Topic
- One story goes with the picture.
- Sense of story is evident: Beginning, middle, and end.
- Many students stay in this stage a while.

Stage 3: Illustration with Letters Randomly Written on the Bottom
- Usually consonants and very few vowels.
- Starting to realize that the letters are used to communicate a story.
- When they read back to you, can match story to letters and can end at end of letters.

Stage 4: Copying Words from Around the Room
- Do have a sense that a word means something—but need to move them along so that the words come from the student.

Stage 5: Write on the Same Topic Day After Day
- Help student with another topic.
- It is important to break this pattern and help student move onto something else.
- Talk through the story first, then encourage the student to write.
- If student has a fear of writing and spelling words, encourage invented or transitional spelling.

Stage 6: Saying Something About the Picture (Not a Story Yet)
- Writes lists to go with the picture or labels the picture.

Stage 7: Invented Spelling With Sound/Letter Correspondence and Is a Sentence
- Spacing between words is still not apparent.

Stage 8: Sentence With a List of Pictures and/or Words
- Example: One day I went to the aquarium. I saw fish, dolphins, and whales . . . (Things in the picture)

Stage 9: A Story: Beginning, Middle, and End
- Share student's work by putting it on the overhead and demonstrating what a sense of story is to the class.

Source: Adapted from The Writing Project: Teacher's College, Columbia University.

Emergent	<ul><li>Pretends to read</li><li>Uses illustrations to tell a story</li><li>Participates in reading of familiar books</li><li>Knows some letter sounds</li><li>Recognizes names/words in context</li><li>Memorizes pattern books and familiar books</li><li>Rhymes and plays with words</li></ul>
Developing	<ul><li>Sees self as reader</li><li>Reads books with word patterns</li><li>Knows most letter sounds</li><li>Retells main idea of text</li><li>Recognizes simple words</li><li>Relies on print and illustrations</li></ul>
Beginning	<ul><li>Relies more on print than illustrations</li><li>Recognizes names/words by sight</li><li>Uses sentence structure clues</li><li>Uses phonetic clues</li><li>Retells beginning, middle, and end</li><li>Begins to read silently</li><li>Uses basic punctuation</li></ul>
Expanding	<ul><li>Begins to read short stories and books</li><li>Reads and finishes a variety of materials with guidance</li><li>Uses reading strategies</li><li>Retells plot, characters, and events</li><li>Recognizes different types of books</li><li>Reads silently for short periods of time</li></ul>
Bridging	<ul><li>Begins to read chapter books of moderate difficulty</li><li>Reads and finishes a variety of materials with guidance</li><li>Reads and understand most new words</li><li>Uses reference materials to locate information with guidance</li><li>Increases knowledge of literary elements and genres</li><li>Reads silently for extended periods</li></ul>

(Continued)

(Continued)

Fluent	• Reads most literature appropriate to grade-level • Selects, reads, and finishes a wide variety of materials • Uses reference materials independently • Recognizes and uses literary elements and genres • Begins to interpret and expand meaning from literature • Participates in literary discussions
Prereader	• Listens to read-alouds • Repeats words and phrases • Uses pictures to comprehend text • May recognize some sound/symbol relationships
Emerging Reader	• Participates in choral reading • Begins to retell familiar, predictable text • Uses visuals to facilitate meaning • Uses phonics and word structure to decode
Developing Reader	• Begins to make predictions • Retells beginning, middle, and end of story • Recognizes plot, characters, and events • Begins to rely more on print than illustrations • May need assistance in choosing appropriate texts
Expanding Reader	• Begins to read independently • Responds to literature • Begins to use a variety of reading strategies • Usually chooses appropriate texts
Proficient Reader	• Reads independently • Relates reading to personal experience • Uses a wide variety of reading strategies • Recognizes literary elements and genres • Usually chooses appropriate texts
Independent Reader	• Reads for enjoyment • Reads and completes a wide variety of texts • Responds personally and critically to texts • Matches a wide variety of reading strategies to purpose • Chooses appropriate or challenging texts

Source: O'Malley, J. Michael; Pierce, Lorraine Valdez, *Authentic Assessment for English Language Learners*, 1st Ed., © 1996. Reprinted by permission of Pearson Education, Inc., New York, New York.

Twenty Three

Overview of Assessment and Evaluation for the English Learner

LEARNING OBJECTIVES

Readers will be able to

- ❖ Define assessment and evaluation
- ❖ Define the Home Language Survey (HSL) and describe its use
- ❖ Describe the use of language assessments for English learner (EL) placement
- ❖ Identify and use formal and informal, formative and summative assessment

While tutoring in the neighborhood after-school program dedicated to struggling learners, Sherrie was assigned to help third grader, Mario, a newcomer to the United States. The program director told Sherrie that Mario is an EL and has excellent math skills. Mario took out his homework and began to do a math worksheet. Wanting to see if he was approaching his work correctly, Sherrie said, "Lea en voz alta." (Read out loud). He started off by reading the numbers 10, 11, 12, 13, 14, 15 as "*Ten, eleben, tweelb, fiftee, sirteen, sixtee . . .*"

Ahmed is a student from Saudi Arabia entering Gibbons Elementary for the first time. The teacher is using a proficiency test to place him in the correct level. The test shows a picture of a young woman in a classroom pointing to a blackboard. As the teacher asks Ahmed who the woman is, he stares at the picture and does not appear to know how to answer.

Mrs. Freeman, the guidance counselor from Lauderway Elementary School, is testing Yoshi to see at what language level he should begin school. Mrs. Freeman shows him a colorful picture with foods such as rice, eggs, bread, bananas, pumpkins, lemons, cherries, and apples. She says, "Name three things in the picture that you might find in pies." Yoshi stares at the picture and does not answer.

Nong, who has had little exposure to English, is being tested for English level placement and is asked to draw a picture of breakfast. She draws rice, a fish head, and soup. Her teacher believes Nong did not understand the question.

Carlos is sitting with his new teacher, who is trying to assess his English knowledge. In her conversation with him, she asks him to complete the following sentence: *My brother and I like to play football. His favorite position is quarterback and my favorite position is*_____. Carlos looks questioningly at his teacher, not understanding what he is being asked.

What problems can you surmise about the previous scenarios?
If you were the teacher of these students, what assumptions would you make about their respective language levels?
Would you be assessing their language or their cultural knowledge?

When Mario says the names of the numbers incorrectly, will his teacher know that his problem is with language, not in calculating numbers? Would you think Ahmed was developmentally delayed because he did not know to label the woman in the picture as a teacher? Would it have occurred to you that boys have only male teachers where he is from, and the concept of having a female teacher is alien to him?

When Yoshi was asked about pies, he could not answer the question because pies are a manifestation of American culture and do not exist as a component of the typical Japanese diet. People in the United States eat a variety of foods for breakfast, but it is probably safe to say fish heads, rice, and soup are not among them. Bacon, eggs, toast, and coffee are more likely to conjure up images of American breakfast foods. However, for Nong, this is a common meal and she prefers the head of the fish to the body.

When Carlos was asked about football, his favorite sport, he was thrilled. He and his brother love the game, but to them, football is *futbol*, the word for "soccer" in Spanish.

Assessment is both the starting point and is an ongoing task in the teaching and learning process. In order for teachers of ELs to adequately identify, design, and implement differentiated instructional strategies, she must first know the language ability levels of her EL students and optimally in as many of the students' languages as possible. That knowledge, in addition to knowing the cultural background and experiences of EL students, is the starting point for instruction because this informs which instructional decisions a teacher can and should make.

WHAT IS ASSESSMENT?

Assessment in the context of education is the formal or informal process of determining what a student knows or has learned. At some level, assessment is both the starting point and is an ongoing task in the teaching and learning process. In order for teachers of ELs to adequately identify, design, and implement differentiated instructional strategies, she must first know the language ability levels of her EL students, and optimally in as many of the students' languages as possible. That knowledge, in addition to knowing the cultural background and experiences of EL students, is the starting point for instruction because this informs which instructional decisions a teacher can and should make.

Classroom teachers need to be accountable for the effectiveness of their teaching. To evaluate students, they need to observe, collect information, and document their students' progress so that they can modify and improve instruction, evaluate the curriculum, and measure the language gains the students make. Assessment of ELs' language proficiency serves the same purpose as assessment of other areas of student learning. The primary goals of assessment are to gain information about the nature and extent of students' learning and to determine the appropriate educational plan for students. Assessment also allows us to conduct both *formative* (ongoing evaluation of student performance to guide teaching and assess learning by collecting and analyzing student work) and *summative* (the end results) of program evaluations. What has to be kept in mind is what is being measured—language or content. Are students being tested on how much content they know, or how much English language they have acquired?

Unfortunately, often too much reliance is placed on a single standardized assessment instrument, when assessment should be an ongoing collection of information gathered during and after instruction to determine the student's overall progress. Additionally, the misuse or misinterpretation of assessment data or cultural bias within the instruments (as exemplified in the scenarios at the beginning of the chapter) result in incorrect diagnoses, student misplacements, inappropriate or inadequate programs, and student underachievement.

Testing and assessment are very different. Sireci and Faulkner-Bond (2015) describe *tests* as single-occasion, unidimensional, timed items, or exercises that are usually in multiple choice or short-answer form. *Standardized* testing involves creating and ensuring that the conditions for every test taker are the same. Because of this, the results of standardized testing allow for comparisons across all test-takers. In contrast, assessment takes place on a broader scale and can consist of a collection or a varied sample of work completed by students to ascertain what they know or can do. Testing can only be one part of an overall assessment of a student. We need to assess rather than test, because testing alone cannot accurately evaluate the EL. Finally, evaluation takes place when we make a judgment based on results of assessment.

A main challenge in the field of EL education is that ELs are often misclassified as having learning disabilities when they are actually in the process of learning English (Baker, 2000; Cook & Linquanti, 2015). In order to determine whether students have a learning disability, ELs must be assessed in the native or first language in addition to English. Teachers should keep records of students' difficulties in both the L1 and the L2 to demonstrate the areas in which students need additional support. Interviews with parents about their child's educational, medical, and personal history will aid in the determination of issues and help with proper placement and educational services (Abedi, 2014). Inappropriate or inadequate testing that leads to misclassifications of ELs results in unfair repercussions for students. If an EL student is misplaced, insufficient instruction takes place, having a negative effect on student learning and academic achievement. Long-term results may include higher dropout rates, thus perpetuating unequal educational opportunities for EL students.

Schools must comply with federal and state laws (*Lau v. Nichols*, 1974; Title VII of the Elementary and Secondary Act, 1968, etc.), which mandate appropriate instruction for non-native speakers of English. This is not possible without assessing how much a student knows upon entry to the school, as well as how the student is progressing throughout the program. To ensure that educators receive a valid picture of the EL, familiarity with the EL's culture, home language, previous educational experience (e.g., level of native language literacy), and ability in English must be considered as well. Administrators must know where to budget monies, what programs to initiate and fund, and what trained personnel need to be hired to teach students. Without accurate and reliable assessment, a grave injustice is done to the future of our English-learning population.

More and more educators of ELs subscribe to the idea that English language proficiency and academic content should be assessed from a holistic viewpoint. Data can be gathered from a great variety of sources such as the following:

1. School records (including previous test records), portfolios (samples of students' work), guidance reports, attendance and health records, and referral forms.
2. Interviews—formal and informal—with students, parents, teachers, and other appropriate school personnel.
3. Anecdotal records or direct observations of students in the classroom, the playground, at "specials" (art, music, physical education [PE], etc.), in the cafeteria, and in daily interactions with native English speakers.

4. Informal instruments such as checklists, rating scales, student self-assessments, peer assessments, cloze testing (a reading and appropriate language use assessment technique in which words have been deleted from a passage and the student must identify them correctly by filling in the blanks), writing samples, and curriculum-based tests constructed by classroom teachers.

5. Standardized tests designed by specialists and administered, scored, and interpreted under standard conditions.

SCENARIO

Mrs. Cooper teaches third grade at Spring Street School in a small town in Massachusetts. The town's population is mostly White, mainstream, and native English speaking. All her students speak English fluently without a discernible accent and are functioning at about grade level. There is nothing to indicate that any of the students has a diverse background. One boy, Roman, is having tremendous difficulty spelling. Although the teacher keeps telling him to sound out the words, his spelling looks like this:

Apul (apple)
Thot (thought)
Eskool (school)
Pipul (people)
Nedd (needed)
Poot (put)

Mrs. Cooper decides to speak to Roman's parents because, in her assessment of the situation, he obviously is not studying for his spelling tests; however, the student teacher, bilingual in English and Spanish, took one look at his test, went over to Roman's desk, and said to him, *"Roman, hablas español?"* Roman's eyes brightened in surprise and answered, *"Si, Señora. Hablamos español en casa."* The student teacher went to her cooperating teacher and said, "Mrs. Cooper, Roman is sounding out his spelling words. Phonetically, these are perfectly sounded out in Spanish!" Mrs. Cooper had no idea that Roman was from a Spanish-speaking family because he had no accent, had no Hispanic surname, spoke fluent English, and did not "look" Hispanic. Assumptions can be misleading and lead to grossly inaccurate judgments about placement, evaluation, and levels of proficiency and achievement in ELs.

WHAT SHOULD A TEACHER KNOW ABOUT THE LANGUAGE LEARNER?

Teachers need to know *as much as possible* about the history of their students for many reasons. First, they need to know what languages are spoken at home and in which languages students and families are literate. Upon entry to many schools, parents and/or caregivers must complete a Home Language Survey (HLS). The HLS is a "screener," which seeks to determine if further testing of English language proficiency is warranted for English for speakers of other languages (ESOL) placement and services. Different states across the United States ask slightly different questions on the HLS, but the main questions asked are:

1. Is a language other than English used in the home? If yes, language used_____.
2. Did the student have a first language other than English?
3. Does the student most frequently speak a language other than English?
   Ideally, we need to know more, like the following information.

If any question is answered in the affirmative, it is a signal that language services might be needed. The HLS should alert administrators and teachers to further evaluate for proper identification placement for the student (see Figures 23.1 and 23.2).

Additional questions that a teacher may ask include:

4. Is the student literate in the home language?
5. Is the student literate in English?

Primary/Home Language Survey for Kindergarten and New Incoming Students

Student Information (The parents or guardians should complete this section.)

First Name: _____

Last Name: _____

Date of Birth: _____
(Month/Day/Year)

Questions for Parents or Guardians	**Response**
What language(s) is (are) spoken in your home?	
Which language did your child learn first?	
Which language does your child use most frequently at home?	
Which language do you most frequently speak to your child?	
In what language would you prefer to get information from the school?	

Figure 23.1: Home Language Survey Sample 1

Source: U.S. Department of Education (US DOE, 2017b)

Student's Last Name:

Student's First Name:

ENGLISH

1. Is a language other than English spoken in your home?
   ☐ No ☐ Yes_____ (specify language)

2. Does your child communicate in a language other than English? ☐ No ☐ Yes_____ (specify language)

3. Which language did your child learn first?_____ (specify language)

4. In which language do you prefer to receive information from the school?_____ (specify language)

5. What is your relationship to the child? ☐ Father ☐ Mother ☐ Guardian ☐ Other_____ (specify)

ESPAÑOL (SPANISH)

1. ¿Se habla otro idioma que no sea el inglés en su casa?
   ☐ No ☐ Sí_____ (especifique idioma)

2. ¿Habla el estudiante un idioma que no sea el inglés?
   ☐ No ☐ Sí_____ (especifique idioma)

3. ¿Cuál fué el primer idioma que aprendió su hijo/a?
   _____ (especifique idioma)

4. ¿En que idioma prefiere recibir comunicaciones de la escuela?_____ (especifique idioma)

5. ¿Cuál es su relación con el estudiante? ☐ Padre ☐ Madre ☐ Guardián ☐ Otro_____ (especifique)

FRANÇAIS (FRENCH)

1. Parle-t-on une autre langue que l'anglais chez vous?
   ☐ Non ☐ Oui_____ (veuillez préciser la langue)

2. Votre enfant parle-t-il une autre langue que l'anglais?
   ☐ Non ☐ Oui_____ (veuillez préciser la langue)

3. Quelle langue votre enfant a-t-il apprise en premier?
   _____ (veuillez préciser la langue)

(Continued)

(Continued)

---

4. Dans quelle langue préférez-vous recevoir les communications de l'école? _____ (veuillez préciser la langue)

5. Quelle est votre lien de parenté avec l'enfant? ☐ Père ☐ Mère ☐ Tuteur ☐ Autre _____ (veuillez préciser)

Figure 23.2: Home Language Survey Sample 2

Source: U.S. Department of Education (US DOE, 2017b).

Consider the following two scenarios related to EL identification and placement:

SCENARIOS

Nico's father is from Colombia. When Nico registered for school, his mother was handed a school form to complete, which included questions with answer boxes to check, such as "Is there a language other than English spoken in the home?" His mother checked the box "yes," although Nico was English dominant. A few days later, Nico was called to the guidance office to be given an oral English placement test.

Lina, a German girl who has moved to the United States to live with her American-born aunt, went to her neighborhood high school with her aunt to register. They were handed a Home Language Survey, on which they indicated that German was Lina's first language. But upon hearing Lina speak English with her aunt, the guidance counselor placed Lina in a regular classroom. The aunt pointed out that Lina had been in the country for only 4 months and still needed ESOL instruction, but the aunt had to make a special request for language services. The guidance counselor incorrectly assumed that because Lina could speak "survival" English (enough to be understood clearly), she could function academically in a class of native-English students.

Often incorrect assumptions are made on the basis of appearances. For example, an individual with a foreign surname such as Chin might not speak a word of Chinese, or a child named Samuel Brown might have been raised in Mexico and not know any English. José Bautista was born in the Dominican Republic, moved to Haiti when he was a baby, and attended a bilingual school where the language of instruction was English. His father was a doctor of Dominican descent, but

(Continued)

spoke only English to José. José learned Haitian Creole from his playmates, but he is English dominant.

If administrators did not know his background, where would he be placed based on his name, his country of origin, or his accent?

Middle/high school ESOL teacher, Katherine Lobo, shares a story about a family from East Africa. The father filled in the Home Language Survey and reported that his daughter spoke Creole—as variation of Portuguese. Consequently, she was placed in the Haitian Creole class and did not do very well. She did not share the culture or language of the students. This was around the time that we received many students from Haiti due to the huge earthquake. Needless to say, when the father went to the school for the parent–teacher conference (at that time his English was improving) the "problem" was sorted out. The lesson is to constantly check assumptions and double check them—a student of color who speaks "Creole" does not always mean a student from Haiti!

Other questions on background knowledge that are critical for teachers to know relate to previous education. Some of those questions include: How much previous education has the student had? Is he or she literate in the native language? Is the native language a written or oral language? (Some native languages are only oral and do not have a written form.) What kind of a student was the child academically in the native language? Was the student's education interrupted by political upheaval, war, economic strife, migration, familial problems, or other forms of unrest? Students with limited or interrupted formal education (SLIFE) are difficult to place in appropriate grade levels. How much education do the parents possess? Do they speak English? Why did the family come to the United States? Was it a happy move? Did it shatter or reunite the family? Did the child know he or she was coming to the United States, or was there no time for the closure of saying goodbye to friends and family? These social and psychological factors carry a powerful influence when it comes to learning another language or living contentedly in another country.

INITIAL PLACEMENT AND ASSESSMENT

As a result of noncompliance with federal laws ensuring equal educational opportunities for all students regardless of national origin, ethnicity, or language, many states or school districts are often mandated by court order to develop and implement strategic plans to deliver comprehensible instruction for EL students. Two examples are the states of Florida and New York.

A good example of a consent decree is the August 1990 ruling passed in the state of Florida. The Florida Consent Decree is a court-enforced agreement between the Florida

Board of Education and a coalition of eight groups represented by Multicultural Education, Training, and Advocacy, Inc. (META) and Florida legal service attorneys. The Consent Decree guaranteed the identification and provision of services for Florida students learning English. The Consent Decree (Florida Department of Education [FL DOE], 1990) settlement terms consist of six principal areas related to the education of ELs:

- Identification and assessment
- Equal access to appropriate programming
- Equal access to appropriate categorical and other programming for EL students
- Personnel
- Monitoring
- Outcome measures

A direct consequence of the Consent Decree is the tremendous importance, value, and consequences of assessment and evaluation. These protections are put into place for EL students and families and to ensure that they receive appropriate and adequate instruction.

SCHOOL REGISTRATION AND ENGLISH LANGUAGE ASSESSMENTS

When a new student registers for school, the administration must determine language proficiency for proper placement and learning. As noted earlier, an HLS is first administered to a parent or caregiver in a language that he or she can understand. If applicable, the next step is to administer an English language proficiency test. Schools and districts across the United States can use a variety of English language proficiency tests. Some of the more common tests used to determine language proficiency include:

- The Language Assessment Scales (LAS)
- The IDEA Proficiency Test (IPT) (http://www.ballard-tighe.com/ipt)
- The Maculaitis Assessment Program (MAC) (http://www.questarai.com)
- The Peabody Picture Vocabulary Test (PPVT) (https://www.pearsonclinical.com/language/products/100000501/peabody-picture-vocabulary-test-fourth-edition-ppvt-4.html)
- WIDA ACCESS Placement Test (WAPT) (https://www.wida.us/assessment/W-APT)

A language proficiency test may test oral or written skills in a language but is primarily given to determine into what language level the student will be placed. One popular oral test that is administered to beginning level students is the Idea Proficiency Test (IPT) published by Ballard & Tighe. By using visuals and a question and answer format, the level of vocabulary, syntax, comprehension, and verbal expression can be measured. A written exam is also available to accompany the oral exam. The written test determines vocabulary, vocabulary in context, reading for understanding, reading for life skills, and language usage.

Testing is an inexact science, but it provides an approximate indication from which the EL can progress. It is very important to give a written as well as an oral test, as ELs may be more proficient in some areas than others.

EL PLACEMENT

Schools are required to place EL students based age- and grade-appropriate levels. Placing students in the appropriate grade level is a complex process, because many factors need to be taken into consideration. It is imprudent to place older EL students in lower grade levels simply because the student is in the process of learning English. For the most accurate placement of the new student, the teacher needs to know as much as possible about the student. After an initial placement test (such as the IPT) is administered to determine the level of English proficiency, assessment of the student's home language proficiency, previous schooling, academic level, family history, background, and any other pertinent information must be considered. These factors can determine future success or failure in the classroom. *The Colorín Colorado* website (2017) describes important factors used to place and assess EL students in classrooms, including the student's home language literacy levels, length of time in the United States, prior education, and the preparation of teachers to work with EL students.

Moreover, because the most common way to assess ELs is through an oral language proficiency test and HLS, a wide range of skills and abilities are not being identified. How will you know if the new young boy can read or write in his native language, or if he ever attended school at all? If he comes from a wealthy Haitian family, it can be assumed the student has attended school, has studied in French, has learned Haitian Creole from speaking with his peers, and maybe has had English training as well. He might even be ahead of his grade-level counterparts in the United States. But for a student coming from a less-advantaged family, formal schooling may never have been an option in the home country. What considerations would you have to make for these students?

In contrast, a 10-year-old student who has escaped from a war-torn country, has had 1 year of formal training before escaping her village, speaks little English, and is now staying in the United States until the war in her country is over. How and where will you place her? She has the academic skills of a first-grader, yet is age 10. Will you place her with the other first-graders where she will not struggle academically, or will you assign her to a fourth or fifth grade class so she can develop socially with her peer group?

Other important factors to consider are the reasons for immigration. The Haitian student who was wealthy in his country has come to the United States because his father is going to practice medicine. The poorer Haitian student has come to the United States to seek economic freedom and a better life. The student escaping her homeland until the war is over probably has expectations of returning home soon. Which student would be encouraged to learn English quickly, aspire to high academic achievement (seen as the key to success in life), and embrace the United States culture?

Obviously, the student who expects to return to her country will have less motivation to learn the language.

What about previous literacy levels? Some cultures do not have a written language, but have very strong oral storytelling traditions. Undoubtedly, the literate student has an easier time than the student with no previous literacy skills, because prior knowledge can be transferred to the new language (Cohen, 2014; Cummins, 2000. The student with no prior literacy skills must learn to read and write through a foreign language, a monumental task for some learners.

Overall, programmatic assessment of the EL student is accomplished by seeking information about the student's prior school experiences, using school records or home country transcripts; interviews with parents, guardians, and interpreters; and any other evidence of the student's previous educational history. Ideally, the student is tested in the home language for content knowledge so that language capability is not confused with content knowledge. If no tests are available for measuring the student's previous academic background, the teacher must devise ways to test prior knowledge.

Once in classrooms, the student must be evaluated to see how much language is being learned, how well he or she is doing in class, and when enough language has been learned to reclassify the student and progress to a higher level (see Chapter 24). Teachers should be careful not to exit an EL before the appropriate time. Students may appear to have a more advanced mastery of English than they really do, often when teachers rely on oral language use and their interactions with other students. Finally, accurate records of assessment must be kept to know when enough progress has been made to warrant exiting the ESOL program and being mainstreamed.

After exiting the ESOL program, assessment must continue in order to ascertain the child's progress for assurance that he or she is functioning at grade level. New federal guidelines under Every Student Succeeds Act (ESSA) suggest that exited EL students should be monitored for 4 full years after exiting the ESOL program (US DOE, 2017b). If the student is having difficulty, other services and counseling should be provided, including support through alternative programs and learning strategies. With accurate, precise, and ongoing assessment, teachers and administrators can differentiate among, and offer proper treatment for, language, academic, psychological, physical, and emotional problems.

TYPES OF ASSESSMENT: FORMAL AND INFORMAL

Testing, both formal and informal, plays a key role in EL teaching and planning by identifying (a) linguistic skills (phonology, morphology, syntax, and vocabulary) and (b) integrated language skills: reading, writing, listening, and speaking (Carrasquillo, 2013). Both linguistic skills and integrated language assessment instruments are similar in that they are designed to measure outcomes based on the academic content being taught; however, there are some major differences.

VALIDITY

Tests must be valid to record accurate results. *Validity* refers to the adequacy and appropriateness of the assessment in what it seeks to measure. It can also refer to interpretations made from assessments in regard to the specific use of assessment results. Does the assessment accurately measure what it is intended to gauge? Because language learning involves mastery of skills in different areas, it is important to test the learner's skills from a global perspective across the four language domains (listening, speaking, reading, and writing) and tasks, considering the total product rather than individual subskills (vocabulary, grammar, pronunciation, inferring meaning, etc.) of language.

Informal testing instruments better serve this purpose than standardized tests, which are often designed to measure outcomes and content common to students who belong to the ethnic majority of the United States. For example, if we ask a child who was raised in the U.S. mainstream culture to finish this sentence: *Jack fell down and broke his_____*, it would be an easy task. However, if we ask a child who has no familiarity with this common nursery rhyme, the child would be unable to answer. The flexibility of informal testing allows adaptation of the content to avoid cultural biases and to measure a greater variety of subskills. At some time within their educational experience, all students will be expected to perform on standardized tests; therefore, it is a good idea to prepare them by teaching test-taking skills that include awareness of the typical American test discourse, format, expectations inherent within standardized tests, language skills, predictable patterns, repetitive questioning phrases, and other strategies that teach ELs how to approach test questions (Table 23.1).

Table 23.1: Types of Assessment: Formal and Informal

Formal Measures	Informal Measures
• are based on statistical norms for representative populations • are designed to compare individuals and groups with norms representative of the general population • are administered according to specific guidelines in terms of seating, test format, response time, and responses made • are administered by trained and credentialed personnel • are usually English language based • are usually composed of questions requiring short answers, or often multiple choice responses • can be interpreted across settings	• can be based on classroom activities and materials • can be designed to determine students' strengths and needs • can be used whenever appropriate • are time consuming and not easily scored • can be used by teachers, assistants, and peer tutors • can incorporate both English and other languages • can use a variety of response modes and contexts • are not easily interpreted across settings

RELIABILITY

Tests do not reflect everything a student knows or is capable of knowing. We need to know the test is a true indicator of achievement. Therefore, it must be reliable. *Reliability* refers to the consistency of assessment results obtained over a given period of time, when scored by different raters, or over different measurements of samples of the same behavior. Does the assessment consistently measure what it is intended to gauge, no matter who administers the test? Reliability is expressed statistically as a correlation coefficient indicating the degree of relationship between two sets of scores, with 1.0 being the greatest degree of correlation, and zero being the lowest. Simply speaking, if we give an achievement test today, will the test scores be consistent if we give the test tomorrow or next week? Consistency makes validity possible and justifies generalizations about assessments (Ariza, 2018).

It is important to remember that although reliability (consistency) of measurement results is necessary to obtain valid results, it is not sufficient in isolation. In other words, it is possible to have consistent results that provide the wrong information, or measurement results that are consistently interpreted incorrectly. While standardized tests are generally quite reliable (between .80 and .95) compared to more accurate informal assessment instruments, the results obviously will not be useful if they are not valid. Decisions about ELs knowledge, achievement, and placement should not be based on one test alone. We need to see an overall composite of skills to truly evaluate the student.

PRACTICALITY

Practicality refers to the economic aspects of the assessment instrument with regard to time, labor, and money. The ideal assessment instrument would include ease of administration and scoring, while producing results that are correctly interpreted by school personnel. For instance, while interview testing may provide a good measure of oral communication proficiency, this type of instrument requires the luxury of time and energy—commodities the typical classroom teacher lacks. Conversely, while standardized tests provide ease of administration and scoring, the results rarely yield true data that are useful for ESOL educators. States continue to define and identify ways to assess their EL students. Importantly, valid and reliable assessments developed for ELs and their multiple language systems, is key to designing strong instructional programs and supporting academic learning.

POINTS TO REMEMBER

✔ Assessment of content learning should not be confused with how much language the student knows. Assessments are used for the following reasons:
- For appropriate student academic and language placement.
- To gain information about the student's learning.

- To conduct formative and summative evaluations.
- For appropriate student placement in ESOL programs, special instruction in English, bilingual education, and so forth.
- To gain information about the student's learning, educational background, literacy level, and so forth.

✔ When evaluating students, we need to collect information about EL progress to modify and improve instruction, evaluate the curriculum, and measure language gains.

✔ Testing and assessment are different. Testing is a single-occasion exercise under specific conditions that are the similar for all students. Assessment is a broader collection of work samples indicating the caliber of work the student is doing.

✔ Inappropriate assessment can lead to inappropriate placement, instruction, and achievement, resulting in minority students dropping out of school.

✔ Teachers must know what languages the student speaks, how much academic background the student possesses, and as much personal information as possible to correctly place, evaluate, and instruct the EL student.

✔ Standardized tests are unfair to the new language learner because they can be culturally and linguistically biased, and they cannot accurately measure how much the student truly knows because of their reliance on language. What they indicate instead is how the EL student measures up to the native English-speaking student.

✔ States still are accountable for the academic performance of ELs under ESSA.

REFLECTION QUESTIONS AND DISCUSSION

1. What is the difference between testing and assessment? Create a Venn diagram to illustrate these two and the relationship between them.

2. Describe the difference between summative and formative assessments. Provide three examples of each.

3. Define reliability and validity with regard to formal and informal tests.

4. José is a 10-year-old boy from Cuba who arrived with his parents and older brother Mario who is 15. Maria is an 8-year-old girl from Kosovo whose parents were brutally murdered in an outbreak of fighting, and who has arrived alone in the United States to stay with an uncle she does not know well. Ju Han is a 12-year-old boy from Korea whose parents are visiting professors of nuclear medicine who will be here for 2 years.

Describe what you would do to place these students in appropriate classes in their new schools in your state. What steps would you take? What would you have to know about them? How could you find out information about them to help you help them?

ACTIVITIES

1. Go to an elementary school, a middle school, and a high school. Interview the administrators and ESOL teachers to find out how they test, assess, and place EL students. Write a comparison report and share it with your group. Use the following page to write your report.

    Name(s) and class time _____
    Elementary school name _____
    City_____
    Tests used_____
    Person in charge of the ESOL program_____
    Report:

2. Interview some teachers to find out how they assess the native language literacy of their ESOL students. Then adapt or develop your own instrument to assess native language literacy.

3. Review the documents in the Appendix used to guide identification and placement of EL students. Prepare an initial placement plan for new ELs arriving at your school. Research and include available entry/exit tests approved by your school district.

WEB RESOURCES

4 Ways to Help ELs Self-Assess Their Writing. http://blog.tesol.org/4-ways-to-help-ells-self-assess-their-writing/

Assessment & Reflection with ELLS—And All Students. http://www.edweek.org/tm/articles/2012/05/01/tln ferlazzo hullsypnieski.html

Assessment of English Learners. http://www.readingrockets.org/webcasts/1003

The Best Free Online Tools for ELs to Use for Assessing Their Language-Level. http://larryferlazzo.edublogs.org/2016/02/26/the-best-free-online-tools-for-ells-to-use-for-assessing-their-language-level

ELL Assessments. https://www.readinga-z.com/ell/ell-assessments

English Language Learners—Classroom Assessment. https://www.pearsonassessments.com/services/solr/search/.api?segmentName=learningassessments&categoryId=40811&requestFrom=categoryLanding&siteContext=ped.ani.us.la&requestFrom=leftnav

Identification, Assessment, and Instruction of English Learners With Difficulties in the Elementary and Intermediate Grades. http://www.ctserc.org/component/k2/item/218-identification-assessment-and-instruction-of-english-language-learners-with-learning-difficulties-in-the-elementary-and-intermediate-grades

Larry Ferlazzo—Assessing English Learners. https://www.teachingenglish.org.uk/blogs/larry-ferlazzo/larry-ferlazzo-assessing-english-language-learners

Needs Assessment and Learner Self-Evaluation. http://www.cal.org/caela/tools/program development/elltoolkit/Part2-5NeedsAssessment&LearnerSelf-Evaluation.pdf

Supporting English Learners With Formative Assessments. http://www.gettingsmart.com/2016/04/supporting-ells-with-formative-assessments

REFERENCES

Abedi, J. (2014). English language learners with disabilities: Classification, assessment, and accommodation issues. *Journal of Applied Testing Technology*, *10*(2), 1–30.

Ariza, E. N. (2018). *Not for ESOL teachers: What every classroom teacher needs to know about the linguistically, culturally, and ethnically diverse student* (3rd ed.). Dubuque, IA: Kendall/Hunt Publishing.

Baker, C. (2000). *The care and education of young bilinguals. An introduction for professionals.* Clevedon, UK: Multilingual Matters, Ltd.

Carrasquillo, A. L. (2013). *Teaching English as a second language: A resource guide.* New York, NY: Routledge.

Cohen, A. D. (2014). *Strategies in learning and using a second language.* New York, NY: Routledge.

Cook, H. G., & Linquanti, R. (2015). *Strengthening policies and practices for the initial classification of English learners: Insights from a national working session.* Washington, DC: Council of Chief State School Officers.

Colorín Colorado. (2017). Reading comprehension strategies for English language learners. Retrieved from http://www.colorincolorado.org/article/reading-101-english-language-learners

Florida Department of Education. (1990). Florida consent decree. Retrieved from http://www.fldoe.org/academics/eng-language-learners/consent-decree.stml

Law, B., & Eckes, M. L. (2010). *The more-than-just-surviving handbook: ELL for every classroom teacher* (3rd ed.). Winnipeg, MB: Portage & Main Press.

Richards, J. C., & Schmidt, R. W. (2014). *Language and communication*. London, UK: Routledge.

Sireci, S. G., & Faulkner-Bond, M. (2015). Promoting validity in the assessment of English learners. *Review of Research in Education*, *39*(1), 215–252.

Tarone, E. E., Gass, S. M., & Cohen, A. D. (Eds.). (2013). *Research methodology in second-language acquisition*. New York, NY: Routledge.

U.S. Department of Education. (2017a). ESSA monitoring guidelines. Retrieved from https://www2.ed.gov/about/offices/list/oela/english-learner-toolkit/chap8.pdf

U.S. Department of Education. (2017b). Tools and resources for identifying all English learners. Chapter 1. Retrieved from https://www2.ed.gov/about/offices/list/oela/english-learner-toolkit/chap1.pdf

Classroom Assessments and Standardized Tests for English Learners

LEARNING OBJECTIVES

Readers will be able to

- ❖ Identify and select classroom assessment practices for an English learner (EL)
- ❖ Describe the need for ongoing assessment of ELs to inform instruction
- ❖ Maintain student assessment documentation on ELs
- ❖ Describe and select alternative assessments for ELs
- ❖ Describe standardized testing practices and procedures related to ELs including bias in assessment

Roody arrived from Haiti as a non-English speaker when he was 10 years old and was placed, age appropriately, in the fourth grade. Although Roody was not a mean-spirited child, his behavior soon became a problem, as he was annoying other children, ignoring the teacher, and making classroom life miserable. The teacher decided to meet with his parents for an academic conference, but was advised by the bilingual counselor not to call Roody's house. In the Haitian culture, parents revere the teacher and are not called to the school, except when the child has a serious behavior problem. This means the child might be punished corporally at home. The teacher did not want the boy to be punished—he only wanted to discover what was bothering Roody so he could help him to learn. Finally, a Haitian-Creole speaking liaison contacted the parents on behalf of the teacher and a school conference was arranged. Through a discussion with the parents, the teacher discovered that Roody was bored and frustrated in class; although he could not understand English well enough to grasp the language arts content, he had learned the math content two grades earlier in Haiti. As a result, an individual educational plan was created for Roody; he would go to the fifth grade teacher's highest math group while a tutor would help him with his academic English. Roody's behavior improved dramatically once his keen mind was challenged and the world in English began to make sense.

HOW DOES A CLASSROOM TEACHER ASSESS AND EVALUATE AN EL IN CLASS?

In Chapter 23, we discussed different types of assessments (such as formal and informal) as well as assessments that are used to screen, identify, and place EL students in appropriate classrooms. In this chapter, we focus on assessments that can be used formally and informally in classrooms for both summative (end point) and formative (to inform teaching and learning) purposes. Note that teachers use a variety of assessment practices in their practice, including observing how students are engaged in an activity, if they have comprehended a task or mastered a concept. Assessment is an integral part of the teaching and learning process.

ELs must receive instruction in basic subject areas that is understandable to them, given the student's level of English proficiency. Assessment of student learning, especially in the content areas, can pose problems for teachers of ELs, because language proficiency and knowledge of content are difficult to discern. Teachers need to distinguish if content has been mastered or if students' English language level masks what students know in the academic content areas. Teachers must remember that every test of academic content is also to some degree a test of language. In fact, many tests that seek to measure academic knowledge actually measure only language proficiency (Holmes, Hedlund, & Nickerson, 2000; Menken, 2000). Just as a second grade mainstream teacher might read a mathematical problem to a poor reader for assessment of the child's understanding of mathematical concepts, teachers of ELs must adapt or differentiate assessment instruments for EL students to appraise actual content knowledge. If we ask a child, "What is the sum of four and four?" the student might not respond because he or she does not know the meaning of the word "sum." How many times do these errors occur for both native and non-native English-speaking children without our knowledge? In fact, these misunderstandings occur between native English-speakers all the time. You hear words and interpret them through the meaning you know, but the meaning is not always what the speaker was trying to imply.

Imagine the misunderstandings that occur when a person is learning a new language. For example, an EL calls the teacher "*teacher*," not knowing the correct way to address a teacher in the United States, yet is politely translating the appropriate form of address from the native language to the target language (English). Again, this is the right information but based on this context, it is the wrong word. The same phenomenon applies to assessment; the language used may interfere with the meaning the student receives. It is impossible to accurately assess a student's content knowledge using standardized testing if the student does not understand the intended meaning of the words.

Teachers must become proficient in learning to assess ELs. Many teachers who are inexperienced in teaching non-native English-speakers are unaware of the complex set of issues and implications these students bring with them. Often the teacher unknowingly refers the student to special services when the difficulty is purely from linguistic interferences. This is why students learning another language are overrepresented in special education programs (Harry & Klingner, 2014). They are referred for testing when the teacher mistakenly believes the child's English language "dis"ability indicates academic, social, emotional, or mental ability. However, sometimes the reverse is true—the teacher, after years of experience, knows the student has serious developmental concerns beyond academic English tasks, and refers the student to special services only to be denied. The reasons for denial could be the particular school's retention policy, inability to test the student in the native language, lack of official documentation of problems, or any number of reasons.

SCENARIO

Mrs. Matsumoto, a teacher with little experience in alternative testing for EL students, was at the end of her patience with Akemi. Nothing had changed in Akemi's academic behavior—she still was not responding as the teacher expected, even after being in the United States for more than 8 months. The other students were busy answering the questions on the Civil War unit test while Akemi had barely made an attempt to read the test questions. In frustration, Mrs. Matsuno grabbed a piece of paper and tossed it on Akemi's desk. "Here, draw a picture." At least she had given the child a way to keep busy. To the teacher's surprise, Akemi started drawing a clear, epic-style depiction of the Civil War, with President Lincoln, soldiers with vivid uniforms representing Northern and Southern armies, and illustrations that clearly showed she had understood the content of the unit. Mrs. Matsuno was overwhelmed! She had unwittingly discovered a successful way to alternatively assess her student.

WHY ALTERNATIVE ASSESSMENTS FOR ENGLISH LANGUAGE LEARNERS?

When assessing ELs, always keep in mind that lack of English fluency does not signify lack of intelligence or knowledge. It should not be assumed that students are below grade level because they cannot do grade level work in English. In fact, English-learning students are often bored or frustrated when forced to sit through lessons addressing academic content they have already mastered in their native language. Such students may respond by acting out or tuning out.

Alternative assessment is the practice of judging student progress by methods, instruments, and documentation other than standardized tests. These methods can include portfolios, journals, interviews, and so forth, that demonstrate the student's ability to complete grade-level work. Authentic assessment, performance assessment, and naturalistic assessment are also valuable indicators because they demonstrate the child's true abilities.

Chamot and O'Malley (1994) describe six basic reasons why alternative assessment is valuable and more accurate in assessing instruction for English for speakers of other languages (ESOL) students.

1. Authenticity—Assessment reflects actual classroom tasks in local curriculum content and provides true information about language acquisition.
2. Variety—Student performance is assessed from a variety of perspectives, instead of relying on a limited number of measurements; this provides a global perspective from which to draw conclusions about progress.
3. Process Orientation—Progress is monitored with respect to learning processes and strategies, as well as product output.
4. Continuity—Student performance is ongoing and monitored throughout the school year.
5. Instructional Assessment—Instruction can be adapted to individual student needs, and feedback on instructional effectiveness is readily provided.
6. Collaborative—Teachers can interact holistically to share their views of students' performance throughout a variety of scenarios.

Authentic assessment incorporates real-life functions. The EL can demonstrate achievement by producing information, such as being able to make a telephone call to the bus company to inquire about a route. Performance assessment requires the student to make a correct response, indicating knowledge of a skill, concept, or method of completing a task. Naturalistic assessment entails observing performance and behavior informally within a natural setting (Ariza, 2018).

Assessment and instruction should go hand in hand, as they are interdependent. Carefully designed assessment should be authentic and conducted in conjunction with developmentally appropriate activities that reflect the ELs' true environment, both in and out of school (Cummins, 1982; O'Malley & Pierce, 1996; Ariza, 2018). Throughout the entire process of teaching and learning, authentic assessment should be ongoing, methodical, and linked to all subjects taught. In this way the instructor can judge the EL's progress holistically, as well as objectively, and accurately analyze reading, writing, listening, speaking, cultural knowledge, and communicative competence.

Although the choices for alternative assessments are comprehensive, we will discuss the most common types in use today.

Portfolios

Probably the most popular example of an alternate assessment is the portfolio. Students, teachers, professors, private and public employees, artists, job seekers, and any number of individuals are expected to showcase their work in the form of portfolios to indicate their progress and competence. Portfolios for ESOL students are collections of information about the student that indicate progress in learning which enable teachers, parents, and administrators to evaluate the student's achievement, growth, and thinking processes. Portfolios can also include communications with students, other teachers, parents, and administrators about the student's progress, with specific representation of his or her work (Ariza, 2018; O'Malley & Pierce, 1996).

In addition to being simply a collection of student work, a portfolio is a purposeful collection of student work that exhibits the student's efforts, progress, and achievement in one or more areas (Ariza, 2018). The collection must include the student's participation in selecting contents of his or her work, the criteria for selection, the criteria for judging merit, and evidence of student reflection. Thus, a collection of student work can only become a portfolio if the student contributes input, allowing the student to play a role in his or her own academic growth.

The advantages of assessment by portfolios are many (Ariza, 2018)and especially so for ELs, including:

- Provides a more holistic picture of student growth and learning gains
- Allows multiple people to view and understand the student's learning, including teachers, coaches, parents, school leaders and staff
- Occurs more naturally in the learning environment
- Acts as a tool for student–teacher conferencing
- Places the child at the center of educational process and decision-making by teachers
- Informs curriculum and instruction
- Can demonstrate bilingual student learning in and across multiple languages and language modalities

WHAT SHOULD BE INCLUDED IN PORTFOLIOS?

There is no right or wrong way to put together a student portfolio, unless a school or district mandates a specific procedure. Typical contents of a portfolio may include:

- Drawings
- Writing samples
- Language Experience Approach (LEA) stories dictated to the teacher
- Poetry, haiku, creative writings, or other assignments

(Continued)

- Letters
- Invitations
- Greeting cards
- Visual representations created by the student, such as charts, maps, semantic maps, webs, graphic organizers, pictures of bulletin boards, and science or other projects
- Evidence of solo or group activities in which the student has participated
- Audio or video of verbal progress
- Video of student participation in dramatic representations, choral readings, role-playing, or skits, or of the student leading the class in some activity, teaching/sharing something about his or her culture, telling or reading a story, interviewing someone, giving a puppet show, dramatizing a commercial, and so forth
- Learning log
- Checklist of achievements, such as a vocabulary list, rubrics of criteria mastered, SOLOM matrix (see references), and so forth
- Reading inventories
- Selected work samples
- Parent/teacher conference report
- Student self-evaluation
- Copies of pertinent data such as report cards and test scores
- Book reports
- A list of books read
- Lab reports submitted
- Research papers
- Evidence of collective group work in which the student took part
- Work dated at the beginning, middle, and the end of the year, to measure self-progress

As we can see, the list of contents for a student's portfolio can be endless. However, it is important that teachers keep portfolios as well, containing student work accumulated throughout the year; these should include cumulative portfolios of the student's long-term records and another portfolio with grades, records, notes, and observations. This is not merely efficient record-keeping, it is also a way to maintain legal documentation for future reference, crises, or substantiation.

Appendix A of this chapter contains a portfolio coversheet that teachers can complete or assist EL students in completing. The cover sheet provides a guide for EL students to identify samples of their best work, their rationale for choosing it, and a self-evaluation of their work. We have found that portfolios make great visual supports for parents and caregivers to view their child's progress in parent–teacher meetings.

Teacher-Made Tests

For students temporarily exempted from standardized tests, teacher-made tests can be substituted for standardized computation/calculation and reading/language exams. However, all substitute testing must be approved by the EL committee, follow the district EL plan, and be tied to the test subject content from which the EL was originally exempted to ensure congruence with the standard test.

Abbreviated Standard Tests

Many school districts have developed alternative tests to assess the skills and benchmarks that are used to measure achievement of goals and standards. These are often called test prototypes. In addition, many private textbook and computer software publishers have marketed test prototypes that correspond to state standardized tests and can be adopted as alternative assessments for individuals exempted from formal testing.

Protocols

When a teacher needs to assess a particular skill or wants to assess a certain content area, students can be assigned a specific academic activity to perform. For example, if a teacher needs to assess skills in oral reading, the student is asked to read aloud. The results are obvious indicators of achievement. Protocols can look like checklists or chronologies of student observations.

Rating Scales/Inventories

Teachers can use these methods to record behaviors and student progress. Daily or weekly behavior, academic progress, or emotional episodes can be recorded. For example, when trying to eliminate a linguistic or grammatical interference, a teacher could write: *Yesterday Wang, who is working on his pronunciation of "th," corrected himself twice, and today he corrected himself five times*. Such documentation should not be judgmental; rather, it should merely report progress.

Anecdotal Records

Anecdotal records are notes jotted in a narrative form at the end of the day or during a free moment. The teacher, paraprofessional, or staff member working with the student can also record what happened in the classroom, on the playground, in "specials," at lunch, with other students, while the student is alone, and so forth. The teacher can clarify student behavior or performance, and major changes can be revealed over time. However, this manner of assessment does have drawbacks, as the teacher must have ample time to collect the data and the perception to make sense of the information collected. Therefore, it might be best to save this method for selected individuals who need more one-on-one attention.

Miscue Analysis

Teachers use miscue analysis as an assessment tool to ascertain how a reader processes the printed word (Ariza, 2018) An analysis of reading weaknesses and strengths can be made by the kinds of errors made. In the case of an EL, the teacher must be sure the "mistakes" are not caused by pronunciation problems but truly represent difficulty in reading. In miscue analysis, the student reads aloud a meaningful passage of about 500 words, while the teacher records the performance. The teacher can hold a copy of the same text to make notes. After the reader finishes, the teacher asks probing questions to see what the child has remembered. Some common miscues can be:

- A reader mispronounces a word read (that is, onset, middle, or finial sounds are not pronounced)
- A reader inserts a word that is not in the text
- A reader omits a word that is in the text
- A reader repeats a word or portion of the text
- A reader substitutes a word in the text when making sense of the text
- A reader reverse the order of the words

The teacher, who knows the students, will be the best judge of their reading comprehension. However, sometimes a student will read aloud beautifully and not understand what he or she has just read; conversely, the student will not read well aloud, but will understand the passage after reading silently. In such cases, the teacher might not realize what is happening. In the first case, the student demonstrates excellent pronunciation, and in the second example, the student cannot pronounce the words correctly, yet comprehends the text. A younger student might have acquired a native-like accent, but not possess vocabulary or academic language (Cognitive Academic Language Proficiency [CALP]; Cummins, 1981), whereas the older student might have excellent prior knowledge and be able to understand, but not be able to speak well. Identifying such reading patterns enables teachers to plan an appropriate reading program for their students.

Informal Reading Inventory

An IRI (Informal Reading Inventory) is an assessment tool that involves teachers recording students as they read passages with varying degrees of difficulty (grade levels). After reading, students are asked comprehension questions. The recording is replayed and the teacher can then conduct a miscue analysis to see if the student's comprehension is reflected in his or her patterns of miscues. The results indicate the reading grade level.

Running Records

A running record is one way to evaluate a student's progress in reading. Usually teachers are trained to conduct running records (Latham Keh, 2017). This method is similar to a miscue analysis, as the student reads while being recorded and the teacher identifies student reading errors. Some teachers prefer not to record the reader, but the recording allows teachers to avoid classroom interruptions, and they can play back the performance at a later date. Unlike IRI's, there is no text to mark, and so the teacher has to write quickly— another reason why recording is useful. Running records are also a way to evaluate text difficulty for EL students, group students, monitor progress, and observe difficulties, while allowing readers to read at their own pace (Zarillo, 2002; Figure 24.1).

Reading a-Z Running Record

Level D

Student's Name _____   Date _____   The Wheel
                                                      99 words

Have the student read out loud as you record.   Assessed by _____

Page	E = errors S–C = self-correction M = meaning S = structure V = visual	E	S–C	E M S V	S–C M S V
3	The wheel comes off the truck.				
4	It rolls down the hill. Faster and faster.				
5	The wheel rolls through the field. It rolls past the cows. Faster and faster.				
6	The wheel rolls through the barn. It rolls past the chickens. Faster and faster.				
7	The wheel rolls toward the river. It rolls over the bridge. Faster and faster.				
8	The wheel rolls into the school. It rolls out the door. Faster and faster. The wheel rolls through the town.				
9	It rolls past the Policeman. Faster and faster.				
10	The wheel rolls into the garage. it stops rolling. The wheel is on the truck.				
	Totals				

Accuracy Rate: [____]   Error Rate: [____]   Self–correction Rate: [____]

Figure 24.1: Miscue Analysis Instrument

Importantly, teachers of EL students using running records or other informal assessments need to remember that many ELs have extensive knowledge of their first (or home) languages and literacies and are not in any way deficient. In fact, bilingual and multilingual children may be processing across multiple languages and/or culturally may speak or read more slowly.

Journals

Journals are an excellent venue for learners to begin practicing their writing. Students usually either love keeping journals or hate it. Journals can be formal notebooks or they can be made of folded and stapled paper. A teacher can make journal writing valuable to ELs, and at the same time have an excellent vehicle for assessing their writing skills.

If given a writing task, even students who appear to have an excellent grasp of English will almost always make errors, and the teacher will find areas that need substantial practice. Ironically, many students (especially from Asian countries) write native-like English, yet cannot speak or understand English well because their past language education focused on literacy, not communicative competence.

Personal Journals

A personal journal may be the first encounter a student has in writing about personal thoughts. Where, when, and how often journal writing is assigned depends on the teacher's preferences and objectives. The teacher may respond if the journal writer wishes, but should not correct. Often students are delighted when the teacher writes back a personal response. This technique works wonders for those who are too shy or timid to talk to the teacher. By responding in writing, the teacher can begin to build a very strong, personal bond with the writer. The journal writer must feel that his or her writing is personal and that trust must be fostered by the teacher.

Dialogue Journals

A dialogue journal (Ariza, 2018) is just that—the student writes and the teacher responds. Students can keep writing about the same topic, or a new topic can be announced at each writing time. This is a great opportunity to encourage new writers to participate in a meaningful activity. Students usually savor reading what their teacher has to say. Be aware, however, that certain topics or language may present problems, and the teacher may need to explain why the writing is inappropriate. Also, teachers may learn distressing details

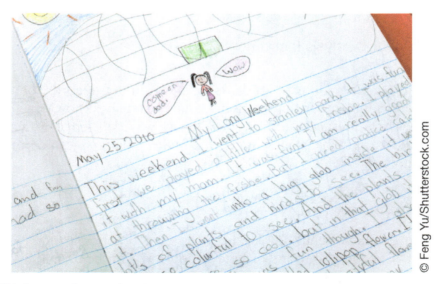

Figure 24.2: Dialogue Journal

about a student's life, such as an abusive relationship, a parent going to jail, or the fact that his or her friend is contemplating suicide, and may need to decide how he or she should intervene because the student's writing might be a legitimate call for help (Figure 24.2).

Buddy Journal

Buddy journals are ongoing conversations between two individuals in written form (Ariza, 2018). The partners can be in the same grade, class, or reading group, or they can be older students in different classes, schools, grades, and with the advent of electronic mail, even in different countries. The students can brainstorm topics, or topics can be assigned by the teacher. This is an ideal way to create a meaningful activity, as the writers are motivated to write because they will receive an answer. Again, the teacher may have to monitor the journals for appropriateness.

Learning Journal

A learning journal is an ideal way to teach metalinguistic awareness, as ELs are encouraged to write about their learning process. This may be a little difficult because students must be taught what to look for and what to write about. For example, *Today I made a mistake and everyone laughed when I said soup instead of soap. I hate it when they laugh at me.* Guiding questions can be posed so that language learners can understand how they are learning and the processes they are going through. Typical questions could be: *What did you learn today?; How did you know you learned it?; How did you feel when you took that reading test today?; What is the hardest part about English?* By reading the journals, teachers are able to cull salient points to focus and build on, while helping students to understand the language learning process.

SOLOM

The California State Department of Education created an oral language observation instrument called the SOLOM (Student Oral Language Observation Matrix). Throughout the year, the teacher has the opportunity to see students in a variety of meaningful and complex communication situations. Because teacher observations are cumulative and free from the stresses of artificial testing situations, the assessment of students yields greater reliability than the one-shot standardized tests. The SOLOM test focuses on oral language traits such as comprehension, fluency, vocabulary, grammar, and pronunciation. Each student is assessed for these traits, and the appropriate box checked off. The SOLOM does consider the sociocultural context of the student's oral language production. However, it is a useful tool that teachers can use to gauge oral language proficiency. With this assessment tool, the teacher must be linguistically sensitive, as the test can be subjective. The SOLOM matrix and information can be found at the Center for Applied Linguistics website: http://www.cal.org/twi/EvalToolkit/appendix/solom.pdf. Other valuable information can be found as well.

Checklists

Checklists are wonderful, fast, and convenient alternative assessment tools for EL students, because they are adaptable for any lesson and can be completed quickly. Checklists include the behaviors or skills that are to be assessed; the teacher simply checks off the appropriate skill. When creating a checklist, the teacher must think about all the behaviors, tasks, skills, and so on, that he wants to see the student master. At the bottom of the checklist, space should be left for additional categories which are certain to present themselves during the process of learning. Checklists can be made for one lesson, or for many throughout the year. The date, the behavior, the task, activity, and so forth, should be recorded for later reference. Because this is a holistic assessment, it is a natural way to document achievement, mastery, or failure. Be cautioned, however, that checklists can be limiting; when teachers focus exclusively on certain things, they may miss other significant occurrences.

Rubrics

A rubric is a predetermined list of criteria to determine the grade for or quality of an assignment, a product, project, or task. For example, the teacher can grade a student on the following basis:

For a grade of A the student must:
    Attend every class
    Receive no less than 90% on the test
    Turn in superior written work on time
    Prepare for and participate in each class

For a grade of B the student must:
    Miss no more than one class
    Receive no less than an 80% on the test
    Turn in very good written work
    Prepare for and participate in most classes

For a grade of C the student must:
    Miss no more than two classes
    Receive no less than 70% on the test
    Turn in good written work
    Prepare for and participate in some classes (Figure 24.3)

Academic Rubric

You can create and customize your own rubric by using the tool found at http://rubistar.4teachers.org/index.php, as well as other websites. Teachers can prepare rubrics for EL students according to the objectives they want to achieve. The rubrics can include language and content area skills and can provide feedback to EL students in both areas.

4. Communicates a purpose or idea in a clear, specific manner. Superior effort.	3. Uses good techniques to communicate ideas; purpose is clear.	2. Demonstrates an attempt to communicate with adequate success. Makes significant errors or omissions.	1. Demonstrates little or no clarity; reason for assignment is unclear.
Examples:	Examples:	Examples:	Examples:

Figure 24.3: Scoring Rubric for Oral Presentation

Electronic Documentation

Audio and video documentation are additional methods of capturing the student's abilities from beginning (placement) to end (exiting the ESOL program). Initial interviews can determine proper placement based on oral proficiency and receptive language understanding, and can be played back at any time to measure progress, evaluate learning, and to plan further instruction. As an additional bonus, students can see and hear their own progress. The teacher can video students as they participate in skits, role-playing, theatrical works, solo and choral recitations, interviewing, presentations, debates, and any number of opportunities that personify the ELs as they engage in language interaction.

Interviews and Conferences

One simple way to judge how much students know is to sit down and talk with them. Teachers can phrase questions to elicit responses that indicate mastery of a grammatical concept. For instance, if a teacher wants to know if the student can use *do* and *did* appropriately, the teacher can ask a specific question requiring that form to answer correctly. Teachers who tell a student, *Tell me what you did during the spring vacation*, will soon learn if the student knows the past tense. If a student is told, *Ask me what I did on my birthday last year*, and the student responds, *What you did on your birthday last year?*, we know there is a problem with the *do* structure in English. In this way, teachers can clearly see where comprehension breaks down and where strengths lie.

Interviews and conferences may be formal or informal, but they involve more than just talking to the student. The aim is to get the student to talk, so teachers must listen and let the student speak. This will be difficult if there are 30 other students clamoring for attention. If teachers want to use this method, they need to plan by choosing a time when they will be able to concentrate on the student and ask questions that require more than a yes or no answer.

Student Self-Assessment

Some students come from countries where the teacher (as master) talks and the learner memorizes, and creativity is not expected or encouraged. ELs in American classes must be prepared to become reflective and to evaluate their own work. Provocative questions such as: *What is my best work this week? What do I need to practice more to improve my spelling? What do I need to become a better writer?* will help learners to assess themselves and see where they have improved, as well as where they need to improve. This procedure will take much practice and guidance, because many students raised in other cultures are not expected to focus on themselves, and they feel uncomfortable doing this.

GRADING THE EL

One of the greatest dilemmas facing the classroom teacher is the issue of fair and accurate grading of ELs, when the categories on their report cards do not truly reflect the EL student's quality of work or academic progress. Sadly, a report card often only reflects the student's work in comparison to the rest of the class. In addition, a poor grade can carry such a social stigma that the children often unfairly judge their own worth by the grades they receive. When grades include absences or behavioral issues, the final tally is skewed, and academic ability is neglected. Compounding the grading issue is the uncertainty and disparity concerning the literacy level in the native language. It is unfair and quite impossible to compare a competent literate with an emerging literate, as there is no common standard to measure standard performance.

Ariza (2018) suggests a number of guidelines that can be used in obtaining more accurate grades. Teachers should grade only:

1. The student's best work
2. Material relevant to the student's learning
3. Progress and end product

Students should:

1. Know what skills and topics will be graded (to ensure their best effort is directed at the right objectives)
2. Be taught to know how to critique their own work and what to learn to improve their grades
3. And, finally, teachers should strive to improve their own grading practices.
4. As previously recommended, extra time can be allowed to provide for delayed language processing; interpreters can be available, and the testing format can be revised to make testing more comprehensible for the second language learner. As grading procedures become more defined and precise, the process of determining accurate grades will become smoother.

Finally, conventional report cards can be replaced by a quarterly summary report that evaluates student performance across the curriculum in narrative form, with corresponding rating scales and written comments about the significance of the grade.

STANDARDIZED TESTS FOR ELS

In Chapter 23, we described standardized testing as creating and ensuring that the conditions of testing are the same for all test takers. In addition, students are assessed against a standard or benchmark. Although there are some standardized tests designed specifically to assess English language proficiency, most are inadequate for target language evaluation. These tests are usually administered once or twice a year, do not monitor students' ongoing progress in language acquisition, and usually cannot measure all the components involved in language learning (reading, writing, listening, speaking, and communicative competence).

While there are distinct advantages to standardized testing, namely the ability to compare test results across students over a period of time, probably the most salient disadvantage in standardized testing is the inability to assess linguistic or communicative competence, skills critical to language acquisition. *Linguistic competence* is the ability to control pronunciation, morphology, and syntax. *Communicative competence* refers to the ability to use language to achieve a particular purpose within different contexts (Richards & Schmidt, 2014). There is no doubt, however, that standardized tests including annual state standards assessments and end-of-course (EOC) examinations, will continue to be used in the near future across the United States.

One problem with standardized tests for ELs is the issue of cultural bias. *Cultural bias* occurs when test items and questions contain cultural knowledge that students may not be familiar with and/or that characterize or stereotype persons from diverse backgrounds. A classic example is asking students about "snow" when they are from a warm climate and may have no knowledge about snow. Cultural bias is especially a problem for EL students. ELs may not be familiar with some test items because they do not have the schema or background knowledge to answer the question. Consider this example:

> *Mr. Jones works at the lumber company. His gross salary is $400.00, but his net pay is $275.00. What is his take home?* (If the student does not know the meaning and concept of terms such as lumber, gross salary, net, and take home, we cannot accurately assess math knowledge.)

Other problems that result from cultural differences stem from the ways in which tests are taken in other countries. The idea of multiple choice questions is unheard of in many other countries. For example, in Haiti the traditional type of test given is the essay test. Among other typical testing procedures in the United States, "bubbling in" answers to a test on a scantron sheet is a foreign concept to students from many other cultures; without guidance and training, new students in the United States will not know what they are expected to do in this new testing situation.

In some other countries it is not considered cheating to work together, ask another student for the answer, or to work in groups. Individual work is prized as a valued commodity in the United States, and if another's work is not cited in the references, it is considered plagiarism. Korean and Chinese students, for example, believe it is an honor to quote another author's work without citation and honestly cannot understand the commotion resulting from submitting a "plagiarized" assignment.

Law and Eckes (2014) believe that standardized tests tend to fragment skills and do not really measure reading ability. Students may demonstrate their knowledge of vocabulary or grammar, but the tests may not measure reading or writing ability as a whole. Additional problems associated with standardized testing include:

- The inability to show whether the student knows the material or not (because of multiple choice answers)
- Only lower-order thinking skills are tested
- They measure correctness based on a single occasion, instead of measuring random competence
- The tests cannot tell where or why the student failed
- All language and thinking skills are tested through the confines of language
- Standard tests have no context from which to draw meaning and inference

In sum, standardized tests are designed to measure students' academic progress and can facilitate comparison across groups of students. However, they are often difficult for EL students because they require knowledge of how to take the test, specific cultural information, might contain cultural bias, and require knowledge of complex academic language (syntax, vocabulary, etc.).

That said, the federal government still holds schools accountable for the achievement of ELs. The "No Child Left Behind Act of 2001" (NCLB) made an impact on standard based high stakes testing for all states. This Act advocated annual testing for all students in grades 3–8, including ELs, regardless of English proficiency. English language development had to be assessed yearly to qualify for Title III (federal) funding for ELs, which was used to develop and implement English language instruction in educational programs.

In December, 2015, NCLB became the "Every Student Succeeds Act" (ESSA). This Act has changed the federal role in education and the accountability of schools. ESSA continues to require performance goals to be reported using standardized tests, with high expectations of students, but allows states to report results according to their own determination of specifics of what is measured and how it is to be reported (Hess & Eden, 2017).

POINTS TO REMEMBER

✔ EL students should be assessed using multiple forms of assessment in order to paint an accurate picture of their content area learning and English language ability.
✔ Every content area test is also a test of language; therefore, teachers need to ensure that test are written at ELs' language ability levels.
✔ Alternative assessments provide ways for ELs to demonstrate their learning.
✔ Alternative assessments can be used for formative (teacher-informed) and summative (student end point) purposes.
✔ Standardized tests can be problematic for ELs because they can contain bias in the assessment content and practice.
✔ Standardized tests can enable comparison across students and student learning over a period of time.

REFLECTION QUESTIONS AND DISCUSSION

1. Describe the role of classroom assessments in EL student learning? How do they relate to alternative assessments for ELs? Describe three examples of each.

2. Based on the previous chapters, how can you use student assessment results to determine teaching strategies for individual students? Explain and share.

3. What are standardized tests? What are four key considerations in the use of standardized testing for EL students?

ACTIVITIES

1. Examine sample proficiency tests used in your district for content, language, and cultural bias. Example: Research PPVT, LAB, LAS, IPT. Describe key aspects of each test.

2. In a group, choose an objective for a classroom ESOL lesson. Show what you would do to assess or ascertain whether or not your objective has been met.

3. In a group, brainstorm how you could teach an EL to self-assess. List your ideas.

WEB RESOURCES

5 Non-test Alternatives for Assessing English Language Learners. https://www.fluentu. com/blog/educator-english/assessing-english-language-learners
Assessing ESL Students in the Subject Classroom. http://www.esl.fis.edu/teachers/support/ eslAssess.htm

Assessment & Reflection With ELLs—And All Students. http://www.edweek.org/tm/articles/2012/05/01/tln_ferlazzo_hullsypnieski.html

Assessment for ELLs. https://www.youtube.com/watch?v=q6fG4FmibEQ

Assessment of English Language Learners. https://www.youtube.com/watch?time_continue=1&v=ysDDfG-enCc

Reading A–Z: ELL Assessments. https://www.readinga-z.com/ell/ell-assessments

Tips for Asessing ELL Students. https://www.youtube.com/watch?v=ILTwEJ8V8d4

Using Informal Assessment for English Language Learners. http://www.colorincolorado.org/article/using-informal-assessments-english-language-learners

REFERENCES

Chamot, A. U., & O'Malley, J. M. (1994). *The CALLA handbook: Implementing the cognitive academic language learning approach*. Reading, MA: Addison-Wesley.

Chittendon, L. (1994). *Teaching writing to elementary children*. Speech presented at the Bay Area Writing Project Workshop, Berkeley: University of California.

Cummins, J. (1981). The role of primary language development in promoting educational success for language minority students. In California State Department of Education (Ed.), *Schooling and language minority students: A theoretical framework*. Los Angeles, CA: Evaluation, Dissemination and Assessment Center, California State University.

Cummins, J. (1982). *Tests, achievement and bilingual students*. Wheaton, MD: National Clearinghouse for Bilingual Education.

Harry, B., & Klingner, J. (2014). *Why are so many minority students in special education?* New York, NY: Teachers College Press.

Hess, F. M., & Eden, M. (2017). *The every student succeeds act: What it means for schools, systems, and states*. Cambridge, MA: Harvard Education Press.

Holmes, D., Hedlund, P., & Nickerson, B. (2000). *Accommodating English language learners in state and local assessments*. Washington, DC: National Clearinghouse for Bilingual Education.

Law, B., & Eckes, M. L. (2010). *The more-than-just-surviving handbook: ELL for every classroom teacher*. Winnipeg: Portage & Main Press.

Menken, K. (2000). *What are the critical issues in wide-scale assessment of English language learners?* (Issue Brief No. 6). Washington, DC: National Clearinghouse for Bilingual Education.

O'Malley, J. M., & Pierce, L. V. (1996). *Authentic assessment for English language learners: Practical approaches for teachers*. New York, NY: Addison-Wesley.

Richards, J. C., & Schmidt, R. W. (2014). *Language and communication*. Hoboken, NJ: Taylor & Francis..

Zarillo, J. J. (2002). *Ready for RICA: A test preparation guide for California's reading instruction competence assessment*. Upper Saddle River, NJ: Prentice Hall.

PORTFOLIO COVER SHEET

Student Name: _____

Date: _____

Class: _____

Type of assignment _____

I have chosen to place this item in my portfolio because _____

_____

From this assignment I learned _____

_____

_____

_____

One thing I want to tell you about this assignment is _____

_____

_____

_____

When I look at this assignment

I like_____

_____

I would improve _____

_____

If I were to give myself a grade on this assignment, it would be a grade of _____

because _____

_____

_____

Teacher signature _____

Comment:

Engaging Families of English Learners

Readers will be able to

- ❖ Define family engagement
- ❖ Describe the importance of family engagement in English learner (EL) students' learning
- ❖ Delineate what educators can do to engage non-English speaking families

SCENARIO

Lucía is a sixth grade immigrant EL. She and her family arrived from war-torn El Salvador and enrolled in a rural school district in the southeast United States in late August. It is mid-October. There are only three other EL children in Lucía's classroom, and her family lives geographically far from them in on a trailer located on the edge of a peanut farm. Lucía receives several notices in her backpack from her school and her teacher. However, neither she nor her parents can read them because they are in English. One is a document that looks like a request for money, and another looks like a calendar. But because they cannot read English, the parents are not sure what to do with them. The following week, Lucía heads out to the bus stop and stands outside waiting for the bus. None of the other children arrive at the bus stop, and Lucía waits for over an hour at the street corner until she finally decides to walk home.

In the scenario above, Lucía and her parents clearly are not informed about the school calendar and events. How could the school communicate with Lucía's parents in a way that makes sense and to which they could respond? What can teachers do specifically to ensure that families are knowledgeable about important school events and information?

Parents and caregivers (or collectively "families") are without a doubt a child's first teacher. Families play one of the most important roles in the educational landscape of a child, and this is true for both native and non-native English speaking students. EL families face unique challenges, given their linguistic and cultural backgrounds, and there are some key differences in the ways that schools and educators must interact with EL families. Understanding and responding to diverse families' needs and engaging them in school activities, communications, and educational expectations and information will make a positive impact on EL students' learning.

REFLECT: Take a minute to reflect and jot down key words that define or describe how your parent or caregiver engaged in your education when you were in school. What assumptions do you bring to the topic of "family engagement?"

In essence, parent engagement is directly related to issues of equity and social justice, because not all families have equitable access to their child's education. Sometimes there are linguistic differences or cultural differences that impede the process of participation, communication, or education decision-making. In this chapter, we review what parent engagement is and why it is important to the educational success of EL students. We also discuss what schools might expect from EL families and what EL families think about schools. Finally, we outline five key principles of effective engagement for EL families.

One of the first activities that educators must undertake is to look into the home languages, literacy practices, and activities that define their EL families. Parents, such as Lucía's, may not read Spanish and they may not speak it either, even though they are recent arrivals to the United States from El Salvador. It is essential that teachers of ELs know exactly what language(s) are used in the homes of their EL students and the language(s) that parents can read, if any. Gathering this information could be part of a short, informal conversation with the EL student or could be a more elaborate, systematic assessment of EL families' backgrounds, histories, and social networking. In this book, we provide a few examples of ways to obtain this key information and how educators can use this to inform their work.

WHAT IS FAMILY ENGAGEMENT OF ELS?

In this chapter, we define family engagement as the process of identifying, communicating, and collaborating with caregivers, parents, and other key adults who are responsible for and contribute to a child's education and overall well-being. Other scholars such as

Ceballo and colleagues describe parental involvement as "resources parents dedicate to their children's education," namely "parents' interactions with schools . . . and with their children to promote academic success" (2014, p. 116). We agree that educators who view families as "resources" in their child's learning promotes the positive and affirming role that parents play in their child's education.

One of the leading scholars who investigates parental engagement has described a comprehensive model with six dimensions of parent involvement. Epstein (2010) views these dimensions as (a) parenting skills, where schools provide resources to help parents establish a positive home environment to foster child development; (b) home–school communication concerning child development; (c) home learning activities—involvement in learning activities in the home; (d) volunteering at school—parent participation in the functioning of the school; (e) decision-making—parent collaboration with the school in making school management decisions; and (f) collaboration with the community—parents' access to community resources to promote child learning and development. Epstein's framework describes activities in which parents can participate in home, school, and community settings. However, these six dimensions are embedded in a Western and United States cultural model of education that promotes home–school "partnerships" and that views parents as active, available, and participatory in nature. It assumes that parents understand the pedagogy (processes of teaching and learning) and that they also have the ability to read and write English. Epstein's model provides a useful outline of ways that schools and educators can build partnership with families. However, schools must modify and rethink models of parental engagement with EL families in mind.

Nontraditional ways of engaging families are key. Historically, educators have viewed parental engagement as parents' attendance at school events, including attending the biannual parent–teacher conference; volunteering in the school office, media center, or classroom; or availability to supervise at school field trips and events. In many cases, these activities are not practical for EL families. One study conducted by Jeynes (2003) investigated types of parental involvement and their association with student learning. Jeynes reviewed research studies that included parents or caregivers from different racial, ethnic, and linguistic backgrounds. Jeynes found that traditional parental involvement, such as parents assisting in school during school hours, or parents attending field trips, did *not* necessarily have a stronger effect on student learning than did other types or nontraditional forms of parental involvement. In fact, Jeynes found that having ongoing, home conversations between parents and child regarding the importance of education and support for the child's education had a stronger impact overall. This finding is important because it suggest that parents from linguistically or culturally diverse backgrounds can support their child's learning and engage in education in more culturally and linguistically responsive ways. Educators can facilitate this by promoting parent–child conversations regarding education in the home.

Educators and legislators in the United States understand the key work of parents in the education of their child. In the United States, the new Every Student Succeeds Act

(ESSA, 2015), written into law in December of 2015, outlines three important requirements of school district with respect to parental notifications. All school districts in the United States must comply with updated ESSA regulations. ESSA regulations require that districts ensure that:

1. All parents receive important notices and notifications regarding their child's education, including assessment results with an explanation and training on how to interpret the results.
2. Parents receive translations of those notifications "to the extent practicable, in a language that parents can understand."
3. District employees are prepared to distribute notifications to parents.

Specifically, ESSA notes that districts must implement a plan that describes how they will outreach to families of ELs. The plan must include how the district will inform families (a) how they can be involved in their child's education and (b) how they can assist their child to learn English and to meet state academic standards. Predictably, over the next few years, schools will need to ensure that they can document how they engage families in culturally and linguistically responsive ways.

Finally, the WIDA group, which we describe earlier in this book, offers a set of "ABCs" of family engagement and working with parents or caregivers of ELs (WIDA, 2017). The As stand for awareness and advocacy; the Bs underscore building trust and "brokering" cultural differences; and the Cs include communication and connecting to learning for ELs.

As educators of ELs, we must begin by meeting and reaching out to families, listening to their stories, and advocating on their behalf (Lawrence-Lightfoot, 2003). This constitutes the WIDA group's letter "A" of family engagement. The more knowledgeable we become of families, the more proficient and adept we can become in terms of brokering cultural differences. To broker cultural differences means that we understand the cultural "lens" through which diverse families see and engage in the world. We also learn how that might be similar to or different from mainstream culture. As brokers, we mediate these two (or more) different sets of cultural knowledge. Finally, communicating and connecting is what we do when we act on our knowledge of families' languages, cultural backgrounds, and literacy practices. Here, educators must truly localize outreach efforts so that they meet families' needs. An example may be to invite EL children's extended families to school events, provide transportation and interpretation to facilitate family involvement in school events, and to always ensure that all of the EL students' languages are visible and represented in school materials, in greetings, and at events. This should go beyond stereotypes and surface level culture and should reflect a deep understanding of values and beliefs.

Now that we know what family engagement for ELs is, it is important to note what it is not. Culturally and linguistically responsive family engagement is not sending home district, school, or classroom information or materials in languages that parents cannot understand. This includes everything from federal documents for free and reduced price lunch to classroom fieldtrip information. *Everything* must be translated or interpreted orally to nonliterate parents, without exception. But providing documents and materials is just the start. Families should be informed and engaged in all decision-making aspects of a child's education as well. This includes annual teacher meetings with an interpreter if necessary, community functions, evening access to computer labs and homework support. Hence, it is *not* family engagement to assume that because families have not responded to requests for information or because they have not attended events that they have been adequately informed and engaged. One way to think about this is to reframe family engagement as "school–home–school" communication. In other words, educators must initiate and follow up with families and are responsible for ensuring that families understand school expectations.

CULTURALLY AND LINGUISTICALLY RESPONSIVE PARENTAL ENGAGEMENT: AN EXAMPLE FROM RURAL SCHOOLS

In our work in *rural* school districts, we have found that EL families are not only geographically isolated, spanning great distances between schools and houses, but are also socially isolated and lack access to basic social services. This is problematic for EL children because they do not have an "even playing field" with native English speakers. It is our jobs as educators to ensure that we support children in nontraditional and creative ways to foster success and lifelong learning. Knowing that 96% of our university-district partner's EL families were Spanish speakers, we sought ways to provide them with educational networking. When we asked families what they felt they needed from schools, more than 50% stated that they wanted to learn English (in evening classes), and they also stated that they wanted to know how to communicate with schools and to obtain basic school information (such as how to read a report card and how they could help their child with home work at night).

Taking these ideas together, we have devised culturally responsive graphic novels called *fotonovelas* (Coady, Coady, & Nelson, 2015). One example of a fotonovela is below (see Figure 25.1). Because we sought to build relationships with families, we also wanted to talk with them and "walk them through" the *fotonovela*, discussing ideas and sharing stories about ways to help their child at home. Finally, we asked families to share the information or to "promote" it among the Spanish speaking community.

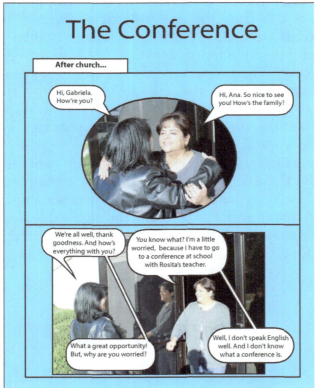

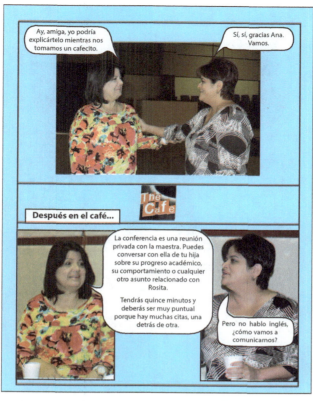

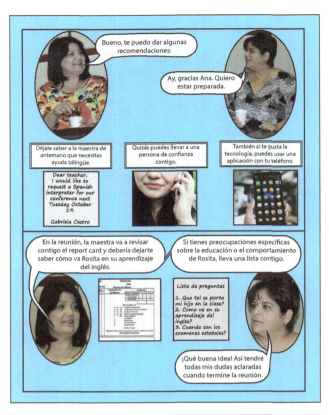

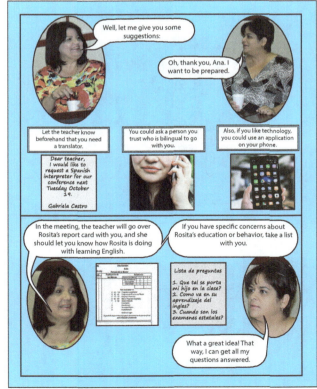

Antes de la conferencia

- Pregúntele a su niño qué le parece la escuela.

- Pregúntele a su niño si hay algo sobre lo que él quisiera que usted le hable a su maestro.

- Indíquele a su niño que usted y el maestro se reúnen para ayudarle.

- Haga una lista de los temas sobre los que desea hablar con el maestro.

Prepare una lista de preguntas como las siguientes: ¿Cuáles son las materias en las que mi niño es más fuerte y más débil? ¿Entrega mi niño la tarea a tiempo? ¿Participa mi niño en la clase? ¿Mi niño parece estar feliz en la escuela? ¿Qué puedo hacer en casa para ayudar?

Durante la conferencia

- Llegue a tiempo (o temprano) a la reunión.

- Termine la reunión a tiempo. Otros padres probablemente tienen programada su conferencia después de la suya.

- Relájese y sea usted mismo.

- Mantenga la calma durante la conferencia.

- Haga las preguntas más importantes primero.

- Si su niño recibe servicios especiales, como clases de inglés, pregunte sobre el progreso de su niño en esas clases.

- Pida que le expliquen lo que no entiende.

- Pídale al maestro que le indique cómo puede ayudar a su niño en casa.

Dele las gracias al maestro.

Después de la conferencia

- Hable de la conferencia con su niño.

- Hable sobre los puntos positivos y sea directo acerca de los problemas.

- Comuníquele a su niño cualquiera de los planes que usted y el maestro hayan hecho.

- Manténgase en contacto con el maestro durante el año escolar.

Figure 25.1: Fotonovela: Consejos/Advice

Before the conference

- Ask your child what he thinks of the school.

- Ask your child if there is anything he wants you to talk about teacher.

- Tell your child that you and the teacher meet to help you.

- Make a list of the topics you want to talk to the teacher about.

Prepare a list of questions such as the following: What are the subjects in which my child is stronger and weaker? Does my child deliver homework on time? Does my child in the class? Does my child seem happy at school? What can I do at home to help?

During the conference

- Arrive on time (or early) at the meeting.

- End the meeting on time. Other parents probably have their conference after yours.

- Relax and be yourself.

- Stay calm during the conference.

- Ask the most important questions first.

- If your child receives special services, such as English classes, ask about progress of your child in those classes.

- Ask them to explain what they do not understand.

- Ask the teacher to tell you how you can help your child at home.

Thank the teacher.

After the conference

- Talk about the conference with your child.

- Talk about the positive points and be direct about the problems.

- Communicate to your child any of the plans you and the teacher have made.

- Stay in contact with the teacher during the school year.

Figure 25.1: Fotonovela: Advice / Advice

WHAT NON-ENGLISH SPEAKING FAMILIES SAY ABOUT U.S. SCHOOLS?

In our work with EL families, we have asked them directly what they wanted teachers to know about their child's education, if they had an opportunity to share and communicate with them. Families/parents spoke boldly and powerfully about the importance of education. Some of them described challenges with communicating with the schools and teachers, and others noted the specific child's needs For example, one non-English speaking parent stated, "Is it true that there's no more homework? There are still 3 weeks left in the school year. Is my child lying to me?" This is a common concern of EL parents, because they do not have regular information from schools in a language they understand, a problem easily resolved with proper planning and channels of communication established. Two other EL parents stated, "I don't always understand the notes the teacher sends me in Spanish" and "I have no idea what happens at a parent-teacher meeting. I don't think I will go." These are other concerns that, with planning for EL parent communication, could be resolved. Finally, one mother noted, "They told me to bring an older child to translate." Although at first this may seem like an adequate strategy, we would strongly advise teachers and administrators of EL students not to rely on older siblings to convey information to parents for multiple reasons, including privacy, adequate translation or interpretation, and disrupting the child–parent relationship by forcing those children to take on the role of parenting.

REFLECT: How would you define "education?" What cultural assumptions does your definition hold? How might non-English speaking families define "education?"

WHAT SCHOOLS EXPECT FROM NON-ENGLISH SPEAKING FAMILIES?

As we noted earlier, schools might expect that non-English speaking families respond to educators and participate in school events in the same ways that native-English speaking families do. This is a misconception that educators must rethink. Family engagement reflects and reveals certain cultural values of a particular social or cultural group. For example, whether or not parents (or caregivers) are expected to attend school meetings with their children's teachers demonstrates one way that culture frames parental involvement. Even the definition of "education" differs across cultural groups. For example, a cognate of education in Spanish is *educación*, yet these terms hold different meaning to distinct cultural groups (Coady & Yilmaz, 2017). To be *bien educado* or well-educated among Latinos includes having respect and being well-behaved. Generally, in the United States this term is equated with level of education, such as holding an advanced degree.

Five Principles for Teachers' Effective Engagement of EL Families

Based on our experiences and our work with EL families, we offer five important principles of how educators—teachers, counselors, and administrators alike—can engage EL families. Remember that schools not only have a legal obligation but there is a moral and ethical responsibility to working with families. There are tremendous benefits to EL student learning, which is our ultimate goal.

1. *Discuss, develop, and implement a plan.* Educators must come together to identify the cultural and linguistic backgrounds of EL children and parents and their learning needs. Who are the EL students' caregivers? Does the school have a strategy to engage EL families?

   Educators can conduct a formal needs assessment or informal conversations or interviews with children to learn about their backgrounds, home languages, and needs. In some cases, educators go "door-to-door" to meet families and learn about their child, as well as see the child in her home environment. In rural settings, this may not be practical, due to geographic distances but in today's education environment, the use of smartphones or other electronic devices and media may be one way to bridge those distances.

2. *Identify and use students' native languages.* In our experience, many of the "problems" of engagement revolve around issues of communication. There are often simple solutions to these issues. For example, educators need to know (a) how to translate all school documents. Many districts use software such as TransAct to ensure that there is good translation for families; however, this should go beyond official school materials and include school policies (absences, grades), newsletters, updates, and announcements. Educators must ensure that the language of all communication is accessible to families, wherever practicable.

   In addition, it's crucial to know if families are literate in that language and/or if an interpreter or key community member can take on the role of communicating orally with parents. Ensuring that a school-based network of educators is available to answer the phone or call a caregiver when a child is critically ill.

3. *Encourage and support the use of the native language.* Families must be reassured that there are tremendous cognitive and social benefits to their child when they use their native language in the home. Reinforcing the importance of bilingualism will help the child succeed academically.

   The opposite side of the communication equation is the opportunity for teachers to learn several key phrases in languages of families. Teachers in our work in Florida, for example, have asked to learn how to communicate key ideas to parents. Even saying "hello," "how are you," and "your child had a good day today," can go a long way in creating a healthy and supportive environment in the school.

4. *Demystify how U.S. schools work in family-friendly terms.* Educators must demystify for EL parents how the U.S. education system works, as well as the cultural assumptions embedded in the U.S. school system. For example, families may not

be aware of mandatory education for all children, nor the need to provide a written note if a child has been absent from school. Some families may not be familiar with the concept of "truancy." The cultural differences about how schools function and the roles that various educators play can be confusing.

Other assumptions are embedded in schools, such as the emphasis on testing practices, and the expectation that parents attend parent–teacher meeting nights at school, or that families need to show a legal form of identification in order to pick a child up early from school. Conveying key information to families and being aware of assumptions or expectations can mitigate future problems. Colorín Colorado (2017) (http://www.colorincolorado.org/article/how-school-system-works) offers some fundamental information, available in English and Spanish, for families on how schools work. Their site reviews various roles that educators can play in schools.

5. *Identify ways that EL families can participate in their child's education.* As noted above, families' conception of education may differ from that of educators', and their resources such as time, experience, knowledge, and skills may not be immediately known to teachers. All families want the best for the children. In our work with families, we are often told that families simply do not know how they contribute to their child's education, particularly when they don't speak English. Identify ways that families can help. Some examples are holding conversations (in the home language) about the child's education and the importance of school, setting up a quiet space in the home where a child can study, having access to print materials in the home language— including nontraditional items such as recipes, graphic novels, and religious texts if used in the home (Coady, 2009a, 2009b). Also, identifying someone in the school who can regularly and systematically communicate with families in their language would ensure that parents and teachers understand the child's specific learning needs.

Ultimately, ELs' success in school is a team effort between teachers, families, and communities as resources. EL families have unique needs, and it is our responsibility as teachers to ensure school–home–school communication is seamless, accurate and timely. In addition, cultural resources and knowledge of cultural differences in the ways families view education is important for teachers to understand. Going beyond "surface" culture of families and gaining insight into how families function—their languages, literacies, and histories—will help to demystify and strengthen home–school relationships and pave the ground for strong partnerships that support EL student learning.

POINTS TO REMEMBER

✔ EL families represent a multitude of linguistic and cultural backgrounds and knowledges.
✔ Educators must know the home language and literacy practices of all of their EL students (and non-EL students); those languages constitute a foundation and *resource* for ongoing learning.

- ✔ Families must *always* receive school information in language(s) that they understand in writing and/or orally.
- ✔ Educators can become responsible advocates for EL students in school functions and at school events.
- ✔ Ongoing home language and literacy development supports EL student learning.
- ✔ Building partnerships with families is a key to student success.

REFLECTION QUESTIONS AND DISCUSSION

1. Define family engagement.

2. What is culturally and linguistically responsive family engagement? Provide three examples.

3. Why is it important to think broadly about "caregivers" of an EL child?

4. Create a network for communicating with non-English speaking families. Who should communicate with whom? For what purposes? You can draw a diagram that links key school personnel to other personnel and/or to families.

ACTIVITIES

1. Take time *outside* of the school environment and go to a place where EL families may go. This might be a discount dollar store, a church, grocery store, or international foods market. Observe how EL families engage with the community. What language(s) do they use? What is the role of the child/children, if any, in this setting? Do they engage in literacy activities? If so, how? Reflect on what you learned and how it might relate to EL students in school.

2. Informally survey (orally) your colleagues in school regarding some of their interactions with EL families. What creative ideas and suggestions can you identify that may engage families? Generate a plan to implement one of those suggestions and follow up with colleagues to learn how that worked for your particular school setting.

WEB RESOURCES

Colorín Colorado: Building Strong Parent–Educator Partnerships (with links to materials on parent conferences and talking with the child's teacher). http://www.colorincolorado.org/article/building-strong-parent-educator-partnerships

Project STELLAR (Supporting Teachers and Educators of English Language Learners Across Rural Settings). https://education.ufl.edu/esol/files/2016/11/Project-STELLAR-Announcement-Web-11-8-16.pdf

WIDA: The ABCs of Family Engagement. https://www.wida.us/get.aspx?id=2055

REFERENCES

Ceballo, R., Maurizi, L. K., Suarez, G. A., & Aretakis, M. T. (2014). Gift and sacrifice: Parental involvement in Latino Adolescents' education. *Cultural Diversity & Ethnic Minority Psychology, 20*(1), 116–127.

Coady, M. R. (2009a). "*Solamente libros importantes*": Literacy practices and ideologies of migrant farmworking families in north central Florida. In G. Li (Ed.), *Multicultural families, home literacies and mainstream schooling* (pp. 113–128). Charlotte, NC: New Age.

Coady, M. R. (2009b). Using families' ways of knowing to enhance student learning. In E. Amatea (Ed.), *Building culturally-responsive family-school partnerships: From theory to practice* (pp. 231–251). Upper Saddle River, NJ: Pearson.

Coady, M. R., Coady, T. J., & Nelson, A. (2015). Assessing the needs of immigrant, Latino families and teachers in rural settings: Building home-school partnerships. *NABE Journal, 6*. Retrieved from https://www2.nau.edu/nabej-p/ojs/index.php/njrp/article/view/42

Coady, M. R. & *Yilmaz, T. (2017). Preparing teachers of ELs: Home-school partnerships. In J. I. Liontas (Ed.), *The TESOL Encyclopedia of English Language Teaching*. Hoboken, NJ: TESOL International Association & Wiley. DOI: 10.1002/9781118784235.eelt0837

Colorín Colorado. (2017). Reading comprehension strategies for English language learners. Retrieved from http://www.colorincolorado.org/article/reading-101-english-language-learners

Epstein, J. (2010). *School, family and community partnerships: Preparing educators and improving schools* (2nd ed.). Boulder, CO: Westview Press.

ESSA. (2015). Every student succeeds act. Retrieved from https://www.congress.gov/114/plaws/publ95/PLAW-114publ95.pdf

Jeynes, W. H. (2003). A meta-analysis: The effects of parental involvement on minority children's academic achievement. *Education and Urban Society, 35*(2), 202–218.

Lawrence-Lightfoot, S. (2003). *The essential conversation: What parents and teachers can learn from each other*. New York, NY: Random House.

WIDA. (2017). *The ABCs of family engagement*. Retrieved from https://www.wida.us/get.aspx?id=2055

Teacher Reflections: Notes From The Field

To help present and future teachers deal with the issues surrounding alternative assessment of ELLs, we thought it would be most helpful to hear from teachers already in the field, dealing with testing and assessment issues on a day-to-day basis.

Marci Maher, who received her ESOL endorsement through her undergraduate teaching program at Florida Atlantic University, is a new fourth grade teacher in Broward County, Florida. She talks about what it is like for her to comply with state mandates, meet the needs of all the students in her charge, and juggle the mind-boggling array of administrative tasks demanded of her as a classroom teacher.

MARCI MAHER:

ESOL students come to the classroom not knowing what to expect. You don't know anything about their academic or personal history. You need to teach them, and they need to learn. Communication is limited. They feel hopeful, you feel hopeful. Then reality sets in. How in the world do you teach a child who cannot speak or understand English? Where do you begin? How do you make them feel a part of the classroom?

From my own experience as a brand new teacher, I can assure you that it is with great apprehension and a little bit of fear that one takes on the challenge of teaching the ESOL child. When you look into the eyes of foreign children, you want to convey so much to them. You want so much for them to benefit from what you have to offer in the classroom, knowing that as hard as you try, without the proper resources, these children will lose precious time in their academic development, leaving gaps where seeds of knowledge need to be planted and nurtured. These children need uninterrupted learning, as do all children. Yet these children's lives were interrupted when they were transported to a new country through no choice of their own. What can teachers do? This situation is here to stay, as more and more people from other countries enter the United States from all over the world.

In all fairness to the teacher and to the ESOL student, the school should provide the teacher with materials such as computer programs, bilingual books, tests to measure the child's academic level in the native language, and bilingual translators who are immediately accessible. This way, not so much time is lost during the adjustment period for the ESOL child. However, the reality is that this might not happen, so a well-prepared teacher will gather his or her resources and prepare material long before the inevitable ESOL child arrives.

I would like to share some of the steps I have taken to aid an ESOL child in my class who is classified "A2." To set the scene, "Pedro" had just arrived from Brazil in January. I had been teaching fourth grade for six weeks. Pedro did not speak, read, or comprehend any English. Where does a teacher begin with a child such as Pedro? I decided to take the following steps:

(Continued)

- First, I tested him on a computer reading program called "The Rosetta Stone." He did fairly well.
- I got some phonics books on a second-grade level to increase his decoding and encoding skills to our fourth-grade level.
- Next, I arranged for him to be in a third-grade reading group. Exposure to reading in a less intimidating level was recommended to me by experienced teachers. He also sits in on my reading groups.
- I scheduled him to have a daily half-hour reading skills session in the computer lab.
- I found a Brazilian peer buddy from the fifth grade who would partner with him, show him around, and explain things to him in his native language.
- Whenever possible, but at least three times a week, I sat with Pedro and read one-on-one with him. Afterwards, we worked with word lists and phonics skills.
- Pedro received a spelling list once a week, as did the other children—but he received words modified to fit his circumstances.
- Pedro had a peer buddy in my class who spoke Spanish. He understood most of what he heard, but not all. I spoke some Spanish and I think he understood some of what I said as well. Pedro participated in all other subjects such as math, science, social studies, art, and physical education. His classmates readily accepted him and socially, the transition has been smooth.

As you can see, teaching the ESOL student requires quite a bit of coordinating and organizing in addition to all the regular classroom duties. It is no easy feat. I am a teacher who is receptive and open to teaching ESOL students and I am ready to go the "extra mile." Individuals who are not open to foreign cultures and believe students should learn English before being placed in the regular classroom may have difficulty teaching ESOL students and might feel resentment. However, the law is clear and we must make modifications for ELL students. What happens to the ESOL child in a negative type of environment? Obviously, there is not one answer, but I suggest that all new teachers prepare for their future ESOL students by knowing the legal issues, knowing what is expected of them as teachers, and preparing themselves to be able to respond to the needs of these lovely children.

Betty Lacayo is a veteran fourth grade teacher in St. Lucie County, Florida, with many years of experience teaching ELL students. She has learned to meet their needs, adapt and modify content areas, and create alternative instruments to assess learning and instruction.

In the following pages, she shares her thoughts, based on her years of experience. She explains what transpires in her school when a new ESOL student registers and how she copes with the day-to-day instructing and assessing of ESOL students.

BETTY LACAYO:

After identifying a new ESOL student through the Home Language Survey, the guidance counselor (the designated ESOL tester) administers the routine test given to ESOL students (the Idea Oral Language Proficiency Test), which will determine for me whether or not the student is a non-English speaker (NES) or a limited English speaker (LES). If a child is LES, a norm-referenced test is administered. My school uses the MAT (Metropolitan Achievement Test). If students score below the 32nd percentile they are placed in an ESOL program. An NES student is immediately placed in an ESOL classroom (that is, mainstreamed in a regular class with a teacher who either is in the process of attaining, or has attained, the ESOL endorsement).

Monitoring during the program includes an annual ELL committee review of the student's current English language proficiency test data, academic achievement record, and current classroom performance to determine if there is a continued need for ESOL services. Students may not exit the program if they score an NES or LES on the IDEA test. In our county we use a classification system of A1, A2, B1, B2, C1, C2 and then exit the ESOL Program. We also conduct an annual ELL committee review before moving up a classification or exiting the program.

St. Lucie County School Board (like other counties) offers an ESOL Quick Reference Guide. These booklets contain key information pertaining to the practical application of ESOL program requirements. They also include a step-by-step outline of school-based procedures, including identification procedures, assessment, placement, parent notification, the ELL plan, exit procedures, and the monitoring of a student's performance after exiting the program.

After the guidance counselor gathers the classification information, she passes along the results to me as the classroom teacher, and then I have to pretty much fend for myself. Once receiving the ESOL child in my class, I sit and have a very informal interview (in a conversational manner) to determine the child's English ability. If the student is Spanish or Haitian-Creole speaking, I have the ESOL teacher assistant speak to them to determine whether or not they have attended school in the past and have learned to read and write in their native language. If I have a student from a country other than a Spanish or Haitian-Creole speaking country, I am at a great disadvantage and can only hope that the county has someone to come help me interpret. Otherwise, I have to start at the "bare bones" basics. When students come into my class as non-English speaking, I start by having them help me label things around the classroom using index cards. This helps to acclimate them to the classroom layout. As they work on the cards, I also observe their writing skills and hand coordination with a pencil and paper. Consequently, the language they speak determines the activities I plan for them. When children speak Spanish, I am able to modify activities and am confident with the tasks I have created for them. I adapt activities to our current theme of study in the classroom so students feel a part of our classroom community. Haitian students

(Continued)

are a bit more difficult, because the majority of the Haitian children we see at our school have never attended school anywhere. With other nationalities, it is extremely difficult to place them at their current level of academic ability, but in my opinion, observation is the most powerful tool. I watch to see if the students know how to hold a book and turn the pages correctly. I look to see how well the student is able to copy the alphabet for some sign of previous writing practice. If students have basic reading and writing skills in their native language, I immediately research the linguistic and grammatical interferences that occur between their native language and English so that I have a good basis for ascertaining where I need to start.

There are numerous ESL books and other books that make you aware of the cultural differences you can expect to encounter with your students from afar. The best plan of action I take is to try to get to know my student's culture so I can understand how the student thinks and why he or she may behave in ways that reflect the values of that culture.

Every teacher with ESOL students has been tormented over the question of what to do about assessing these students. Wanting to be fair and grade according to ESOL students' abilities, teachers are forever in search of new methods to adapt their assessment procedures to fit the needs of these students.

Knowing traditional assessments have not been effective in my assessment of ESOL students, I have searched for alternative methods. I have adapted several methods of assessment of reading and language arts. Because I integrate subject areas across curriculum, most science and social studies grades are pulled from reading and language arts lessons and assignments. Math, being the great equalizer, is graded separately and is only modified when word problems are involved.

Because every ESOL student comes into my classroom with different needs, I tailor my curriculum and methods of assessment accordingly. Fortunately, my experience has been that the "typical" ESOL student coming into my fourth/fifth grade classroom has some (limited) English and is able to read and write in his or her native language. The following ESOL assessment adaptations are for this type of ESOL student.

An example of a reading assessment I use is what I refer to as a "backward S." I use this assessment method when I want to determine if a student has comprehended the main events and sequence of a story plot. After reading a story in a whole-group setting, I will have the students brainstorm the events that have taken place. Once these events are charted, I have the students place story events along the "backward S" in the order in which they have occurred.

The ESOL adaptation of this lesson begins after the ESOL students have participated in the brainstorming session. I meet with them as a group and have them recall story events orally to me (typically ESOL students will not participate in whole-class brainstorming sessions; they listen intently but do not like to volunteer answers until they are comfortable with speaking English). The ESOL students are usually eager to participate at this point, because they have had the process and format modeled for them by their fellow students. After listing the events, they illustrate the recalled events and construct a simple sentence or two placed under the illustration describing the story event. Next, they paste these illustrations along the "backward S" in proper sequence. This lesson enables me to assess their ability to sequence a story, recall events, and construct a simple sentence.

Using adaptations of books is another way I assess an ESOL student's comprehension of a story. After reading a short story, we discuss events in the book and any connections they have made with the story line. Next, we discuss how to change the text of the book to make an entirely new story. Once we have discussed the new plot, I help the students write the story using a Language Experience Approach. After the dictation is written on chart paper, the ESOL students work to construct a new book, making illustrations and composing text.

When working with non-fiction material, I teach research reporting. Using a matrix, I outline the research in matrix form and students use the format to construct a research paper. When adapting the report for ESOL students, I use a basic matrix. I pluck basic facts from the non-fiction book they are reading and have them fill out this matrix. After completing the basic matrix, ESOL students will construct sentences from researched material and compile the report.

When using alternative methods of assessment, I am sensitive to the efforts of my ESOL students and celebrate any work they produce. Every year I partner with a primary (K–2) teacher and establish "little buddy readers" for my ESOL students. The choice of buddies is generally determined by the grade levels at which my ESOL student and the buddy are reading. (Typically, the buddy's reading level is just below the current level of my ESOL student.) Work produced by my ESOL students is always shared with their buddy, along with the primary grade classes.

Another great benefit of the "buddy system" is that it allows my ESOL students to go into the primary classroom as a "teacher assistant." The time spent in the primary classroom allows the ESOL student to be exposed to guided reading lessons that are filled with helpful reading strategies.

Adaptations of vocabulary lists have proven to be effective when integrating an ESOL student's native language with English. Although the method I use is limiting, my ESOL students enjoy vocabulary time. When constructing a weekly vocabulary list, I use words that relate to our current theme of study. Because the vocabulary words are used in content, it is crucial that their meanings become real to my students. I adapt vocabulary lists for my ESOL students by choosing between five and eight vocabulary words having root meanings that come from their native language.

When I assign vocabulary words, the class finds the definitions for homework, and the next day we collectively compose the list of words with their meanings. During this process, I ask my ESOL students to point out and underline root meanings they may recognize in their native language. For example, my Hispanic students recognize the word *dentures* from the Spanish word *dentadura*. I illustrate that *diente* means *teeth* in English. This example not only gives Spanish-speaking students a chance to

(Continued)

feel a part of the lesson, it also helps the English-speaking students to learn the root meaning of dente, which will expand their vocabulary as they search for new words with that root meaning, e.g., *dentist, dental, orthodontist*, etc.

"Cloze" assignments prove to be quite helpful for practice in correcting grammatical points and assessing an ESOL student's grammar acquisition. After practice in correcting common syntactical errors (by having the students fill in the blanks with the correct grammar), I can determine their awareness of the proper syntax in English. But I make sure to always have them practice before I actually give a cloze activity as an assessment.

Over the years, I have observed ESOL students participate with more success in smaller cooperative groups than in a large, whole-group setting; but many critics erroneously believe cooperative grouping does not allow opportunities to assess students. When I have cooperative groups in my classroom, I discuss the grading criteria with my students before we break into groups. Whether I am grouping my students homogeneously or heterogeneously, the ELL student typically does well in the group. I believe students learn from their peers and cooperative groups help to alleviate anxiety the English learning students may feel in a group setting. It also helps to keep the learning environment diverse and interesting. Literature circles (a cooperative grouping method) are a prime example of getting students to discuss the books they have read. In literature circles, students choose the books they want to read, and through a series of questions, they discuss different elements of the story. My ESOL students typically tend to gravitate toward books that are on their current level and are quite proud to be able to discuss the book, rather than being asked to "write a book report." As literature circles are taking place, I circulate to make sure everyone has a role in the group. The students do well as facilitators in this academic setting.

As you probably can surmise, my classroom practices are very functional. I use manila folders to record anecdotal records. It is a simple and extremely manageable process. I try to have a conference with my students once a week and alternate reviewing independent reading and writing projects. I divide the class into four groups: Monday Group, Tuesday Group, Wednesday Group, and Thursday Group. Fridays are reserved for any students who were absent on their conference day. During a writing conference, the students bring what they would like to discuss or share with me. Sometimes it is a daily journal entry or a writing project they are working on (such as a research report, etc.). We talk for about five minutes and discuss any problems they may be having with their writing. I only edit things they are to publish (we consider published work as work written for others to read). I never edit their daily journals. After their conference, I pull their manila folder and write a quick comment on what I observed during the conference. For example, if I observed the student having difficulty with verb tense, I will note that on the anecdotal record (e.g., *Susie has changed tense in her narrative story about the party she had over the weekend*). The following week we review the comments on the anecdotal record and I look for improvement in the area.

For a reading conference, students bring selections they want to share with me. I have them read to me aloud, and then we discuss what they are reading. It can be a chapter book we are reading together as a class, a book they are reading independently, or any other reading material. It is at this time that I observe if they are using decoding strategies when coming to an unfamiliar word and if they are employing comprehension strategies. I make brief notes of what I observe (e.g., Johnny used good word attack strategies when reading the word *accomplish*).

As an educator who knows traditional assessments do not work for this diverse population, creating alternative methods of assessment has proven to be a challenging experience. I have learned that I must respect the native culture of my ESOL students as I familiarize them with their new culture. I must also be considerate of their sense of pride in their accomplishments, as I continue to search for new methods of assessment that will uplift their learning spirits and reflect their true academic abilities. If I am able to inspire my English-learning students to be excited about the work they produce in my class, I believe they will feel like they are an integral part of our classroom community.

Appendices of Rubric Samples

Your Name:_____ Group Topic: _____

Group Members: _____

Collaboration Rubric

	Beginning 1	Developing 2	Accomplished 3	Exemplary 4	Score
Contribute					
Research and Gather Information	Does not collect any info that relates to the topic.	Collects very little info—some relates to the topic.	Collects some basic info—most relates to the topic.	Collects a great deal of info—all relates to the topic.	
Share Information	Does not relay any info to teammates.	Relays very little info—some relates to the topic.	Relays some basic info—most relates to the topic.	Relays a great deal of info—all relates to the topic.	
Be Punctual	Does not hand in any assignments.	Hands in most assignments late.	Hands in most assignments on time.	Hands in all assignments on time.	
Take Responsibility					
Fulfill Team Role's Duties	Does not perform any duties of assigned team role.	Performs very few duties.	Performs nearly all duties.	Performs all duties of assigned team role.	
Share Equally	Always relies on others to do the work.	Rarely does the assigned work—often needs reminding.	Usually does the assigned work—rarely needs reminding.	Always does the assigned work without having to be reminded.	
Value Others' Viewpoints					
Listen to Other Teammates	Is always talking—never allows anyone else to speak.	Usually doing most of the talking—rarely allows others to speak.	Listens, but sometimes talks too much.	Listens and speaks a fair amount.	
Cooperate with Teammates	Usually argues with teammates.	Sometimes argues.	Rarely argues.	Never argues with teammates.	
Make Fair Decisions	Usually wants to have things their way.	Often sides with friends instead of considering all views.	Usually considers all views.	Always helps team to reach a fair decision.	

	Beginning 1	Developing 2	Accomplished 3	Exemplary 4	Score
Value Others' Viewpoints					
Behavior	Interrupts class while teacher is speaking.	Talks while teacher is talking or reading.	Listens quietly but talks a little.	Listens quietly and raises hand if they have a question.	
Posture	Not sitting properly in their seat or space.	Sits in spot but is touching or annoying others around them.	Sitting in spot slouching or leaning to the side.	Sitting up straight in their spot.	
Contributions	Always calls out questions and answers posed.	Sometimes calls out questions and answers posed.	Answers and asks questions but calls out rarely.	Raises hand to ask and answer questions.	
Contributed by Bianca Swanson, Student in TESOL 4081, Florida Atlantic University.					

SUMMARY EVALUATION GUIDELINES

Student _____ Date _____

This Student	Never	Sometimes	Often	Always
• Identifies the topic	1	2	3	4
• Identifies the main idea	1	2	3	4
• Combines/chunks similar ideas	1	2	3	4
• Paraphrases accurately	1	2	3	4
• Deletes minor details	1	2	3	4
• Reflects author's emphasis	1	2	3	4
• Recognizes author's purpose	1	2	3	4
• Stays within appropriate length	1	2	3	4

Source: O'Malley, J. Michael; Pierce, Lorraine Valdez, *Authentic Assessment for English Language Learners*, 1st Ed., © 1996. Reprinted by permission of Pearson Education, Inc., New York, New York.

ANALYTIC ORAL LANGUAGE SCORING RUBRIC

Focus/ Rating	1	2	3	4	5	6
Speaking	Begins to name concrete objects	Begins to communicate personal and survival needs	Begins to initiate conversation; retells a story or experience; asks and responds to simple questions	Initiates and sustains a conversation with descriptors and details; exhibits self-confidence in social situations; begins to communicate in classroom settings	Speaks in social and classroom settings with sustained and connected discourse; any errors do not interfere with meaning	Communicates competently in social and classroom settings
Fluency	Repeats words and phrases	Speaks in single-word utterances and short patterns	Speaks hesitantly because of rephrasing and searching for words	Speaks with occasional hesitation	Speaks with near-native fluency; any hesitations do not interfere with communication	Speaks fluently
Structure			Uses predominantly present tense verbs; demonstrates errors of omission (leaves words out, word endings off)	Uses some complex sentences; applies rules of grammar but lacks control of irregular forms (*e.g., runned, mans, not never, more higher*)	Uses a variety of structures with occasional grammatical errors	Masters a variety of grammatical structures
Vocabulary		Uses functional vocabulary	Uses limited vocabulary	Uses adequate vocabulary; some word usage irregularities	Uses varied vocabulary	Uses extensive vocabulary but may lag behind native-speaking peers
Listening	Understands little or no English	Understand words and phrases, requires repetition	Understands simple sentences in sustained conversation; requires repetition	Understands classroom discussions with repetition, rephrasing, and clarification	Understands most spoken language, including classroom discussion	Understand classroom discussion without difficulty

Source: O'Malley, J. Michael; Pierce, Lorraine Valdez, *Authentic Assessment for English Language Learners*, 1st Ed., © 1996. Reprinted by permission of Pearson Education, Inc., New York, New York.

_____

(Date)

Dear parents:

Your child, (Student's Name), will be putting together a portfolio this year. This portfolio will contain samples of his or her work that show what he or she is learning. I will use the portfolio to identify each student's strengths and weaknesses and to plan appropriate instructional activities.

    At various times throughout the year, I will be asking you to review the portfolio and to comment on your child's work. After you have reviewed your child's portfolio, please make comments on the Portfolio Summary Sheet and initial it at the bottom. Please call me if you have any questions or would like to come in for a parent–student portfolio conference. I am looking forward to working closely with you.

Sincerely,

(Teacher's Name)

(Teacher's Telephone Number)

Source: O'Malley, J. Michael; Pierce, Lorraine Valdez, *Authentic Assessment for English Language Learners*, 1st Ed., © 1996. Reprinted by permission of Pearson Education, Inc., New York, New York.

PORTFOLIO EVALUATION SUMMARY

Student _____ Grade _____ Date _____

Teacher _____ School _____

First Language (L1) _____ Second Language (L2) _____

Directions: Circle L1 or L2 to indicate if student meets the standard			
Curriculum/ Assessment Area	Does Not Meet Standards	Meets Standards	Exceeds Standards
Oral Language	L1 L2	L1 L2	L1 L2
Written Language	L1 L2	L1 L2	L1 L2
Reading	L1 L2	L1 L2	L1 L2
Overall Summary	L1 L2	L1 L2	L1 L2

Comments

SELF-ASSESSMENT OF COMMUNICATION STRATEGIES IN ORAL LANGUAGE

Name _____ Date _____

Circle the answer that shows how often you do the following things.			
When I have problems talking in English, I			
1. Use my native language.	Never	Sometimes	Often
2. Ask for help.	Never	Sometimes	Often
3. Use gestures or facial expressions.	Never	Sometimes	Often
4. Avoid communication totally or partially.	Never	Sometimes	Often
5. Use a synonym or a description.	Never	Sometimes	Often
6. Make up new words.	Never	Sometimes	Often
7. Simplify what I want to say.	Never	Sometimes	Often

Source: O'Malley, J. Michael; Pierce, Lorraine Valdez, *Authentic Assessment for English Language Learners*, 1st Ed., © 1996. Reprinted by permission of Pearson Education, Inc., New York, New York.

SELF-ASSESSMENT OF SPEAKING ABILITY

Name _____ Date _____

Part 1: Place an X on each line to show how much you agree or disagree.

This week I used English to talk with _____.

1. I think that I was successful.   Disagree |—|—|—|—| Agree

2. The person I spoke to understood me.   Disagree |—|—|—|—| Agree

3. I felt comfortable speaking with another person in English.   Disagree |—|—|—|—| Agree

4. I understood everything that this person said to me.   Disagree |—|—|—|—| Agree

5. I could do this again with no problem.   Disagree |—|—|—|—| Agree

Part 2: Complete the sentences below.

6. When someone doesn't understand me, I _____

7. When I don't understand someone, I _____

8. Now I know _____

Source: O'Malley, J. Michael; Pierce, Lorraine Valdez, *Authentic Assessment for English Language Learners,* 1st Ed., © 1996. Reprinted by permission of Pearson Education, Inc., New York, New York.

Glossary of Professional Terms

Allomorphs: A variant form of a morpheme /z/→/z/, /s/, /ɪz/.

Audio-Lingual Method: A method of foreign or second language teaching based on the notion that second language learning should be regarded as a mechanistic process of habit formation.

Automatic Processing: When a language learner demonstrates the abilities of expert learners who manage many types of information simultaneously, because certain subskills have become automatic to them.

Auxiliary Verb: A verb that precedes a regular or main verb; it is also called a helping verb (*Susan has left*).

Behaviorism: An empiricist position that focuses on human behavior that is determined by specific environmental factors. With respect to language, a child learns a language through a stimulus, response, and reinforcement chain.

BICS: An acronym for Basic Interpersonal Communicative Language, also known as social language.

Borrowing: Process by which a language adopts words or phrases from another language.

CALP: An acronym for Cognitive Academic Language Proficiency, or academic language proficiency. (Cummins, 1986)

Categories: Words are organized into different groups according to their behavior.

Cognates: Words that are derived from the same source and typically have similar form and meaning.

Cognitive Academic Language Learning Approach (CALLA): An approach of learning English through a strategy that promotes the acquisition of academic language skills.

Cognitive Strategies: Direct strategies which learners apply to the language or the task itself, for example, remembering more effectively or compensating for missing information.

Common Underlying Proficiency (CUP): In second language learning, Cummins assumes that content and skills learned in the primary language will transfer to the target language.

Communicative Competence: This term refers to learners' ability to understand what is being said and to use language appropriately in a variety of contexts. This requires competence in four areas: grammatical, sociolinguistic, discourse, and strategic competence.

Consonants: Sounds formed when airflow is partially or completely obstructed in the mouth by the placement of the tongue and position of the lips.

Constituents: Building blocks of a sentence.

Context: The real world information that helps us fill in the details that are not available in the discourse, enabling us to interpret what is said. (See also *epistemic, linguistic, social* and *physical context* in Chapter 10.)

Controlled Processing: When a learner first learns a language, he or she is limited in the way he or she handles the basic elements of the language.

Derivational Morphemes: Morphemes that are formed from root words, usually through affixes, for example, /dirt/, /dir*ty*/.

Developmental Errors: Errors naturally produced by children in the process of acquiring a language that fade away once speakers become more proficient in the language.

Dialect: A language variety defined by geographic location and social factors such as class, religion, or ethnicity.

Direct Method (DM): Direct Method focuses on the promotion of communication in the target language where students learning English as a second language or foreign language are not allowed to use their native language in their learning process.

Direct Speech Acts: Utterances that perform their functions in a direct and literal manner.

Discourse: A continuous stretch of speech or written text beyond the sentence level.

EFL; English as a Foreign Language: This term is widely employed when referring to English taught to speakers of other languages and where English is not the primary language of instruction.

When using this term a number of assumptions are often made:

- The learner's native language is not English.
- The learner is in a school environment where a language other than English is the primary language of instruction.
- Proficiency in English is necessary for success in this particular subject, but not for success in school or for upward mobility.
- The majority language is not English.
- The dominant language is not English.
- The learner lives in a neighborhood where a language other than English is widely spoken.

ELs; English Learners (also English Language Learners, ELLs): This term is widely employed to refer to students who are in the process of acquiring English in schools where English is the primary language of instruction.

When employing this term, a number of assumptions are made;

- The learner's native language is not English.
- The learner is in a school environment where English is necessary for success and upward mobility.
- Although the learner may live in a neighborhood where English is not widely spoken (enclave community), the majority language is English.
- English is the dominant language.

ENL; English as a New Language: This term is found in the most recent literature when referring to students who are in the process of acquiring English in schools where English is the primary language of instruction. This term is synonymous to EL. The same assumptions made for EL are made for students who are identified as learning English as a new language.

ESL; English as a Second Language: This term is widely employed to refer to the teaching of the English language to speakers of other languages when English is the primary language of instruction. The same assumptions made for ELs and ENLs are made for ESL students.

ESOL; English to Speakers of Other Languages: This term is widely employed when referring to the teaching of the English language to non-native speakers of English. It is assumed that the "learner" hears and speaks a language other than English at home.

Global Errors: Errors produced by learners that interfere with communication. Global errors may involve substitution of incorrect sounds or words and jumbled up sentences.

Grammar Translation Method (GTM): A method of foreign and second language teaching that focuses on reading, writing, translation, and the conscious learning of grammatical rules; its primary goal is to develop a literary mastery of the target language.

Grice's Conversational Maxims: Conversational rules that regulate how speakers should comply with certain cooperative principles.

Home Language Survey (HLS): A screener used in the United States to determine if a student requires initial language ability testing for placement into ESL/ESOL programs and services.

Homonyms: Different words with the same pronunciation and spelling but different meanings (such as baseball *bat* and *bat* the animal).

Implicatures: Inferences based on certain warranted conditions.

Indirect Speech Acts: Utterances that perform their functions in an indirect and nonliteral manner.

Inflectional Morphemes: Modify a word's form to make it fit the grammatical category to which it belongs, for example, /walk/→/walk*ed*/, present tense to past tense form.

Interlanguage: The dynamic language system that is unique to L2 learners as they go through a number of states of grammar along a continuum, starting with their native language and ultimately approaching the target language.

Intonation: Rising and falling pitch in a language that does not change word meaning, but changes the function of a sentence.

Language Minority Students: This term refers to (a) individuals who were not born in the United States or whose native language is a language other than English; (b) individuals who come from environments where a language other than English is dominant; and (c) individuals who are Native Americans or Alaskan natives who come from environments where a language other than English has had a significant impact on their level of English language proficiency and who have sufficient difficulty speaking, reading, writing, or understanding English that they would not have the opportunity to learn successfully in classrooms where the language of instruction is English, or to fully participate in our society. Language *minoritized* students is a term used to reflect the positioning of students by society, as imposed upon them (Sensoy & DiAngelo, 2012).

Learning Styles: The way we learn things in general (see multiple intelligences and cognitive styles in Chapter 19).

LEP; Limited English Proficient or Language Enriched Pupil: This term is widely employed when referring to students whose native language is not English and who are acquiring English as a second language. Under the terms of the Florida Educational Equity Act of 1984, a limited English proficient student is defined as a student whose home language is other than English as determined by a home language survey and whose English aural comprehension, speaking, reading, or writing proficiency level is below that of English speaking students of the same age and grade level.

Some professionals in the field of second language acquisition argue that this term has a negative connotation because students are referred to as "limited." These students can typically communicate in their native language; thus, the fact that they are acquiring a second language should be viewed as an asset, not as a limitation.

Lexical Ambiguity: A word that has two or more possible meanings.

Linearity: Words are strung together in a linear form, for example, *she goes to work every day* instead of *goes she work to every day*.

Local Errors: Errors that do not hinder communication—incorrect inflections on nouns and verbs, incorrect use or omission of articles, and other errors that involve single elements of the sentence.

Metacognitive Strategies: Indirect strategies in which learners manage or control their own learning process, for example, managing your emotions, organizing and evaluating your learning.

Minimal Pairs: Words that differ by one phoneme, for example, /*pin*/ vs. /*bin*/.

Morphemes: Minimal meaningful units, for example, /boy/ vs. /boys/.

Morphology: The study of word formation that deals with the internal structure of words in a language.

Multiple Intelligence: Intelligence is not a single construct or static, but a set of distinct intelligences that can be developed over a lifetime. (Such as linguistic, bodily kinesthetic, musical, logical/mathematical, spatial/visual, interpersonal, intrapersonal, and naturalist intelligences.)

Nativism: Also known as the mentalist perspective. This position focuses on the fact that children acquire a language by constructing their own grammar through a process of hypothesis-testing and not purely imitating adults' speech.

Overgeneralizations: A term used to describe developmental errors attributed to an application of a rule in instances where the rule does not apply. *Overgeneralization* is a broader term than *narrowing*. (See first and second language acquisition in Chapter 15.)

Phonemes: Distinctive sound units that make a difference when sounds form words.

Phonemic Sequence: Permissible way in which phonemes can be combined in a language.

Phonology: The study of sound systems that deals with pronunciation rules in a language.

Pragmatics: The study of how the meaning of utterances depends on the context in which they are used (such as time, place, social relationship between speaker and listener, speaker's assumptions about listener's beliefs).

Silent Language: Meaning that is conveyed through gestures, eye contact, space, and touch.

Social Interactionist: A theoretical position that focuses on the critical role of caregivers in facilitating innate abilities for language acquisition.

Social Affective Strategies: Strategies for mediating and interacting with others, also considered as communication strategies.

SOLOM: Student Oral Language Observation Matrix—an informal oral language ability tool used by teachers of EL.

Speech Register: The various ways of speaking that are marked by degrees of formality. Also known as *speech style*.

Strategies: Specific "attack-skills" that learners employ in problem-solving, including both learning and communication strategies. Learning strategies are typically receptive strategies for processing linguistic input (see *metacognitive, cognitive, and social affective strategies* in Chapter 19). Communication strategies perform an expressive function.

Structural Ambiguity: Sentences that contain two or more meanings.

TESOL; Teaching English to Speakers of Other Languages/Teachers of English to Speakers of Other Languages: This term is widely employed when referring to the teaching of English to non-native speakers of English or when referring to teachers who teach English to second language learners. The term TESOL is employed in a variety of other contexts as well, for example, *TESOL strategies.* In this context, the term refers to strategies teachers use when teaching English to speakers of other languages and to non-native speakers of English. See tesol.org

Translanguaging: A process whereby multilinguals strategically utilize their languages as an integrated language system (see García and Kleyn, 2016).

Vowels: Sounds formed when airflow in the mouth is not blocked.

WIDA (sometimes Worldwide Instructional Design and Assessment): A national and international consortium and framework for ELs. The WIDA framework includes EL students' ability levels, "Can Do Descriptors" to guide instructional decision making, standardized language proficiency testing, and Model Performance Indictors (MPIs). See wida.us

World Englishes: The term refers to the use of English for international and intranational purposes and assumes that there are many varieties of English spoken by native and non-native speakers of English. These varieties, although based on a native speaker's model, have distinct and systematic features at various linguistic levels (syntactic, morphological, lexical, stylistic, and discoursal) that reflect the sociolinguistic underpinnings of their use.

References

Abdelaal, N. M. (2017). Instrumental analysis of the English stops produced by Arabic speakers of English. *International Journal of Education and Literacy Studies*, *5*(3), 8. doi:10.7575/aiac.ijels.v.5n.3p.8

Abedi, J. (2004). Inclusion of students with limited English proficiency. In *NAEP: Classification and measurement issues: CSE Report 629, Graduate School of Education and Information Studies*. Los Angeles, CA: University of California.

Abedi, J. (2014). English language learners with disabilities: Classification, assessment, and accommodation issues. *Journal of Applied Testing Technology, 10*(2), 1–30.

Acuña-Fariña, J. C. (2009). Aspects of the grammar of close apposition and the structure of the noun phrase. *English Language & Linguistics, 13*(3), 453–481.

Ager, S. (2017). *Nüshu*. Retrieved from https://www.omniglot.com/writing/nushu.htm

Akmajian, A., Farmer, A. K., Bickmore, L., Demers, R. A., & Harnish, R. M. (2017). *Linguistics: An introduction to language and communication*. Cambridge, MA: MIT Press.

ALAS! (2008). Cartoon: Immigrants are ruining the economy. Retrieved from http://www.amptoons.com/blog/?p=4113

Alghizzi, T. M. (2014). Critical period hypothesis. *Language in India, 14*(1), 15–22.

Alhawiti, M. M., & Abdelhamid, Y. (2017). A personalized e-learning framework. *Journal of Education and e-Learning Research, 4*(1), 15–21.

Almehmadi, M. M. (2012). A contrastive rhetorical analysis of factual texts in English and Arabic. *Frontiers of Language and Teaching, 3*, 68–76.

Altan, M. Z. (2001). Intelligence reframed: Multiple intelligences for the 21st century: Howard Gardner. *TESOL Quarterly, 35*(1), 204–205.

Ambridge, B. (2013). How do children restrict their linguistic generalizations? An (un)grammaticality judgment study. *Cognitive Science, 37*(3), 508–543. doi:10.1111/cogs.12018

American Educational Research Association. (2004). *English language learners: Boosting academic achievement. Essential Information for Education Policy* (Vol. 2(1)). Washington, DC: Author.

Anderson, R. C., Reynolds, R. E., Schallert, D. L., & Goetz, E. T. (1977). Frameworks for comprehending discourse. *American Educational Research Journal, 14*(4), 367–381.

Ariza, E. N. (2010). *Not for ESOL teachers: What every classroom teacher needs to know about the linguistically, culturally, and ethnically diverse student* (2nd ed.). Boston, MA: Allyn & Bacon.

Ariza, E. N. (2018). *Not for ESOL teachers: What every classroom teacher needs to know about the linguistically, culturally, and ethnically diverse student* (3rd ed.). Dubuque, IA: Kendall/Hunt Publishing.

Asher, J. J. (1969). The total physical response approach to second language learning. *The Modern Language Journal, 53*(1), 3–17.

Backes, J. (1993, May). The American Indian high school dropout rate: A matter of style? *Journal of American Indian Education, 32*(3), 16–29.

Baker, C. (2000). *The care and education of young bilinguals. An introduction for professionals*. Clevedon, UK: Multilingual Matters, Ltd.

Bankston, C. L., & Zhou, M. (2002). Being well vs. doing well: Self-esteem and school performance among immigrant and nonimmigrant racial and ethnic groups. *International Migration Review, 36*(2), 389–415.

Batalova, J., & McHugh, M. (2010). Top languages spoken by English language learners nationally and by state. ELL Information Center Fact Sheet Series. No. 3. Migration Policy Institute.

Baytar, B. (2014). Implicit and explicit grammar teaching. In B. Baytar (Ed.), *Linguistics, culture and identity in foreign language education* (p. 365). Sarajevo, Bosnia: IBU.

BBC. (2014). *A guide to Thai*. Retrieved from http://www.bbc.co.uk/languages/other/thai/guide/alphabet.shtml

Benson, P., & Voller, P. (2014). *Autonomy and independence in language learning*. New York, NY: Routledge.

Bialystok, E. (1978). A theoretical model of second language learning. *Language Learning, 28*, 69–84.

Bialystok, E., & Mitterer, J. (1987). Metalinguistic differences among three kinds of readers. *Journal of Educational Psychology, 79*(2), 147–153. doi:10.1037/0022-0663.79.2.147

Bialystok, E., & Sharwood Smith, M. (1985). Interlanguage is not a state of mind: An evaluation of the construct for second-language acquisition. *Applied linguistics, 6*(2), 101–117.

Bick, A., Goelman, G., & Frost, R. (2011). Hebrew brain vs. English brain: Language modulates the way it is processed. *Journal of Cognitive Neuroscience, 23*(9), 2280–2290. doi:10.1162/jocn.2010.21583

Boberg, C. (2003). Review of "The Handbook of Language Variation and Change". *English World-Wide, 24*(1), 109–113. doi:10.1075/eww.24.1.08bob

Bohas, G., Guillaume, J. P., & Kouloughli, D. E. (2016). *The Arabic linguistic tradition*. New York, NY: Routledge.

Bowles, M., & Stansfield, C. W. (2008). *A practical guide to standards-based assessment in the native*. Language. NLA—LEP Partnership. Bethesda, MD: Second Language Testing.

Brown, D. (1994). *Principles of language learning and teaching*. Upper Saddle River, NJ: Prentice Hall.

Bunch, G. C. (2010). Preparing mainstream secondary content-area teachers to facilitate English language learners' development of academic language. *Yearbook of the National Society for the Study of Education, 109*(2), 351–383.

Caballero, R., & Diaz-Vera, J. E. (2013). Metaphor and culture: A relationship at a crossroads? *Intercultural Pragmatics, 10*(2), 205. doi:10.1515/ip-2013-0009

Caine, G., & Caine, R. (1991). *Making connections: Teaching and the human brain*. Alexandria, VA: Association of Supervision and Curriculum Development.

Caine, G., & Caine, R. (1997). *Mind/brain learning principles*. Retrieved from http://www.newhorizons.orgofc_21clicaine.html

Canale, M. (1983). From communicative competence to communicative language pedagogy. In J. Richards & R. W. Schmidt (Eds.), *Language and communication*. New York, NY: Longman.

Cao, L., Xu, K., & Ariza, E. N. W. (2018). Chinese, Japanese, South Korean, and Indian. In *Not for ESOL teachers* (3rd ed., pp. 1–36). Dubuque, IA: Kendall Hunt.

Carrasquillo, A. L. (2013). *Teaching English as a second language: A resource guide*. New York, NY: Routledge.

Casasanto, D. (2014). Experiential origins of mental metaphors: Language, culture, and the body. In M. Landau, M. D. Robinson, & B. P. Meier (Eds.), *The power of metaphor. Examining its influence on social life* (pp. 249–268). Washington, DC: American Psychological Association.

Casasanto, D. (2014). Experiential origins of mental metaphors: Language, culture, and the body.

Cazden, C. B. (1986). Classroom discourse. In Wittrock, M. C. (Ed.), *Handbook of research on teaching* (3rd ed., pp. 432–463). New York, NY: Macmillan.

Ceballo, R., Maurizi, L. K., Suarez, G. A., & Aretakis, M. T. (2014). Gift and sacrifice: Parental involvement in Latino Adolescents' education. *Cultural Diversity & Ethnic Minority Psychology, 20*(1), 116–127.

Center for Applied Linguistics. (2017). *Dual language programs*. Retrieved from http://www.webapp.cal.org/duallanguage/

Center for Applied Linguistics. (n.d.). Retrieved from http://www.cal.org

Chakorn, O. O. (2006). Persuasive and politeness strategies in cross-cultural letters of request in the Thai business context. *Journal of Asian Pacific Communication, 16*(1), 103–146.

Chakrabarti, A., & Sengupta, M. (2012). Second language learning anxiety and its effect on achievement in the language. *Language in India, 12*(8), 50–78.

Chamot, A. U. (2014, December). Developing self-regulated learning in the language classroom. Knowledge, skills and competencies in foreign language education. *Proceedings of the Sixth Centre for Language Studies (CLS) International Conference* (pp. 4–6). Singapore.

Chamot, A. U., & O'Malley, J. M. (1986). *A cognitive academic language learning approach: An ESL content-based curriculum*. Washington, DC: National Clearinghouse for Bilingual Education.

Chamot, A. U., & O'Malley, J. M. (1994). *The CALLA handbook: Implementing the cognitive academic language learning approach*. Reading, MA: Addison-Wesley.

Chapman, S. (2013). Grice, conversational implicature and philosophy. In *Perspectives on pragmatics and philosophy* (pp. 153–188). New York, NY: Springer.

Chater, N., McCauley, S. M., & Christiansen, M. H. (2016). Language as skill: Intertwining comprehension and production. *Journal of Memory and Language*, 89, 244–254.

Cheung, K. K. (2017). *Chinese American literature without borders: Gender, genre, and form*. New York, NY: Springer.

Chittendon, L. (1994). *Teaching writing to elementary children*. Speech presented at the Bay Area Writing Project Workshop, Berkeley: University of California.

Chizzo, J. (2002). Acculturation and language acquisition: A look at Schumann's acculturation model. Retrieved from http://gse.gmu.edu/assets/docs/lmtip/vol3/J.Chizzo.pdf

Chomsky, N. (2000). Linguistics and brain science. In A. Marantz, Y. Miyashita, & W. O'Neil (Eds.), *Image, language, brain: Papers from the first mind articulation project symposium* (pp. 13–28). Cambridge, MA: The MIT Press.

Chomsky, N. (2015). *Aspects of the theory of syntax*. Cambridge, MA: The MIT Press.

Chu, N. H. S., Yao, C. K., & Tan, V. P. Y. (2017). Food therapy in Sinosphere Asia. *Journal of Clinical Gastroenterology, 52*, 105–113.

Clapper, C., Mitsch, J., & Tamati, T. (2017). Effects of phonetic reduction and regional dialect on vowel production. *Journal of Phonetics, 60*, 38–59. doi:10.1016/j.wocn.2016.11.002

Coady, M. R. (2009a). "*Solamente libros importantes*": Literacy practices and ideologies of migrant farmworking families in north central Florida. In G. Li (Ed.), *Multicultural families, home literacies and mainstream schooling* (pp. 113–128). Charlotte, NC: New Age.

Coady, M. R. (2009b). Using families' ways of knowing to enhance student learning. In E. Amatea (Ed.), *Building culturally-responsive family-school partnerships: From theory to practice* (pp. 231–251). Upper Saddle River, NJ: Pearson.

Coady, M. R., & Ariza, E. (2010). Struggling for meaning and identity (and a passing grade): High-stakes writing in English as a second language. *MEXTESOL, 34*(1), 11–27.

Coady, M. R., Coady, T. J., & Nelson, A. (2015). Assessing the needs of immigrant, Latino families and teachers in rural settings: Building home-school partnerships. *NABE Journal, 6*. Retrieved from https://www2.nau.edu/nabej-p/ojs/index.php/njrp/article/view/42

Coady, M. R., Hamann, E. T., Harrington, M., Pacheco, M., Pho, S., & Yedlin, J. (2007). Successful schooling for ELLs: Principles for building responsive learning environments. In L. S. Verplaetse & N. Migliacci (Eds.), *Inclusive pedagogy for English language learners: A handbook of research-informed practices* (pp. 245–255). New York, NY: Lawrence Erlbaum Associates.

Coady, M. R., Harper, C., & de Jong, E. (2016). Aiming for equity: Preparing mainstream teachers for inclusion or inclusive classrooms? *TESOL Quarterly, 50*(2), 340–368. doi:10.1002/tesq.223

Coady, M. R., & Yilmaz, T. (2017). Preparing teachers of ELs: Home-school partnerships. In J. I. Liontas (Ed.), *The TESOL encyclopedia of English language teaching*. Hoboken, NJ: TESOL International Association & Wiley. doi:10.1002/9781118784235.eelt0837

Cohen, A. D. (1990). *Second language learning: Insights for learners, teachers, and researchers*. New York, NY: Harper and Row.

Cohen, A. D. (1996a). Second language learning and use strategies: Clarifying the issues. Retrieved from http://www.carla.umn.edu:16080/ strategies/resources/SBlclarify.pdf

Cohen, A. D. (1996b). The impact of strategies-based instructions on speaking a foreign language. Retrieved from http://www.carla.umn.edu/about/profiles/CohenPapers/SBlimpact.pdf

Cohen, A. D. (2014). *Strategies in learning and using a second language*. Alexandria, VA: Routledge.

Colorín Colorado. (2017). Reading comprehension strategies for English language learners. Retrieved from http://www.colorincolorado.org/article/reading-101-english-language-learners

Comrie, B., Matthews, S., & Polinsky, M. (Eds.). (1996). *The atlas of languages: The origins and development of languages throughout the world*. London, UK: Quatro Publishing PLC.

Connor, U. (1987). Argumentative patterns in student essays: Cross-cultural differences. In U. Connor & R. B. Kaplan (Eds.), *Writing across languages: Analysis of L2 text*. Reading, MA: Addison-Wesley.

Connor, U., & Connor, U. M. (1996). *Contrastive rhetoric: Cross-cultural aspects of second language writing*. Cambridge, UK:Cambridge University Press.

Cook, H. G., & Linquanti, R. (2015). *Strengthening policies and practices for the initial classification of English learners: Insights from a national working session*. Washington, DC: Council of Chief State School Officers.

Cook, V. (2013). *Second language learning and language teaching*. New York, NY: Routledge.

Crawford, J. (2004). *Educating English learners: Language diversity in the classroom*. Houston, TX: Bilingual Education Serv.

Crawford, J. (2004). *No Child Left Behind: Misguided approach for school accountability for English language learners*. Washington, DC: NABE. http://www.languagepolicy.net/articles.html.

Crookes, G., & Schmidt, R. W. (1991). Motivation: Reopening the research agenda. *Language learning, 41*(4), 469–512.

Crystal, D. (2007). *English as a global language*. Cambridge, UK: Cambridge University Press.

Cummins, J. (1981). The role of primary language development in promoting educational success for language minority students. In California State Department of Education (Ed.), *Schooling and language minority students: A theoretical framework*. Los Angeles, CA: Evaluation, Dissemination and Assessment Center, California State University.

Cummins, J. (1982). *Tests, achievement and bilingual students*. Wheaton, MD: National Clearinghouse for Bilingual Education.

Cummins, J. (1986). Empowering minority students: A framework for intervention. *Harvard Educational Review, 56*(1), 18–36. doi:10.17763/haer.56.1.b327234461607787

Cummins, J. (1992). Language proficiency, bilingualism, and academic achievement. In P. A. Richard-Amato & M. A. Snow (Eds.), *The multicultural classroom: Readings for content-area teachers* (pp. 16–26). New York, NY: Longman.

Cummins, J. (1996). *Negotiating identities: Education for empowerment in a diverse society*. Los Angeles, CA: California Association for Bilingual Education.

Cummins, J. (2016). Reflections on Cummins (1980), "The cross-lingual dimensions of language proficiency: Implications for bilingual education and the optimal age issue." *TESOL Quarterly, 50*(4), 940–944.

Cummins, J., & Sayers, D. (1997). *Brave new schools: Challenging cultural illiteracy through global learning networks*. London, England: Palgrave Macmillan.

Cummins, J., & Swain, M. (2014). *Bilingualism in education: Aspects of theory, research and practice*. New York, NY: Routledge.

Das, J. P., Janzen, T., & Georgiou, G. K. (2007). Correlates of Canadian native children's reading performance: From cognitive styles to cognitive processes. *Journal of School Psychology, 45*(6), 589–602. doi:10.1016/j.jsp.2007.06.004

de Jong, E. (2006). Integrated bilingual education: An alternative approach. *Bilingual Research Journal, 30*(1), 23–44.

de Oliveira, L., & Shoffner, M. (Eds.). (2016). *Teaching English language arts to English language learners: Preparing pre-service and in-service teachers*. New York, NY: Springer.

Dehbozorgi, E. (2012). Effects of attitude towards language learning and risk-taking on EFL student's proficiency. *International Journal of English Linguistics, 2*(2), 41–48.

Diaz-Rico, L. T. (2013). *The crosscultural, language, and academic development handbook: A complete K-12 reference guide*. New York, NY: Pearson Higher Ed.

Diaz-Rico, L. T. (2017). *The cross cultural, language, and academic development handbook: A complete K-12 reference guide* (6th ed.). New York, NY: Pearson.

Diaz-Rico, L. T., & Weed, K. Z. (1995). *The crosscultural language and academic development handbook: A complete K–12 reference guide*. Massachusetts, MA: Allyn and Bacon.

Dobrin, L. M. (2009). SIL international and the disciplinary culture of linguistics: Introduction. *Language, 85*(3), 618–619.

Dörnyei, Z. (1995). On the teachability of communication strategies. *TESOL Quarterly, 29*(1), 55–85.

Dörnyei, Z. (2014). *The psychology of the language learner: Individual differences in second language acquisition*. Mahwah, NJ: Routledge.

Dulay, H., Burt, M., & Krashen, S. (1983). *Language two*. New York, NY: Oxford University Press.

Dunn, R. (1983). Learning style and its relation to exceptionality at both ends of the spectrum. *Exceptional Children, 49*, 496–506.

Dunn, R. (1984). Learning style: State of the scene. *Theory into Practice, 23*, 10–19.

Durgunoğlu, A. Y. (2002). Cross-linguistic transfer in literacy development and implications for language learners. *Annals of Dyslexia, 52*(1), 189–204.

EAL Journal. (2016). What is translanguaging? Retrieved from https://www.ealjournal.org/2016/07/26/what-is-translanguaging/

Ebbers, S. M. (2017). Morphological awareness strategies for the general and special education classroom: A vehicle for vocabulary enhancement. *Perspectives on Language and Literacy, 43*(2), 29.

Eggington, W. G. (1987). Written academic discourse in Korean: Implications for effective communication. In U. Connor & R. B. Kaplan (Eds.), *Writing across languages: Analysis of L2 text*. Reading, MA: Addison-Wesley.

Epstein, J. (2010). *School, family and community partnerships: Preparing educators and improving schools* (2nd ed.). Boulder, CO: Westview Press.

ESSA. (2015). Every student succeeds act. Retrieved from https://www.congress.gov/114/plaws/publ95/PLAW-114publ95.pdf

Ethnologue, G. B. F. (2009). *Languages of the world*. Dallas: SIL International.

Eunice Kennedy Shriver National Institute of Child Health and Human Development, NIH, DHHS. (2000). Report of the national reading panel: Teaching children to read: Reports of the subgroups (00-4754). Washington, DC: U.S. Government Printing Office, National Reading Panel Publications—NIC.

Every Student Succeeds Act (ESSA). (n.d.). Retrieved from https://www.ed.gov/ESSA

Fischer, S. R. (2001). *History of language*. London, UK: Reaktion Books.

Florida Department of Education. (1990). Florida consent decree. Retrieved from http://www.fldoe.org/academics/eng-language-learners/consent-decree.stml

Florida Department of Education. (1990). Office of Multicultural Student Language Education. *Consent Decree*. Retrieved from http://www.firn.edu/doe/bin00011/restatem.htm

Freeman, D., & Freeman, Y. (2007). *English language learners: The essential guide*. New York, NY: Scholastic.

Fries, C. C. (1963). *Linguistics and reading* (Vol. 2). New York, NY: Holt Rinehart and Winston.

Galloway, N., & Rose, H. (2015). *Introducing global Englishes*. New York, NY: Routledge.

Gándara, P., & Orfield, G. (2012). Why Arizona matters: The historical, legal, and political contexts of Arizona's instructional policies and US linguistic hegemony. *Language Policy, 11*(1), 7–19.

Garcia, B. (1995). Florida Department of Education. *Issues regarding the education of LEP students … A restatement*. Retrieved from http://www.firn.edu/doe/bin/restatem.htm

García, O., & Kleifgen, J. A. (2010). *Educating emergent bilinguals: Policies, programs, and practices for English language learners*. New York, NY: Teachers College Press.

García, O., & Kleyn, T. (Eds.). (2016). *Translanguaging with multilingual students: Learning from classroom moments*. New York, NY: Routledge.

García, O., & Lin, A. M. (2017). Translanguaging in bilingual education. In O. García, A. M. Lin, & S. May (Eds.), *Bilingual and multilingual education* (pp. 117–130). New York, NY: Springer.

García, O., & Wei, L. (2013). *Translanguaging: Language, bilingualism, and education*. New York, NY: Palgrave.

García O., & Wei, L. (2014). Translanguaging and education. In *Translanguaging: Language, bilingualism and education*. London, UK: Palgrave Macmillan.

Gardner, H. (1983). *Frames of mind: The theory of multiple intelligences*. New York, NY: Basic Books

Gardner, H. (2017). Taking a multiple intelligences (MI) perspective. *Behavioral and Brain Sciences, 40*, 183–184.

Gardner, R. C., & Lambert, W. E. (1972). *Attitudes and motivation in second language learning*. Rowley, MA: Newbury House.

Gass, S., & Selinker, L. (2008). *Second language acquisition: An introductory course*. New York, NY: Routledge.

Goodman, K. (1986). *What's whole in whole language*. Richmond Hill, ON: Scholastic TAB.

Goodwyn, A. (2016). Still growing after all these years? The resilience of the "personal growth model of English" in England and also internationally. *English Teaching-Practice and Critique, 15*(1), 7–21. doi:10.1108/ETPC-12-2015-0111

Great Schools Partnership. (2017). Glossary of education reform. Retrieved from http://edglossary.org/english-language-learner

Greenfader, C. M., & Brouillette, L. (2017). The arts, the common core, and English language development in the primary grades. *Teachers College Record, 119*(9). Downloadable pdf: http://www.tcrecord.org/library, ID Number: 21915.

Grey, S., Williams, J. N., & Rebuschat, P. (2015). Individual differences in incidental language learning: Phonological working memory, learning styles, and personality. *Learning and Individual Differences, 38*, 44–53.

Grice, H. P. (1989). *Studies in the way of words*. Cambridge, MA: Harvard University Press.

Hakuta, K. (1986). *Mirror of language. The debate on bilingualism*. New York, NY: Basic Books.

Hamilton, V. (2018). International English: A guide to varieties of English around the world. *Reference Reviews, 32*(2), 16–17.

Harry, B., & Klingner, J. (2014). *Why are so many minority students in special education?* New York, NY: Teachers College Press.

Haslam, N., Loughnan, S., & Sun, P. (2011). Beastly: What makes animal metaphors offensive? *Journal of Language and Social Psychology, 30*(3), 311–325. doi:10.1177/0261927X11407168

Hasler, B. S., Salomon, O., Tuchman, P., Lev-Tov, A., & Friedman, D. (2017). Real-time gesture translation in intercultural communication. *Ai & Society, 32*(1), 25–35. doi:10.1007/s00146-014-0573-4

Hernandez, A. E. (2013). *The bilingual brain*. New York, NY: Oxford University Press.

Herrera, S. G., & Kavimandan, S. K. (2017). *Accelerating literacy for diverse learners: Classroom strategies that integrate social engagement and academic achievement, K-8* (2nd ed.). Boston, MA: Pearson.

Herrera, S. G., & Murray, K. G. (2015). *Mastering ESL/EFL methods: Differentiated instruction for culturally and linguistically diverse students* (3rd ed.). New York, NY: Pearson.

Hess, F. M., & Eden, M. (2017). *The every student succeeds act: What it means for schools, systems, and states*. Cambridge, MA: Harvard Education Press.

Hirsch, J., Moreno, D. R., & Kim, K. H. S. (2001). Interconnected large-scale systems for three fundamental cognitive tasks revealed by functional MRI. *Journal of Cognitive Neuroscience, 13*(3), 389–405. doi:10.1162/0898929015113742

Holmes, D., Hedlund, P., & Nickerson, B. (2000). *Accommodating English language learners in state and local assessments*. Washington, DC: National Clearinghouse for Bilingual Education.

Horbury, A., & Cottrell, K. (1997). Cultural factors affecting the acquisition of reading strategies in bilingual children. *Education 3–13, 25*(1), 24–26.

Hymes, D. (1974). *Directions in sociolinguistics*. Philadelphia, PA: University of Pennsylvania Press.

Hymes, D. (2013). Country: Toward linguistic competence in the United States. In *The Sociogenesis Of Language And Human Conduct* (pp. 189–224).

Iverson, P., & Evans, B. (2009). Learning English vowels with different first-language vowel systems II: Auditory training for native Spanish and German speakers. *Journal of the Acoustical Society of America, 126*(2), 866–877. doi:10.1121/1.3148196

James, C. (2013). *Errors in language learning and use: Exploring error analysis*. New York, NY: Routledge.

Jeynes, W. H. (2003). A meta-analysis: The effects of parental involvement on minority children's academic achievement. *Education and Urban Society, 35*(2), 202–218.

Kachru, B. (1985). *Standards, codifications, and sociolinguistic realism: The English language in the outer circle*. Cambridge, UK: Cambridge University Press.

Kamińska, P. M. (2014). *Learning styles and second language education*. London, UK: Cambridge Scholars.

Kaplan, R. B. (1988). Contrastive rhetoric and second language learning: Notes towards a theory of contrastive rhetoric. In A. C. Purves (Ed.), *Writing across languages and cultures: Issues in contrastive rhetoric* (pp. 275–304). Newbury Park, CA: Sage Publishers.

Kern, R., & Kramsch, C. (2014). Communicative grammar and communicative competence. In C. A. Chapelle (Ed.), *The encyclopedia of applied linguistics*. Malden, MA: Wiley.

Klein, A. (2016). Under ESSA, states, districts to share more power. *Education Week, 35*(15), 10–12.

Kleinke, S. (2010). Speaker activity and Grice's maxims of conversation at the interface of pragmatics and cognitive linguistics. *Journal of Pragmatics, 42*(12), 3345–3366.

Knowles, M. S., Holton, E. F., III, & Swanson, R. A. (2014). *The adult learner: The definitive classic in adult education and human resource development*. New York, NY: Routledge.

Kovalyuk, Y. (2014). American English idioms: Semantics and culture. *British and American Studies, 20*, 137.

Krashen, S. (1977). The monitor model for adult second language performance. *Viewpoints on English as a second language*, 152–161.

Krashen, S. (1981). *Second language acquisition and second language learning*. Oxford, UK: Pergamon Press.

Krashen, S. (1982). *Principles and practice in second language acquisition*. Oxford, UK: Pergamon.

Krashen, S. D. (1996). *Under attack: The case against bilingual education*. Culver City, CA: Language Education Associates.

Krashen, S. D., & Terrell, T. D. (1983). *The natural approach: Language acquisition in the classroom*. Hayward, CA: Alemany Press.

Kubota, R., & Lehner, A. (2004). Toward critical contrastive rhetoric. *Journal of Second Language Writing, 13*(1), 7–27.

Kucher, A. (2016). "If you need help, they are always there for us": Education for refugees in an international high school in NYC. *The Urban Review, 49*(1), 1–25. doi:10.1007/s11256-016-0379-4

Kuczok, M. (2011). The *interaction* of *metaphor* and *metonymy* in *noun*-to-*verb* conversion. In B. Bierwiaczonek, B. Cetnarowska, & A. Turula (Eds.), *Syntax in cognitive grammar* (pp. 41–54).

Kupisch, T., Barton, D., Hailer, K., Stangen, I., Lein, T., & van de Weijer, J. (2014). Foreign accent in adult simultaneous bilinguals. *Heritage Language Journal, 11*(2), 123–150.

Lamar, D., & Dixon, R. (2008). SETESOL 2008: A baker's dozen: 13 sweet treats for content teachers. In *Session presented at SETESOL 2008*, Birmingham, AL.

Language Files. (2017). *Skaau.com*. Retrieved from http://www.skaau.com/vb/showthread.php?t=694370

Latifi, M., Ketabi, S., & Mohammadi, E. (2013). The comprehension hypothesis today: An interview with Stephen Krashen. *E-FLT: Electronic Journal of Foreign Language Teaching, 10*(2), 221–233.

Lau v. Nichols (1974). 414 US 563.

Law, B., & Eckes, M. L. (2010). *The more-than-just-surviving handbook: ELL for every classroom teacher* (3rd ed.). Winnipeg, MB: Portage & Main Press.

Lawrence-Lightfoot, S. (2003). *The essential conversation: What parents and teachers can learn from each other*. New York, NY: Random House.

Leisman, G., Maulem, R., & Mughrabi, S. K. (2015). The neurological development of the child with the educational enrichment in mind. *Educational Psychology, 21*, 79–96. doi:10.1016/j.pse.2015.08.006

Lennenberg, E. (1967). *Biological foundations of language*. New York, NY: John Wiley & Sons.

Linguistics 001 (2017). UPenn. Retrieved from http://www.ling.upenn.edu/courses/ling001/acquisition.html

Liu, A. H., & Sokhey, A. E. (2014, June 18). When and why do U.S. states make English their official language? *Washington Post*. Retrieved from https://www.washingtonpost.com/news/monkey-cage/wp/2014/06/18/when-and-why-do-u-s-states-make-english-their-official-language/?utm_term=.4f7b38621dab

Liu, X., & Allen, T. J. (2014). A study of linguistic politeness in Japanese. *Open Journal of Modern Linguistics, 4*(05), 651.

Lombardi, J. (2008). Beyond learning styles: Brain-based research and English language learners. *The Clearing House: A Journal of Educational Strategies, Issues and Ideas, 81*(5), 219–222.

López, M. G., & Tashakkori, A. (2006). Differential outcomes of two bilingual education programs on English language learners. *Bilingual Research Journal, 30*(1), 123–145.

Makalela, L. (2015). Bilingualism in South Africa: Reconnecting with *Ubuntu* translanguaging. In O. García & A. Lin (Eds.), *Encyclopedia of bilingualism and bilingual education*. New York, NY: Springer.

Maslow, A. (1970). *Motivation and personality* (2nd ed.). New York, NY: Harper & Row.

McClelland, J. L., Rumelhart, D. E., & Hinton, G. E. (1986). The appeal of parallel distributed processing. In D. E. Rumelhart, J. L. McClelland, & PDP Research Group (Eds.), *Parallel distributed processing: Explorations in the microstructures of cognition Vol. 1: Foundations*. Cambridge, MA: MIT Press.

McFarland, J., Hussar, B., de Brey, C., Snyder, T., Wang, X., Wilkinson-Flicker, S., … Hinz, S. (2017). *The condition of education 2017. NCES 2017-144*. Washington, DC: National Center for Education Statistics.

McLaughlin, B. (1980). On the use of miniature artificial languages in second-language research. *Applied Psycholinguistics, 1*, 357–369.

McLaughlin, B., Rossman, T., & McLeod, B. (1983). Second language learning: An information-processing perspective. *Language Learning, 33*, 135–158.

Menken, K. (2000). *What are the critical issues in wide-scale assessment of English language learners?* (Issue Brief No. 6). Washington, DC: National Clearinghouse for Bilingual Education.

Messick, S., & Associates (Eds.). (1976). *Individuality in learning*. San Francisco, CA: Jossey-Bass.

Migration Policy Institute. (2013). The limited English proficient population in the United States. Retrieved from http://www.migrationpolicy.org/article/limited-english-proficient-population-united-states#LEP%20Children

Migration Policy Institute. (2015). Top Languages Spoken by English Language Learners Nationally and by State. ELL Information Center Fact Sheet Series. No. 3. *Migration Policy Institute*. Retrieved from http://www.worldatlas.com/articles/the-most-spoken-languages-in-america.html

Migration Policy Institute. (2017a). Largest U.S. immigrant groups over time, 1960–present. Retrieved from http://www.migrationpolicy.org/programs/data-hub/charts/largest-immigrant-groups-over-time

Migration Policy Institute. (2017b). U.S. immigrant population and share over time, 1850–present. Retrieved from http://www.migrationpolicy.org/programs/data-hub/charts/immigrant-population-over-time

Mihalicek, V., & Wilson, C. (2011). *Language files: Materials for an introduction to language* (11th ed.). Columbus, OH: Ohio State University Press.

Moeller, A. K., & Nugent, K. (2014). *Building intercultural competence in the language classroom* (p. 161). Faculty Publications: Department of Teaching, Learning and Teacher Education. Retrieved from http://digitalcommons.unl.edu/teachlearnfacpub/161

Moghaddam, A. N., & Araghi, S. M. (2013). Brain-based aspects of cognitive learning approaches in second language learning. *English Language Teaching, 6*(5), 55.

Mohammadipour, M., & Rashid, S. M. (2015). The impact of task-based instruction program on fostering ESL learners' speaking ability: A cognitive approach. *Advances in Language and Literary Studies, 6*(2), 113–126. doi:10.7575/aiac.alls.v.6n.2p.113

Montgomery, M., Reed, P. E., Anderson, B., & Bernstein, J. B. (2016). *The archive of traditional Appalachian speech and culture*. Columbia, SC: University of South Carolina.

Moore, K. D. (2014). *Effective instructional strategies: From theory to practice*. Los Angeles, CA: Sage.

Moskovsky, C., Alrabai, F., Paolini, S., & Ratcheva, S. (2013). The effects of teachers' motivational strategies on learners' motivation: A controlled investigation of second language acquisition: The effects of teachers' motivational strategies. *Language Learning, 63*(1), 34–62. doi:10.1111/j.1467-9922.2012.00717.x

Moyer, A. (2014). Exceptional outcomes in L2 phonology: The critical factors of learner engagement and self-regulation. *Applied Linguistics, 35*(4), 418–440.

National Center for Education Statistics. (2016). Retrieved from https://nces.ed.gov/programs/digest/d16/tables/dt16_204.20.asp

National Center for Education Statistics. (2017a). Digest of education statistics. Retrieved from https://www.nces.ed.gov/programs/digest/d16/tables/dt16_216.55.asp

National Center for Education Statistics. (2017b). English language learners in public schools. Retrieved from https://www.nces.ed.gov/programs/coe/indicator_cgf.asp

National Center for English Language Acquisition (NCELA). (2016). Dual language education programs: Current state policies and practices. Retrieved from https://www.ncela.ed.gov/files/rcd/TO20_DualLanguageRpt_508.pdf

National Center for English Language Acquisition (NCELA). (2017). Fast facts on English learners. Retrieved from http://www.ncela.us/fast-facts

National Clearinghouse for Bilingual Education. (1992/2002). Retrieved from https://ncela.ed.gov/publications/archived2002

National Clearinghouse for English Language Acquisition. (2016). NCELA. Retrieved from https://ncela.ed.gov/

Neuner, S. (2002). Learning as information processing: Reflections on cognitive theory in second language instruction. *Babylonia, 10*(4), 35–39.

Nevárez-La Torre, A. A. (2012). Transiency in urban schools: Challenges and opportunities in educating ELLs with a migrant background. *Education and Urban Society, 44*(1), 3–34.

Nguyen, A., Shin, F., & Krashen, S. (2001). Development of the first language is not a barrier to second-language acquisition: Evidence from Vietnamese immigrants to the United States. *International Journal of Bilingual Education and Bilingualism, 4*(3), 159–164.

No Child Left Behind. (2002). Retrieved from http://www.wrightslaw.com/news/2002nclb.sign.htm

NPR.org. (2017). *Why you probably shouldn't say "Eskimo"*. Retrieved from www.npr.org/sections/goatsandsoda/2016/04/24/475129558/why-you-probably-shouldnt-say-eskimo

Nyikos, M. (1991). Prioritizing student learning: A guide for teachers. In L. Strasheim (Ed.), *Focus on the foreign language learner*. Lincolnwood, IL: NTC.

Ockey, G. (2011). Self-consciousness and assertiveness as explanatory variables of L2 oral ability: A latent variable approach. *Language Learning, 61*(3), 968–989. doi:10.1111/j.1467-9922.2010.00625.x

O'Grady, W., Dobrovolsky, M., & Aronoff, M. (1989). *Contemporary linguistics: An introduction*. New York, NY: St. Martin's Press.

O'Grady, W., & Hattori, R. (2016). Language acquisition and language revitalization. *Language Documentation and Conservation, 10*, 45.

O'Malley, J. M., & Chamot, A. U. (1990). *Learning strategies in second language acquisition*. Cambridge, UK: Cambridge University Press.

O'Malley J. M., & Pierce, L. V. (1996). *Authentic assessment for English language learners: Practical approaches for teachers*. Boston, MA: Addison-Wesley.

Osterman, K. F. (2000). Students' need for belonging in the school community. *Review of Educational Research, 70*(3), 323–367.

Oxford, R. L. (2016). *Teaching and researching language learning strategies: Self-regulation in context*. New York, NY: Taylor & Francis.

Oxford, R. L., & Carmen, M. A. (2017). *Language learning strategies and individual learner characteristics: Situating strategy use in diverse contexts*. London, UK: Bloomsbury.

Pandya, J. Z. (2011). *Overtested: How high-stakes accountability fails English language learners*. New York, NY: Teachers College Press.

Park, H. (2014, October 21). Children at the border. *The New York Times*. Retrieved from https://www.nytimes.com/interactive/2014/07/15/us/questions-about-the-border-kids.html

Parker, F., & Riley, K. L. (2005). *Linguistics for non-linguists: A primer with exercises*. Boston, MA: Pearson/Allyn and Bacon.

Pena-Correall, T., & Robayo-Castro, B. (2007). B.F. Skinner's verbal behavior: 1957–2007. *Revista Latinoamericana De Psicologia, 39*(3), 653–661.

Pennycook, A. (2017). *The cultural politics of English as an international language*. New York, NY: Taylor & Francis.

Petrey, S. (2016). *Speech acts and literary theory*. London, UK: Routledge.

Pew Research Center. (2014). *Fact tank*. Retrieved from http://www.pewresearch.org/fact-tank/2014/08/18/u-s-public-schools-expected-to-be-majority-minority-starting-this-fall

Platt, J., & Weber, H. (1980). *English in Singapore and Malaysia: Status, features, functions*. Kuala Lumpur: Oxford University Press.

Ploquin, M. (2013). Prosodic transfer: From Chinese Lexical tone to English pitch accent. *Advances in Language and Literary Studies, 4*(1), 68–77. doi:10.7575/aiac.alls.v.4n.1p.68

Pourkalhor, O., & Esfandiari, N. (2017). Culture in language learning: Background, issues and implications. *Language, 5*(01), 23–32.

Rabab'ah, G. (2005). Communication problems facing Arab learners of English. *Grazer linguistische Studien, 3*(63), 63–75.

Radick, G. (2007). *The simian tongue: The long debate about animal language*. Chicago, IL: University of Chicago Press.

Radwan, A. A. (2014). Gender and learning style preferences of EFL learner. *Arab World English Journal, 5*(1), 21–32.

Ramsay, G. (2000). Linearity in rhetorical organisation: A comparative cross-cultural analysis of newstext from the People's Republic of China and Australia. *International Journal of Applied Linguistics, 10*(2), 241–256.

Reed, M., & Levis, J. M. (2015). *The handbook of English pronunciation*. Chichester, UK: Wiley-Blackwell.

Reid, J. (1987). The learning style preferences of ESL students. *TESOL Quarterly, 21*(1), 87–111.

Reid, J. (1998). Learning styles. In P. Byrd & J. Reid (Eds.), *Grammar in the composition class*. Boston, MA: Heinle and Heinle.

Reppen, R., & Grabe, W. (1993). Spanish transfer effects in the English writing of elementary students. *Lenguas Modernas, 20*, 113–128.

Richards, J. C., & Rodgers, T. S. (2014). *Approaches and methods in language teaching*. New York, NY: Cambridge University Press.

Richards, J. C., & Schmidt, R. W. (2014). *Language and communication*. London, UK: Routledge.

Richards, K., & Seedhouse, P. (Eds.). (2016). *Applying conversation analysis*. Basingstoke, UK: Springer.

Roberge, M., Siegal, M., & Harklau, L. (Eds.). (2009). *Generation 1.5 in college composition: Teaching academic writing to US-educated learners of ESL*. New York, NY: Routledge.

Robertson, K. (2017). *Reading 101 for English language learners*. Colorín Colorado. Retrieved from http://www.colorincolorado.org/article/reading-101-english-language-learners

Rodd, J., Gaskell, G., & Marslen-Wilson, W. (2002). Making sense of semantic ambiguity: Semantic competition in lexical access. *Journal of Memory and Language, 46*(2), 245–266.

Rogers, T. T., & McClelland, J. L. (2014). Parallel distributed processing at 25: Further explorations in the microstructure of cognition. *Cognitive Science, 38*(6), 1024–1077. doi:10.1111/cogs.12148

Ruiz-de-Velasco, J., Fix, M., & Clewell, B. C. (2000). *Overlooked and underserved: Immigrant students in U.S. secondary schools*. Washington, DC: The Urban Institute. Retrieved from http://www.urban.org/UploadedPDF/overlooked.pd

Ryder, J. F., Tunmer, W. E., & Greaney, K. T. (2008). Explicit instruction in phonemic awareness and phonemically based decoding skills as an intervention strategy for struggling readers in whole language classrooms. *Reading and Writing, 21*(4), 349–369. doi:10.1007/s11145-007-9080-z

Samovar, L., & Porter, R. (2004). *Communication between cultures* (5th ed.). Belmont, CA: Wadsworth.

Samson, J. F., & Collins, B. A. (2012). *Preparing all teachers to meet the needs of English language learners: Applying research to policy and practice for teacher effectiveness*. Center for American Progress. Retrieved from https://files.eric.ed.gov/fulltext/ED535608.pdf

Sánchez-Gutiérrez, C., & Rastle, K. (2013). Letter transpositions within and across morphemic boundaries: Is there a cross-language difference? *Psychonomic Bulletin & Review, 20*(5), 988–996.

Schmidt, R. W. (1990). The role of consciousness in second language learning. *Applied linguistics, 11*(2), 129–158.

Schmidt, R. W. (1994). Deconstructing consciousness in search of useful definitions for applied linguistics. *AILA Review, 11*, 11–16.

Schrank, J. (n.d.). *The language of advertising claims*. Sunset.backbone.olemiss.edu. Retrieved from http://home.olemiss.edu/~egjbp/comp/ad-claims.html

Schumann, J. (1978). Social and psychological factors in second language acquisition. In J. Richards (Ed.), *Understanding second and foreign language learning: Issues and approaches*. Rowley, MA: Newbury House.

Sebastian, R., Laird, A. R., & Kiran, S. (2011). Meta-analysis of the neural representation of first language and second language. *Applied Psycholinguistics, 32*(4), 799–819. doi:10.1017/S0142716411000075

Selinker, L. (1972). Interlanguage. *IRAL—International Review of Applied Linguistics in Language Teaching, 10*(1–4), 209–232

Sensoy, O., & DiAngelo, R. (2012). *Is everyone really equal? An introduction to key concepts in social justice education*. New York, NY: Teachers College Columbia University.

Shiyab, S. (2017). *Patterns of thinking across languages*. Translation Directory.com. Retrieved from http://www.translationdirectory.com/article619.htm

Simmons, G. F., & Fennig, C. (Eds.). (2017). *Ethnologue: Languages of the world* (20th ed.). Dallas, TX: SIL International.

Sireci, S. G., & Faulkner-Bond, M. (2015). Promoting validity in the assessment of English learners. *Review of Research in Education, 39*(1), 215–252.

Skinner, B. F. (1957). *Verbal behavior*. New York, NY: Appleton-Century-Crofts.

Smiley, P., & Salsberry, T. (2007). *Effective schooling for English language learners: What elementary principals should know and do*. Larchmont, NY: Eye On Education.

Snyder, T. D., & Dillow, S. A. (2012). *Digest of education statistics 2011 (NCES 2012-001)*. Washington, DC: National Center for Education Statistics Institute.

Spradley, J. P. (2016). *The ethnographic interview*. Long Grove, IL: Waveland Press.

Stern, H. H. (1992). *Issues and options in language teaching*. Oxford, UK: OUP.

Stockall, N. (2007). Time well spent: Phonemic awareness training or paired associate learning for children with language impairments? *Forum on Public Policy: A Journal of the Oxford Round Table, 1*, 1–44.

Sullivan, A. (2015). *Native American learning styles* (Unpublished doctoral dissertation). University of Minnesota, Duluth.

Swan, M., & Smith, B. (2007). *Learner English—A teacher's guide to interference and other problems*. Cambridge, NY: Cambridge University Press.

Tahaineh, Y. (2014). A review of EFL Arab learners' language: Pitfalls and pedagogical implications. *International Journal of English Linguistics, 4*(1), 84–102. doi:10.5539/ijel.v4n1p84

Tarone, E. E. (1981). Some thoughts on the notion of communication strategy. *TESOL Quarterly, 15*, 285–295.

Tarone, E. E., Gass, S. M., & Cohen, A. D. (Eds.). (2013). *Research methodology in second-language acquisition*. New York, NY: Routledge.

Terry, N. (2014). Dialect variation and phonological knowledge: Phonological representations and metalinguistic awareness among beginning readers who speak nonmainstream American English. *Applied Psycholinguistics, 35*(1), 155–176. doi:10.1017/S0142716412000276

TESOL Global Partners. (n.d.). Retrieved from http://www.tesol.org/

Thomas, W. P., & Collier, V. P. (1997, December). *School effectiveness for language minority students*. Washington, DC: National Clearinghouse for English Language Acquisition (NCELA) Resource Collection Series, No. 9.

Thomas, W. P., & Collier, V. P. (2002). *A national study of school effectiveness for language minority students' long-term academic achievement*. Santa Cruz, CA: Center for Research on Education, Diversity and Excellence, University of California-Santa Cruz.

Tremblay, P., Darwill, B., & McCarthy, J. (2018). *The exorcist tradition in Islam: Exorcism; Hadith* [Online]. Retrieved from https://www.scribd.com/document/369954376/The-Exorcist-Tradition-In-Islam-pdf

U.S. Department of Education. (2008). Retrieved from https://www2.ed.gov/nclb/accountability/index.html

UNESCO. (2003). *Perspective on literacy*. Retrieved from http://unesdoc.unesco.org/images/0013/001318/131817eo.pdf

United Nations High Commissioner for Refugees (UNHRC). (2016). *Data on Syrian refugee crisis*. Retrieved from http://www.data.unhcr.org/syrianrefugees/regional.php

United Nations High Commissioner for Refugees (UNHRC). (2018). The UN Refugee Agency. UNHCR. Retrieved from http://www.UNHCR.org

U.S. Department of Education. (2008). *A nation accountable: Twenty-five years after a nation at risk*. Washington, DC. Retrieved from https://www2.ed.gov/rschstat/research/pubs/accountable/accountable.pdf

U.S. Department of Education. (2017a). ESSA monitoring guidelines. Retrieved from https://www2.ed.gov/about/offices/list/oela/english-learner-toolkit/chap8.pdf

U.S. Department of Education. (2017b). Tools and resources for identifying all English learners. Chapter 1. Retrieved from https://www2.ed.gov/about/offices/list/oela/english-learner-toolkit/chap1.pdf

Vahidi, S. (2008). The impact of EFL learners' rhetorical organization awareness on English academic/expository text comprehension. *Pazhuhesh-e Zabanha-ye khareji, 41*, 145–158 [*Journal of Language, Culture, and Translation (LCT), 1*(2) (2012), 49–67].

Varghese, M. M. (2005). An introduction to meeting the needs of English language learners. Retrieved from http://www.newhorizons.org/spneeds/ell/varghese.htm

Varghese, M. M., & Park, C. (2010). Going global: Can dual-language programs save bilingual education? *Journal of Latinos and Education, 9*(1), 72–80. doi:10.1080/15348430903253092

Ventriglia, L. (1982). *Conversations of Miguel and Maria: How children learn a second language*. Reading, MA: Addison-Wesley.

Verplaetse, L. S., & Migliacci, N. (Eds.). (2008). *Inclusive pedagogy for English language learners: A handbook for research-informed practices*. New York, NY: Lawrence Erlbaum.

Wade-Woolley, L. (2016). Prosodic and phonemic awareness in children's reading of long and short words. *Reading and Writing, 29*(3), 371–382. doi:10.1007/s11145-015-9600-1

Wertsch, J. (2008). From social interaction to higher psychological processes. A clarification and application of Vygotsky's theory. *Human Development, 51*(1), 66–79. doi:10.1159/000112532

White, L. (2003). *Second language acquisition and universal grammar*. Cambridge, UK: Cambridge University Press.

Whorf, B. L., & Veretennikov, A. (2016). Language, mind, and reality. *Epistemology & Philosophy of Science, 50*(4), 220–243.

WIDA. (2017). *The ABCs of family engagement*. Retrieved from https://www.wida.us/get .aspx?id=2055

WIDA. (n.d.). Retrieved from https://www.wida.us

Williams, M., Mercer, S., & Ryan, S. (2016). *Exploring psychology in language learning and teaching*. Oxford, UK: Oxford University Press.

Wilson, J., Fang, C., Rollins, J., & Valadez, D. (2016). An urgent challenge: Enhancing academic speaking opportunities for English learners. *Multicultural Education, 23*(2), 52.

Wolf, P. S., David, A., Butler-Barnes, S. T., & Zile-Tamsen, V. (2017). American Indian/Alaskan native college dropout: Recommendations for increasing retention and graduation. *Journal on Race, Inequality, and Social Mobility in America, 1*(1), 1.

Yates, L. S. (2004). Plyler v. Doe and the rights of undocumented immigrants to higher education: Should undocumented students be eligible for in-state college tuition rates. *Washington ULQ, 82*, 585.

Youn, H., Sutton, L., Smith, E., Moore, C., Wilkins, J. F., Maddieson, I., & Bhattacharya, T. (2016). On the universal structure of human lexical semantics. *Proceedings of the National Academy of Sciences, 113*(7), 1766–1771.

Yule, G. (2016). *The study of language*. Cambridge, UK: Cambridge University Press.

Zafar, S., & Meenakshi, K. (2012). A study on the relationship between extroversion–introversion and risk-taking in the context of second language acquisition. *International Journal of Research Studies in Language Learning, 1*(1), 33–40. doi:10.5861/ijrsll.2012. v1i1.42

Zarillo, J. J. *Ready for RICA: A test preparation guide for California's reading instruction competence assessment*. Upper Saddle River, NJ: Prentice Hall, 2002.

Zellermeyer, M. (1988). An analysis of oral and literate texts: Two types of reader-writer relationships in Hebrew and English. In B. Rafoth & D. Rubin (Eds.), *The social construction of written communication*. Norwood, NJ: Ablex.

Zen, E. L., & Apriana, A. (2015). Contributing factors toward first and second language acquisition: A manifestation of Krashen's affective filter hypothesis. *Engaging Linguistics and Literature: Perspectives and Insights Beyond the Curriculum*, 256–264.

Zeng, F. (2012). Tonal language processing. *Acoustics Today, 8*(2), 26–28. doi:10.1121/1.4729576

Index